CIVIC DISCIPLINE

Studies in Historical Geography

Series Editor: Professor Robert Mayhew, University of Bristol, UK

Historical geography has consistently been at the cutting edge of scholarship and research in human geography for the last fifty years. The first generation of its practitioners, led by Clifford Darby, Carl Sauer and Vidal de la Blache presented diligent archival studies of patterns of agriculture, industry and the region through time and space.

Drawing on this work, but transcending it in terms of theoretical scope and substantive concerns, historical geography has long since developed into a highly interdisciplinary field seeking to fuse the study of space and time. In doing so, it provides new perspectives and insights into fundamental issues across both the humanities and social sciences.

Having radically altered and expanded its conception of the theoretical underpinnings, data sources and styles of writing through which it can practice its craft over the past twenty years, historical geography is now a pluralistic, vibrant and interdisciplinary field of scholarship. In particular, two important trends can be discerned. Firstly, there has been a major 'cultural turn' in historical geography which has led to a concern with representation as driving historical-geographical consciousness, leading scholars to a concern with text, interpretation and discourse rather than the more materialist concerns of their predecessors. Secondly, there has been a development of interdisciplinary scholarship, leading to fruitful dialogues with historians of science, art historians and literary scholars in particular which has revitalised the history of geographical thought as a realm of inquiry in historical geography.

Studies in Historical Geography aims to provide a forum for the publication of scholarly work which encapsulates and furthers these developments. Aiming to attract an interdisciplinary and international authorship and audience, Studies in Historical Geography will publish theoretical, historiographical and substantive contributions meshing time, space and society.

Civic Discipline
Geography in America, 1860–1890

KAREN M. MORIN
Bucknell University, USA

ASHGATE

© Karen M. Morin 2011

All rights reserved. No part of this publication may be reproduced, stored in a retrieval system or transmitted in any form or by any means, electronic, mechanical, photocopying, recording or otherwise without the prior permission of the publisher.

Karen M. Morin has asserted her right under the Copyright, Designs and Patents Act, 1988, to be identified as the author of this work.

Published by
Ashgate Publishing Limited
Wey Court East
Union Road
Farnham
Surrey, GU9 7PT
England
www.ashgate.com

Ashgate Publishing Company
Suite 420
101 Cherry Street
Burlington
VT 05401-4405
USA

British Library Cataloguing in Publication Data
Morin, Karen M.
Civic discipline : geography in America, 1860-1890. --
(Studies in historical geography)
1. American Geographical Society of New York--Presidents--
Biography. 2. Daly, Charles P. (Charles Patrick),
1816-1899. 3. Daly, Charles P. (Charles Patrick),
1816-1899--Influence. 4. Geographers--United States--
Biography. 5. Geography--United States--History--19th
century. 6. Civic leaders--New York (State)--New York--
Biography. 7. Arctic regions--Discovery and exploration--
American. 8. Congo (Democratic Republic)--Colonization.
9. Belgium--Colonies--Africa.
I. Title II. Series
910.9'2-dc22

Library of Congress Cataloging-in-Publication Data
Morin, Karen M.
Civic discipline : geography in America, 1860-1890 / by Karen M. Morin.
p. cm. -- (Studies in historical geography)
Includes bibliographical references and index.
ISBN 978-1-4094-0143-8 (hardback) -- ISBN 978-1-4094-0144-5 (ebook)
1. American Geographical Society of New York. 2. Daly, Charles P. (Charles Patrick), 1816-1899. 3. Geography--United States--History. 4. Geography--Philosophy. I. Title.
G3.A5M67 2010
910.97309'034--dc22

2010037090

ISBN 9781409401438 (hbk)
ISBN 9781409401445 (ebk)

Printed and bound in Great Britain by the MPG Books Group, UK

Contents

List of Figures

Acknowledgments

In this book I draw upon archival records of the New York-based American Geographical Society (AGS) and its 35-year President Charles P. Daly (1864–1899) to interpret nineteenth-century American geography as a popular "civic discipline" that served commercial, reformist, and scientific interests of the day. The ideas presented here sporadically unfolded for me over many years, at some point along the way taking on a life of their own. I did not set out to write the book that this one became, but such is the nature of archival research. I would have to trace my initial interest in the AGS to a conference session (almost a decade ago now) at which I was asked to comment on some papers devoted to geography's "society women"– the typically elite, exceptional women who made contributions to geographical societies such as the AGS in their earliest years. As Jan Monk and others argued, women were welcome at the AGS, and made lasting contributions to it, before or in more significant ways than women involved with other such societies. That conference session sparked my curiosity and led to my reading of the society's institutional archives at its headquarters on New York's Wall Street beginning in 2003. At the time I was lucky to meet former AGS cartographer Miklos Pinther, who gave me my introductory lesson on the society, its archives, and its influential nineteenth-century leader, Charles P. Daly. It was really the discovery of the Daly Papers at the New York Public Library that changed the direction of this research, so I first and foremost owe a debt of gratitude to Miklos for providing me initial insights into the organization and his incredibly helpful tips on the Daly archives.

The AGS staff – especially former Director Mary Lynne Bird and Archivist Peter Lewis – have been extraordinarily tolerant in allowing me open access to the archives and assisting me in my research, especially in its early stages. Many people affiliated with the AGS in years past have given me additional insights – a special thank you to David and Mary Alice Lowenthal for their warm hospitality (and good stories) in London, and to reference librarian Jovanka Ristic of the AGS library in Milwaukee. The staff at the Manuscripts and Archives Division at the New York Public Library have been graciously and expertly supportive of my research over the years, and I thank them, as well as Alice Hudson in the NYPL Map Division. The lovely Mrs. Harold Hammond, widow of Charles Daly's biographer Harold Hammond back in the 1950s – thank you for taking the time to discuss the project with me by phone, if only after 9:00 pm and clarinet practice finished. I am also immensely indebted to Alicia Clarke of the Sanford Museum in Sanford, Florida, for supplying me with the valuable Congo correspondence and documents I draw upon in Chapter 6.

I have waltzed around this material for so many years that I likely will not remember all the many institutions and individuals that helped me along the way. Some stand out obviously. Institutional assistance for this project came in the form of two grants from the National Science Foundation, a Senior Scholar Fellowship from the Gilder Lehrman Institute of American History in New York, and generous support from Bucknell University's Provost's Office, Arts & Sciences Dean's office, and the Geography Department. I could not have completed the research without the grants, leaves, and course releases over the years provided by Bucknell, and I thank in particular for their support Jim Rice, Chris Zappe, and Paul Susman. My friends and colleagues Maria Antonaccio, Annie Randall, and Paula Closson Buck, thank you for occasionally checking in on my woman cave to ask how the book's coming along. I also have had Bucknell support with so many unappealing tasks – from Kim Dirocco, who kindly chased down all the permissions; Deb Cook-Balducci, who produced all the images almost overnight; librarians Dan Heuer and Candice Hinckley, who unflinchingly tracked down all the obscure historical sources; and my indispensible research assistants over the years, especially Alex Bothwell and the amazing Liz Marut, who patiently muddled through so much boring microfilm. All of you are sincerely appreciated.

Research on geography's role in European (especially British) empire building in the nineteenth century greatly influenced how I framed this project, and I have consequently leaned very heavily on colleagues in the UK for advice about it. Above all I would like to thank Mike Heffernan for providing intellectual support for the project and reading the entire manuscript; and I am also deeply grateful to Robert Mayhew for sticking with the project long enough for it to see the light of day with Ashgate's Historical Geography Series. Thanks to Val Rose and the whole team at Ashgate for bearing with this persnickity author. Others who read chapters and provided invaluable feedback include Felix Driver, Michael Bravo, John Enyeart, David Lambert, Charlie Withers, Miles Ogborn, and, on an earlier version of Chapter 2, Matt Hannah, Cheryl McEwan, Jeanne Kay Guelke, and Susan Schulten. So many helped keep the project moving forward in other ways, most especially Jan Monk but also thanks to Don Mitchell, Tamar Rothenberg, Neil Smith, Phil Steinberg, David Wishart, Mona Domosh, Lawrence Berg, Leslie Patrick, Anne Tlusty and my good sister Ann Baker.

This material was presented at a number of conferences and seminars over the years and I appreciate all the insightful feedback that participants at those venues offered. I am singularly indebted to those who organized and attended my 2009 seminars at the University of Bristol, University College London, Nottingham University, and Queen Mary University of London, who gave me the push I needed to finish the project. Alex Vasudevan, Wenfei Winnie Wang, Jenny Robinson, Adam Dixon, Paul Glennie, James Kneale, and David Pinder, thanks for all your hospitality.

On a more personal level, it is a cliché but also a truism, that those closest in, who have lived with this book, and me inside it, for such a long time, are the ones I owe the most. So especially to the most patient and forgiving soul on earth, thank you Dan Olivetti for the blessed routines of our days together. I, Olive H. Morin, will never forget everything you have done to help make this book happen. And to my children Nina Olivetti and Nick Olivetti – thank you – every kindness, curious question, text message, and happy homecoming, these are what really kept me going in my work, and in my life. Finally, as a woman-identified woman it still feels a bit strange to have written a book around a nineteenth-century male protagonist, a gentleman's life to be studied rather than admired, and I couldn't help but be constantly reminded of my own father, T.R. Morin, a more contemporary version of the so-called "self-made man," throughout the process. So to the man who passed on to me those qualities of tenacity and resourcefulness that I needed most to complete this project, thank you Dad, this one's for you.

* * *

Versions of Chapters 2 and 7 originally appeared in the following publications, and I thank the editors (Audrey Kobayashi and Sharmistha Bagchi-Sen) for their help and gratefully acknowledge permission from Taylor and Francis to reprint those works here. Chapter 2: "Charles P. Daly's Gendered Geography, 1860–1890" *Annals of the Association of American Geographers* 98 (4, 2008): 897–919; and Chapter 7: "Unpopular Archives," The *Professional Geographer* 62 (4, 2010): 534–543.

Chapter 1
Introduction: Geography as Civic Discipline in Nineteenth-Century America

Introduction

The American Geographical Society (AGS), established in 1851, is the oldest and was the pre-eminent professional geographical organization in the nineteenth-century United States.[1] Before the National Geographic Society (NGS) came along in the late 1880s, the AGS, together with the United States Geological Survey, carried nearly all of geography's institutional power in the United States in the decades after the Civil War.[2] Taking a look back at the origins and development of the AGS, Charles Patrick Daly, the society's President for 35 years (1864–1899), emerges as key figure in the shaping of the goals, practices, and procedures of the AGS and thus of American geography more broadly in the post-Civil War era. This book explores how early American geographical knowledge and practices were understood, took shape, and made publicly available via Charles Daly and the AGS; and in turn, how the ideals and programmatic interests of the AGS itself were closely linked to the interests, goals, and work of its main protagonist – Daly's personal subjectivity and role as New York civic leader, scholar, revered New York judge, and especially, popularizer of geography.

Charles Daly appears in newspaper accounts, biographies, and in his own writings and speeches as a classic example of the allegedly "self-made man" who emerged triumphantly from early nineteenth-century American mercantile capitalism. Daly was a prominent public figure in New York and among business and geographical communities throughout the United States and Europe. He was leader of numerous scholarly, literary, philanthropic, and social reform societies in New York, working primarily on behalf of foreign-born or first-generation Irish immigrants (like himself). His "day job," though, was as judge of the New York Court of Common Pleas – the highest court in New York City in the nineteenth century – a position he was elected to continuously for 42 years, the last 27 of them as Chief Justice. As I argue in this book, Charles Daly was also an influential and popular geographer of the second half of the nineteenth century, albeit a little-known one today.

In its first two decades, under the leadership of shipping magnate Henry Grinnell, the AGS primarily focused on Arctic exploration and development of the first U.S. transcontinental railroad. The Civil War halted operations for a time, but following it, Charles Daly almost single-handedly revived the organization, continuing these projects while adding to them the development of the Central American Isthmus canal in the 1870s, and later, with exploration and trade in Central Africa (among many others). With a unique combination of business acumen, scholarly erudition, and a carefully crafted touch of showmanship, Daly turned the AGS into a commanding public presence. He quickly ascended from member of the AGS in 1855, to councilor three years later, and to President from 1864 until his death in 1899, at age 83. Daly greatly expanded the AGS membership, publications, and library, and increased AGS correspondence with numerous geographical and scientific societies around the world (details below). The society today describes Charles Daly as the first individual to have launched it onto the "world stage."[3]

Daly was a prolific writer and speaker on many topics (a biographical profile appears below). He published over 40 geographical papers, on topics ranging from physical geography to cartography to mineral resource and trade potential at home

Figure 1.1 Cooper Union – Astor Place Hotel, Cooper Square (East 7th Street – Astor Place)

Source: Milstein Division of United States History, Local History & Genealogy, The New York Public Library, Astor, Lenox and Tilden Foundations.

Figure 1.2 Chickering Hall, North East corner of Fifth Avenue and 18th Street (*ca.* 1888)

Source: Eno Collection, Miriam and Ira D. Wallach Division of Art, Prints and Photographs, The New York Public Library, Astor, Lenox and Tilden Foundations.

and abroad. He privately and publicly hosted and supported the expeditions of many famous (and infamous) explorers of the day, those leading expeditions in the Arctic such as Isaac Hayes and Robert Peary as well as the explorers of Africa such as Henry Morton Stanley and his close personal friend, Paul du Chaillu (who came to live with Daly after Daly's wife's death). Daly's geographical meetings were enormously popular public events, drawing crowds of 2,000 or 3,000 spectators to venues such as the New York Historical Society, the Cooper Union, and Chickering Hall. He was especially known for his signature annual addresses on the "state of geographical work of the world" for each year. He often impressed upon his audiences that they lived in a "great geographical age," and it was for these annual addresses that he received most praise and public recognition as a geographer.[4] These and others of Daly's geographical events popularized geography among the public, and, as I show in this book, served powerful business interests of New York as well as political communities in the U.S. and internationally.

While it may already appear otherwise, this book is not really "about" Charles Daly. I draw upon Charles Daly's life and contributions to geography as a means to cast light upon the nature of nineteenth-century American geography within broader institutional, societal, and spatial contexts. Rather than biography, this book is better thought of as a sociology of Charles Daly's geography – a social geography. The men who founded and promoted geographical societies such as the AGS – those gentlemen's clubs of the nineteenth century – are important sites of inquiry as they served to direct and fund research and exploration, collect and define geographical knowledge, disseminate this knowledge to the public, and, of course, impact material cultures and infrastructures on the ground. The projects and practices of such learned societies arose out of a particular nexus of intellectual, commercial, social, and personal interests.[5] This book thus demonstrates the constructed or "produced" nature of geographical knowledge and practice historically, casting geography's history within a critical or structural biography of its main protagonist.[6] To borrow Matt Hannah's language from another context, Daly is enlisted here as a "relationally dense node at which to tie together and render coherent a much wider set of logics, circumstances, and political dynamics."[7] The historian Linda Colley uses critical biography of an "unknown" travel writer of the eighteenth century to examine large-scale social transformations in technology, commerce, international politics, and gender roles. Like Colley's, this book "charts a world in a life and a life in the world."[8]

Also let me be clear at the outset that my purpose is not to argue that Charles Daly necessarily thought of his life and work in the geographical and other terms I set forth here (in fact, he may not have). I am not interested in delving into his personal psychology, inner struggles, and habits to find out; nor does my analysis depend on such factors. I treat Daly as a social subject, well connected to many intellectual, philanthropical, legal, diplomatic, and business spaces who accomplished a great deal personally and civically in all of them. In my research I did not find Charles Daly to have been driven by a single disciplinary or scientific concern; he was an individual with a wide range of interests, networks, talents, and accomplishments. Nonetheless in this book I attempt to draw out Daly's overarching geographical sensibilities and his public persona as geographer, and the ways these influenced not only his own life and work, but also the work of the AGS and thus of nineteenth-century American geography more generally.

In this study I trace Charles Daly's "thinking geographically" in three ways: through analysis of his influence on geography as a *professional field* or discipline, coalescing institutionally at the American Geographical Society; as an *epistemology* – an intellectual domain or arena of knowledge; and as a set of professional skills or *practices*. Charles Daly's geography took a representational and discursive form in his speeches and writings, and it also manifested as a material practice – he created what Edward Said has referred to as "imaginative geographies" of peoples and places for his audiences that had real, material effects on the ground.[9] I want to make explicit the links between the "representational force" of the imaginative geographies Daly created for his many constituents and their effects in producing and transforming actual spaces; local ones in New York to those more far flung, in the American West, Central America, and in the Arctic and Africa.

In order to do this I examine the relationship between Daly's social subjectivity and its material effects, making clear how Daly and his AGS colleagues were able to institutionalize personal ideas and goals. Charles Daly's geographical work supported important social reform improvements as well as U.S. commercial and state power, at home and overseas. If Daly's geography – his sense of what constituted geographical knowledge itself – centered largely on successfully attracting public interest to exploration, imaginative geographies, and "filling in" spaces on the map; his geography also involved creating, transforming, and producing spaces through settling immigrants, improving their housing and streets, establishing parks, building towns and railroads, and helping establish the infrastructures necessary for American commercial development and empire-building at home and abroad.

Geography and the American Commercial Empire

Historians and sociologists of science now recognize the development of scientific inquiry of every sort – from natural history to medicine to physics – as social constructions; that is, as situated and produced within particular social and cultural milieus. Scholars have studied the sites of scientific knowledge production; the uneven distribution and diffusion of ideas; the process of constituting fields in and through which science was gathered; the rise of scientific subcultures and networks among them; and the institutionalization and policing of the sites of these subcultures. Many human geographers have successfully traced the constructed or produced nature of geography's disciplinary knowledge historically, connecting it to broader social milieus.[10] Their works admonish us to move away from taken-for-granted definitions of geography as a subject with a particular tradition and history, to flesh out both what people in different times and places thought of as geography, and/or what kinds of knowledge and activities might now be considered "geography" through were not considered as such by practitioners in various times and places. David Livingstone, for instance, calls for the writing of new histories of geography that are attuned to the various and contingent factors that shaped geography intellectually, socially, and politically. He argues that writing geography's history will mean,

> locating particular geographical theories, methodologies, representations, schools of inquiry, and so on, in their intellectual context, their social space, their physical setting. And it will mean resisting the tendency to privilege certain definitions of the subject's conceptual terrain over others.[11]

Other scholars remind us too that all geographical knowledge is "local," with both categories of meaning and credibility of knowledge claims secured through the workings of local causes.[12] Subsequent chapters illustrate the importance of this localness to the work of the AGS; I cast Charles Daly as an "armchair geographer" who moved through a number of local sites and networks – physical sites such as the study, the library, the lecture theater, AGS offices, New York City, and the halls of Congress; to those more discursive, such as newspaper accounts, maps, published lectures, books, and so forth – which collectively became sites of both the production of geographical knowledge and the consumption of it, by AGS members, businessmen, and the public at large.

The most important theoretical advance in the historiography of nineteenth-century geography in my view came about through works that demonstrated its relationship to colonialism, imperialism, and empire. Felix Driver's work on "geography and empire," for instance, ushered in a mini-industry of research examining institutional geography's support of British Empire building in the nineteenth century.[13] Many geographical societies, perhaps most prototypically London's Royal Geographical Society (RGS), are now understood as having supported colonial or imperial relationships of power in the nineteenth century – such as by cataloguing data or mapping colonies for territorial acquisition or military control, extracting resources, or opening trade markets for home goods – even if such organizations publicly stated their primary purpose as advancement of scientific knowledge or education in geography. Much of the discussion of geography's historiography has been based on British geographical archives, though, so the present study, which centers on an American geographer and U.S. archives, will hopefully serve as an important intervention in these debates. Moreover, geographers and scholars of popular culture have sustained a voluminous record of interest in the National Geographic Society (NGS), but I think it safe to say that studies of the relationships between American institutional geography and nineteenth-century American imperialism and empire in particular have lagged behind their (our) European counterparts. It is my hope, then, that this book also serves as something of a corrective to most critical studies of American geographical societies that begin only in 1888 with the NGS and subsequently formal or "official" U.S. expansionism in the Caribbean and Pacific. Meanwhile I acknowledge that a different emphasis is required for examining the interests and reach of the American Geographical Society, with its more commercial interests.

In 1875 the AGS was the fifth largest geographical organization in the Euro-American world in terms of membership,[14] with the larger ones in London, Paris, Berlin, and St. Petersburg (there were 31 such organizations in 1873, and 51 by 1880).[15] The critical role that geographical institutions and organizations played historically in shaping and reinforcing state and commercial power is centrally relevant to the present case. While the fact of an American "commercial empire" in the nineteenth century is not a new idea, geography's relationship to it is in need of further study.[16] My initial interest in the AGS began with the question of whether its explicit and unapologetic business and commercial orientation produced for it a somewhat different set of programs than those for other geographical societies; for a brief comparison, the AGS was neither colonial in orientation like the RGS, nor as nationalistic as the NGS (see below). While other geographical societies also carried strong commercial goals in the nineteenth century – most notably those in France and Brazil, as well as some smaller, provincial societies throughout Britain[17] – the links between the geographical knowledge and practices of the

AGS and its origins in New York City allow for a deepened understanding of the spatiality of knowledge production.

A number of social and spatial processes of mid- to late-nineteenth-century America directly impacted the organizational mission of the AGS. At the broadest scale these included the American Civil War and Reconstruction; rapid U.S. territorial expansion and its associated immigration and settlement patterns; and industrialization and urbanization and the changes these brought about in urban neighborhoods and workplaces. More specifically, much should be made of the AGS's emplacement in New York City, central node of an exploding American industrial capitalism in the mid-nineteenth century. By 1830 New York City had become the largest city in the Americas, and by 1860 was the unchallenged center of American commerce. New York City ranked first in the nation in population, industrial production, bank deposits, and wholesale trade. As early as 1850, 71 percent of all U.S. import-export trade passed through New York harbor. The city's locational advantages reinforced one another, such that by the early part of the nineteenth century New York was the pre-eminent port of entry for immigrants to the United States. Europeans arrived in such numbers during the 1840s and 1850s that by 1860 nearly half of the city's residents were foreign-born, mostly Irish and German. In 1850, 26 percent of the city's population had been born in Ireland, making up the city's largest immigrant block.[18] As I explore in Chapter 3, some of Charles Daly's most influential geographical work in New York City, what I call his "social reform geography," was in making infrastructural improvements to the urban neighborhoods of many of these recent arrivals – in buildings, streets, as well as in sites of pleasure and reprieve such as the Bronx Botanical Gardens. This book is thus, in many ways, a New York story.

The AGS began its operations in rented rooms at New York University and Clinton Hall in the 1850s; continued at Cooper Union in the later 1860s and early 1870s; and moved to its own building at 15 West 29th Street in 1876 (remaining there until 1901).[19] A New York "business elite" established the AGS in the midst of the city's rapid urban changes; they were men interested primarily in the commercial advantages that geographical knowledge of the globe offered them (detailed in Chapter 2). The projects the society supported, expeditions it sponsored, public events it held, and documents it published resonated closely with its organizational mission; its maxim from the beginning, "Geographical Exploration is Commercial Progress."[20] Like London's RGS in the nineteenth century, the AGS was "part social club, part learned society, part imperial information exchange center and part platform for the promotion of sensational feats of exploration."[21] But unlike the RGS, the men who founded the AGS were explicit about the contributions geography could make to commercial development, either directly or through the influence of governments. In its early decades frequent mention was made in council and society meetings to the various needs of the commercial classes and mercantile community, and projects lacking obvious economic advantage were discouraged.[22]

Large U.S. corporations were emerging during the so-called "second industrial revolution" of heavy industry, steam, and railroads, post-1870 – and this was the stage for the rise of large U.S. corporations (e.g. Nabisco and Standard Oil), which were for the first time engaged in large-scale production, mass-marketing, and shipping, domestically and abroad. Alongside this new phase of capitalist expansion beginning in the 1870s was a "geography" to support it. While this study hinges on the geographical practices as conceived by Charles Daly and the AGS, and not on the development of American companies per se, the two are deeply intertwined. As noted in the society's "Transactions for 1873," for instance, New York insurance companies – the Atlantic Mutual Insurance Company, the Mercantile Insurance Company, the Union Insurance Company, and the Orient Insurance Company – conditionally gave an aggregate sum of $500 that year to the AGS in order to,

> complete and maintain its collections of maps and charts, and works upon foreign countries … [with the] sole condition [that] the collections of the Society be held, at all reasonable hours, subject to the inspection and study of the officers and agents of the above-mentioned companies.[23]

Many individuals – particularly businessmen and government officials – used the society's facilities in such ways. Businessmen came to AGS meetings to be informed as well as entertained, and, as I detail in subsequent chapters, the geographical knowledge provided to them both satisfied and stimulated their interests. In what follows I link U.S. business and commercial interests at home and abroad – for instance in locating and extracting resources, cementing spheres of influence, and developing transportation and trade routes – with those of Charles Daly and the AGS. It is worth emphasizing then, that this study is not just about how historical events shaped geography, but probably more importantly, how geography shaped historical events.[24] The AGS and Daly played an influential role in field exploration, social reform, in American expansionism and foreign policy; and these, by directly funding projects, by serving as a pressure group on governments, and by serving as an influential space of study and discussion.

A Civic Discipline

Charles Daly practiced a "popular" or public-oriented geography; a type of geography still associated with the AGS today (Chapter 7). Daly's geography was popular both in terms of its non-academic nature as well as its extensive reach to a broad audience. A number of scholars have recently turned their attention to such geographies, calling for more histories of geography as popular or "ordinary" practice.[25] While Daly was not among the grass-roots practitioners, such as school field instructors studied by Hayden Lorimer,[26] for instance; his geography was popular in its appeal among (principally) New York businessmen, other professionals, and the public. One of Daly's primary "contributions" to geography was the hold he had over the popular imagination about distant locations such as in the Arctic and Africa. Academic geography was tiny in the U.S. during Daly's most active and influential period, meanwhile the sort of populist understanding of "geography as exploration" began to be challenged by influential figures such as William Morris Davis by the end of the century, who supported a more "expert" or "scientific" definition of the subject. As a number of scholars have pointed out, the telling of geography's history has frequently revolved around such moves to secure the academic credibility of the subject in a way that has left out of the story – even dismissed – popular geographers such as Charles Daly as having made few lasting contributions to the discipline. Charles Withers and others have made a convincing case that we ought not privilege academic geography in considering the important sites of geography's production and consumption historically; especially important as we consider that "popularization [has always been] integral to geography."[27] These are themes to which I return in some detail in the Postscript (Chapter 7).

Coinciding with the rise of early commercial capitalism in the nineteenth-century U.S. was an emerging (mostly) urban, literate bourgeoisie desiring knowledge of the "modern" sciences, including geography. As Jurgen Habermas has argued, knowledge formerly exchanged through a "world of letters" in the eighteenth century became publicized in the nineteenth, exchanged via a new sociability in coffee houses, lecture theaters, and salons.[28] Within this context we might think of Charles Daly as something of a "public intellectual": his public lectures and meetings, newspaper coverage of the same, and his widely disseminated reports and publications comprised a career influential in the public teaching of geography (albeit with little impact on school geography).[29] And, among so many other sites of geographical knowledge production in Daly's sphere was his own home, a salon of sorts, which, according to his niece, filled nightly with "notables" from many arenas of New York and Washington social life – leading explorers, diplomats, philanthropists, and literary figures among them.[30]

Newspaper reportage was essential to Daly's ability to popularize geography, a point stressed throughout the volume. His savvy management of the emerging print press, more than anything else, helped him popularize the AGS and its programs while contributing to the public education of the world beyond (see especially Chapters 3 and 5). Daly had a keen appreciation for the potential of the popular press to advance himself and his many causes, such that scores of New York newspapers closely followed his judicial decisions, reform work, as well as his staging of spectacular geographical meetings and events. Praise for Daly as judge, civic leader, and geographer appeared in hundreds of newspaper articles throughout the 1870s, 1880s, and 1890s. He shrewdly coordinated and garnered a great deal of support for his many geographical, legal, and civic projects through newspapers such as The *New York Times*, *New York Daily Tribune*, *New York Herald*, *The World*, *New York Sun*, *Evening Telegram*, and the London *Times*. He

Figure 1.3 Charles Patrick Daly, L.L.D. Chief Judge of the New York Court of Common Pleas. President of the American Geographical Society. Etching by H.B. Hall, 1869

Source: Print Collection, Miriam and Ira D. Wallach Division of Art, Prints and Photographs, The New York Public Library, Astor, Lenox and Tilden Foundations.

appears for the most part a sweetheart of the New York press, usually depicted in newspapers as one of the city's most "honored and learned judges." The *Evening Post* wrote of Daly in 1864,

> All can approach him, all find him the same engaging gentleman, and all draw profit from his society, rich as it is in the inculcation of ennobling sentiments and the practice of manly virtues … Judge Daly is found to be a man of peculiar fitness to do justice to all the noble impulses which impart honor to manhood.[31]

Daly's "manly" virtues greatly influenced the exploratory field geography he promoted through the AGS, as I argue in Chapter 2. Such worked in tandem with those masculine virtues typically associated with those of the legal profession – judiciousness, neutrality, and a strong ethical code – to provide Daly credibility and authority over the knowledge fields he claimed, especially so when widely publicized through a "friendly" media. This became especially important when Daly weighed in on scientific questions of the day, convincingly "holding court" as armchair geographer on physical geography issues such as the Open Polar Sea debate in the Arctic, for which he had no first-hand experience (Chapter 5).

By 1873 the *New York Herald* declared that Daly had become the "only geographer in the country of any eminence"; and in 1876 asserted that no other scholar in the country had "given more attention to the geographical science" than Judge Charles Daly.[32] Another newspaper, *The Hour*, referred to Daly's lectures as "ranking foremost among the geographical literature of the day."[33] When Daly secured funding for the construction of a new building for the society late in his life, the *New York Tribune* referred to him as the "oldest living geographer" who had saved the organization from dissolution when he took it over, to almost single-handedly amassing sufficient funds to undertake the building project ($400,000). The *Tribune* gushed, "President Daly has not only been the official head of the [AGS] for more than a generation, but he has almost been the society itself, devoting much of his time to his pet educational institution."[34] The burgeoning newspaper industry, and competition among papers, meant that such reportage carried considerable cultural power to influence public opinion in the nineteenth century.[35]

Much of Daly's ability to popularize geography rested on his speechifying – delivering speeches meant not to be studied but heard, filled with useful, practical (if sometimes tedious) data, widely considered both eloquent and interesting. While the significance of local site or location in the production and dissemination of scientific knowledge has brought a new dimension to recent work on the sociology of science, as Livingstone observes, the importance of speech in scientific enterprises has been less well developed. Several of the chapters in this volume explore the evocative power of Daly's "spaces of speech" and their newspaper coverage, and thus underscore important connections between "location and locution": what can be said in different venues; how it is said; and how it is heard.[36]

Geography for the "Public Good"

As noted earlier, in this work I consider Charles Daly's geographical work in its capacity as an institutionalized profession, an epistemology, and as a practice. In so doing I frame Daly's geography as a "civic discipline." Civic here refers simply to a public sphere or public arena (at a variety of scales), and implies a geography put to use in the "service" of that public. Much of Daly's and the AGS's work was cast as civic improvement or as civic good through engagement with geographical knowledge. I consider in the subsequent chapters how the AGS organization, and the man Charles Daly, portrayed and enacted civic responsibility – to the municipality and/or community at various scales, including the neighborhood, city, and nation – via the collection, dissemination, and application of geographical knowledge. The study thus grapples with the question of how an organization ostensibly neutral to the advancement of science would portray its civic responsibility. Daly often declared himself to be offering a neutral AGS venue for discussion of competing geographical theories and researches, for instance, but his and his colleagues' vested interests (literally stock-holding with various associated commercial enterprises) were anything but that (Chapter 4). Daly's interests were not so much geo-political as "geo-commercial," for instance in advocating for an inter-oceanic isthmus canal through Nicaragua during the site selection process (of what eventually became the Panama Canal) – and this via diplomatic negotiations, legal battles, and through special AGS meetings. Along with so many others the Nicaragua project illustrates how Daly's and the AGS's spatial and financial "civic missions" were closely linked.

Charles Daly's own immigrant, ethnic, and class background combined into an intense sense of upward mobility that hinged on his own personal commercial and other successes. Writ large, his support of American expansionism was above all, too, of a commercial impulse. It is not surprising that elite men such as Charles Daly who invested heavily in a successful American economic empire were primarily free-marketers fixated on their own returns (and careers), making no particular distinctions between "customers" of their end products. As Mona Domosh puts it, doing business for such men "required a flexible view of world order." She asserts that:

> In the more commercial worldview that characterized American international companies, foreign nations as potential consumers were considered similar in kind, if not in fact, to each other and to the United States, with no clear delineation between colonizer and colonized.[37]

In this book then I tell a story about such "fixations" of AGS men, contributing a critical appraisal of the role of particular geographical actors, institutions, and practices connected to American empire building in the nineteenth century.

Geography's role in serving "the public interest" appears as a common trope throughout the chapters of this book. It probably goes without saying that there is nothing particularly exceptional about elite, powerful members of society casting their (oftentimes self-serving) work in such terms. In that sense I do not consider Charles Daly to have been particularly exceptional in his civic life and career: indeed to *be* a civic person of the professional social class he moved within during the American Gilded Age meant acting in the ways Daly did, professionally, philanthropically, and commercially. His gentle, patrician persona; his Irish working-class background and deep sense of upward mobility; his revered intellect and popular legal decisions; and his personal stake in numerous commercial enterprises, all informed the geographies he produced. Yet Daly's working-class background and self-education – his characteristically (Irish) American civic career – does represent something unique to geography. In that sense his is perhaps a bit more of an appealing story than that of the more privileged men who dominated other – especially European – geographical societies of the period. Also unlike other men who fill the pages of geography's history, Daly's sensibilities tended to be more transnational than national – in addition to advocating for things like Irish home rule he cast himself as indifferent to the "race to the [North] Pole" (Chapter 5) – which allows for an important appraisal of how ideas generated from geographical work traveled into civic work, and vice versa, within this particular historical (American) milieu.[38]

While "civic" in this book refers to public service or public good, the phrase "civic discipline" carries a double meaning. Inspired primarily by the insights of Michel Foucault, "civic discipline" refers both to geography as a body of thought and practice institutionalized into a professional-scientific discipline or field of study; as well as a way of thinking geographically, a way of controlling or "disciplining" how people think about the world and then act upon it.[39] Something of a revolving door existed between the two, where ideas generated from geographical work found their way into numerous civic projects which, in turn, depended upon support from a host of different factions. Daly's close association with Belgian King Leopold II's colonization of the Congo, for instance, found reinforcement from New York's Chamber of Commerce as well as from U.S. senators hoping for a "safety valve" solution for freed American slaves (Chapter 6). Daly also played an important role as purveyor of Arctic science in the mid-nineteenth century, which provided a "happy distraction" from the politics of American expansionism and the tensions of the Civil War and the war with Mexico.[40] Daly was one of America's most influential "access points" to the Arctic in the later decades of the nineteenth century. He argued for AGS involvement there that effected infrastructural improvements and national prestige and rank within the scientific community (Chapter 5).

Charles Daly's position as geographical President allowed him to weigh in differently in a number of different civic spaces: as city planner in neighborhoods of New York City; as diplomat arguing geographical questions of national import before Congress in Washington, D.C.; as judge and lawyer debating commercial geographical questions in the courts; and as armchair explorer studying and weighing evidence of physical geography patterns in the AGS offices. These, in turn, became important sites of geographical knowledge production further influenced by the range of respective epistemologies inherent in such sites – such as gender norms and masculine traits associated with fieldwork (Chapter 2); moral reform and uplift of the needy (Chapter 3); scientific credibility and legal judiciousness (Chapters 4 and 5); and business profits and margins (Chapter 6), among others.

Having already said a great deal about Charles Daly I would like to provide a bit more systematic background on his life, career, and geographical interests in the next section. (Many other such details appear in subsequent chapters, as appropriate.) Following this brief biography I conclude with a chapter-by-chapter outline of the remainder of the book.

Charles P. Daly: A Select Biography

Charles Daly was born in 1816 on the lower east side of New York City two years after his parents had immigrated to New York from Galway, Ireland (where his father worked as a hotel manager and carpenter, respectively). His biographer describes Daly's early life as unstable; his mother died when he was three years old, and at age 12 when his father also died, young Charles left home and school for Savannah, Georgia, to earn a living as a quill maker.[41] He subsequently spent three years "at sea," during which time he is said to have fought with pirates and rescued a nun off the coast of Holland. (Few details are available about these adventures.[42]) Returning to New York City in his late teens Daly served as apprentice to a master carpenter. His membership in a literary society led to employment as a clerk in a law office at age 20, and by age 23 he was admitted to the New York Bar, having served only three of the seven years of apprenticeship customarily required at the time for the bar exam. Daly would go on to lecture at Columbia Law School throughout his life, including delivering its commencement address in 1865, even though he had almost no formal education beyond a few years at a primary (parochial) school.

Charles Daly was among the Irish in New York, but in many ways, not of them. Most Irish immigrants in New York worked as unskilled laborers: by 1860, 200,000 of the city's 800,000 people were Irish, comprising 87 percent of the foreign-born, unskilled laborers. Daly was one of the few Irish born or first generation Irish-Americans to become a successful entrepreneur or professional; only 1 percent of New York's hundreds of lawyers at mid-century, for example, were Irish.[43] With a license to practice law behind him, Daly considered a political career for a time; he was elected to a term as New York State assemblyman to Albany in 1842 (during which time he proposed the legislation that established New York's Central Park). In 1844, at age 28, he was appointed Judge of the Court of Common Pleas, on which he served (was elected) continuously until 1885 (that is, he served from age 28 until he retired from the bench at age 70).[44] The all-male legal profession was considered one of the two most "learned" of the time (the other, the ministry), its men comprising the "most cultivated" of American society.[45]

Throughout his legal career Daly made some newsworthy decisions, particularly during and in the aftermath of the Civil War. He advised Abraham Lincoln on southern trade at the ports ("privateering") and on southern prisoners of war, but as a Union Democrat he was anti-abolition and otherwise opposed to Lincoln (Chapter 3). Two of his most celebrated cases were the Astor Place Theater Riots case (in 1849) and the impeachment trial of Mayor A. Oakey Hall (in 1872), during the "Tweed Ring" scandals.[46] Daly was known as an "incorruptible judge" and, though himself serving as an on-again-off-again leader of the Irish political machine Tammany Hall, fought Tweed and his cohorts despite the potential risks to his (elected) judicial position.

It was Daly's decision in the Astor Place Theater Riots case that gained him a national reputation, as the case hinged on American troops firing on American citizens, killing 22 and resulting in the imprisonment of dozens of others.[47] Daly's decision in the case set a new precedent for criminalizing rioting; a decision that only further inflamed already tense ethnic and class conflict in the city among Irish immigrants and their Native-born neighbors, most of whom were Protestant English.[48] Most of the dead and imprisoned in the Astor Place case were Irish immigrants who had protested the performance of a British actor, and who were variously described in anti-Irish newspaper accounts as "gang members" and a "drunken Irish mob," or, by Irish sympathizers, murdered "innocent bystanders." Daly sided with the likes of Horace Greeley in the case, in justifying military force to maintain law and order. As Daly was well on his way to accumulating a large fortune via investments in land, railroads, and other real estate (Chapter 4), it is not surprising that his legal verdict reflected interests similar to those of a New York established elite with whom he was increasingly identifying. Some of the most vehement anti-Daly rhetoric found in the archives today is that written by Edward Z.C. Judson, who was jailed for a year for his participation in the Astor Place fighting. Judson, a.k.a. Ned Buntline, wrote against Daly on this and other topics in his New York weekly, *Ned Buntline's Own*.[49]

The Astor Place Theater case gained Daly a reputation for "tough" decisions on the bench, and because it went against working-class Irish (whom Daly supported in other ways), it set the stage for the extensive press coverage he would receive for work in the courts as well as for his geographical work. As noted above, Daly had a deep understanding of and appreciation for the potential of the popular press to advance himself and his many causes. While a rapidly expanding discourse on "exploration of the unknown" could be conveyed through numerous social nodal points – through government reports, scholarly papers delivered at the meetings of the proliferating learned societies, published travel books, journals, magazines, imaginative literature and so on[50] – I am especially interested in how Daly shrewdly coordinated and garnered a great deal of support for his many geographical (and other) projects through newspapers. (He collected hundreds of newspaper articles about himself in 21 large scrapbook volumes now held among his other papers at the New York Public Library.)

In addition to his geographical writing, Daly wrote several books on the history of the courts and was author of numerous biographical, political, literary, scientific, and legal papers, most of them issued in pamphlet form. Topics included everything from world's fairs and markets, to Jewish settlement in the U.S., antiquity, New York City politics, the Civil War, Christopher Columbus, the Monroe Doctrine, botanical gardens, Shakespeare, theater in America, and poetry. His books include *Common Pleas for the City and County of New York* (1855) and *The Settlement of Jews in North America* (1893); other works include, among many others, "Historical Sketch of the Judicial Tribunals of New York from 1623 to 1846" (1855); "History of Naturalization and its Laws in Different Countries" (1860); "Are the Southern Privateersmen Pirates?" (1862); "Origin and History of Institutions for the Promotion of Useful Arts by Industrial Exhibitions" (1864); "Reports of Cases in the Court of Common Pleas, City and County of New York" (13 vols., 1868–1887); "Want of a Botanical Garden in New York" (1891); "Is the Monroe Doctrine Involved in the Controversy between Venezuela and Great Britain?" (1896); and "The First Theater in America, When Was the Drama First Introduced in America?" (1896).[51]

Daly and his wife Maria attracted much attention within New York's social scene, due to Daly's rising professional status but also owing to Maria's "old money" connections in the city. Charles and Maria had married relatively late in life, in 1856 (he was 40), and not without a great deal of familial ethnic, class, and religious tensions.[52] Evidence of their wide social net can be found in the hundreds of condolence letters to Daly, from diplomats, businessmen, politicians, and explorers, throughout the U.S. and Europe, on the occasion of Maria's death in 1894.[53]

In addition to – or perhaps despite – his well-publicized role in court proceedings, Daly led several reform efforts and aid societies in the city, mostly for Irish and Jewish immigrants. He was active in the Hebrew Benevolent Orphan Asylum, for example, and the St. Patrick's Society (which provided, among other things, relief against the Irish famine). Daly also led tenement house and street sanitation reform in the city, and was active in the Working Women's Protective Union, arguing in favor of a united, organized movement to promote fairer wages for seamstresses. His relatively progressive views on women included advocating the single life as potentially more "happy and useful" than the married.[54]

Daly met Alexander von Humboldt in Germany during a European trip in 1851, and shortly after his return – "fired about geography" – he joined the American Geographical Society.[55] In his over 40-year association with the society Daly greatly expanded its bank account; its membership – which rose from a couple of hundred in the early 1860s to approximately 1,400 by 1874; and library. The AGS library became the largest privately maintained geographical research library and map collection in the western hemisphere, its purpose "for the benefit of the scholar, the merchant, and the statist." Daly donated 700 volumes from

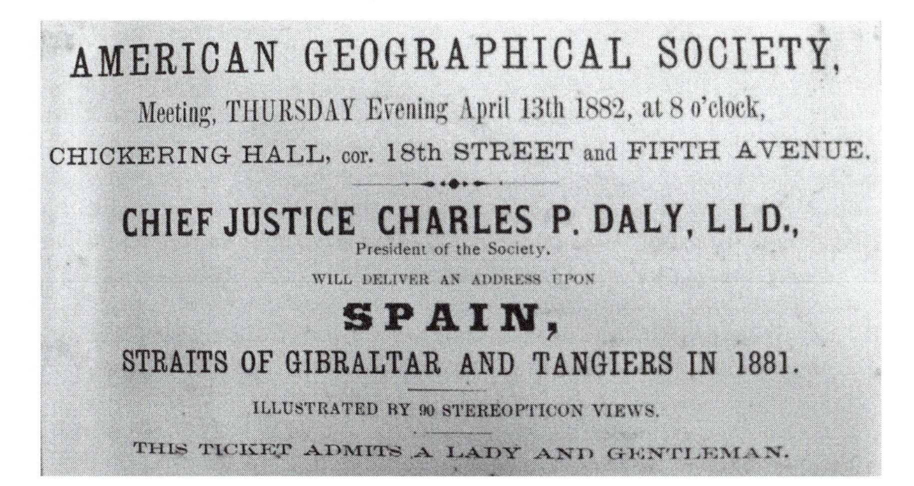
AMERICAN GEOGRAPHICAL SOCIETY,

Meeting, THURSDAY Evening April 13th 1882, at 8 o'clock,

CHICKERING HALL, cor. 18th STREET and FIFTH AVENUE.

CHIEF JUSTICE CHARLES P. DALY, LL.D.,

President of the Society.

WILL DELIVER AN ADDRESS UPON

SPAIN,

STRAITS OF GIBRALTAR AND TANGIERS IN 1881.

ILLUSTRATED BY 90 STEREOPTICON VIEWS.

THIS TICKET ADMITS A LADY AND GENTLEMAN.

Figure 1.4 Admission Ticket, Meeting of the American Geographical Society featuring a lecture by Charles P. Daly

Source: Charles P. Daly Papers, Vol. 9. Manuscripts and Archives Division, The New York Public Library, Astor, Lenox and Tilden Foundations.

his own personal library (of 12,000 volumes) to the AGS on his 75th birthday, bringing its total to 14,000 volumes by 1874. He increased AGS correspondence with numerous geographical and scientific societies around the world, meanwhile becoming an honorary member or fellow of most – the RGS as well as the Italian, Berlin, Imperial Russia, and Madrid geographical societies. His guest appearance at the RGS in June 1874 was widely praised in the London newspapers (and this despite his avid Irish republicanism; see Chapter 3).[56] As a degree of evidence that Daly's influence on American geography went well beyond New York, the London papers referred to him as the "president of the geographical society of the United States."[57]

Daly invigorated the society's published journal with professional articles (beyond the former practice of simply reprinting lectures), and as noted above, was himself a prolific author on geographical topics, publishing 40 papers and commentaries on topics ranging from "Recent Developments in Central Africa and the Valley of the Congo" (1884) to "The History of Physical Geography" (1890) to "Have We a Portrait of Columbus?" (1893) among a wide variety of other subjects.[58] As noted above, it was his annual addresses though, lasting roughly from 1865–1893, on the "state of geographical knowledge" for each year, for which Daly received most recognition as a geographer. The addresses, which the AGS council referred to as "highly instructive and entertaining," enumerated or collated researches of the previous year, exhaustively and elaborately detailing scientific advances gained by voyages of discovery, surveys, navigational achievements, and other topics of interest.[59] These arguably adopted the style and content of the annual addresses of RGS President Sir Roderick Murchison, whom Daly held as the "ideal type of geographer."[60] These addresses were typically delivered at society meetings, published in the society's *Journal*, and oftentimes published verbatim in the newspapers. The content and reception of Daly's lectures and publications serve as the basis for each of the chapters in the volume, and Maria Daly's diary offers glimpses into their impact. In February of 1879 she noted:

> Last evening was the Geo. Soc. monthly meeting … the audience was remarkable for so inclement an evening! It was listened to with great attention. The [stereopticon] views much appreciated and Chas. [t]his morning most complementary notices in all the papers.[61]

Charles Daly died of a ruptured blood vessel, "apoplexy," in 1899, after suffering numerous unspecified health problems from overwork and exhaustion (see Chapter 2). Upon his death the society held a special meeting in his memory, something they had only done for him, Alexander von Humboldt, Karl Ritter, and one or two others.[62] A number of sites in the Arctic were named after Daly (Chapter 5), and the society established the Charles P. Daly Gold Medal in 1902, which recognizes "valuable or distinguished geographical services or labors."

Book Outline

Chapters of this book are (generally) arranged by the spaces of Daly's impact on geographical knowledge and practice, as well as by what I consider to be "foundational moments" or events within each.

In Chapter 2, *Charles P. Daly's Gendered Geography*, I further introduce Daly's personal subjectivity and social milieu, and link these to the practices and goals of the AGS. The chapter's driving question is why an explicit interest in collecting statistics was contentiously eliminated from the AGS's mission when Daly took over its leadership – it was founded as the American Geographical and Statistical Society. I argue that Daly's notion of geography was shaped by, among others, the social contours of masculinity and manhood inherent in mid- to late-nineteenth-century America. Daly shifted the AGS's focus from the interpretive "center" (e.g. AGS headquarters) to the exploratory "field," a move that reflected the challenges to elite men's manhood and social position in the urban workplace following the Civil War. The gender dynamics associated with the center versus the field is a useful way to contrast both sides of Charles Daly's persona – as a scholar performing detached, careful study yet as an "armchair explorer" who also derived a great deal of personal authority by staging popular and dramatic spectacles in New York City, speech-ifying and presenting himself on stage at geographical society meetings with returning heroic explorers from the Arctic, Africa, and elsewhere.

In Chapter 3, *New York City's Friend of Labor: Geography and Urban Social Reform*, I situate Charles Daly's life and work within the spaces of New York City and the nineteenth-century Age of Reform. This social movement coalesced around ideologies and activities aimed at eradicating or counteracting the ill effects of rapid industrialization, urbanization, and immigration; particularly addressing environmental clean up and the uplift of a number of target populations. This chapter focuses on Daly's leadership in a number of civic and reform causes that resonated closely with his work as geographer, with the programmatic interests and practices of the AGS, and with the material geographies he created on the ground in New York City. It therefore offers new perspectives on nineteenth-century reform movements and their connection to geography and geographical societies.

Daly forthrightly cast himself as a "friend of labor." As the son of foreign-born Irish immigrants, he worked particularly for Irish relief causes, in New York as well as in Ireland. The centerpiece to the chapter is Daly's considerable influence as city planner in improving the spaces of poor and working-class Irish and Jewish immigrants in New York – especially in tenement housing and street sanitation reform. Daly played a prominent role in battles for civic improvement, and as such I cast him as an early "city planner" – helping as he did develop a platform for subsequent urban development in housing, waste disposal, and street cleaning. It is worth underscoring the ideological appeal to geographical intervention – an intervention we can now see to be "geographical" – with contemporaries' appeal to geography as a practice *and* as a subject that could ameliorate the condition of the urban poor.

Chapter 4, *Transporting American Empire: Rails, Canals, and the Politics of the "Geo-Personal,"* explores links among Daly's work as judge, attorney, and diplomat, with that of his role as geographer. While Daly received a great deal of public praise for his work on behalf of those in need, in this chapter I raise questions about some of the personal motivations for his civic agenda, and for use of AGS venues to promote them. Daly's wife's family profited enormously by Daly's swaying the city council to cite the Bronx Botanical Gardens on their land, for example, basing his arguments on the needs of the working classes and the "well being of even the poorest man."

This chapter focuses on Daly's geographical work in North and Central America, detailing his involvement with companies influential in the development of two important, large-scale transportation systems: the Northern Pacific Railway Company (NPR) in the western United States, and the Nicaragua Canal Company, a company that competed for, but ultimately lost, the rights to build a shipping canal across Central America at Nicaragua.

Development of the railroad held personal interest for Daly; he was a major stockholder in the NPR, and worked extensively with agents to solicit potential immigrants from Germany to settle on land bought and sold from its (federally-endowed) right of way. In turn, the western routes of the Northern Pacific were researched, debated, and published by the AGS – a nexus of interests that explicitly tied personal gains, civic duties and responsibilities, and American expansionism with geographical knowledge and practices of the day. Daly also worked on behalf of the Nicaragua Canal Company, a company of which he became Vice President and legal counsel, and for which he fought for a federal charter to build in Nicaragua what eventually became the Panama Canal. From 1854 onwards, the AGS was the primary venue in the United States for discussions of a proposed ship canal through Central America, offering their resources in the form of lectures, publications, and lobbying of governments; within what they argued was a "fair minded, scientifically-based" discussion of the proposed routes. In this chapter I critically examine such debates within the commercial, political-expansionist, and physical geography arguments put forth; as well as the personal gains and losses Daly experienced by throwing his legal weight around (and despite the fact that "his" route was not ultimately selected).

In Chapter 5, *Arctic Space and the Jurist-Geographer*, I examine Charles Daly's professional "credentialing" that allowed him to shape the cognitive content of Arctic spaces and peoples for his many audiences, while influencing infrastructural development necessary for Arctic exploration and commercial ventures in the region. Such activities included pressuring the U.S. government for support of various expeditions; providing expeditionary equipment and cartographic support; and debating travel routes, physical geography, and ethnographical questions via AGS venues. This chapter analyzes Daly's and the AGS's roles in these endeavors, primarily via the expedition of Frederick Schwatka (1878–1880), an 11-month overland (sledge) journey in search of the remains of the perished Franklin expedition. Subsequent AGS President Robert E. Peary (1903–1907), disputed "discoverer" of the North Pole, was also a recipient of much of Daly's patronage during his expeditions to Greenland and points north in the 1890s.

While such activities structurally push the chapter, I am most interested in how Daly cast himself as a "jurist-geographer" when maneuvering through public, business, and scientific communities in order to secure Arctic exploration as a valuable civic enterprise. The nexus of Daly's social roles as judge, lawyer, and geographer allowed him to "hold court" on physical geography debates – such as on the Open Polar Sea theory – in influential ways: hearing and weighing the "evidence" obtained from Arctic explorations in highly schematic ways; staging spectacular events featuring the arrival of glorified explorers and Inuit "witnesses" in careful, calculated ways; and exerting a powerful influence over press coverage and thus the public culture of Arctic exploration more generally. Though Daly's and the AGS's commercial geography generally lacked a strong nationalistic component, underlying his civic agenda for Arctic exploration was a highly nationalistic end – not by participating in the cruder, masculinist world of "firsts" that so typifies our histories of geography, but rather by casting polar research as disinterested science that would ensure national prestige and rank within the international scientific community. Daly's insistence on the scientific benefits to Arctic exploration informed geography as a practical science, with ends that would nonetheless mediate and delimit Arctic commerce, national and multi-national diplomatic relations, and race relations with Inuit. Daly's understanding of the public culture of scientific travel and exploration gives us a picture that was, among other things, shrewd in its cross-cultural politics.

Chapter 6, *"Geographical Exploration is Commercial Progress": In the Congo*, begins with the enduring leitmotif of the AGS: the support of a commercial or business geography. As judge, civic leader, and AGS President Charles Daly perhaps more than anything else made his mark by advancing American commercial development, particularly in transportation and resource development, within U.S. borders and outside of them. Geographical knowledge discovered, discussed, and advanced by the AGS links to an extensive number of American commercial ventures. This chapter focuses on one particular geo-commercial colonial project with which the AGS was deeply involved in Central Africa.

Unbeknown to most, through the AGS the United States participated in the nineteenth-century colonization of Africa, with Charles Daly serving as the American mouthpiece, cheerleader, and institutional point man for King Leopold II of Belgium, ruthless colonizer of the African Congo in the later nineteenth century. Leopold heavily recruited Daly's support for his plan, and Daly in turn provided an American platform for Leopold, organizing support among the mercantile community, lobbying the U.S. Congress and the President, and hosting geographical meetings about current explorations in Africa, primarily with the object of setting up Leopold's trading stations for rubber and ivory. Daly was unlikely tricked by Leopold's supposed humanitarian efforts in the Congo (suppression of the slave trade); he likely went along with Leopold and Leopold's envoy, Henry S. Sanford, for the commercial advantages he hoped to gain for American business interests. "Geographical knowledge" thus constituted and deployed by the AGS for such purposes – such as reports to influential civic and political bodies, as well as events honoring explorers of Africa such as the infamous Henry Morton Stanley – deserves careful attention in its capacity to shed light on American involvement in colonial Africa as well as geography's role in American commercial empire building there in the nineteenth century.

Finally, in Chapter 7, *Postscript: Reclaiming Charles P. Daly, Prospects and Problems*, I reflect on the politics and implications of undertaking archival research about historical figures such as Charles P. Daly who have been considered irrelevant or unimportant to geography's history. As well, perhaps paradoxically, I want to draw out the implications for today's audiences in marking the previously unmarked white male subjects of geography's history, thus making visible how geographical knowledge, and the so-called dominant traditions in geography, come to be considered as such.

Endnotes

1 Throughout the book I refer to the organization as the "American Geographical Society," even though it was known as the "American Geographical and Statistical Society" until 1871, a change that drives my discussion in Chapter 2.

2 Despite this, and unlike other American and European geographical organizations, the nineteenth-century AGS remains virtually unstudied. Among the works that discuss geographical societies established and functioning in the nineteenth-century United States see Preston E. James and Geoffrey J. Martin, *All Possible Worlds: A History of Geographical Ideas*, 2nd ed. (New York: John Wiley, 1993); Catherine Lutz and Jane Collins, *Reading National Geographic* (Chicago: University of Chicago Press, 1993); Julie Tuason, "The Ideology of Empire in National Geographic Magazine's Coverage of the Philippines, 1898–1908," *Geographical Review* 89 (1999): 34–53; Susan Schulten, *The Geographical Imagination in America, 1880–1950* (Chicago: University of Chicago Press, 2001); and Tamar Y. Rothenberg, *Presenting America's World: Strategies of Innocence in National Geographical Magazine, 1888–1945* (Burlington: Ashgate Publishing, 2007). Very few secondary works are available on the AGS. They include John K. Wright's institutional history, *Geography in the Making: The American Geographical Society 1851–1951* (New York: American Geographical Society, 1952); Ernesto E. Ruiz, "Geography and Diplomacy: The American Geographical Society and the 'Geopolitical' Background of American Foreign Policy, 1848–1861" (PhD dissertation, Northern Illinois University, 1975). Neil Smith's *American Empire: Roosevelt's Geographer and the Prelude to Globalization* (Berkeley: University of California Press, 2003) focuses on the influential twentieth-century AGS director, Isaiah Bowman, beginning *ca.* 1915; and several works detail women of the AGS, including Janice Monk, "Women's Worlds at the American Geographical Society," *Geographical Review* 93 (2, 2003): 237–257 and Douglas McMannis, "Leading Ladies at the AGS," *Geographical Review* 86 (1996): 270–277. Other works make only brief mention of the AGS: e.g. Schulten, ibid., and Tim Inwin, *The Place of Geography* (New York: John Wiley & Sons, 1992).

3 American Geographical Society website (www.amergeog.org), date last accessed 16 June 2010. Wright, ibid., 75–111 argues that Daly was one of three influential AGS leaders of his era: the others George Cullum (an army general), Vice President for many years under Daly who handled many of the business aspects of the organization; and Francis Stout, an American "blue blood" who focused on the society's links with Europe.

4 References to the "great geographical age" appear in, for instance, Charles P. Daly, "Annual Address. The Geographical Work of the World for 1875," *Journal of the American Geographical Society of New York* 7 (1875): 34; "Annual Address. The Geographical Work of the World in 1876," *Journal of the American Geographical Society of New York* 8 (1876): 95; and "Annual Address. Geographical Work of the World in 1878 & 1879," *Journal of the American Geographical Society of New York* 12 (1880): 103.

5 Good examples include David N. Livingstone, *The Geographical Tradition* (Oxford: Blackwell, 1992); Felix Driver, *Geography Militant* (London: Blackwell, 2001); Charles W.J. Withers, *Geography, Science and National Identity: Scotland Since 1520* (Cambridge: Cambridge University Press, 2001).

6 See, for instance, David N. Livingstone, *Nathaniel Southgate Shaler and the Culture of American Science* (Tuscaloosa: University of Alabama Press, 1987); Matthew Hannah, *Governmentality and the Mastery of Territory in Nineteenth-Century America* (Cambridge: Cambridge University Press, 2000); Smith, *American Empire*; and David Lambert, "'Taken Captive by the Mystery of the Great River': Towards an Historical Geography of British Geography and Atlantic Slavery," *Journal of Historical Geography* 35 (2009): 44–65.

7 I make the case that the nineteenth-century AGS projects were equally as important as those undertaken in the twentieth century under Isaiah Bowman, so aptly brought forward by Neil Smith in his *American Empire*. Bowman made his mark during the post-WWI Paris Peace Conference and on post-WWII global geo-politics, partly by making AGS resources available to the federal government. Some of the same observations made of Smith's treatment of Bowman apply here: Matthew Hannah, "'In Full View Yet Invisible': On Neil Smith's American Empire," *Political Geography* 24 (2005): 240, argues that Smith's treatment of Bowman is quite apart from whether or how Bowman himself understood the overarching geographical logic of American empire. Smith wants us to pay attention to wider patterns and tensions as well as Bowman's agency and impact.

8 Linda Colley, *The Ordeal of Elizabeth Marsh: A Woman in World History* (New York: Pantheon Books, 2007), xix.

9 Edward Said, *Orientalism: Western Conceptions of the Orient* (London: Kegan Paul, 1978); and *Culture and Imperialism* (New York: Alfred A. Knopf, 1993).

10 Felix Driver, "Geography's Empire: Histories of Geographic Knowledge," *Environment and Planning D: Society and Space* 10 (1992): 23–40; David Livingstone, *Geographical Tradition*, 16; Mike J. Heffernan, "The Science of Empire: The French Geographical Movement and the Forms of French Imperialism, 1870–1920," in *Geography and Empire*, eds. Anne Godlewska and Neil Smith (Oxford: Blackwell, 1994), 92–114; Morag Bell, Robin Butlin and Michael Heffernan, eds. *Geography and Imperialism, 1820–1940* (Manchester: Manchester University Press, 1995); Jan Golinski, *Making Natural Knowledge: Constructivism and the History of Science* (Cambridge: Cambridge University Press, 1998); Driver, *Geography Militant*; Withers, *Geography, Science and National Identity*, 12–14; Charles W.J. Withers and Robert J. Mayhew, "Rethinking 'Disciplinary' History: Geography in British Universities, *c.* 1580–1887," *Transactions of the Institute of British Geographers* 27 (2002): 11–29; Robert J. Mayhew, "Materialist Hermeneutics, Textuality and the History of Geography: Print Spaces in British Geography, *c.* 1500–1900," *Journal of Historical Geography* 33 (2007): 466–488.

11 David N. Livingstone, "The Spaces of Knowledge: Contributions Towards a Historical Geography of Science," *Environment and Planning D: Society and Space* 13 (1995): 5–34, quote on 28.

12 Feminists (including feminist geographers) were among the first scholars to acknowledge the "situatedness," partiality, and localness of all disciplinary knowledge; see for example, Donna Haraway, "Situated Knowledges: The Science Question in Feminism and the Privilege of Partial Perspectives," *Feminist Studies* (1988): 575–599; and Gillian Rose, *Feminism and Geography: The Limits of Geographical Knowledge* (Minneapolis: University of Minnesota Press, 1993). Also see Steven Shapin, *The Scientific Revolution* (Chicago: University of Chicago Press, 1996); Steven Shapin, "Placing the View from Nowhere: Historical and Sociological Problems in the Location of Science," *Transactions of the Institute of British Geographers* 23 (1998): 5–12; Withers, *Geography, Science and National Identity*, 16–24.

13 Driver, "Geography's Empire."

14 Daly, "Annual Address," 7 (1875): 34. Other U.S.-based societies came later, the National Geographic in 1888; the Geographical Society of Chicago in 1898; the Geographical Society of Philadelphia, Geographical Society of the Pacific, and the Geographical Society of California in 1891; the Geographical Society of Baltimore in 1902; and the Association of American Geographers in 1904, among others. Many were short-lived. There was also a great deal of competition among them, particularly the NGS and AGS in the early years, and the NGS and AAG later. See Roger E. Downs, "Popularization and Geography: An Inseparable Relationship," *Annals of the Association of American Geographers* 100 (2, 2010): 444–467; Rothenberg, *Presenting America's World*; Gary Dunbar, ed. *Geography: Discipline, Profession and Subject Since 1870* (Dordrecht, Netherlands: Kluwer Academic, 2001); Brian W. Blouet, ed. *The Origins of Academic Geography in the United States* (Hamden: Archon Books, 1981); Wright, *Geography in Making*, 144, 167.

15 These are by Charles Daly's own accounting: "Annual Address. Subject: The Geographical Work of the World in 1872," *Journal of the American Geographical Society of New York* 4 (1873): 116, and "Annual Address," 12 (1880): 1. Also see Ruiz, *Geography and Diplomacy*; James and Martin, *All Possible Worlds*, Wright, *Geography in the Making*. Much of the early AGS meeting minutes focused on foreign correspondence, descriptions of what was being done to initiate and stay in contact with geographical societies overseas. The society saw itself as a link between "the old world" and the new, as well as a link between the U.S. federal government and foreign countries, particularly in the exchange of information that "may be of interest to the mercantile community"; e.g. see "Committee on Foreign Correspondence and Exchange," *Bulletin of the American Geographical and Statistical Society*, Vol. II (1856): 57–83.

16 For works by geographers, see for instance, John Agnew, *Hegemony: The New Shape of Global Power* (Philadelphia: Temple University Press, 2005) and Mona Domosh, *American Commodities in an Age of Empire* (New York: Routledge, 2006).

17 Heffernan, "The Science of Empire." For discussion of the Commercial Geographical Society of Paris, for example, see William H. Schneider, *An Empire for the Masses: The French Popular Image of Africa, 1870–1900* (Westport: Greenwood Press, 1982).

18 Mona Domosh, *Invented Cities: The Creation of Landscape in 19th Century New York and Boston* (New Haven: Yale University Press, 1996), 12–15. Ronald H. Bayor and

Timothy J. Meagher, eds. *The New York Irish* (Baltimore: Johns Hopkins University Press, 1996).

19 The society continued its move uptown, to 15 West 81st Street in 1901, a decade later to 156th and Broadway, and in the later twentieth century moved back downtown to its present location on Wall Street (see Chapter 7).

20 For example, Charles P. Daly, "Recent Developments in Central Africa and the Valley of the Congo," *Journal of the American Geographical Society of New York* 16 (1884): 89.

21 Driver, *Geography Militant*, 25.

22 For example, "Memorial to the Secretary of the Navy," *Bulletin of the American Geographical and Statistical Society*, Vol. I (1, 1852): 66.

23 AGS, "Transactions of the Society for 1873," *Journal of the American Geographical Society of New York* 5 (1873): 45. Among such men was William Henry Moore, President of Atlantic Mutual Life Insurance Company, who was AGS Councilor from 1869–1906.

24 Compare to Schulten, *Geographical Imagination in America.*

25 Hayden Lorimer, "Telling Small Stories: Spaces of Knowledge and the Practice of Geography," *Transactions of the Institute of British Geographers* 28 (2003): 197–217; Hayden Lorimer and Nick Spedding, "Excavating Geography's Hidden Spaces," *Area* 34 (2002): 294–302; Alastair Bonnett, "Geography as the World Discipline: Connecting Popular and Academic Geographical Imaginations," *Area* 35 (2003): 55–63. Also see Downs, "Popularization and Geography."

26 Lorimer, "Telling Small Stories."

27 Downs, "Popularization and Geography," 445.

28 Jurgen Habermas, *The Structural Formation of the Public Sphere: An Inquiry into a Category of Bourgeois Society* (Cambridge: Cambridge University Press, 1989). Withers, *Geography, Science and National Identity*, 4, outlines the many critiques and advances on Habermas' basic argument.

29 For context see Charles Withers, "Towards a History of Geography in the Public Sphere," *Hist. Sci.* xxxvi (1998): 1–39, quote on 2; W.A. Koelsch, "Academic Geography, American Style: An Institutional Perspective," in Dunbar, ed. *Geography: Discipline, Profession and Subject*, 245–279. For background on U.S. school geography see Bruce A. Harvey, *American Geographics: U.S. National Narratives and the Representation of the Non-European World, 1830–1865* (Stanford: Stanford University Press, 2001). Harvey, 28, calls school geography a "patriotic genre" during the antebellum period.

30 Mrs. Henry R. Hoyt, in an interview with Daly's biographer Harold Hammond. Transcribed interview, 2 November 1947, 42. Box 10, Charles P. Daly Correspondence and Papers, Manuscripts and Archives Division, New York Public Library (NYPL), New York. Maria Daly's diaries, both published and unpublished, are also an important source of such information. Harold Hammond, ed. *Maria Lydig Daly, Diary of a Union Lady 1861–1865* (New York: Funk & Wagnalls Company, Inc., 1962); Maria L. Daly Correspondence and Papers, Vols. 25, 26, 27, and 28, Charles P. Daly Correspondence and Papers, NYPL.

31 Unidentified article, *Evening Post*, 1 September 1864. Scores of similar statements appeared in the papers upon Daly's retirement from the bench; for instance, "Chief-

Justice Daly," *New York Times*, 15 November 1884; and "Forty-one Years a Judge: The Honorable Career of a Wise and Upright Jurist," *New York Times*, 15 November 1885.

32 "The Chief Justice-ship," *New York Herald*, 16 September 1873. The quote comes from an article advocating that President Grant appoint Daly to the United States Supreme Court. In addition to pointing out Daly's many positive virtues – his stainless career, the fact that he is patron of the arts and "entertains all the foreigners who come to our shores" – the article further noted that Judge Daly "has a considerable fortune which would adorn the office." Second quote from a *Herald* article of 13 October 1876, cited in Harold Hammond, *A Commoner's Judge: The Life and Times of Charles Patrick Daly* (Boston: Christopher Publishing House, 1954): 275.

33 "Chief Justice Daly," *The Hour*, 29 January 1881. Subsequent chapters provide a more in-depth analysis of media responses to Daly's lectures and other geographical events.

34 "To Have a New Home," *New York Tribune*, 26 September 1897.

35 Schneider, *Empire for the Masses*; Michael Heffernan, "The Cartography of the Fourth Estate," in *The Imperial Map: Cartography and the Mastery of Empire*, ed. James R. Akerman (Chicago: University of Chicago Press, 2009): 261–299.

36 David N. Livingstone, "Science, Site and Speech: Scientific Knowledge and the Spaces of Rhetoric," *History of the Human Sciences* 20 (2, 2007): 71–98; see 71, 75. Among the many notable recent books on this topic see Miles Ogborn, *India Ink: Script and Print in the Making of the English East India Company* (Chicago: University of Chicago Press, 2007).

37 Domosh, *American Commodities*, 22–23.

38 I thank Mike Heffernan for his insightful observations on this point.

39 See for example, Michel Foucault, *The Order of Things: An Archaeology of the Human Sciences* (1970; rpt. New York: Vintage, 1994) and Michel Foucault, *The Archaeology of Knowledge and the Discourse on Language* (New York: Pantheon, 1972).

40 After Michael Robinson, *The Coldest Crucible: Arctic Exploration and American Culture* (Chicago: University of Chicago Press, 2006).

41 In addition to Hammond's biography, *Commoner's Judge*, see H.W.H. Knott "Charles Patrick Daly," *Dictionary of Biography* 5 (1973): 41–42; Hammond's *Maria Daly, Diary of a Union Lady 1861–1865*, especially xl–xli; Miklos Pinther, "Charles Patrick Daly 1816–1899," *Ubique: Notes from the American Geographical Society* 23 (2, 2003): 1–4; and Barry Ryan's law entry on Daly in John Garraty, ed. *The American National Biography* (Cary, N.C.: Oxford University Press, 1999). As to Daly's family genealogy, see "New York Celebrities, Chief Justice Daly," *The Sun*, 3 January 1885.

42 Max Kohler, *Chas. P. Daly: A Tribute to His Memory* (New York: *The American Hebrew*, 1899), asserted that Daly enjoyed the mystique surrounding his early years and so kept them obscure. Kohler also claimed that it was these early travels that sparked Daly's interest in geography.

43 Leo Hershkowitz, "The Irish and the Emerging City: Settlement to 1844," in Bayor and Meagher, *New York Irish*, 20.

44 The Common Pleas Court was considered the highest court in New York City during the nineteenth century, existing by that name from 1821 until 1896, when it was dissolved

and its jurisdiction divided between the Supreme Court, the Superior Court, and the General Sessions Court.

45 E. Anthony Rotundo, *American Manhood: Transformations in Masculinity from the Revolution to the Modern Era* (New York: Basic Books, 1993): 170–172.

46 For details on these cases see Kohler, *Chas. P. Daly Tribute*, 4, and Hammond, *Commoner's Judge*, 153–156.

47 Edward K. Spann, "Union Green: The Irish Community and the Civil War," in Bayor and Meagher, *New York Irish*, 207.

48 Only one other case in the U.S. history had dealt with rioting, and this in Philadelphia, in which "an occasional riot was to be tolerated as a safety-valve for the people"; Hammond, *Commoner's Judge*, 66, also see Michael Kimmel, *Manhood in America: A Cultural History*, 2nd ed. (New York: Oxford University Press, 2006): 40–42.

49 "Ned Buntline" was a dime novelist who helped create the legend of Buffalo Bill Cody, "Wild Bill." He spent his boyhood in Danville, Pennsylvania, coincidentally near where I now live. After prison he resurfaced as an organizer in the "No Nothing" political movement, whose platform was primarily opposition to immigrants coming to America.

50 After Driver, *Geography Militant*, 28–29.

51 Full citations for the books are: Charles P. Daly, *The Settlement of Jews in North America*, ed. Max Kohler (New York: Philip Cowan, 1893) and *Common Pleas for the City and County of New York, With an Account of the State and Its Tribunals, from the Time of Its Settlement by the Dutch in 1623 until the Adoption of the State Constitution in 1846* (New York: R. Delafield, 1855).

52 In addition to the tensions stemming from their vastly different economic backgrounds, Maria's ethnic heritage was Dutch and German, and as Episcopalian, her family disdained Daly's Irish Roman Catholicism. According to Hammond, *Commoner's Judge* and *Diary of a Union Lady*, Maria's father disapproved of the marriage and assumed Daly was marrying Maria for her money; Daly did in fact become wealthy through the marriage, as well as through his many real estate properties and other investments (see Chapters 3 and 4). They did not bear any children.

53 Hundreds of condolence letters, from explorers, politicians, businessmen, neighbors and friends, as well as European colleagues especially from Germany, France, Holland, and Belgium, are archived in Box 7 (1894–1897, particularly see the file for 1894), Charles P. Daly Papers, NYPL.

54 "Judge Daly's Address," *Home Journal*, 8 November 1862.

55 Hammond, *Commoner's Judge*, 98. Von Humboldt's letter of 18 July 1851, written to his friend Freiherr von Bunsen of Daly, Box 1, Charles P. Daly Papers, NYPL.

56 Daly was "much cheered on rising to address the company," and in his remarks spoke of the efforts of the AGS "open[ing] out the resources of the American continent for the uses of Americans and [all] mankind." "Royal Geographical Society," *Morning Post*, *Daily News*, the London *Times*, and the *Daily Telegraph*, all 23 June 1874.

57 Both the *Times* and *Daily News* quoted explorer George Schweinfurth's reference to Daly as President of the "geographical society of the United States."

58 Daly, "Recent Developments in Central Africa," *Journal* 16 (1884); "Annual Address. On the History of Physical Geography," *Journal of the American Geographical Society of New York* 22 (1890): 1–55; "Have We a Portrait of Columbus? Annual Address, January 9, 1893," *Journal of the American Geographical Society of New York* 25 (1893): 1–63. Daly also lectured on Spain and Christopher Columbus just after he returned from purchasing a portrait of Columbus in Madrid in 1882. See "A New Yorker's Views on Spain," *New York Times*, 14 April 1882. Ticket from Vol. 9, Charles P. Daly Papers, NYPL.

59 AGS Council, "Transactions of the Society for 1873," *Journal of the American Geographical Society of New York* 5 (1874): 35–45; quote on 37. Daly delivered annual addresses on a great range of topics throughout his tenure as AGS President, though those specifically on "the geographical work of the world," lasted from 1869 until 1880, with one other so-titled in 1888. His "Geographical Results of 1869" were covered in the *Naval and Military Gazette*, 23 February 1870. In the address Daly noted 13 geographical "accomplishments" for that year including completion of the U.S. transcontinental railroad and Suez Canal. As discussed in subsequent chapters, the news media closely followed Daly's annual addresses, with headlines such as "Geographical Progress," *New York Times*, 28 February 1878. Wright, *Geography in the Making*, notes that Daly delivered his first annual address on 16 March 1865, though it was not published.

60 Felix Driver, personal correspondence, 21 June 2010. See Daly's "Annual Address," *Journal* 4 (1875): 34.

61 Maria L. Daly, diary entry dated 12 February 1879, Vol. 28, Charles P. Daly Papers, NYPL. In another entry dated 24 March 1880, ibid., Maria noted, "Last night went … to hear the Judge's annual address on the work of the world for 1878–79. It was very much liked no one felt it too long … he was in good voice, easy and natural. It was a great success. I felt quite proud of him."

62 John K. Wright, "British Geography and the American Geographical Society, 1851–1951," *Geographical Journal* 118 (2, 1952): 153–167; see 159. AGS, "Transactions of the Society, January–February, 1900," *Journal of the American Geographical Society of New York* 32 (1, 1900): 88–100.

Chapter 2
Charles P. Daly's Gendered Geography

Introduction

Until 1871, the AGS was known as the American Geographical and Statistical Society, and during its first two decades, as the name implies, its work was cast as both "geographical" and "statistical" in nature. This bifurcation of interests allows a unique window into the study of the relationship between the calculation sciences and geography as field exploration, and both as particular types of gendered discourses, knowledges, and skills. In this chapter I examine the relationship between statistics and geography, as perceived by AGS men, and argue that the content of the knowledge they produced was shaped at least in part by the social contours of masculinity and manhood inherent within their milieu.

David Livingstone reminds us that "the task of geography's historians, at least in part, is … to ascertain how and why particular practices and procedures come to be accounted geographically legitimate and hence normative at different moments in time and in different spatial settings."[1] Livingstone emphasizes that it is not enough to simply acknowledge that geography was practiced in particular social contexts, but rather that social conditions "insinuated their way" into the very heart of theorizing. "This suggests," he writes, "that the geographer's traditional craft-skills … cartographic competence, regional survey, statistical methods and so on, turn out to be rhetorical devices of persuasion by which geographers have reinforced the authority of their assertions."[2]

With such admonitions in mind, my narrative hinges on one traditional craft-skill of the geographer – "geo-statistics" – a particularly contested one in historiographies of western geography as well as contemporary U.S. geography.[3] The first question that arises is why an explicit interest in statistics was eliminated from the AGS's agenda after its first two decades. I suggest that this had to do with the gender dynamics of the men running this homo-social organization – their so-called crisis of manhood or crisis of masculinity – as much as anything else.[4] Although scholars of masculinity such as Michael Kimmel persuasively argue that social relations during this period thrust male masculinity into "crisis," I am also sympathetic with Gail Bederman's position that to call the obsession with manhood during this era a crisis perhaps overstates the case, as gender systems are always in a state of "constant contradiction, change, and renegotiation."[5] I maintain the notion here, though, to propose that there are certain social spaces within which issues of gender become more punctuated than others, and those of mid- to late-nineteenth-century American geography seem to be one of them.

The "manliness" of the calculation sciences – conducted "at home" – versus narratives of field experience – conducted "away" – takes on particular salience with respect to the AGS. Charles Daly's role in shifting the AGS's albeit partial emphasis from geographical statistics to field exploration is closely connected to the shifting ideological contours of male masculinity at the time and its public performance. It should become clear that gendered individuals and gendered knowledge are mutually constituted; the differently gendered subject positions of individual actors were intimately connected to both the knowledge they created and the way they outwardly expressed or performed their manhood in their public, professional lives.

A substantial body of work has established connections between the valorization and celebration of exploration and fieldwork in geography in the nineteenth and early twentieth centuries and shown how it was related to, and constitutive of, ideas of manliness and masculinity. Much of this work, however, focuses on the British context. In mid- to late-nineteenth-century American geography, a different set of parameters was at play. An American empire based on commerce rather than on distant colonies lent a different cast to the relationship among exploration, geographical science, and manliness.

When the AGS and Charles Daly came onto the scene, the country was just beginning to recover from the devastations of the Civil War and the militaristic mindset it engendered: male life as warfare or battlefield. Continental expansion westward in the latter half of the nineteenth century, the "taming" of the American West, also provided a fertile environment for development of an adventurous, "expansive" American manhood.[6] The West, as both reality and idea, contained the epitome of masculine culture and manly virtues embodied by, among others, the ambitious, risk-taking speculator of land and resources or the strong, silent cowboy as the quintessential American hero.

Other dramatic social forces likewise shifted ideas of manliness in the second half of the nineteenth century. Rapid industrialization and urban growth, and unprecedented numbers of immigrants from Europe, combined to provoke major structural changes and competition in society, especially in the urban workplace. This is specifically germane to the study of the AGS and its origins in New York City, central node of an exploding American industrial capitalism in the mid-nineteenth century.[7] The New York business elite who founded the AGS were explicit about the contributions geography could make to commercial development. These men's "marketplace manhood,"[8] set against other expressions of masculine culture in northeastern U.S. cities (those both more genteel and more valiantly intrepid), combined to shape "commercial" American geography in unique ways. While this chapter focuses on tensions between geographical statistics and field exploration, I should note that Charles Daly's geography also found expression in urban social reform and as such, the uplift of target populations in New York City (Chapter 3).

I begin this chapter with a discussion of relationships between mid-nineteenth-century statistical and other forms of geographical knowledge, emphasizing the ways that both commerce and male masculinity worked through the production of such knowledge. This sets the stage for my analysis of Charles Daly's "gendered geography" – as a realm of knowledge, a set of skills, a set of discourses, and as phenomena materially produced "on the ground." It is worth noting that although I cast the AGS as a homo-social male organization – as men indeed held the power and leadership positions throughout the nineteenth century – from its beginning the AGS admitted women as members (unlike London's RGS), and many women appear to have attended meetings. The first woman member was likely admitted in 1869, though by 1893 probably only nine of the 1,400 members were women (this changed significantly after 1915).[9] In the early twentieth century the AGS began inviting occasional woman mountaineers and explorers as speakers, such as Isabella Bird, May Sheldon, Fanny Bullock Workman, and Annie Peck (the latter two were rivals at the time for the women's mountaineering climbing record). Although it is beyond the purview of this book to draw conclusions about the AGS as a "woman-friendly" organization, others have done so,[10] especially in terms of staffing. For my purposes, I speculate that the earlier "Daly era" may well have set the stage for women's significant participation at the AGS, especially when considering Charles Daly's own relatively progressive ideas about women.[11]

Through study of the early AGS and Charles Daly's life and contributions to geography I am able to cast light on the gendered nature of the discipline within broader institutional and societal contexts, particularly by asking how challenges to male masculinity helped shape U.S. geography in the later nineteenth century. The AGS, and Daly in particular, turns out to be one important node in the performance and signification of American geography's hegemonic masculinity.

A Statistical-Geographical Society

The leitmotif of the American Geographical Society has always been the support of a sort of "business" geography; its maxim stated as "Geographical Exploration is Commercial Progress."[12] The AGS served its own particular niche in bringing geography to businessmen and professionals, men who for the most part were not connected either directly to universities or to federal or state bureaucracies; nor, like the National Geographic Society decades later, did they reach out explicitly to a public or mass audience in order to legitimate national interests abroad. For the most part, AGS men were wealthy patrons of geographical research and exploration, who advocated research (although rarely practicing it themselves), mostly for the commercial advantages it afforded. Ernesto Ruiz identified and grouped the known professions of all but nine of the 59 members of the AGS governing board (council and officers) in its first decade, from 1851 to 1861. He grouped these into six categories: 14 were entrepreneurs (in telegraph, shipping, promotion, land speculation, insurance, and manufacturing); 13 belonged to the Foreign Service; 11 were editors and publishers; 10 were specialists in earth science; six were clergymen; and five were lawyers, judges, and politicians.[13] Although the founders of other geographical societies also tended to represent such coalitions of interests, one might nonetheless characterize AGS men as particularly oriented towards business compared to, for example, the RGS, with its much higher representation of founding members who were career diplomats from the British Admiralty and Navy;[14] or the Paris Geographical Society, comprised mainly of aristocrats and military men "following narrow scientific pursuits," until its spin-off groups such as the Commission of Commercial Geography likewise turned towards the business community.[15] Professional and merchant-class men, such as those in the insurance industry, joined the AGS and served on its council, meanwhile profiting from use of AGS maps, charts, and information supplied about foreign countries.[16]

For the industrialist and merchant, "geography" and "statistics" were indispensable tools for locating foreign customers and analyzing the potential of new markets and profits, and the AGS thus became the means towards those ends for many of its founders. The seal of the AGS in its first decades imaginatively linked these threads of interest, combining the systematic lines of latitude and longitude imprinted on a globe overlaid with the term "Ubique" ("everywhere") – denoting confidence in the ability to order, contain, and dominate space – with that of the book of the Census, denoting a simultaneous statistical control of populations existing within those lines.[17]

Figure 2.1 Seal of the American Geographical and Statistical Society, *ca.* 1860

The AGS first distinguished itself in the mid-nineteenth century through its two principal objectives, the collecting and disseminating of information, and serving the business interests of New York. These were accomplished by hosting lectures, developing a research library, and publishing geographical and statistical findings. The original charter of the organization, passed by the New York State Legislature in 1852, defined its purpose as simply "collecting and diffusing geographical and statistical information"[18] and indicating that members were to have distinguished themselves in one or the other field. The procedure for and logic behind collecting and diffusing particular types of information was largely unsystematic and idiosyncratic, however, and depended upon individual members' interests. Thus the AGS can be characterized as a loose "center of information compilation" or "center of information exchange." This organization was of a different nature than Latour's well known (1987) "centers of calculation" that required a great deal more ordering, interpretation, and control of information collected.[19] As I discuss later, Charles Daly's staging of geographical meetings can be viewed as an attempt to comprehensively compile heterogeneous data about the polar regions or the geographical work of the world for a given year into coherent descriptive narratives for the public, although he also advanced interpretations of information collected when it suited his purposes.

In addition to collecting and exchanging information, the society's other main activity was sponsoring expeditions and supporting related exploratory activities, through funding, training, and preparing of explorers; publishing their findings; and acting as a pressure group lobbying governments for the support of particular expeditions. The society's principal exploratory interests in the nineteenth century were in the western U.S., South and Central America, Africa, and the Arctic. Certainly one of their more visible functions was in hosting explorers – providing a venue for their lectures, organizing receptions for them, and publishing their findings. While businessmen dominated the society's council, they also recognized the need for explorers to serve on the governing board and thus sought them out and elected them. One such explorer was the Scottish missionary David Livingstone, whose African letters to the AGS were featured at its second meeting.

Whereas much has been written about the roles of other geographical societies in polar expeditions and research,[20] little has been written about the AGS and its support of Arctic exploration in the nineteenth century. Certain figures in the annals of Arctic exploration stand out as beneficiaries of AGS support, such as Edwin de Haven, Elisha Kane, Isaac Hayes, and Charles Hall, who were among the American Arctic explorers during the period (Chapter 5).[21]

The founding members of the AGS set up special subcommittees to support exploration. Others were to collect statistical information from local, state, and national governments, foreign correspondents, and approximately 30 other scientific societies. Explicit interest in the collection of statistics can be seen in the first volume of the council's meeting minutes, in which committees were appointed for procuring lectures and papers on topics as diverse as "Regions of Vegetation & Statistics of Lighthouses," the "Topography of Texas & Statistics of Agriculture," and the "Statistics of Steam Navigation."[22] During the 1860s, when the Civil War halted much of the society's activities, the most active subcommittees worked on "statistical projects" dealing broadly with fisheries; cotton production and manufacture; iron, gold, and silver; soils; and so on. At this juncture, "statistical projects" involved the counting and enumerating of resources and populations in the form of figures, tables, and numbers, although not involving any manipulation of those numbers.

The content of the society's publications and lectures also attests to its statistical interests. Through 1859 the society's flagship publication, the *Journal* (both previously and subsequently called the *Bulletin*), carried separate "geographical" and "statistical" departments (although after 1870 this practice was abandoned). During the organization's first two decades, 170 papers were read at monthly meetings, and approximately one-fifth of these were considered statistical.[23] In all, 30 of the 170 papers were statistical, with 12 of those contributed by councilors themselves, a much higher proportion than they contributed to geographical papers. Another 12 of the 170 included but did not focus on numbers and tables; and the remainder focused on a wide ranging set of topics broadly identified as "geography," including exploration, ethnography, natural history, meteorology, and astronomy. Considering the diffuse nature of topics considered geography, "statistics" would appear to be the single most coherent subarea of interest, by the society's own reckoning.

Anglophone geography in the high Victorian period continued the eighteenth-century preoccupation with filling in the "blank spaces" on maps with empirical description, and, of course, the competition in doing so. Importantly, however, it was less a coherent, unified academic field than a set of emerging discourses and practices situated in various contexts and evolving from them. Geography in the nineteenth century included a heterogeneous array of activities, including exploration and travel, navigation, cartographic survey, regional inventory, collection of artifacts, geopolitical taxonomy, and resource compilation, often completed locally through fieldwork and discursively through the production of texts and images about places.[24]

How and why certain practices and discourses achieved authority, and audiences, is a critical question. The influence of Alexander von Humboldt on American geography of the period is important to recognize, particularly because Humboldtian science was a method numerical in orientation – an attempt to conduct fieldwork and describe the natural world in numerical terms. As many scholars have observed, von Humboldt's grand synthesizing project entailed precise and accurate measurement and then mapping every feature of the earth, with an aim not just to describe features, but to discover their relationships and the manner by which physical processes interacted. A panoply of instruments was used: barometer, chronometer, telescope, compass, quadrant, sextant, and thermometer. Ethnographic data was also supplied in numerical terms; for example, in comparing technologies of different culture groups. Michael Bravo describes this kind of work as "topographical mapping": "[r]eading signs on the surface of the landscape (the sources of rivers, oases, cloud patterns) provided the key for piecing together the landscape's inner propensities for imperial commerce – the direction and flow of its waters, the moral qualities of its populations and the caravan routes for the traffic in humans," all of which could be further combined with other forms of geographical knowledge such as that of the manners and customs of local inhabitants.[25] Michael Dettlebach adds that the result of such work was often encyclopedic, "embracing botany, mineralogy, zoology, geology, meteorology, terrestrial magnetism, atmospheric chemistry and tides, and topography, but only insofar as these were capable of *numerical* expression, arrangement, and comparison" (italics added).[26]

Significantly, when Charles Daly assumed leadership of the AGS in 1864, one of the first things he did was oversee the dropping of the society's "official" statistical orientation. An amended charter of 1871 defined in greater detail the purpose of the organization, and it was at this juncture that the word *statistical* was dropped from the organization's title, despite the fact that the amended charter did not reflect any particular change in emphasis.[27]

Wright speculates that the name was changed simply for brevity's sake, because the new statement retained the previous commitment to statistics. Correspondence about the collection of statistical information such as the federal census did continue to flow through the society office. Yet, statistics ceased to be one of the society's major interests after 1871.[28] Explicitly why this is so remains unclear. Unfortunately, and rather mysteriously, the only volume from a century's worth of councilor meeting minutes, the one covering the period 1866–1871, is missing from the AGS archives. This volume would have documented discussions about changing the name of the organization. (It has been missing since the 1880s.) We will never know the discussions or debates that took place at these meetings, although other archival sources give credible evidence as to the perceptions held by Charles Daly and other AGS men regarding the organization's purpose and function and thus suggest an explanation for the move away from an explicit interest in collecting and disseminating statistics. While Charles Daly's conception of geography included counting and enumerating resources globally, he gradually began to associate himself more fundamentally with explorers' experiences in the field. This shift, I detail momentarily, occurred simultaneously with the "crisis" in masculinity among elite American men in the second half of the nineteenth century.

Meanwhile, documentary evidence portrays a sense of betrayal among some of the original members of the society when statistics ceased to be a primary interest of its leadership. John Disturnell, for example, a tourist agent and publisher of guidebooks, maps, and railroad distance tables, was one of the organization's founding members and had provided building space for the first AGS meetings. He wrote numerous letters to the society in the 1860s, complaining that the new leaders were "not popular with lovers of exact science." In a book about New York City, Disturnell declared that the society's name change "annull[ed] in part the object of its original founders."[29] Thus it would seem correct to observe with Wright that statistics appealed in particular ways to many of the men who established the organization but less so to those who came after: "The avenues of investigation and promotional activity implied by the word 'and Statistical' recommended the institution to businessmen ... who might not have been interested [in a geographical society] had these words been omitted."[30]

"Colonial" Statistics and its Advocates

From the mid-eighteenth century, two main types of statistics were regularly collected by the U.S. federal government: those dealing with international trade and the decennial census statistics.[31] By the middle of the nineteenth century, various special interests had converged at the federal level to expand collection to three types: (1) census and other official state statistics, developed for administrative control of the state and economy; (2) vital statistics, especially health statistics, stemming from epidemiological research and demographic calculations of insurance actuaries; and (3) "moral statistics," designed to address urban social problems[32] such as pauperism, alcoholism, prostitution, mental illness, judicial decisions and rates of incarceration, and levels of education of various social groups, among others.

The interests of AGS men in its first two decades coincided with those of the federal government only in the first of these types, as both institutions were concerned with America's imperial intentions at home and abroad. The AGS focused largely on economic conditions in the United States, Latin America, and Europe, broadly defined, on everything from soils and agriculture to the postal services. Most statistical data gathered and published centered on enumerating resources such as crop production and manufacturing output; extractive mineral production (including imports and exports of various countries); statistical tables dealing with communication and transportation technologies that would facilitate commercial development (such as development of the telegraph and railroad); and census and population profiles. Attention to these topics came from several influential AGS members. John Jay, one of the founders and subsequently one of its most prominent members and councilors, delivered papers on the statistics of agriculture, showing the deterioration and loss of soil in 1859 and arguing for an improved 1860 agricultural census. Another founder, Archibald Russell, author of *Principles of Statistical Inquiry* (1839), was assistant to a special committee of the U.S. Senate in preparing the agricultural schedule for the federal census of 1850.

As many scholars have noted, interest in statistics paralleled the expansion of industrial capitalism and the process of enumerating resources, the exact wealth of the state, and target populations, to control them and secure governing of that state. Talal Asad emphasizes the importance of statistics in colonial administration, calling them, in fact, the "strongest language of all" among the discursive interventions of colonialism, since statistical figures and reasoning are employed in the attempt to reconstruct the moral and material conditions of target populations in order to measure relative "progress."[33] Kalpagam further argues that accounting was the most important discursive practice of colonial discipline, in that for colonization to proceed, colonial administrators needed standardized measurements of land, commodities, and money. Statistics were not merely a means of representing the colonized world, according to Kalpagam, "but were crucial in their construction as well, and enabled the development and accumulation of instrumental capability" – that is, of certain kinds of intervention. In that sense they became the most important language in the narrative legitimation of modernity; for "telling stories about progress, of accumulation of wealth, control of nature, the wellbeing of humanity, and equally to counter those stories as well."[34] Both Asad and Kalpagam underline the relationship between statistics and notions of progress in colonial settings, as both moral and material "progress" presupposes the continuous use of comparative statistics.

Casting statistics as "agents of empire" in this way highlights the nature of statistical knowledge as the enumeration of that which has been, or could be, colonized. Although not devoted to the supposed uplift of target populations through statistics per se, much of the AGS work in its early decades nevertheless followed this colonial science model – or more specifically, a political-economic imperial model of non-territorial domination over global regions through enumeration and comparison of raw materials, ultimately to benefit domestic manufacturing and industrialization.

From this perspective, statistical modes of representation can be understood as one type of knowledge acquired through exploration and discovery, with statistics and geography two sides of the same coin, complementarily geared towards economic, political, or cultural control over people and place. As one founder of the AGS noted at the time, statistics is "geography's kindred and almost inseparable companion."[35] Lectures and papers that quantified and compared resources place to place were common in AGS discourse. John Jay's paper on American agriculture just mentioned, for example, simultaneously enumerated the 1850 U.S. population (23 million), the population employed in agriculture (45 percent), the amount of capital derived from it compared with other industries ($5 billion, "5/6ths of the whole"), taxes funneled through this segment of the economy, areas suitable and unsuitable for agriculture, and so on, compared with such information for the countries in Europe. He concluded, on a Malthusian note, that Europe would quickly come to depend on U.S. agriculture.

The movement, then, of a geographical society away from statistical or mathematical enumeration to concentrate its efforts on field exploration is worth analyzing. It should be made clear here, though, that enumerating statistical data and conducting field exploration are not oppositional geographical exercises (the former might be considered a subset of the latter), but they can construct different representations of the world. Statistics – a mathematical conception of the world – are quite a different form of representation than other forms of exploratory knowledge – such as narrative description, drawings, maps, specimen collections, and so on. Yet statistics and these others all need to be collected in the field, and all need to be compiled, manipulated, and interpreted at a "center." Nevertheless, the common perception of statistics lays stress on its interpretive aspect – conducted "at home," at society headquarters, a university, government office, and so on – whereas the common perception of exploration lays stress on the field observation aspect.[36]

Furthermore, as Edney[37] notes in his example of colonial India, different values were attached to the field versus centers of compilation, dissemination, and calculation, emphasizing the importance of where geographical information acquires its supposed objectivity. The shift from statistical to exploratory knowledge at the AGS can be seen in this light as a shift from a focus on the interpretive "center" to a focus on the exploratory "field." Associated with this shift to the field is the accompanying exploratory narrative that oftentimes foregrounds and indeed pivots on the embodied experience of the explorer in that field, whereas the experience of compilation or interpretation of statistical facts by the neutral, detached social scientist at the center rarely appears at all in representations of statistics. Thus associated with these different representations of the field are different protagonists and interpreters of it, each with differently positioned gendered identities. As I discuss in the next section, the (manly) acts of observation in the field were quite different from the (manly) acts of compilation and synopsis, at AGS headquarters or elsewhere.

Statistics' "Hard Facts" and Exploration's "Hard Bodies"

The American Civil War, U.S. expansionism in the West, industrialization, and immigrants' and (middle-class) women's movements in the urban workplace all combined to challenge gender identities that had been associated with elite American men's cultural and intellectual authority in the Gilded Age.[38] Kimmel[39] refers to the social effect of these men's beleaguerment as a "crisis of masculinity." How manliness and masculinity were shaped in the mid- to late-nineteenth-century United States provides a useful context for analyzing the ideologies, activities, and goals of Charles Daly as AGS President. As scholars of masculinity have discovered – informed as they are by decades of feminist scholarship that has shown a similar case for women – the differently gendered subject positions of individual men were intimately connected to both the knowledge they created and the ways that they outwardly expressed or "performed" their manhood in their public, professional lives.

In his study of American governmentality in nineteenth-century America, for example, Matt Hannah extends Michel Foucault's thesis of government discursive formations by usefully focusing on the gender dynamics inherent in the work of Francis Walker, one of the pre-eminent statisticians in the United States and superintendent of the 1870 and 1880 censuses. (Walker was also Commissioner of Indian Affairs in 1871 and, not incidentally, honorary member of the AGS.) To simplify a nuanced analysis, although Walker was known for his impartiality, honesty, loyalty, strength of will, and strict personal work regime in the "rational mastery of national territory,"[40] he was also someone with a near obsession with his own manhood. Hannah argues that Walker's fear of a "besieged masculinity" shaped his views on the census, which he consequently ran rife with military analogies that emerged after the Civil War.

Walker was among the pedigreed, wealthy elite from the northeastern United States whose intellectual authority would, by the latter nineteenth century, be challenged and replaced by academic and bureaucratic social science experts. The gender, class, and ethnic or race mobility of various "others" into public social life – especially professional class white women and immigrant men – challenged the old elite's sense of social, economic, and cultural control. As Hannah summarizes it, they responded to this potential usurpation by attempting to preserve the familiar gender, race or ethnic, and class hierarchies, and thus means of social control and power, in whatever ways they could. Some strategies were around self-government, and some were directed towards these others. One strategy was to create and empower new coalitions of nativist ("stakeholding") men as men; coalitions including industrial capitalists, emerging professionals, elite social reformers, and clergy, who would unite themselves against the "unmanly" and dependent immigrants and women ("non-stakeholders").[41] They did this partly by escaping into homosocial, racially exclusive social settings, including the many historical, geographical, philosophical, and other learned societies that emerged in the nineteenth-century United States as part of larger developments in educational reform and the growth of universities. These homosocial gentlemen's clubs were also where men "networked" with one another, seeking new business clients and trade. Such had particular salience for Charles Daly, President not only of the AGS but President, councilor, member, and frequent invited lecturer to a number of other learned and reform societies. (Daly's civic duty manifested itself in a number of ways through these reform organizations, as discussed in Chapter 3. Certainly part of what it meant to be a civic individual in the first instance was to embody a patrician duty to the unmanly and dependent.)

The overarching concern of these new coalitions of men was to prove manhood through outward, observable, and individual achievements. As Kimmel describes it, men thus solved their "crisis" of masculinity in a variety of ways:

> They went to work, making sure to keep women out of the workplace and ensure it as a homosocial preserve. They went to war … [they] pitt[ed] their manly will and resolve against the raging desires and animal lusts that their bodies experienced. And they went west, to start over, to make their fortunes, to escape the civilizing constraints of domestic life.[42]

Although all (emancipated) men could arguably partake to some degree in a communal manhood in the earlier decades of the nineteenth century, "the self-made man" arose as a mid-century American bourgeois cultural ideal in eastern cities. This cultural ideal, concomitant with the rise of the middle class and in line with the basic prerogatives of American capitalism, emphasized independence, personal success, and competition.[43] Michael Kimmel describes the rise of the self-made man ideal as coinciding with the decline of the land-owning "genteel patriarchy" and that of the "heroic artisan" as secure anchors for male identity. To him, self-made manhood was built on two things: virtuous character and will power. Virtuous character meant a strong sense of duty, steadiness, self-control, loyalty, and industriousness. A man could benefit most if he could control and channel his prodigious willpower for use at proper moments and activities. These character traits were performed in their various aspects in the many spheres of social life – the home, church, social clubs, and so on – as well as within various professional contexts.

Carried over into the urban workplaces of the professional classes, these same character traits could be used to prove men's manhood by applying them to the social problems and issues facing the industrializing society. It is at this intersection that an alignment with statistics' hard empirical facts and a display of impartiality towards them emerged as important signifiers ("observable achievements") of one type of masculinity and a means by which one's insecurity about manhood could be lessened. Dana Nelson argues that this process articulated a relationship between white men and science itself, showing that white middle-class men's move from merchant to manager "claim[ed] for its own particular provenance the terms of rational objectivity and scientific, civic management."[44] As Hannah elaborates, "a new skepticism [emerged] toward (implicitly feminine) 'lofty ideals' in favor of the (explicitly masculine) hard empirical facts."[45] Acquiring and reporting on objective facts and figures, and making meticulous reference to established authorities in support of them, was one way of maintaining one's impartiality and disinterestedness (and as compared with the expertise intrinsic to those elites embedded in the former patronage system, who required no such outside validation).

In this way impartiality flowed not from the man but from his methods. Statistical experts thus acquired the necessary credentials and authority that allowed them to interrogate and intervene in social systems that operated through the rationality they embodied.[46] Many scholars have, of course, meanwhile identified the alternative career and educational paths of privileged (white) women entering the public sphere in the later nineteenth century as well; such "public mothers" worked in professions that ideologically aligned them with nurturing and care-giving. To over-generalize a complicated and of course contested process, women became social workers while men became social scientists.[47]

Interestingly, Charles Daly's principal profession was legal: he was a judge and later chief justice in the New York Court of Common Pleas for 41 years, and upon retiring from the bench he opened his own law practice. One might consider those values, behaviors, and attributes that counted most in the legal professions as similar in many ways to the preceding description of the manly statistician: qualities of judiciousness, neutrality, impartiality, and a particularly strong code of ethical conduct. Men in the all-male legal profession were also to epitomize traits of dominance and reason against "social undesirables" and women; their world of the courtroom centered on the magisterial, patriarchal figures of attorneys and judge, cloaked in a robe.[48] As judge, Charles Daly was often labeled "magisterial" in newspaper accounts, yet he also went to great lengths to appear self-deprecating and to avoid any appearance of courting popular favor from the bench. Indeed, as I discuss in the next section, Daly was known for exhibiting the qualities of virtuous character to an extraordinary degree. But what about Kimmel's other important signifier of masculinity at the time – willpower?

Many scholars of masculinity point to the importance of the Civil War in shaping American men's notions of manliness in the second half of the nineteenth century. Rotundo argues that the war's cultural influence worked slowly; in its immediate aftermath the horrors of the war were fresh, reinforcing a new militarism in everyday existence – life as "battlefield" or warfare (see Hannah above, on Francis Walker). Yet by the 1880s, memories dimmed and the "benefits" of war stood out, with the martial virtues of intrepidy, courage, strength, endurance, duty, and self-sacrifice valued over the soft, pampered lives of the business and professional classes. As Rotundo importantly adds, however, "the older qualities of manhood such as independence and reason weren't supplanted, but they were cast in a shadow by more physical, primitive qualities."[49]

The physical, primitive, "passionate" qualities enshrined in the context of the Civil War align closely with other valued attributes of male culture at the time that likewise focused on the physical body. New attention to male sports culture, rigorous outdoor activities, and narratives of the hardships involved in "frontiering" in the American West provide a few examples. Such resonate with a particular type of heroic masculinity that pervaded the Victorian adventure tale itself, a deeply gendered myth about a male hero who was strong, courageous, and persistent, in search of gold, land, or other imperial dreams. As Lisa Bloom points out, the hardship and struggle depicted in such tales of adventure served as "trophies" of masculinity.[50]

Here one should observe that a quite different type of masculinity was required of the explorer in the field compared with that of the manly statistician. The explorer's masculinity assumed a "hard body"; he embodied strength, fortitude, and glorified athleticism that endured extreme hardship, and in fact thrived on adventure, daring, and danger. This would seem especially the case for explorers of the Arctic regions and poles, exceptionally cold, dark, barren landscapes upon which, as Bloom notes, could be written a hypermasculinized conquest. Narrating endurance, unexpected winterings through the long Arctic nights, frostbite, starvation, diseases such as scurvy, and death all functioned to heighten the explorer's manhood; as Bloom puts it, such activities "symbolically enacted men's own battle to become men."[51] Thus the poles functioned much like other wilderness areas in the later nineteenth century, as male testing grounds, sites within which the discourse of virile, tough, self-controlling masculinity could be recovered and stabilized and used to ward off the feminizing effects of the city. (Bloom's analysis notwithstanding, of course, a range of discourses of masculinity

Figure 2.2 Hard Facts of Charles P. Daly. "Law and Geography," from Men of the Hour

Source: *The Hour Cartoon Supplement*, 29 January 1881.

Figure 2.3 Hard Body of American Explorer Robert E. Peary, President of the American Geographical Society (1903–1907). Peary on main deck of steamship "Roosevelt," 1909

Source: Prints and Photographs Division, Library of Congress, LC-USZ62-8234.

emerged out of such polar explorations, inflected as they were simultaneously with discourses of national and class identification.[52])

This brief outline of cultures of masculinity in nineteenth-century America provides a useful frame for a close examination of Charles P. Daly's gendered geography and what is says about geographical statistics, field exploration, and the nexus between the two in Daly's uniquely "armchair" version of geography. In the following sections, then, I examine in some detail the gendered geography he produced via AGS-sponsored activities. Particularly through his staging of elaborate geographical spectacles, Daly associated himself explicitly with masculine exploratory field experiences and, in so doing, "reconciled" various parts of his own manhood. Meanwhile, he served as an important node in the reproduction of masculine culture and ideals among his many New York (and other) audiences.

Charles P. Daly's Gendered Geography

As noted above, it was relatively early in Daly's AGS presidency that the official orientation of the society moved away from its statistical focus. His quick ascension from member of the AGS in 1855, to councilor three years later, and to President until his death, says much about his personal appeal to AGS men, and this despite the schism over the neglect of statistical matters wrought by the likes of John Disturnell. Moreover, in my research I detected little explicit concern on Daly's part for this ensuing conflict. Although many geographical issues of the day attracted his attention, his primary interest was in "exploration of the unknown," particularly of those "blankest" spaces on the map to the western imaginary, the Arctic and Central Africa. His was a geography focused intently on filling in the remaining blank spaces, an enterprise that was both encyclopedic and Humboldtian in nature. Daly spent hours pouring over maps and planning the voyages of men supported by the AGS, the federal government, or private entities. The AGS only directly supported one major expedition during Daly's tenure, though – the purported final search for the remains of the lost Franklin expedition led by Frederick Schwatka in 1878–1880 (see Chapter 5). Daly's influence on exploration, however, stretched well beyond this formal type of support. He was a prolific writer on geographical topics, expansive host to geographers and explorers, and newsworthy speaker in his own right.

Daly's Arctic meetings were enormously popular. He presided over more meetings and receptions devoted to the Arctic than to any other place, including a reception honoring survivors of Charles Hall's *Polaris* North Pole attempt in 1874 (especially newsworthy due both to Hall's death as well as to its extraordinary survival story, which I discuss momentarily). Another such event that received a great deal of press coverage was the 1878 AGS meeting featuring the Earl of Dufferin, governor-general of Canada and President-elect of the RGS, at which was discussed a plan to establish a permanent research station (the Howgate Polar

Colony) on the border of the North Polar Sea.[53] Such meetings typically opened with remarks by Daly, followed by speeches from each of the principals.

It was Daly's annual addresses though, lasting roughly from 1869 to 1893, on the "state of geographical work of the world" for the year, for which he received most recognition as a geographer and considerable press coverage in New York newspapers.[54] These addresses were typically delivered at society meetings and published in the society's *Journal*. Significant portions of the speeches were devoted to Arctic exploration. These popular discourses were written (and delivered) in accessible, plain language, typically (but not always) without any reference to the sources of information. The addresses enumerated or collated researches of the previous year, exhaustively and elaborately detailing scientific advances gained by voyages of discovery, surveys, navigational achievements, and so on, but also covering practically any subject dealing with study of the Earth – geology, astronomy, and meteorology – or topics simply of interest to him, such as prehistoric archaeology and curiosities found by explorers. Theirs was a "geographical age," Daly frequently reminded his audiences, an idea manifested in annual addresses oriented to field exploration.[55] For their duration, Daly's unique annual addresses can be considered important and influential works of geography in themselves, as later chapters attest.

Daly's annual report of 1880, just to take one example, in its published form in the society's *Journal*, is 107 pages (single-spaced); in it Daly identified an approximately equal number of expeditions (there were 91) and significant geographical achievements for the years 1878–1879.[56] The *New York Herald* covered the speech in their 24 March 1880 issue, stating that Daly "delivered a long and elaborate address" with stereopticon illustrations. The phenomenal amount of detail in the newspaper article, much of it verbatim from that printed in the *Journal*, suggests that Daly simply supplied the newspaper with a copy of the address. Although his approach was often encyclopedic – descriptive lists of accomplishments or findings – others of his speeches were more "synthetic" – Humboldtian – in their attempt to integrate and analyze such findings. One example of the latter appears as part of his 1870 annual report, in which he spoke at length (30 single-spaced printed pages of the *Journal*) attempting to disprove the existence of an open polar sea. In this report, Daly integrated evidence of gulfstream patterns, seasonal variations in temperature, and eye witness accounts to attempt to disprove existence of such open waters (discussed again later and in Chapter 5).[57]

Although Daly was clearly concerned with social progress via the uplift of immigrants, women, and others of the disenfranchised in other aspects of his career, "geographical progress" meant filling up the blank spaces of the map with physical description – with coastlines, temperatures, wildlife, resources, and so on – and again, such description constituted in large part the content of his speeches. By this measure, Daly concluded in 1873 that the world was not more than half known. In 1880 he commented, "As long as there remain large portions of the earth to be discovered or more fully explored the same reasons apply [to do so]

BULLETIN

OF THE

AMERICAN GEOGRAPHICAL SOCIETY

Vol. XX **1888** **No. 1**

ANNUAL ADDRESS

OF

CHAS. P. DALY, LL.D., PRESIDENT.

RECENT GEOGRAPHICAL WORK OF THE WORLD.

INTRODUCTION.

When I began, many years ago, to give, in an annual address, an account of the geographical work of the world, what was then done was so small, and the information to be obtained respecting it within a year was so limited, that I had to fill out my address with some other geographical subject.

In the course of time, however, the field of exploration became so great, and the amount of information to be obtained within a year so extensive, that I found it difficult to compress an adequate account of it within the narrow limits of such an address.

Minor details could be omitted when there was such geographical information to impart as was supplied by the Russian invasion of Eastern Asia, which made us acquainted with those long inaccessible cities of Bok-

Figure 2.4 First page of Charles P. Daly's "Annual Address: The Geographical Work of the World in 1888"

Source: *Journal of the American Geographical Society of New York* 20 (1, 1888): x.

that existed in the fifteenth century … Prince Henry, the Navigator's motto then adopted, 'Talient de bien faire,' meant the desire to be useful, and it today expresses the object and aim of geographical societies."[58]

Importantly though, when Daly discussed American benefits from exploration, they were typically cast as commercial or business in nature. Infused with the Enlightenment ideal of uniting scientific knowledge with progress, Daly overarchingly defined geographical knowledge acquired from voyages of discovery as that which ultimately would be commercially useful. The AGS's *raison d'etre* to Daly – as directly or indirectly developing resources and trade networks through which to transmit them – interestingly lacks any noblesse oblige rhetoric one might expect to cloak such a bald capitalist-expansionist agenda. In his 1884 annual address Daly explained that he selected exploration of Central Africa as his topic for the evening's speech because such exploration "will be followed by very important commercial results, and already indicates the necessity of adopting … a policy [based on the demands of] our future interests and that of other maritime nations."[59] His association with African exploration, particularly his avid political support for King Leopold II's colonization plan for the Congo, was based on commercial links to be developed there (see Chapter 6). How one might connect the AGS's interest in Arctic exploration to its explicitly commercial orientation – a place seemingly devoid of commercial potential in its cold, dark expanse of snow and ice – is taken in up Chapter 5.

Creating Spectacle through Armchair Explorations

In 1851, Alexander von Humboldt wrote to his friend Freiherr von Bunsen of Daly:

> I cannot close these hurried lines without thanking you, from the bottom of my heart, for the acquaintance I made with Judge Charles Daly … Few men leave behind them such an impression of high intellect upon the great subjects that influence the march of civilization; … Moreover, what is uncommon in an American, and still more uncommon in the practical life of a greatly occupied magistrate, is that this highly intelligent and upright man, has a deep and lively interest in the fine arts, and even poetry.[60]

Von Humboldt's effusive words about Daly align with the hundreds of accounts of Daly's subjectivity documented in the archives. Newspaper articles consistently described "a fine gentleman, quiet, unobtrusive, a man of intellectual cast and countenance … A few minutes with him convinces you are with a person of refined and active mind, that you are with a well bred man of the world."[61] Daly is depicted as courteous, gentle, dignified, learned, noble, and scholarly, with the highest moral standards, fair-dealing, philanthropic, and industrious. Even his "sweet tenor voice" heard after an evening's meal made it into the news. The *New York Times* (1885) wrote of Daly:

> To a well-poised mind and a vigor of body which has enabled him to do a tremendous amount of work he has added the peculiar judicial faculty which is best expressed by the term 'fairness' … Lawyers have often said of him that he 'tried the case for both sides' … It is not enough, however, for a Judge to have learning and the judicial frame of mind. He must be honest and fearless and of high principle. Judge Daly has been all of this … he has gone his way doing his duty and faithfully serving the public regardless of praise or blame.[62]

The *Albany Law Journal* concurred, asserting that Daly's "public and private conduct has been grounded in morality, clothed with dignity and simplicity, and permeated by a hearty good-will toward his fellow-men."[63]

Within the context of intensifying anxieties over the manliness of elite American men, Daly presents an interesting figure, especially considering his working-class, Irish Catholic immigrant background. On one level he appears as the American prototype of the self-made man, a member of the new bourgeoisie who had "arrived" due to his own diligence and hard work; one among the first men to uproot the foppish, feminized genteel patriarch ideal embodied by the British aristocracy following the American Revolution.[64] Yet, Daly also identified himself strongly with the values and habits of that old elite. With no recourse to pedigree, Daly nonetheless attempted to stress an almost aristocratic gentility, developing eclectic and refined intellectual interests such as poetry. The longer Daly remained in public life, the more elevated and romanticized his background became. His physical stature was likewise inflated by reporters; for example when they depicted Daly as embodying "leonine massiveness." Since Daly was only 5 feet, 8 inches tall, this effect was most likely produced by his long, ample beard and "shaggy eyebrows"; coincident with the larger proliferation of men's beards and moustaches mid-century as a reaction to fears of feminization.[65]

Through his many reform activities Daly fostered a patrician relationship to New York Irish immigrants, yet assiduously aligned himself against the stereotype of physically rough and primitive Irish manliness. In this patrician capacity Daly seems to have united himself with other men in the dutiful service to the unmanly or dependent. Thus his gentility can be connected both to his personal embodiment and identity, as well as to the national and class affiliations – modeled after the British aristocracy, perhaps – that he wished to foreground in his professional life. Meanwhile, references to attributes such as his "sweet tenor voice" and his domesticity – the *New York Times* reported that Daly was a "thoroughly domestic man, and when not engaged on the bench or in attending some scientific meeting, he can always be found at home"[66] – align Daly's gender identity with an almost dandified masculinity. This is nowhere more apparent in the press than in the frequent references to Daly's extreme loquaciousness. Numerous reports and biographies depict Daly as nothing if not chatty. One debate rebuttal early in his career lasted for three hours, and in the courtroom his attention to minute detail and specificity often delayed proceedings, apparently even for years. As one biographer described him:

> As a judge he was distinguished by one peculiar failing. When presiding at trials or hearing motions he was a most patient and attentive listener, saying little, but in the appellate branch of the court it was impossible to make a continuous and connected argument before him because of his talkativeness.[67]

As I have already noted, his lengthy annual speeches on geography were in print often over 100 pages long (single spaced). The speeches, many simply listing annual global accomplishments and discoveries, carried a magisterial tone of mastery and control over an information field; they were similar to other speeches and sermons of the period – including those of Presidents of other geographical societies – sometimes lasting for hours. Yet the length of his speeches also seems to have bordered on the tiresome or hysterical, a unique combining of the talkativeness associated with femininity and the more masculinist attempt at mastery and control. While the AGS council seemed aware of the tediousness of his work, they nonetheless counseled Daly that he could better reach the public and AGS members through lecturing, rather than in print, and speeches did become his preferred medium.[68]

How might Daly's rather ambivalent, perhaps "softer," masculinity have affected his vision for geography? In one respect, I suggest that he must have derived much personal gain from associating himself with manly, "hard-bodied" explorers and the willpower they exuded. With later nineteenth-century American manliness associated so closely with strength, passion, and physicality, such explorers' manliness arguably compensated for Daly's lack of the same. Aside from a couple of years at sea as a teenager, and several short trips to Europe and the American West, Daly traveled outside of the U.S. East Coast very little. He might easily be characterized as an "armchair explorer" who lived the life of adventure vicariously through his many friends and associates and through his staged geographical spectacles. This is not all that surprising or exceptional, as most members of the AGS were industrialists likewise more interested in learning about exotic, far off places than experiencing them firsthand. If Daly was an armchair explorer, he was an influential one, perhaps mostly by advocating the support of expeditions among the privately wealthy of New York and state and federal governments, but also by influencing the way knowledge derived from expeditions was received by large public audiences. (In addition to the many Arctic explorers with whom Daly associated, he was a close, personal friend of the controversial African explorer Paul du Chaillu, who came to live with Daly after Daly's wife's death in 1894.[69])

Daly gained a great deal of personal authority through the lectures, speeches, and other geographical spectacles he created, literally casting himself "on stage" with returning heroic adventurers and explorers. His personal authority was further amplified through rhetorical association with explorers he cited in such speeches. Daly's annual addresses were popular in part because, as executive of the AGS, he had access to knowledge of existing or planned expeditions, scientific advancements, and so on that were not yet available to the public; though generating public enthusiasm for geography and affecting government policy was, after all, his job.[70] The sheer popularity of these events suggests that they also served as influential nodes in the advancement of particular types of masculinity. The more theatrical or spectacular geography could be made to appear, the more legitimacy such displays of masculinity could garner – to a point. In the case of the RGS, as Driver notes, this theatrical approach carried a significant downside. Joseph Hooker, of London's Hooker Museum/Kew Gardens, criticized the RGS when he cried, "I hate the claptrap and flattery and flummery of the Royal Geographical, with its utter want of Science and craving popularity and excitement, and making London Lions of the season of bold Elephant hunters and Lion slayers, whilst the steady, slow and scientific surveyors and travelers have no honour at all."[71] Hooker's observations are instructive, especially when one makes explicit the relative "gender capital" that men obtained through these very different efforts.

Anxieties of Acquisition and Representations of the Field

Daly's vicarious "armchair explorations" raise some interesting questions about how field exploration can be represented – via statistics, maps, drawings, narrative description of embodied experience, and so on – and each method's relationship to manhood and masculinity. On one hand, collecting and discoursing on an exhaustive, encyclopedic array of "exploration facts" does not seem all that different in substance or nature from collection and disseminating of the "hard facts" of numerical or statistical tables of the period. In fact, results from voyages of discovery in Daly's lectures often appeared in the form of lists, collections of facts, "a counting" or "an accounting" of explorers' accomplishments and achievements. In his annual speech in 1870 for example, Daly listed 23 (numbered as such) geographical and scientific "events" for that year, which included: the discovery of trees of enormous height and magnitude, some 69 feet in circumference, in Australia; the invention and practical use of a self-registering compass; the discovery, through the spectroscope, of a method for determining the proper motion of the stars; the French expedition up to the Mekong river; the completion of the geological survey of New Jersey; the return of Captain Hall from the Arctic, bringing interesting mementoes of the lost Franklin expedition; and the completion of the Pacific railroad.[72]

Daly's references to technology and instrumentation are particularly noteworthy. Reaching beyond encyclopedic lists towards a more Humboldtian synthesis of earth processes in others of his speeches carried a particular saliency for Daly as an armchair explorer. At such junctures he synthesized reports and measurements taken by those in the field, deriving authority from them, without any direct observations of his own. Yet, lacking in such direct observation, Daly's ability to make authoritative claims about geographical knowledge would require him to somehow associate directly with those events and experiences that took place in the field. Daly's speeches on expeditions and surveys in particular are filled with an encyclopedic cataloging and descriptive details of their routes and destinations, including place names and retelling of the difficulties and obstructions faced by explorers. Casting such exploratory and scientific facts as accurate and complete, meanwhile documenting the strenuous embodied experiences and difficulties faced in obtaining them, not only helped ensure the heroic stature of such accomplishments, but also helped Daly associate himself with such accomplishments in the public eye.

For a typical case in point, we might return to the Arctic Meeting of 1874, devoted to honoring the surviving crew of Charles Hall's ill-fated *Polaris* expedition. A virtual cottage industry of scholarship exists on the voyages of Charles Hall, his first in 1860–1862, an attempt to find remains of the Franklin expedition; as well as his five years living among the Native Inuit (1864–1869); the shipwreck of the *Polaris* on his second Arctic voyage; and his poisoning by a crew member and subsequent death.[73] Hall had brought back an Inuit family with him after his first voyage, the famous Joe Ebierbing and his wife Hannah

(Ipirvik and Tookoolito Taqulittuq), whom he then paraded around Europe and the United States – including featuring them as attractions at the Barnum circus – in attempts to generate interest and funds for his subsequent expeditions. The Ebierbings accompanied Hall on his fund-raising efforts in 1862–1864 and again in 1869–1871, and settled in Groton, Connecticut, before joining him on his second (*Polaris*) voyage, on which they served as interpreters, guides, culture-brokers, and hunters.

The 1874 AGS meeting honoring the surviving *Polaris* crew was held at the Cooper Union, with an immense crowd of 3,000 in attendance. The Ebierbings were exhibited on stage alongside Daly and the other principles, and large maps served as backdrop (this was the Ebierbings' second appearance at an AGS meeting, the first after Hall's first voyage). At the meeting, Daly recounted the fate of the *Polaris* as it attempted but failed to reach the North Pole. The ship got stuck in the ice north of Melville Bay, sprang a leak, and the crew – including Joe and Hannah Ebierbing – became stranded on an ice floe for 194 days. (They later adopted the child Punna, who was born on the ice floe.) The 19 survivors were later rescued off the coast of Labrador, having survived principally by the efforts of Hannah and Joe Ebierbing. In his speech Daly recounted their story, enunciating the following:

> [T]hink of it ladies and gentlemen … that nineteen persons in all, men, women, and children, floated upon a cake of ice, in darkness from the 15th of October until the 1st of May – 194 days – six months and a half – at one time reduced to a biscuit apiece and a small portion of pemmican; saved from the most horrible of deaths, famine, by the accidental capture of a bear; when you think of them thus floating from the 80th to the 59th degree of north latitude, why, there is nothing like it in the whole history of maritime disaster. (Applause).[74]

Through this recounting of adventure and near-death experiences, Daly aligned himself with the "hard" masculinity of such survivors – and thus these men's strength, fortitude, and glorified athletic bodies that endured extreme hardship, famine, cold, and darkness. (The fact that some were Native women and children does little to disrupt this gender dynamic since Natives already "belonged" to this natural landscape.)

It is important to recognize here that "mere" armchair explorers were susceptible to being derided or challenged by "real" explorers in the field (or their representatives) – as not manly enough, as not doing the real work of exploration. Those whose authority and credibility were challenged might thus attempt to divert such criticism in whatever ways were open to them. For example, it is noteworthy that the AGS published articles on the methodology of fieldwork during Daly's tenure (such as on how to achieve accuracy during fieldwork),[75] yet nearly all readers of their publications were also armchair explorers like himself. What use did such information serve?

Documentary evidence shows the occasional harsh public criticism Daly received from explorers and newspapermen, for making assessments about explorations for which he had no direct knowledge, such as happened with debates over the existence of an open polar sea (Chapter 5). A writer for the *New York Tribune*, for instance, described him as a mere "library geographer … whose Arctic travels have been made chiefly in the rooms of the American Geographical Society."[76] The reporter proceeded to argue that his readers ought to believe the direct observers – the real explorers. Daly, meanwhile, in his guise as a Humboldtian man of science and drawing on other sources of information arbitrated through the AGS, insisted that there was no evidence for the supposed warm ocean currents beyond a certain northern latitude. He was eventually vindicated on the issue.

Daly frequently reiterated his allegiance to those in the field, even when contradicted by their "field expertise." Although I have found no documentary evidence to suggest that Daly was particularly plagued by accusations that he lacked experience in the field, evidence does show him increasingly troubled and anxious about his inability to construct a coherent narrative for geography; that is, by comprehensively collating and disseminating the geographical knowledge for which he was responsible. For example, by the 1880s he admitted to having trouble managing the exhaustive amount of detail usually provided in his annual addresses. In 1884 Daly claimed that the "work had now become so extensive and involves such a quantity of details, that a complete yearly account of it would, I fear, prove too technical as well as too monotonous for a public address." In that case, he decided to avoid the yearly "account" and instead devoted his annual speech to the much more containable topic of the commercial advantages of central Africa. Similarly, in 1888, Daly claimed that, "the field of exploration [has become] so great, and the amount of information to be obtained within a year so extensive, that I [find] it difficult to compress an adequate account of it within the narrow limits of such an address."[77]

Daly appears in these passages as acknowledging the loss of magisterial control over the subject that promised geographical progress in the world – the facts overcame the man. One might ask what happens when a knowledge field becomes too large, too diverse, and still expanding to be discursively conquered and mastered. Such loss of control, combined with Daly's reputation as workaholic, suggests a correlation of these with the occasional health problems he suffered. Many of his letters begin with apologies for absences due to unspecified health problems, and his wife's diary substantiates some of them. Maria reports in her diary on 28 May 1879, for example, that Charles suddenly collapsed from overwork and was threatened with "congestion of the brain," an episode described by his biographer as a breakdown.[78] The couple subsequently retreated to their seaside home at Sag Harbor, with his doctor forbidding Daly to do any work during his convalescence. Such nervous exhaustion or neurasthenia, as it was understood at the time, is discussed by scholars as a "cultural disease of masculinity" attributable to the excessive strains and demands of manhood, particularly the strains caused by, among others, too much thinking, self-sacrifice, and impartiality.[79] He eventually died of a ruptured blood vessel, "apoplexy," in 1899.

Charles P. Daly: A Man of His Times

If some of the anxieties Daly experienced from attempts to contain and master intractable facts eventually physically overcame him (overtaxing his body's supply of "nerve force"), I would argue that such anxieties could also to a degree be "relieved" through armchair associations with more physically vigorous, adventurous men in the field. Charles Daly's gentlemanly interest in poetry and theater, his persona as a man of letters, his membership within the New York business and professional elite, and his gentle, patrician attitudes towards the dependent, casts his masculinity as rather "soft" compared with that of the courageous and adventurous masculinity displayed by explorers in the field. Physical prowess of the right sort – and as compared with the manliness associated with the controlled rationality of the statistician or judge – worked well in the later nineteenth century as an outward visible achievement by which men might shore up a heroic manhood otherwise bordering on the effeminate.

The lengths to which Daly went in staging dramatic geographical spectacles while otherwise embodied in the public eye as the gentle judge compellingly suggests that he must have derived a great deal of personal advantage in orienting the AGS towards the exploratory field. As a man ensconced within the urban center of geographical compilation and dissemination, Daly could reconcile the manhood associated with that center (virtuous character and controlled rationality) with the manhood associated with field (hard body and strength of will), ultimately defining that which constitutes geography as well as augmenting his own legitimate status as geographer in the process. Daly relied on the skills, knowledge, and science available at the center of compilation and dissemination to tame the facts into a coherent narrative for geography, and was applauded by newspapers for his "Herculean" efforts to do so. Yet when questions surfaced over the armchair nature of his knowledge or his (in)ability to authoritatively perform Humboldtian synthesis of the facts, he linked himself with explorers in the field who could stand in for his lack of experience. The gender dynamics associated with the center versus the field provide a useful frame for contrasting both sides of Daly's persona – as a scholar and explorer, performing both the careful knowledge derived from study as well as the oftentimes sensationalism of the field.

A key figure in nineteenth-century American geography, Charles Daly embraced particular geographical endeavors and forms of geographical knowledge, outcomes that, I am suggesting, reflected wider societal shifts in values placed on American manhood. Expressions of masculinity that had previously served as secure anchors for elite men's gender identities were challenged, along with, of course, the power and prestige those identities carried in society, especially in the workplace. The move by the AGS to overshadow (though not do away with) statistical knowledge with that of explorers' narratives of adventure in the field can be understood within the context of the increased value placed on men's physicality, passion, and bodily exploits and achievements, themselves embedded within the larger cultural shifts brought about by the Civil War, American continental expansion in the West, and changes in the urban workplace with regard to competition and "threats" posed by immigrants and women. "Hard facts" and "hard bodies" united in Daly's and the AGS's imperialist endeavor to advance commercial geography. The gender dynamics associated with the two sides of geography's information field – home and away – complement the two sides of Daly's persona, as a scholar performing detached careful study and the ersatz-explorer who derived a great deal of cultural cachet by staging dramatic spectacles at the large, well-publicized AGS meetings.

An examination of the social roles, relationships, and professional interests of AGS men illuminates the processes by which gendered geographical knowledge was produced. It is fundamentally the case that by "marking" and socially locating the unmarked white male subjects of geography's history, men who have previously occupied transparent positions of power seemingly from "nowhere," we will be better able to understand the social production of geographical knowledge as not only gendered but also as particularly masculinist in nature.

What I find so important about Daly's embodiment as geographer was his ability to use public events to reinforce and reproduce not only certain types of masculinity but also a masculinist geography. The field of firsts in our historiographies of geography – being the first to find a route or draw a map, going the farthest, or collecting the most, or in Daly's case, associating himself with those who did, by soliciting funds for their support, writing about them, hosting them, and especially drawing attention to them in speeches and lectures – has been one of the most basic tropes of our deeply masculinist American geographical tradition. (Not incidentally, the AGS continues to concentrate on such firsts; for example, through their "Fliers' and Explorers' Globe" project which celebrates the achievements of today's explorers, such as astronauts.) The AGS's early association with American resource development and economic expansion also links to one of the two most important social developments that fostered and codified what we might think of as American "geographical knowledge" – industrial capitalism (the other being war). The geography that Daly and the AGS helped institutionalize – fostering and codifying activities and knowledge that advanced American commercial development – must be recognized as an almost paradigmatic masculinist geography. I am not arguing that statistical or exploratory geography was any more or less inherently "macho" than the other; indeed Asad's and Kalpagam's insights (above) about colonial discipline make that clear.[80] I would simply underline again that the AGS, through Daly, served as an important "node" in the reproduction of masculine culture – as a center not only for information exchange but for the propagation and reinforcement of masculine ideals in the nineteenth-century United States as well.

Endnotes

1 David N. Livingstone, *The Geographical Tradition* (Oxford: Blackwell, 1992): 28–29.

2 Ibid., 29; see also David N. Livingstone, "Climate's Moral Economy: Science, Race and Place in Post-Darwinian British and American Geography," in *Geography and Empire*, eds. Anne Godlewska and Neil Smith (Cambridge: Blackwell, 1994): 132–154; see 133.

3 Matthew Hannah, *Governmentality and the Mastery of Territory in 19th century America* (Cambridge: Cambridge University Press, 2000); Jeremy Crampton, "Cartographic Rationality and the Politics of Geosurveillance and Security," *Cartography and Geographic Information Science* 30 (2, 2003): 135–149; Jeremy Crampton and Stuart Elden, "Space, Politics, Calculation: An Introduction," *Social and Cultural Geography* 7 (5, 2006): 681–685.

4 Michael Kimmel, *The History of Men: Essays on the History of American and British Masculinities* (Albany: State University of New York Press, 2005): 63–73 and Michael Kimmel, *Manhood in America: A Cultural History*, 2nd ed. (New York: Oxford University Press, 2006). Also see E.A. Rotundo, *American Manhood: Transformations in Masculinity from the Revolution to the Modern Era* (New York: Basic Books, 1993); Gail Bederman, *Manliness & Civilization: A Cultural History of Gender and Race in the United States, 1880–1917* (Chicago: University of Chicago Press, 1995); Athena Devlin, *Between Profits and Primitivism: Shaping White Middle-Class Masculinity in the U.S., 1880–1917* (New York: Routledge, 2005); and John Tosh, *Manliness and Masculinities in Nineteenth-century Britain: Essays on Family, Gender and Empire* (Harlow: Pearson Longman, 2005).

5 Bederman, ibid., 12.

6 Rotundo, *American Manhood*, 233; Kimmel, *History of Men*, 74–75.

7 Mona Domosh, *Invented Cities: The Creation of Landscape in 19th Century New York and Boston* (New Haven: Yale University Press, 1996).

8 Kimmel, *History of Men*, 38.

9 See D. McMannis, "Leading Ladies at the AGS," *Geographical Review* 86 (1996): 270–277.

10 Janice Monk, "Women's Worlds at the American Geographical Society," *Geographical Review* 93 (2, 2003): 237–257; McMannis ibid.

11 Harold Hammond, *A Commoner's Judge: The Life and Times of Charles Patrick Daly* (Boston: Christopher Publishing House, 1954) and Harold Hammond, ed. Maria Lydig Daly, *Diary of a Union Lady 1861–1865* (New York: Funk & Wagnalls Company, Inc., 1962). Daly's feminism should not be overstated, however. In a newspaper account of an address he gave at the commencement of the Twelfth Ward High School (*Home Journal*, 8 November 1862) he emphasized that women should not inhabit the same spaces as men, due to their special roles as their "civilizers." He advocated for working-class women's jobs and pay, while he admonished middle-class women to stay home.

12 For example, see Charles P. Daly, "Recent Developments in Central Africa and the Valley of the Congo," *Journal of the American Geographical Society of New York* 16 (1884): 89–159.

13 Ernesto Ruiz, "Geography and Diplomacy: The American Geographical Society and the 'Geopolitical' Background of American Foreign Policy, 1848–1861." (PhD dissertation, Northern Illinois University, 1975): 24.

14 Felix Driver, *Geography Militant: Cultures of Exploration and Empire* (London: Blackwell, 2001): 26, 34, 46.

15 William H. Schneider, *An Empire for the Masses: The French Popular Image of Africa, 1870–1900* (Westport: Greenwood Press, 1982): 21–29. Mike Heffernan points out that the Paris Geographical Society was also strongly statistical in its early phase in the 1820s and 1830s, inspired in part by some French developments in political economy and statistical manipulation/mapping that emerged in that same era in connection with the general fears and anxieties about urban and industrial development. But it dropped this concern quite quickly, and began to focus more or less exclusively on exploration by the 1840s and 1850s, i.e. precisely the same maneuver that took place decades later in New York. See Heffernan, "Geography, Empire and National Revolution in Vichy France," *Political Geography* 24 (2005): 731–758.

16 For the insurance industry example, see American Geographical Society, "Transactions of the Society for 1873," *Journal of the American Geographical Society of New York* 5 (1874): 45.

17 Helena Michie and Ronald R. Thomas, *Nineteenth-Century Geographies: The Transformation of Space from the Victorian Age to the American Century* (New Brunswick: Rutgers University Press, 2003): 1–9.

18 John K. Wright, *Geography in the Making: The American Geographical Society 1851–1951* (New York: American Geographical Society, 1952): 82–83.

19 Driver, *Geography Militant*, 46–47, characterizes the RGS as an information exchange center, or interest group, because its concerns and membership were so large and diverse: "a site where competing visions of geography were debated and put into practice"; whereas work of the Linnean Society or Hooker Museum/Kew Gardens, by contrast, could be characterized as a "center of calculation" – highly centralized collecting and control centers. After Bruno Latour, *Science in Action: How to Follow Scientists and Engineers Through Society* (Milton Keynes: Open University Press, 1987). Also see Matthew Edney, *Mapping an Empire: The Geographical Construction of British India, 1765–1843* (Chicago: University of Chicago Press, 1997).

20 For example, Lisa Bloom, *Gender on Ice: American Ideologies of Polar Expeditions* (Minneapolis: University of Minnesota Press, 1993) and W.G. Ross, "Nineteenth-Century Exploration of the Arctic," in *North American Exploration, Volume 3: A Continent Comprehended*, ed. John L. Allen (Lincoln: University of Nebraska Press, 1997): 244–331.

21 Wright, *Geography in the Making*, 14–70; Ruiz, *Geography and Diplomacy*, 143–170; W.G. Ross, ibid.; David Chapin, *Exploring Other Worlds: Margaret Fox, Elisha Kent Kane, and the Antebellum Culture of Curiosity* (Amherst: University of Massachusetts Press, 2004).

22 American Geographical Society, Council Meeting Minutes (1854–1915), 16 vols. 1 November 1854. New York: AGS.

23 Wright, *Geography in the Making*, 46.

24 Livingstone, *Geographical Tradition*, 27; Driver, *Geography Militant.*

25 Michael Bravo, "Ethnological Encounters," in *Cultures of Natural History*, eds. N. Jardine, J. Secord, and E. Spary (Cambridge: Cambridge University Press, 1996): 339–357; quote from 347.

26 Michael Dettlebach, "Humboldtian Science," in *Cultures of Natural History*, ibid., 287–304; quote from 287.

27 The amended charter of 1871 read: "The object of said Society shall be the advancement of geographical science; the collection, classification, and scientific arrangement of statistics and their results; the encouragement of explorations for the more thorough knowledge of all parts of the North American continent and of other parts of the world which may be imperfectly known; the collection and diffusion of geographical, statistical, and scientific knowledge, by lectures, printed publications, or other means." *Journal of the American Geographical Society of New York* 3, 1872.

28 Wright, *Geography in the Making*, 44, 83.

29 John Disturnell's letter from AGS Correspondence, by author last name. John Disturnell, *New York as it Was and as it Is ...* (New York: Van Nostrand, 1876): 105.

30 Wright, *Geography in the Making*, 69.

31 Hannah, *Governmentality and Mastery of Territory*, 30.

32 R.C. Davis, "The Beginnings of American Social Research," in *Nineteenth Century American Science*, ed. G. Daniels (Evanston: Northwestern University Press, 1972): 152–178; cited in ibid., 30.

33 Talal Asad, "Ethnographic Representation, Statistics, and Modern Power," *Social Research* 61 (1, 1994): 55–87; see 78.

34 U. Kalpagam, "The Colonial State and Statistical Knowledge," *History of the Human Sciences* 13 (2, 2000): 37–55; see 46–47.

35 Reverend J.P. Thompson, "The Role of Geography to the Scholar, Merchant, and Philanthropist," *Journal of the American Geographical Society of New York* 1 (4, 1859): 98–107.

36 I thank Matt Hannah for his insightful comments on this section.

37 Edney, *Mapping an Empire.*

38 Bederman, *Manliness & Civilization*; Kimmel, *Manhood in America*; Dana Nelson, *National Manhood: Capitalist Citizenship and the Imagined Fraternity of White Men* (Durham: Duke University Press, 1998); Kristin L. Hogason, *Fighting for American Manhood: How Gender Politics Provoked the Spanish-American and Philippine-American Wars* (New Haven: Yale University Press, 1998); Rotundo, *American Manhood.*

39 Kimmel, *History of Men*, 63–73.

40 Hannah, *Governmentality and Mastery of Territory*, 3, 12, 81.

41 Hannah, ibid., 72, 86–92; Nelson, *National Manhood*, 103; Rotundo, *American Manhood.*

42 Kimmel, *History of Men*, 39.

43 Rotundo, *American Manhood*, 1–7, 195–196; Kimmel, *Manhood in America*, 11–53.

44 Nelson, *National Manhood*, 103.

45 Hannah, *Governmentality and Mastery of Territory*, 97–98.

46 Hannah, ibid., 30, 63, 98; after W.G. Ross, *Origins of American Social Science*.

47 See, for instance, Paula Baker, "The Domestication of Politics: Women and American Political Society, 1780–1920," in *Unequal Sisters: A Multicultural Reader in U.S. Women's History*, eds. Vicki Ruiz and Ellen C. DuBois (New York: Routledge, 1994), 66–91. At the same time, I thank Jeanne Kay Guelke for questioning whether female "school geographers" were less statistically inclined than men. She argues (personal correspondence August 2005) that "probably not – deploying statistics might have been a way in which female geography textbook authors such as Emma Willard could register some authority." Felix Driver further points out (personal correspondence August 2005) that men as social scientists and women as social workers might be a starting proposition, but this relationship does not fully unlock the complexities of gender and social knowledge in the late nineteenth century. He notes that "social science" enabled as much as it restricted opportunities for middle-class British women to widen their role in the public sphere, in local government, education, medicine, and journalism.

48 Rotundo, *American Manhood*, 172, 196, 212.

49 Ibid., 232–234.

50 Bloom, *Gender on Ice*; also see Richard Phillips, *Mapping Men & Empire: A Geography of Adventure* (New York: Routledge, 1997); Karen M. Morin, "Peak Practices: Englishwomen's 'Heroic' Adventures in the 19th century American West," *Annals of the Association of American Geographers* 89 (1999): 489–514; and Jeanne Kay Guelke and Karen M. Morin, "Gender, Nature, Empire: Women Naturalists in Nineteenth Century British Travel Literature," *Transactions of the Institute of British Geographers* 26 (2001): 306–326.

51 Bloom, ibid., 6.

52 For example, John Wylie, "Earthly Poles: The Antarctic Voyages of Scott and Amundsen," in *Postcolonial Geographies*, eds. Alison Blunt and Cheryl McEwan (New York: Continuum, 2002): 169–183, argues that narratives of competition to be first to reach the South Pole in the early twentieth century, between Norway (Roald Amundsen) and Britain (Robert Falcon Scott), reveal the manner in which gender and national identities worked together to produce different embodied experiences, landscape vision, and field methodologies (the Norwegian technical and militaristic mode versus the British imperial mode that emphasized strain and celebration). For an alternative reading of heroic masculine fieldwork by "scientific explorers," see K. Maria D. Lane, *Geographies of Mars: Seeing and Knowing the Red Planet in an Imperial Age* (Chicago: University of Chicago Press, 2010).

53 H.W. Howgate, "Arctic Meeting at Chickering Hall, Plan for Exploration of the Arctic Regions," *Journal of the American Geographical Society of New York* 10 (1878): 276–298. This meeting received extensive news coverage, in the *New York Herald*, *New York Times*, and *New York Tribune*, all 1 February 1878.

54 Daly's first such address, in 1869, was not published by the AGS as the others, but was covered by the newspapers. See "Geographical Results of 1869," *Naval and Military Gazette*, 23 February 1870. The article lists 13 geographical "accomplishments" for the year including completion of the U.S. transcontinental railroad and Suez Canal.

55 Daly makes references to the "great geographical age" in his annual reports of 1875 (34), 1876 (95), and 1880 (103). From 1895 onwards the AGS's focus moved away from exploration to professionalism and education.

56 Charles P. Daly, "Annual Address: Geographical Work of the World in 1878 and 1879," *Journal of the American Geographical Society of New York* 12 (1880): 1–107. These were categorized under the headings: "Introduction" (work of geographical societies); "General Geographical Work" (which included such topics as the Arc of the Meridian and unsurveyed coasts of the world); "Physical Geography" (covering such topics as meteorology and the severity of recent winters in Europe); "Ethnological" (discoveries of prehistoric remains at several sites in Asia, Europe, and America); with another 13 major categories listing work by location: the Arctic, British America, the United States, West Indies, Central and South America, Europe, Asia, Africa, Borneo, Java, Sumatra, New Guinea, and Australia.

57 Charles P. Daly, "Annual Address. Subject: Review of the Events of the Year and Recent Explorations and Theories for Reaching the North Pole," *Journal of the American Geographical Society of New York* 2 (1870): lxxxiii–cxxvi.

58 Charles P. Daly, "Annual Address. Subject: The Geographical Work of the World in 1872," *Journal of the American Geographical Society of New York* 4 (1873): 63–118; see 65–67. Daly, *Journal* 1880, 2–4 (also covered in the *New York Herald*, 24 March 1880).

59 Charles P. Daly, "Recent Developments in Central Africa," 89.

60 New York Public Library (NYPL). Manuscripts and Archives Division, Charles P. Daly Correspondence and Papers. Correspondence Boxes 1–12. New York Public Library, New York. Von Humboldt letter, Box 1.

61 "Personal Reflections of Distinguished Statemen and Politicians: Judge Charles P. Daly," *New York Leader*, 1 May 1858.

62 "Chief Justice Daly," *New York Times*, 15 November 1885.

63 "The Retirement of Chief Justice Daly," *Albany Law Journal*, 28 November 1885.

64 Kimmel, *Manhood in America*, 14–20.

65 "Off-hand Portraits VIII: Charles P. Daly," *The Knickerbocker*, 15 June 1882. Kimmel, *History of Men*, 21.

66 "Chief Justice Daly," *New York Times*, 1885.

67 H.W.K. Knott, "Charles Patrick Daly," *Dictionary of American Biography* 5 (1973): 41–42.

68 American Geographical Society, Council Meeting Minutes for 1862–1865, Vol. 5.

69 Letters from du Chaillu (NYPL, Box 12) depict an intimacy between the two friends that likely influenced Daly's views on exploration of Africa as well as his geopolitics. Daly wrote in defense of du Chaillu as discoverer of the diminutive people ("pygmies") in the Congo, with the main intent to expose Henry Morton Stanley's claims to the same as fraudulent.

70 Driver, *Geography Militant*, 45.

71 Quoted in Driver, ibid., 48.

72 Daly, "Annual Address," 1870.

73 Brian Henderson, *Fatal North: Adventure and Survival Aboard the USS* Polaris (New York: Signet, 2001); R. Parry, *The True Story of Murder and Survival on the 1871* Polaris *Expedition* (New York: Ballantine, 2001).

74 I.I. Hayes, J.O. Buddington, G.E. Tyson, H.C. Chester and W. Morton, "Proceedings of the Arctic Meeting in Relation to the Voyage of the *Polaris*," *Journal of the American Geographical Society of New York* 6 (1874): 93–115; see 94.

75 For example, W.J. Hamilton, "Method of Geographical Observation," *Bulletin of the American Geographical and Statistical Society* 1 (1852): 77–79.

76 "Reception to Lieut. Greely," *New York Tribune*, 22 November 1884.

77 Daly, "Recent Developments in Central Africa," 89; Charles P. Daly, "Annual Address: Recent Geographical Work of the World," *Journal of the American Geographical Society of New York* 20 (1888): 1–38; see 1–2. This 1888 address was to be Daly's last; the AGS subsequently began to publish "Geographical Notes" instead.

78 New York Public Library (NYPL). Manuscripts and Archives Division, Charles P. Daly Correspondence and Papers. Scrapbook Volumes 1–28. New York Public Library, New York, Vol. 28.

79 Bederman, *Manliness & Civilization*, 99; Rotundo, *American Manhood*, 191.

80 Asad, "Ethnographic Representation"; Kalpagam, "The Colonial State and Statistical Knowledge." As Heffernan points out, "Geography, Empire and National Revolution," the Paris Commercial Geographical Society provides a good example, as it became far more imperialist, racially-motivated, and generally right-wing than its "parent" society by the twentieth century, notably so in the Vichy period.

Chapter 3
New York City's Friend of Labor: Geography and Urban Social Reform

Introduction

In Chapter 2 we saw how Charles Daly's management of "geographical progress" centered largely on exploration and development of the distant and the foreign. As geographer, he was influential in helping create both imagined and real geographies of the Arctic, Africa, and the Americas for the public and his many constituents. In much of his public life Daly also aligned himself closely with social reform movements of the day that were concerned with the "social progress" of the working classes and immigrants, which generated their own public interest demands and sets of imagined and real geographies. This chapter focuses upon Daly's participation in a number of these philanthropic, civic, and reform initiatives of the second half of the nineteenth century, those targeted to the social uplift of disadvantaged groups in Daly's "spaces of home" in New York City.

In addition to Charles Daly's high profile work as judge and geographer (and, early in his career, as state legislator), much of his public influence and appeal derived from his work with a number of philanthropical, civic, literary, and historical societies. He served as President of the New York Historical Society; President of the Friendly Sons of St. Patrick; President of the Working Women's Protective Union; was on the Executive Committees of the Emigrant Aid and Sanitary Reform societies; served as Vice President of the League for the Protection of American Institutions (which worked for the separation of church and state); was executive board member to a number of other organizations including the Society of Mechanics and Tradesmen and the American Jewish Historical Society; and these in addition to his membership in a half dozen or so other literary and historical societies.

Daly's interests and publications in literature, theater, and history cast him as honored member and lecturer before many of the city's prestigious (Anglo-centric) "high culture" societies (such as the Century Club and Adelphi Society). Among these, as his biographer notes, he earned a reputation as a "patron of the arts, philanthropist, Shakespearean scholar, and sage."[1] Yet Daly also aligned himself with a number of civic organizations whose ambitions focused on improving the workplaces and neighborhoods of the laboring classes and immigrants. On their behalf Daly cultivated a reputation as a "friend of labor, or of the common man, of the poor man, of the debtor."[2] As a "friend of labor," Daly's efforts were principally directed towards those first or second generation Irish immigrants with family backgrounds like Daly's own, who flooded into New York's lower East Side neighborhoods in the 1840s and 1850s and became the city's most notorious needy or working poor. He also fought for working women's rights and against anti-Semitism, yet as a Union Democrat was also anti-abolition (a subject to which I return in Chapter 6).

The legitimacy Daly enjoyed as a friend of labor derived from his own background as a former laborer, and from the fact that he advanced into the professional class. In many speeches and interviews Daly referred to the importance of his background as a carpenter and mechanic's apprentice for his self-development. The Society of Mechanics and Tradesmen, an influential group of labor employers (akin, according to Daly, to an "ancient guild"), was one labor organization with which Daly maintained strong affiliation. In presiding over the 100-year anniversary celebration of the society in 1885, he remarked that he was indebted to the society "for the privilege of its library when [he] was a mechanic's apprentice 57 years ago." He reiterated this message when interviewed by newspapers upon his retirement from the bench, observing that it was as an apprentice to the Society of Mechanics and Tradesmen that he found his direction in life; that his self-education began with access to their library.[3] This background also undoubtedly inspired Daly's life-long efforts for civic reform.

Daly's judicial work had numerous reform components, but also many geographical consequences as well, particularly with respect to the social spaces afforded immigrants and workers. His arguments and cases dealing with naturalization laws and inheritance rights of immigrants provide a good example. Daly published *Naturalization: Embracing the Past History of the Subject* (1860), a book outlining the history and description of citizenship and naturalization statues for over 40 countries, from antiquity to the present, with an elaborate discussion of the U.S. case. While this text is largely a description of existing laws rather than advocacy to change them, in this work Daly nonetheless cites the importance of his own legal jurisdiction in such matters – "it is to the Superior Court and Court of Common Pleas where all applications are made for naturalization." In particular he noted his 1847 decision to lower the age of naturalized citizenship from 23 to 21 if an individual had been a United States resident since age 15.[4] As the decision dealt with the right to succeed to an estate based on the naturalization status of one's father, it helped ensure better property rights for recent immigrants.

This chapter focuses on how Daly's selected reform efforts and affiliations, as well as several of his judicial decisions, resonated closely with his work as geographer. His leadership in an eclectic array of civic and reform causes coalesced with his work in geography, and also, as the naturalization decision illustrates, had considerable presence "on the ground" in New York. Particularly with respect to city improvement in street sanitation and tenement housing Daly attempted to direct and improve the lives of target groups largely by improving the spaces they inhabited. What follows unravels some of the personal motivations and institutional parameters that played into his and others' social reform efforts, and connects them to both their material effects and to geographical practices and knowledge; what I term Daly's "social reform geography."

In this chapter I am attempting to offer new perspectives on American nineteenth-century reform ideology and practice, and their relationship to American geography and geographical societies. Such connections have been by and large overlooked in studies of nineteenth-century geographical societies, except with respect to the influential impact of Christian reform networks on modern science, exploratory missionary work, and/or geographical practices.[5] While a substantial body of scholarship examines nineteenth-century social reform in the United States, and another, the history of geographical societies, few works have connected the two, either ideologically or empirically. Those that have made this kind of connection focus primarily on the widespread and influential impact of Christian reform networks on geographical practices, linked primarily but not exclusively to European missionaries in the colonies. The mid-century explorations of Scottish missionary David Livingstone in Africa provide a good example; his work was simultaneously connected both with Christian philanthropical reform networks of the period and with the agenda and goals of London's Royal Geographical Society.[6]

Charles Daly, like most of the upwardly mobile men of his generation, portrayed and enacted his civic responsibility throughout his public life. While it is debatable whether such men (and some women) were successful in the reforms they hoped to achieve, a view open to various interpretations,[7] it is clear that unlike many men of his generation, Daly was not motivated by religion, at least not in any explicit sense. Even though a rare reference to "the words of Isaiah" or "the Creator" did on occasion crop up in Daly's speeches,[8] he steadfastly distanced himself from Christianity and his Roman Catholic religion in his public and personal lives. What is clear is that he drew his reform ethic from other aspects of his identity, such as his Irish ethnicity, working-class background, and intense sense of upward mobility – and, as I hope to show, from his promotion of geographical work. This chapter considers in some detail the obvious overlap between Daly's attention to geography as a subject (in and through the AGS) and his "thinking geographically" in his efforts to establish spaces of improvement – and self-improvement – for the New York Irish and émigré community: these, in the form of parks, better property rights, and improved housing and streets, among others.

It should be noted that reform or civic work appears infrequently as such in AGS publications in the nineteenth century. Brief mentions and announcements are made in the society's "Transactions" or "Notes from Washington" of various civic society meetings, and only an occasional paper dealing explicitly with social reform or the activities of a civic organization was published during the decades of Charles Daly's leadership at the AGS. And yet, AGS work supported such social reform efforts in numerous ways: especially with respect to immigrants and workers, the AGS supplied relevant data on immigration trends, movements, and developments, as well as on the related status and profile of manufacturing inputs and outputs.[9]

Charles Daly's work occupies a unique place in the annals of New York City as he combined his vision for social reform within early urban geography and city planning. In this way he provides a useful lens through which to reconsider what is meant by "geographical history," "geographical knowledge," and "geographical practice" themselves. A number of historiographers write of geography's history as a "contested enterprise," one that today challenges and opens up the boundaries of what we might consider geography itself – as a discipline or subject, as an epistemological framework, and as a practice.[10] The following offers opportunities to analyze the tension between popular and academic geography (also see Chapter 7) with respect to geography's potential to impact a wide range of social issues. Specifically in this chapter I foreground and underscore the ideological appeal to geographical intervention as a subject *and* as a practice that could ameliorate the condition of the urban poor.

Civic Reform: The Message and the Media

Charles Daly lived and worked within what has come to be known as the Age of Reform in the United States, a period of social change that laid the foundation of what would later coalesce as the Progressive Movement of the 1920s. The mid- to late-nineteenth-century reform movement aimed at eradicating or counteracting the ill effects of rapid industrialization, urbanization, and immigration, focused particularly on the effects of environmental degradation and the social uplift of a number of target populations. During the Antebellum period social reform was primarily a movement in support of abolition and women's rights, but following the Civil War expanded to a wide range of social issues such as temperance, prison reform, debt forgiveness, occupational health and safety, street sanitation, universal education, and child and dependent welfare.[11]

Early nineteenth-century social reform in the United States principally arose out of Protestant Evangelicalism. The movement began with a small group of elite Republican men from New England who had some affiliation with abolition. Most notable reformers came from religious families that cultivated a stern Protestant consciousness and a patriarchal moral authority to articulate elite men's civic duty to care for the "unmanly" and dependent – slaves or former slaves, immigrants, women, and the poor. Indeed to *be* a civic person at mid-century, to be a political actor at all, "one was necessarily a man."[12]

To generalize a complex set of actors and activities: by the last third of the nineteenth-century men who did not follow a career path into the ministry or missionary work channeled their manly Christian evangelical impulses into secular reform initiatives. They were responding to the excesses of what Mark Twain famously referred to as "the Gilded Age": that period from the 1870s through the 1890s when rapid wealth accumulation of industrial and commercial giants negatively coalesced into a horrific set of urban social and environmental problems, and to many, "moral bankruptcy" itself. Meanwhile, middle-class women began moving into the public arena with careers that included participation in a number of reform efforts, particularly women's suffrage, temperance, child welfare, and workplace safety. They relied on their own feminine "moral authority" as women to do so, rather than on the rhetoric of the muscular Christianity of Protestant men.[13] Thus elite churchmen's initial plea for a social return to traditional, paternalistic values of religious obedience gradually gave way to the ideals of a more pluralistic secular reform movement of the later nineteenth century, and indeed, to a "culture of reform" itself. Activists from a wide range of social spheres including the legal, political, medical, and cultural fields combined to generate organizations, legislation, and debates aimed at increasing public participation in civic life, honest political leadership, individual rights, health and medical care, workplace safety and security, and municipal services such as clean water, safe and affordable housing, electricity, and sewage treatment. As Cecelia Tichi argues, though the patrician upper- and middle-class reform leaders believed that the working classes and poor needed guidance to acquire higher pay, better working conditions, and better housing, it was those most affected by unfair practices and conditions who forced the more privileged to take up the mantle of labor rights (etc.).[14]

The newspaper industry centered at Park Row served an important conduit in sustaining this culture of reform in New York City. From the 1830s onwards, "penny press" and four-page daily papers competed for readers by both articulating the need for social reform, and reporting on advances in it.[15] The early New York press primarily offered sensationalist "yellow journalism" in reporting on crime, human-interest catastrophes, celebrated divorces, and stories about brothels, murders, trials, fires, bankruptcies, and other disasters. The *New York Sun* led the way, followed by James Gordon Bennett's sensationalist *New York Herald*, Horace Greeley's more reform-minded *New York Tribune*, and Joseph Pulitzer's *The World*, among others. Competition for subscriptions meant that the new industry needed to create new readers, principally among the working classes, so the more sensationalist a story could be made, the more papers sold. The *Herald* and the *Tribune* were two of the main competitors for readers by mid-century (papers that would eventually merge in the early 1920s as the *New York Herald-Tribune*). Bennett's successful *Herald* in particular was criticized for playing on people's base instincts. His were contentious views that sold papers; a flagrant U.S. expansionist, he opposed unions, immigration, and women's rights. Meanwhile Horace Greeley, a well-known editor, reformer, and politician, attempted to provide readers with a social conscience above the more sensationalist *Sun* and *Herald*. His *Tribune* provided a more staid voice of liberal Republicanism and workers' rights, and he carried more influence during the Civil War years than any other newspaperman.[16] Among many other aspects of his career Greeley became known for inventing the editorial form we know today, writing in support of workers' rights and labor unions, women's rights, temperance, and municipal improvements. His *Tribune,* along with all the largest leading newspapers of the day, including the *Herald*, *Evening Star*, and later, the *New York Times*, nevertheless all adopted nativist, anti-Irish attitudes (though Greeley did advocate for Irish Home Rule).

Despite such mainstream prejudices against the Irish, Charles Daly enjoyed many close links to the New York press, with scores of newspapers following his judicial decisions, reform work, as well as his staging of spectacular geographical meetings and events. Daly's influence on the press was widely accepted among AGS men.[17] Praise for Daly as judge, civic leader, and geographer appeared in hundreds of newspaper articles throughout the 1870s, 1880s, and 1890s. In 1877 a widely distributed biography described Daly as "popular with the masses [and] a fervent orator in all the great union gatherings."[18] He appears for the most part a sweetheart of the press, usually depicted as one of the city's most "honored and learned judges" as well as pre-eminent geographer; meanwhile as reformer, was characterized as someone performing work that was extensive and practical, but not necessarily visionary.[19] Daly acknowledged the usefulness of these attributions in an 1885 interview:

> I have been the recipient of much kindness from the press and the general public throughout the many years that I have been in official life … These expressions have often come to me in a very flattering form. I never have sought for the public favor in any other way than by the simple discharge, to the best of my ability, of the duties which my station imposed upon me; yet I have never been wanting for the kindly support and approval of those whose servant I have been.[20]

With the important exception of his position opposing abolition, in many ways Daly's reformist vision aligned with that of Horace Greeley; both men advocated for municipal improvements, for example. They served together on a number of committees, and Greeley supported Daly's re-election as judge at crucial points. Greeley also defended Daly's decision in the Astor Place Riots case, though he disagreed with others of Daly's legal decisions.[21]

Along with many churchmen, leading newspapermen of the day were founders or early benefactors of the American Geographical Society. Greeley, a leader in agrarian reform and ever the "farmer's friend," spoke at the AGS on the topic of the opening of the West in 1859 (unfortunately, however, his lecture, "The Pacific Railroad: Its Importance and Practicability," was never published). The *Herald*'s Bennett (both James Gordon senior and his namesake son) took an even more active role in the AGS and geographical exploration. They helped outfit northern expeditions such as that of Frederick Schwatka, and of course it was Bennett's marketing gimmick to send Henry Morton Stanley to Africa in 1871 to "rescue" David Livingstone – a ploy that won him both praise and contempt from the public and the geographical community. Undoubtedly, in the process, he sold many newspapers (in 1860s the *Herald* boasted a circulation of 77,000, while the *Sun*'s was 60,000 and the *Tribune*'s 55,000).[22]

Such close ties among geography, reform, and the print media provide a useful backdrop to a consideration of how Charles Daly's own "geographies of reform" were popularized and carried out in New York City. To four of these efforts I turn next: Daly's efforts in establishing the Bronx Botanical Gardens; his work against anti-Semitism; his attempts to improve the Irish slums of the lower East Side; and his fight for working women's rights.

Geographies of Social Reform

The Bronx Botanical Garden: A Garden for the Masses

> The necessity of a botanical garden in the City of New York may be presented from two points of view. 1, Its scientific importance and utility for the development, improvement and preservation of the vegetable kingdom, and 2, Its value as a place of recreation and instruction for all classes of the people, and especially for the working classes, who have little leisure for recreation, and whose means do not admit of their indulging in much expense.
>
> Charles P. Daly, *Want of a Botanical Garden in New York* (1891)[23]

To take an example of what I mean by Charles Daly's "social reform geography," the subheading above is taken from a pamphlet Daly wrote and published – and quoted from often in his speeches – in support of the creation of the Botanical Gardens in Bronx Park, New York, initiated by an act of the New York State Legislature in 1891. One of Daly's (and his wife Maria's) pet projects grew from his association with the Bronx Park – as commissioner in the citing process, as chairman of the Committee of the Botanical Garden, as prominent member of the Torrey Botanical Club, as well as member of the park's Board of Managers and Finance Committee. Daly was influential in establishing what is still today one of the city's most important landmarks, akin to another important landmark in the city which he also helped found – Manhattan's Central Park. As New York state assemblyman he introduced the bill to establish it in 1843.

The Bronx Botanical Park and Gardens overlook the Hudson River and include a conservatory, vast rose garden, forest, and various themed plots. Daly was instrumental in selecting the site for the park and gardens, lobbied the state government to pass legislation for its establishment and support, and for years solicited funds for the purchase of land and buildings. Newspapers closely followed the development of the project and Daly's involvement in it, reporting on its history, progress, and status. In 1891 *Lippincott's Magazine* carried Julian Hawthorne's "An American Kew," an argument repeated by many that the gardens would serve as the American rival to London's Kew Gardens.[24] As with many of Daly's civic projects, he published a pamphlet on the subject, *Want of a Botanical Garden in New York*. This begins with a discussion of the gardens of European monasteries in the Middle Ages, the preservation of species, their medicinal uses, and their importance in feeding the growing population. Daly noted that only one other botanical garden then existed in the United States, in St. Louis, and inflected with environmental concerns of the day, discussed the implications of species eradication through urban and industrial development. He argued that as the population increased, "the resources of the country will be more carefully husbanded, and it is for that work now that botanical gardens are so necessary … the most useful species ... perish from neglect [and] wanton destruction … and the botanical gardens will arrest and prevent this."

The arguments Daly made in support of the gardens also rested significantly on the benefits that would accrue to the working classes. In *Want of a Botanical Garden* he wrote passionately about the needs of workers, arguing that the welfare of those without leisure time or opportunities for enjoyment in life – "the greater part of the New York community" – should be provided for by the wealthy:

> It is especially so at this period, when we hear so much about the conflict between capital and labor, of the hostility to the building up of colossal fortunes, and the keeping and transmitting them without doing any thing for the public welfare, or for the working classes, whose labor made the making of them possible; … the antidote … is the willingness of the rich to devote a portion of their wealth in loving consideration of what may promote the welfare and add to the enjoyment of their less fortunate fellow-citizens. A great botanical garden in this large metropolis would accomplish a great deal in this way. The poorest man can enjoy what it offers as much as the richest.… In the ordering of our lives, recreation and amusement is as necessary to our well-being as labor.[25]

The Botanical Gardens promised a democratic, enriching experience for all: they would reconcile the classes and stem potential class conflict, something of the "highest importance to the maintenance of public order."

Daly's motivations appear in line with those of William Hooker, founder of London's Kew Gardens, who solicited support for Kew in the early nineteenth century first by emphasizing the public good to come of them. The Victorian Era was, after all, the "great age of the public garden," with gardens promising wholesome recreation, instruction, and gratification for the public, and complementing a view of the city itself as gentle and prosperous, with generous benefactors.[26] Richard Drayton presents Hooker's strategy as utilitarian: while Hooker publicly boasted about the large numbers of visitors to Kew, he privately "disliked the throngs." By the 1840s Hooker's rhetoric about serving the public good gave way to one that emphasized the economic benefits of botany to merchants and manufacturers, realizing as he did that scientific arguments for their own sake would not go far with benefactors.[27] Writing half a century later and immersed within the exigencies of America's own industrial revolution, Daly rhetorically fused the public, economic, and scientific goods to come of the Bronx gardens.

Moreover Daly's civic interests in gardens and botany were supported by his geographic work. His close friend, Professor N.L. Britton, Director of the Garden, spoke at the AGS commemoration of Daly's death in 1900, and his remarks were published in the society's *Journal*.[28] Meetings of the Botanical Gardens' Board of Managers were held at the AGS headquarters. And, like many natural history topics that captured Daly's attention (as well as that of many other lecturers before the society), he often reported in his annual speeches on the botanical finds of various expeditions and surveys. In 1874, for instance, he noted that Lieut. George Wheeler's survey in the American southwest provided "results, especially in botany … [that] have never probably been exceeded by any exploring or surveying expedition in the west."[29] While imperial visions similar to those of the Hookers did not come into play for Daly, AGS men did hope to reap the mercantilist advantages afforded through botanical profiles of foreign places relayed back to AGS headquarters. For his part, Daly seemed more interested in the direct value of the gardens to New Yorkers. Moreover in his arguments he reiterated that they would provide work for flower growers – noting that women owned 300 of the 5,000 establishments then raising flowers and plants. As with others of his reform projects, Daly appears keen to assist in working women's issues and careers.

Daly's efforts on behalf of the botanical gardens should also be framed by the personal advantages he realized in advocating for them, however. Daly wielded considerable political and cultural power in New York, which he used to enhance his and his wife's already substantial personal wealth during the site selection process for the botanical gardens. Six sites were under consideration, and Daly was able to sway the selection (appraisal) committee towards his father-in-law's (Philip Lydig's) estate. This consequently meant that he, his wife, and his wife's relatives gained considerably from the land sale; the $577,000 deal meant Maria personally earned $79,000.[30] Thus, like many of Daly's reform interests, his interest in botanical gardens and in botany more generally, coincides with a number of personal, geographical, and social concerns.

Popularizing Spaces of "The Jewish Question"

If Charles Daly's principal "objects of reform" were the New York Irish (below), and he was attentive too, to the circumstances of German Americans (Chapter 4), it is noteworthy that his social and intellectual interests also embraced Jewish communities. Daly became an active or honorary member or leader of a number of Jewish organizations, such as the Hebrew Benevolent Orphan Asylum and the Jewish Historical Society. Daly often spoke at notable Jewish gatherings, "ever ready," he claimed, "to express his admiration for the Jewish race," his interest in its history, and his indignation at narrow and degrading anti-Semitic prejudice."[31] He wrote and spoke frequently against anti-Semitism, and the Jews' relative status or discrimination internationally. Many of his speeches outlined persecutions against Jews in various places, and these were often serialized in Jewish publications. In a speech commemorating the 50th anniversary of the Hebrew Orphan Asylum in 1883 – at which Daly reported 31 synagogues and 80,000 Jews in the city – he underlined his view that the Jewish people always assimilate wherever they go, unless "prevented by obstructive laws." It is not clear where Daly's interest in Jewish history and experience began, but one friend attributed it to his teenage years, when Daly briefly lived in Savannah, Georgia, and had "intimate relations with some Jewish residents who were leading citizens of the community." Presumably these were among the quill makers to whom Daly apprenticed himself, after running away from New York following both of his parents' deaths.[32]

One might consider Daly a high-profile historical geographer of the Jews in North America as well, as in addition to the above activities he published the leading historical geography scholarship of the day on Jewish migration and settlement patterns, *The Settlement of the Jews in North America* (1893). This book focused particularly on the colonial period – migrants' origins, rights, livelihoods, synagogues, and persecutions. He often liked to reiterate his position that "no event has been more beneficial to the Jewish people than the discovery of America," since "in no city have they experienced so full an intellectual and material development as in New York." Jews had been an integral element of the population of New York for over 200 years, he noted, and had made valuable contributions to the city's commercial and social growth. Leading Jews of New York considered Daly a "pioneer" in constructing the history of the Jews, and one went so far as to claim that Daly's work on Jewish history was the "starting point and basis of American Jewish history-writing."[33]

From early in his career Daly fought anti-Semitism from the bench as well. An 1852 editorial in *The Asmonean*, a New York Jewish newspaper, covered a case tried before Daly at which a lawyer and preacher named Chauncey Shaffer "repeatedly exhibited anti-Semitic prejudice of the most flagrant sort." The editor of the newspaper commented at length on Shaffer's behavior, and quoted Daly's reprimanding counsel as he delivered an *obiter dictum* (nonbinding remarks) on the subject of prejudice. Daly pointed out that all faiths are equal before the law in America, and he paid tribute to those "who are at least entitled to respect for the unshaken and courageous constancy with which they have clung to a faith connecting them by history and tradition with the remotest antiquity."[34]

For such work, Daly was often honored by New York's Jewish leaders, and at his death it was Jewish scholar Max Kohler who edited the memorial volume about him. Kohler asserted that it made sense that the Jewish community would choose to offer a special tribute to Judge Charles Daly, since he "espouse[d] so zealously the Jewish cause, and so conspicuously and signally enriched the Jewish communal life and thought by means of important contributions to Jewish history, to the extinction of anti-Semitic prejudice and to the elevation and amelioration of American Jewish life in all its phases."[35]

Charles Daly exercised considerable power and position to incorporate "the Jewish question" into public discourse in New York. He fought anti-Semitism in many of the venues open to him: his judicial forum, his public support of a Jewish orphanage, and his scholarly geographical writing on Jewish settlement and migration patterns. These together illustrate a foundational view of a "social reform geography" that, as discussed next, made deeper impacts within the city's Irish communities.

Figure 3.1 Charles P. Daly, Sketch by Juror, October 1877
Source: Charles P. Daly Papers, Vol. 7. Manuscripts and Archives Division, The New York Public Library, Astor, Lenox and Tilden Foundations.

Civic Identity and Spaces of the New York Irish

It was especially within New York City's poor and working-class Irish neighborhoods that Charles Daly found his reform ideology and practice in full flourish – and predictably so, as the exigencies of the day demanded attention to a population in political, cultural, and economic crisis. New York was the world's largest Irish city in the 1870s, and as such it was a city divided, Protestant and Catholic. Large-scale Irish immigration to the United States began with the potato blight in 1844, and by 1850, 26 percent of New York's population had been born in Ireland, making up the city's largest immigrant block.[36] The Irish population continued to represent approximately a quarter of New Yorkers through the 1860s.

Charles Daly's annual reports to the AGS oftentimes outlined such immigration patterns and population densities. By 1873, Daly reported, the Native born in New York numbered 523,198 and foreign born 419,094; with the Irish accounting for 201,999 and the German 151,216.[37] These were the men and women who would enable economic growth via an increasingly labor-intensive manufacturing sector to explode in the later nineteenth-century Northeast – the mostly unskilled or semi-skilled dockworkers, porters, drivers, weavers, printers, masons, carpenters, slaughterhouse workers, seamstresses, fruit sellers, and domestic laborers. Yet it was ethnic prejudice against the Irish, combined with inequitable labor practices and changing market conditions, which fueled disparities between rich and poor that were unprecedented in the history of New York City.

Charles Daly fostered reform of the increasingly debased Irish slums in lower Manhattan through a number of philanthropic, governmental, and political organizations. He served in leadership capacities in several reform efforts, aid societies, and labor organizations in the city, including the St. Patrick's Society, the Working Women's Protective Union, the Emigrant Aid Society, and the Emigrant Savings Bank. He served many years as President of the St. Patrick's Society, whose purpose was to "celebrate St. Patrick's Day and bring relief against the Irish famine." He was also President of the fraternal lodge, the Friendly Sons of St. Patrick, and the Irish Relief Society, both influenced by Irish Republicanism and aimed at eradicating the dire conditions in Ireland.[38] Because Daly was widely acknowledged as "the best Gaelic authority in America," his first task when elected President of the Friendly Sons of St. Patrick (1860–1862) was to write the group's history.

Daly's frequent lectures about Irish Americans and the situation in Ireland were widely covered by the New York newspapers. He received extensive press coverage on St. Patrick's Day especially as he presided at banquets following the elaborate, hugely popular St. Patrick's Day parades every March 17th. Newspaper reports detailed the parade routes, participants, banquet speakers, toasts, and commemorative proceedings.[39] Daly often spoke publicly on the subject of famine relief in Ireland, as well as in favor of Irish Home Rule. He argued in 1885 that it was British oppression that caused the famine, and made the case that Ireland should remain a component part of the British Empire but with independent statehood:[40]

> I think the [present] agitation will result in a local Parliament for administering the affairs of Ireland in the sense in which our State legislatures are local in respect of the general government. I do not think anything short of that will satisfy the Irish people. When the English people become thoroughly convinced that this is the general sentiment of the Irish people I believe the concession will be made.

Daly's position on Home Rule had hardened considerably a year later when he was quoted by the *Herald* as stating that England's view was always, "how best can we crush these people who dare to remonstrate?"[41]

Charles Daly's civic interest in recent Irish immigrants to New York was played out in venues mostly outside of the "official" geographical ones. Yet they entailed numerous geographical practices. For instance, during the Civil War Daly helped establish the 69th Regiment, the first all-Irish unit of the New York State Militia to fight with the Union Army in the Civil War. On 23 April 1861, the regiment marched to Washington and, later, fought in the Battle of Bull Run. The regiment symbolized patriotic Irish involvement in the war generally, and hence, these men's sought-after inclusion in the emerging American nation at a time when bitter anti-Irish sentiment was reaching peak proportions, compounded by Anglo-centric nativism frequently pitting "orange" (Protestant) and "green" (Catholic) Irish against one another in violent street conflict. Daly often led the regiment's parades and marches through the city (although he did not fight in the war). His leading of Irish military and St. Patrick's Day parades, along with his public support of Irish home rule, were important public demonstrations of Irish solidarity, respectability, and community power. Such also constituted the geographical imprint of Daly's "diasporic nationalism."[42]

Charles Daly was among the New York Irish, but in many ways, not of them, since the city's small "Irish aristocracy" – merchants, bankers, doctors, and other professionals – was predominantly Protestant. Daly was one of the very few Irish-born or first generation Catholic Irish-Americans to become a successful entrepreneur or professional; and indeed, only one percent of New York's lawyers at mid-century, for example, were Irish of any sectarian orientation, and only a tiny number of Irish Catholics became members of societies such as the elite Century Club.[43] In such ways Daly managed to create social space for influential, high-profile Irish Catholics, and to in fact claim a part of Yankee identity itself *as* Irish Catholic.

Daly's work on behalf of the Irish grew out of his strong sense of Irish (trans) nationalism rather than from Roman Catholicism, even if the two were usually conflated among northern white Irish immigrants. Daly was not a practicing Catholic, in fact refusing a priest on his deathbed.[44] Though he kept a cordial connection to many of the city's high placed clergy, he did not advocate a pro-Catholic stance on political matters; for example he opposed use of public school money for Catholics. Daly was on the board of managers of the House of Refuge (a juvenile reformatory), and though stating in his arguments that "he was a Catholic himself," aligned himself with the Protestants in opposition to the Freedom of Worship Bill, introduced to the state legislature by Jesuits which would have allowed Catholic Mass to be said there.[45] Most likely Daly's marriage into a wealthy New York merchant family with German/Dutch Lutheran and Episcopal roots – a marriage that caused considerable conflict between Daly's wife and her family – explains why he downplayed his religious background in favor of a more ecumenical approach that would offer a better route to social advancement.[46]

Daly's work on behalf of the Irish was also shaped by the rise of the Irish political machine Tammany Hall, and by tense race relations in New York. Daly's membership and participation in Tammany began in 1838, which at the time was a patriotic and philanthropic fraternal organization that raised funds for debtors, fire victims, and the poor.[47] Gradually, however, as has been well documented, the Tammany organization and the Democratic Party in New York City merged into one and by the mid-nineteenth century it became associated with any number of corrupt or illegal partisan activities. Irish immigrants in particular became deeply dependent on the organization, or, as some scholars would have it, they became adept at using the municipal political machine for their own ends. With control of the city's Democratic Party, Tammany became a champion of the working class and latterly, of immigrants, giving millions of dollars of aid to the Irish poor. Meanwhile Tammany "bought" Irish votes by illegally granting citizenship to immigrants, bestowing city jobs to its followers, and providing services to the newcomers and the poor. These methods of getting votes were used most intensively in the 1860s when William M. Tweed, "Boss of New York," was the Tammany leader. He was known to give jobs to thousands of Irishmen, particularly in public works and civil service, in exchange for their votes. Many Irish increasingly demanded and received jobs, food, shelter, loans, recreation, and solidarity in exchange for party loyalty. Tammany was subsequently accused of election fraud, bribery, and extortion. After misappropriation of massive amounts of public funds in 1871, Tweed fell and Tammany's influence was reduced, but it was revived in the 1880s, with Daly becoming its Vice President in 1886.

Daly's sometimes strained but dependent relationship to Tammany was felt throughout his career. One of his most celebrated legal cases involved the impeachment trial of Mayor A. Oakley Hall in 1872, during the Tweed ring scandals. Daly fought Tweed and his cohorts, and though Tweed came out in opposition to Daly's re-election as judge, Daly managed to maintain Tammany support for re-election.[48] His re-election as judge to the Court of Common Pleas for over 40 years owed greatly to Irish supporters and likely necessitated an association with Tammany. Daly nonetheless liked to emphasize his distance from Tammany, and argued that he was also favored by other minority populations in the city, such as the German Democratic Club. For an elected official, his somewhat defensive comments in an 1885 *New York Times* interview are instructive:

> It is generally assumed that I owe my continuance on the bench to the support of the Irish people. That is not the fact.... Of course I have been associated with the social and political interests of the Irish people; I have always co-operated with them, and always will, for I believe that Ireland has an undoubted right to self-government. But I have never sought their support, nor cultivated their good will with any view to my personal concerns. Their votes, likes those of other classes in the community, have been cast for me at the time, during the forty-two years, I have been a candidate for re-election.[49]

Maria Daly's diary offers many insights into her husband's Civil War-time activities, those related to Tammany, his many personal and professional political associations, as well as Charles' participation in establishing the 69th Regiment. The Irish "rush to service" had arguably more to do with high unemployment rates than it did with support for the Union cause; scholars who have written on this topic note that the war helped the Irish, especially with military pay for the unemployed and their families. Tensions heightened in the city, though, when it appeared the Irish poor were bearing the brunt of the war. To encapsulate a many layered story: the U.S. Conscription Act of 1863 proposed an exemption from service for those who could purchase one for $300. The four-day Draft Riots of 1863 ensued, with mostly Irish workers attacking draft headquarters and burning buildings. There was as well a racial component to the riots, as Irish men attacked the homes and businesses of African-Americans who were their main competitors for jobs when the Irish went to war. As most of them were unskilled laborers, free blacks or emancipated slaves represented their biggest threat to integration and survival, a situation only inflamed by employers using African-American workers as strikebreakers.[50] When the riots broke out, Irish workers claimed that

Figure 3.2 Departure of the 69th Regiment, 23 April 1861, the Irish Headquarters around St. Patrick's

Source: Lithograph by Sarony, Major & Knapp. Collection of the New York Historical Society. Negative no. 45149.

they themselves "are for three hundred dollars whilst (men) pay one thousand dollars for negroes." Thus one of the principal ways that Irish immigrants were acculturated into the United States was through their "embrace of American racism," in addition to their fighting with the Union Army.[51] As the draft riots illustrated, Irish racism against African-Americans, and their mixed views on abolition itself, stemmed primarily from a lack of job security.

For his part, Charles Daly opposed the $300 conscription waiver, and though disapproving of the riots – he had, after all, written the precedent-setting U.S. legal decision that criminalized rioting (the Astor Place decision) – he sided with the Irish laborers,[52] refusing to serve his appointment as Commissioner of the Draft Board because of the waiver. Daly and his wife viewed the question of slavery with considerable ambivalence. Maria, whose parents were slave owners, shared the view of many Irish (and German) immigrants that "the Negro was the natural enemy of the Irish laborer," and she detested abolitionism, stating that it was a "menace imported from England." She declared that she was "no friend of free blacks" … they are "innocent animals" and "insolent."[53] Charles seems to have merely disapproved of the abolitionists' Calvinist-leading ideologies, generally supporting the Civil War "to keep the union together." He agreed with those who argued that slavery ought to be confined to states where it already existed and gradually eradicated.[54]

Overall it seems a complex mix of Daly's ethnic prejudices, his Irish trans-nationalist patriotism, and the political culture of the day complementarily shed light on his reform mentality and subsequent activities. Daly's civic activity made on-the-ground infrastructural improvements in Irish communities' housing, sanitation, labor relations, and wages. He was deeply involved both in tenement house and street sanitation reform, issues which affected poor Irish immigrant groups more than any other in the city. As the middle classes were moving northward and settling into the single-family brownstones, burgeoning numbers of poor immigrants were packed into tenement houses in the lower East Side and elsewhere in grossly overcrowded, unsanitary conditions, the worst slum conditions the city had known. In these ways I see Charles Daly's impact primarily as a forceful participant in early American city planning.

Estimates vary, but sources indicate that in 1871, half of the inhabitants of New York City lived in tenement houses ("from which proceeds three-fifths of crime and three-fourths of mortality," according to a leading reformer[55]); and that by 1879, more than two-thirds of the entire population of New York City were living in approximately 83,000 tenements. The conditions found in the Sixth Ward district, near City Hall, were especially bad:

> Here immigrants usually lived in dilapidated, crowded wooden tenements, while children played in and around slaughterhouses, stables, packing houses, and foundries. Horses, cattle, dogs, pigs were all about.… On Park Street near City Hall there were 50 families in a seven-story tenement filled with sickening smells, garbage, and filth. There were no indoor water closets and no sewerage

Figure 3.3 "Lodgers in a Crowded Bayard Street Tenement – Five Cents a Spot"

Source: Jacob A. Riis, *How the Other Half Lives* (1890; rpt. Boston: Bedford Books of St. Martin's Press, 1996): 105.

> … Bishop John Hughes remarked that the slum dwellers were "the poorest and most wretched population that can be found in the world – the scattered debris of the Irish nation."[56]

The wretched, dark, unventilated rooms, surrounded by filth, wastes, open sewage, odors, and other defiling conditions, led to or exacerbated a panoply of health problems and infectious diseases, including yellow fever, Asiatic cholera, typhoid, typhus, scarlet fever, and diphtheria. In the summer of 1878 alone, 5,000 deaths in the city were attributed to such unhealthy conditions. Because the Irish were disproportionately represented in the tenements, poverty's attendant social problems led to many of the city's largest newspapers adopting anti-Irish attitudes, often in vociferous tones.

To address tenement problems, in 1879 the mayor of New York called a mass meeting at the Cooper Union, where he announced the appointment of a committee of nine men, the "Tenement House Committee," to begin a movement for reform of

New York's tenement houses and law.[57] Judge Daly was among the nine appointed (William Astor and Cornelius Vanderbilt were also on the committee). The earlier *Tenement House Act of 1867* had prescribed the current standards for construction, building codes, and occupancy limits (etc.) of tenements, and reform of it was desperately needed. The committee appointed by the mayor was charged with writing new legislation, as well as with forming a building association that would carry out the on-the-ground improvements.

In reflecting in 1900 on its work, Lawrence Veiller, secretary to the committee, asserted that these reformers knew that "the causes of uncleanliness, poverty and sickness were not so much to be found in the 'innate depravity' of the people as in the environments in which they were compelled to live."[58] Scientific understandings of how infectious diseases were spread drew primarily on empirical environmental factors; contagious agents spread under filthy conditions that were themselves products of the rapid urbanization and congestion, and industrialization. Advancements in health science at the time came together in a movement for preventative sanitation, known as "Sanitary Reform" (and this, a precursor to germ theory and bacteriology that would become widely accepted in the Progressive Era). Sanitary reforms were directed towards making ample provision for pure and abundant light, air, water; for drainage and sewage; and for street paving and cleanliness. They advocated the systematic, large-scale reshaping of housing, streets, neighborhoods, and cities. In this way, according to Jon Peterson, sanitary reformers served as antecedents to city planners. They,

> established a platform, of sorts, for all subsequent urban development … [they] vivified the social norm of cleanliness … [and] demonstrated how a modernizing society could generate planned responses to its needs while simultaneously cultivating the public values essential to justifying large-scale remedial action.[59]

The Tenement House Committee's inspectors (comprised of physicians, engineers, and chemists) – cynically dubbed the "sanitary police" by detractors – examined over 22,000 tenement houses. Based on their findings, the committee proposed a number of measures that prescribed the conditions under which new tenements could be built; the required alterations to existing buildings; and the procedures and content of housing inspections. Perhaps most significantly, they drafted a new *Tenement House Law of 1879* to the Albany state legislature that outlined radical changes to existing standards. Their bill established new lighting and ventilation codes for buildings: it directed that houses should not occupy more than 65 percent of a given lot, requiring 10 feet between the rear of the building and the end of the lot and thus allowing for proper ventilation and lighting; and it required that each tenant had 600 cubic feet of air space individually.[60] The law's new building code also demanded larger air shafts, better fire proofing and hallway lighting, increased size of living spaces, and required that each tenement have a bathtub or shower. Strident opposition ensued, from "slum lords" but also from

Figure 3.4 "Dens of Death"
Source: Jacob A. Riis, *The Battle with the Slums* (New York: Macmillan, 1902): 21.

housing occupants who were scraping by from the meager incomes derived from boarders' rents. Nonetheless, according to the monthly magazine, *The Sanitarian*, "with the powerful aid of the New York Press … and under Divine Providence," the law was passed that same year, 1879.[61]

The 1879 law also included the creation of a number of reform organizations. Foremost among them was the New York Sanitary Reform Society, comprised of a more permanent version of the committee of nine and others (Daly chaired its board of directors, and meetings), and another called the Improved Building Association.[62] This latter association (a.k.a. the Improved Dwelling Association) was to select a model plan for future tenement houses, a procedure in which Daly took a highly visible role. Various architects submitted plans for a low-rent, new style of tenement, detailed in great length in *The Sanitarian* of 1881. Commissioner Lawrence Veiller argued that this would be a "strictly commercial enterprise," limited by law to earning no more than 5 percent dividends on the houses built.[63] Meanwhile the Sanitary Reform Society published a circular in 1880 that explained its purpose and aims. This included oversight and enforcement of the *Tenement House Law* as well as a broad agenda to deal with "all matters affecting the health of people in the city." The society argued that "its purely philanthropic labors for the welfare of the poor must still be its chief duty and pleasure." Its immediate agenda was to work with the Department of Health on plumbing and drainage in poor neighborhoods, the licensing of plumbers, laws for inspectors, and street cleaning. Rather paternalistically the society also recognized its mediating role in the city:

> [We] serve as a connecting link between the health authorities on the one side and the citizens on the other. If the usefulness of the Board of Health is threatened by adverse legislation or by the officious meddling of selfish politicians, they have an organized body of influential citizens to turn to for support. And, on the other hand, such an association can educate and arouse public opinion far more effectively than can be expected of an official body.[64]

Charles Daly presided at the Sanitary Reform Society's first annual meeting, widely reported by New York newspapers (the *New York Times*, *Tribune*, *Herald*, and *World*, among others). He opened the meeting with remarks about the history and objects of the society; the new standards of construction they advocated; their recommendations for ventilation, cleanliness, diet, and the care of sick; as well as their suggestions for effective cleaning of the streets. Newspapers widely quoted Daly's declaration that, based on his "personal inspection of most of the large cities of the world," there was a wider field of work to be done in New York City than in any other city in the world, and its difficulties greater. Since Daly had not, in fact, traveled much outside of the American Northeast and parts of Europe, he seems to have made up this claim, shoring up his authority to do so based mainly on his position as head of the American Geographical Society. In any case the public and press seem to have accepted his assertion. The papers noted that the state legislature "dare not oppose such men as Chief Justice Daly" in passing and funding the new law.[65] These articles also detailed the President of the Board of Health's speech declaring that sanitary reform in the city had already led to lower rates of infant mortality and other epidemics.

A year later, in March 1881, the Sanitary Reform Society made front page news again, around the issue of street cleaning and the mud, dirt, and dust accumulating in the city streets and flowing into New York Harbor. The *New York Herald* reported that:

> Cooper Union never held such an audience as gathered there last night. In point of respectability it was unrivalled by anything that New York has ever known … It is a matter of regret that such a meeting could not be held to celebrate and rejoice over a clean city instead of one which is overwhelmed with mud and filth. But the enthusiasm of last night sprang from a prospect of a reform and a glorious possibility of a wholesome future.[66]

The meeting was intended to "collect views of citizens of different occupations," and address a problem "Albany was ignoring." Daly served as chairman of the meeting, declaring in his opening statements his familiar slogan that New York was "the dirtiest city in the universe of equal extent," noting that the death rate was increasing and malignant fevers would likely increase in the warmer weather. He charged that the city, the Board of Health, and the Board of Police were not doing their jobs; an assertion that the *Evening Telegram* bolstered when reporting on the "cowardliness" of police commissioners who left the meeting without addressing the crowd, and who thus had "received the contempt of honest, straightforward, manly men" such as Charles Daly.[67] Throughout the meeting newspapers reported applause that was "turbulent," "thunderous," and "tumultuous." The keynote to the meeting was struck, according to the *Evening Telegram*, when Daly announced to great applause that he and the others "meant business."

The meeting resulted in the election of slate of men to lobby the legislature to move the jurisdiction of street cleaning to the mayor's office and to reform street cleaning procedures. A follow-up meeting was held in April 1881, before which Daly had taken out advertisements in the city's newspapers to invite citizens' participation. He wanted issues to come before the public. The *Citizens Street Cleaning Bill* had been defeated in the Albany legislature, and at the April meeting Daly encouraged the issue to come before the public, "the highest power known under our government – the power of public opinion."[68] His efforts were ultimately successful, as the following year saw passage of the *Consolidation Act of 1882*. Among other structural changes to municipal government and infrastructural changes to the physical environment, the Act provided for new procedures for street improvement as well as the inspection and collection of city refuse.[69] Charles Daly clearly had played a prominent role in this battle for civic improvement.

Working Women's Protective Union

In addition to working for reform of houses and streets, Charles Daly also advocated for better wages and fair labor practices, particularly for Irish immigrant women. Burdened under three depressions from 1854 to 1873, and given their low position in the strata of the city's economy, the Irish among the poorest were the hardest hit by the economic downturns.[70] In the workforce Irish women predominated as seamstresses, domestic workers, and hotel workers, while many sold fruit and vegetables and/or took in boarders. Maria Daly had worked to resettle widows and orphans onto Catholic farm colonies of sorts during the Civil War. The needs of poor women during the war also led to one of Charles Daly's most significant reform activities, in establishing and heading an organization called the Working Women's Protective Union. The union provided support for seamstresses, teachers, dressmakers, and other workers throughout the war, in 1865 forming the first known Catholic day nursery for working mothers.[71] The union also provided *pro bono* legal protection, collected wages due the women, as well as helped women find employment. When it came to women's labor Daly aligned himself loosely with socialist reformers and thinkers of the day such as the women's rights advocate John Stuart Mill.[72]

As the head of the board of directors of the Working Women's Protective Union – whose large, public meetings were held at the Cooper Union and covered widely by the New York press – Daly was principally known to argue for a united, organized movement for fair wages for seamstresses, and he became involved in working women's labor disputes. At the first anniversary meeting of the union in 1864, newspapers quoted him as asserting that women needed to be protected from unscrupulous employers, from the "frauds of designing men." He argued that an adjustment was needed at the time between capital and labor: "the women were earning .16 per shirt, and the capitalist was selling them for $3.50, but the total cost to the capitalist was only $1.59." Daly remained involved with the group throughout his public life, appearing in the news late in his life (in 1893), still arguing for fair wages for seamstresses.[73]

Daly was often asked to speak at meetings of women's organizations and schools, at which his ideological views on gender relations would become apparent. To a graduating class of girls from the Twelfth Ward High School in 1862, for instance, he claimed that "women may be happy and useful without ever getting married."[74] "Single women have a very noble and wide field of exertion, both moral and intellectual," he told the girls, adding that it is "a great mistake of your sex to do nothing to further your education after leaving school." Daly's support for women clearly emerged from his class consciousness. Like many professional reformers he somewhat contradictorily asserted that middle-class married women should retire and let those "who need the money more" take the jobs. He asserted that middle-class women ought to keep to their separate sphere of influence and exert power appropriate to it, arguing that women are the "fountain of morality" and as such, should not try to take men's place in society. In fact he declared that he was against women's rights advocates who tried to do this; otherwise, "to whom is to be committed the cares and duties of the household? … The character and manners of American women have been deteriorating for some years, and if a change is not produced, the effect will be very injurious to the national character."

Certainly such remarks carried a great deal of spatiality, as women of different social classes to him ultimately "belonged" in different domestic or work places. Yet is seems clear that upwardly mobile men of Charles Daly's milieu *would* make this kind of argument, as this was an era of an emerging bourgeois class, when men and women attempted to display their middle-class identity and culture precisely through women's manners, morality, domesticity, and even idleness. It should not be surprising therefore that Daly made this distinction, that middle-class married women's roles were as feminine "civilizers" of men and those of lower classes were as workers who deserved fair wages and working conditions. Ultimately such class distinctions should not detract from his efforts at bringing the issues of fair wages (etc.) for working women to the public arena.

Discussion: Geography and Urban Social Reform

Interviewed about her uncle's interest in the New York slums, Charles Daly's niece spoke of his self-advancement as an instance of more general sought-after improvement:

> We took a great many walks, he and I, down in what is now called the Village, he was always interested … but you know in those days, there were slums, we all knew about the slums, but there was a vitality about the people there, they were sure that some day they would have a palace on Fifth Avenue. It was extraordinary.… Most of them were perfectly sure that things would get better. And, look at his own life; he came up.[75]

Mrs. Hoyt's observation is helpful not only in describing Charles Daly's everyday experience in impoverished New York neighborhoods, but also hints at the persona as upwardly mobile role model he nurtured through his many links with civic and reform organizations. While Charles Daly identified himself as a "self made man" of the late nineteenth century, he also always maintained deep, public connections to his un-pedigreed past. (He did not, incidentally, like others of his means, move "uptown" when he could afford it, but remained living at Clinton Place, in lower Manhattan, throughout his career.)

As bourgeois, genteel, conservative civic leader and judge, Charles Daly, not surprisingly, came to embody the paternalistic, duty-bound reformer of the Gilded Age. To many of his audiences he cast his role as mediator between the community and selfish politicians, as responsible protector of citizens, effective at educating and influencing them.[76] The botanical gardens he advocated for would educate and pacify workers; his admonitions to single and widowed seamstresses encouraged them to work hard and fight for fair wages; and his calls upon the public to voice their concerns about polluted streets sought to empower individuals at the community level. Notably, though, the first entry in the first of Daly's hand-written diaries, dated 4 July 1864, begins with a reflection on his rising position among the ruling elite. He boldly began: "The end of government is to let people feel that they have their own way, while you control them." He apparently questioned the wisdom of recording his own complicity in such class divisions, though, and subsequently scratched out the words "while you control them," softening them to "while in reality they are controlled."[77]

Charles Daly lived and worked during a precedent-setting era of reform in New York City, where (mainly) bourgeois men and women who were connected to the (mainly) Protestant churches became actively involved in the spiritual as well as material uplift of the urban poor. The "civilizing" mission of professional reformers – missionaries, northeastern philanthropists, sympathetic ethnographers, and so on – was to transform the social and cultural lives of the downtrodden with Christianization, education, and bourgeois domestic standards and professional ideals. Meanwhile, most displayed a humanitarian sympathy to the injustices brought about by the imperatives of industrial capitalism, slavery, and sexism (albeit recognizing the many differences among the agendas and world views of men and women reformers as well as those of different social classes, geographic locations, and religious preferences).

This chapter has focused on a number of Charles Daly's selected reform efforts and affiliations, as well as on their limits – such as his views on abolition. (His "objects of reform" likewise did not include Native Americans; see Chapter 4.) Nevertheless, Daly clearly worked for the "public good" insofar as he used his considerable influence to improve the conditions of many urban communities. His motivations and goals were many-faceted. He advocated, among other things, education of the working classes (as well as environmental protection) through the establishment of the Bronx Botanical Gardens; an end to ethnic prejudice of New York's Jews; home rule in Ireland and improved housing and clean streets in New York's Irish neighborhoods; improved inheritance laws for recent arrivals; and better wages for seamstresses. His platform – lectures and events – as well as his scholarly writings, historical research, and legal decisions, aided by a New York press amenable to disseminating them, all made material "imprints" on the city.

Perhaps surprisingly, Daly did not focus his civic vision on public schools, which would have aligned neatly with the nationalistic needs of newly arrived immigrant children, as happened in Europe from the 1870s onwards and propelled to a large extent by geographical societies.[78] Certainly study of early geography textbooks would offer another entrée into geography as a "civic discipline" in the nineteenth century.[79] The AGS as an organization, though, distanced itself from the emerging professionalism of school and university geography, explicitly avoiding pedagogical issues in their work and publications (something that would change with the organization from 1895 onwards).[80] Thus Charles Daly was not an educator in the formal sense. Yet, as an influential public intellectual his work included and even demanded the education of the public on a range of civic issues, through many formal and informal venues, as well as through the media outlets available to him.

Daly's is a unique American story, and offers a commentary on a particular, and characteristically (Irish) American civic career in New York City. His self-education and lack of pedigree perhaps makes Daly a more appealing historical figure than the likes of many of the more privileged men who fill the pages of the history of geography. Also unlike most of those other men, Daly's politics and sensibilities were more *trans*-national than national – his advocating for Irish Home Rule providing an important example but there are others (discussed in subsequent chapters). The fact that a leading American geographer openly sympathetic to Irish nationalism and republicanism was held in such high esteem within British geographical circles is noteworthy. (For instance, when serving as an American delegate to the International Geographical Congress held in London in 1895, Daly received a "great standing ovation" when called upon to preside over one of its sessions.[81])

What should not be overlooked in analyzing Daly's many activities is that his civic motivations and goals complemented his personal ones (ethnic to financial); and these in turn produced a set of geographical practices and associated knowledges. This chapter has advanced the notion of "social reform geography," connecting Daly's reform efforts both to the platform offered by his presidency of the American Geographical Society and to the material geographies of the city with which he was engaged. The human habitat to Daly was not simply the context for social understanding; rather it was an "integral element of … major social transformation."[82] His geography favored infrastructural improvements in the urban environment, and thus challenges accepted wisdom that mid- to late-nineteenth-century American geography was only or mainly concerned with field exploration and commercial development.

While historiographers of geography are right to pay attention to the historical contexts that produced geography as a particular set of ideas, skills, and practices, we must also ask what influences geography exerted on civil society as thus produced? Certainly geography's support of Empire has been widely acknowledged, particularly in the British case, but nineteenth-century American geography, as evidenced by the work and career of Charles Daly, also exerted a great deal of influence over such things gender norms, race relations, commercial development at home and abroad, but also, significantly, infrastructural development and reform of cities. In recent years geographers have moved away from taken-for-granted definitions of the subject as one concerned with maps and exploration to understandings of geographical knowledge as a set of discursive practices and social meanings that at any time were used to make sense of the world geographically, including a wide range of popular understandings and civic practices.

Archival evidence points to the fact that Charles Daly's reform work was tied to geography less as a discipline than as a set of practices. While in his capacity as its President Charles Daly directed the AGS towards field exploration of the foreign and the unknown, his was also an urban geography, clearly expressed as urban development of the spaces of home. In this capacity I contend that Daly displayed a way of "thinking geographically." Geographical knowledge was to him a civic enterprise, producing a "civic consciousness" among the public in the Civil War and post-Civil War era United States. Public interest and civic culture played an enormous role in Charles Daly's geography, as it did for most urban elites who sought to legitimate their policies by reference to the common good (and even if a measure of altruism also pervaded their work).[83] Daly's efforts at building community identity and solidarity through public demonstrations; his scholarly study of migration and settlement patterns; a number of his legal decisions; and his work as city planner and informal city surveyor all demonstrate geography as a means to rectify contemporary social problems. Daly's reform work was tied closely to the city's legal, political, journalistic, and philanthropical elite, but most certainly, as the decades-long President of the premier geographical society in the country at the time, and especially of New York City, his voice and knowledge carried considerable influence in matters affecting the city's infrastructure as well as the "Irish cause." Casting the work of social reform within the context of the geographical practices it required, as well as within the geographies it produced, allows for a better understanding of the norms, goals, and procedures of social reform itself.

Endnotes

1 Harold E. Hammond, ed. *Maria Lydig Daly, Diary of a Union Lady 1861–1865* (Lincoln: University of Nebraska Press, 1962; rpt. 2000): xl.

2 The phrase, "friend of labor" derives from Daly's niece, Mrs. Henry R. Hoyt, in an interview with Daly's biographer Harold Hammond. Transcribed interview, 2 November 1947, 42. Box 10, Charles P. Daly Correspondence and Papers, Manuscripts and Archives Division, New York Public Library (NYPL), New York.

3 "Justice Daly Retires. An Affecting Scene Yesterday in the Court of Common Pleas: A Chat with the Judge," *The Daily Telegraph*, 20 November 1885, Box 9, Daly Papers, NYPL; "Ladies Sit at the Tables," *New York Tribune*, 17 November 1885. Daly added that, "no member of this society had ever gone to the poorhouse." This organization also held a banquet for Daly and Paul du Chaillu on their return from a European trip late in his life; see Harold E. Hammond, *A Commoner's Judge: The Life and Times of Charles Patrick Daly* (Boston: Chrisopher Publishing House, 1954): 384, 391.

4 Charles P. Daly, *Naturalization: Embracing the Past History of the Subject, and the Present State of the Law in the United States [Etc.]* (From the *New American Cyclopedia*. New York: John F. Trow Printer, 1860); see 21–23.

5 For instance, David L. Livingstone, *The Geographical Tradition: Episodes in the History of a Contested Enterprise* (London: Blackwell, 1992); Felix Driver, *Geography Militant: Cultures of Exploration and Empire* (London: Blackwell, 2001); Amy DeRogatis, *Moral Geography: Maps, Missionaries and the American Frontier* (New York: Columbia University Press, 2003); and Karen M. Morin and Jeanne Kay Guelke, eds. *Women, Religion, & Space: Global Perspectives on Gender and Faith* (Syracuse: Syracuse University Press, 2007).

6 Driver, *Geography Militant*, 73–77. Mike Heffernan (personal correspondence 3 July 2009) notes that many leading members of the RGS were ambivalent about religiously-motivated research, due to its potential to compromise scientific credibility. He notes that the Paris Geographical Society was also rather anti-clerical. Nonetheless, churchmen did serve on the councils of such organizations and would have influenced their agendas accordingly. John K. Wright discusses churchmen on the AGS council in his *Geography in the Making: The American Geographical Society, 1851–1951* (New York: The American Geographical Society, 1952): 1–14, 81.

7 For a useful overview of the categories by which one might interpret social reform as genuine reform, see Alexander Missal, *Seaway to the Future: American Social Visions and the Construction of the Panama Canal* (Madison: University of Wisconsin Press, 2008).

8 Charles P. Daly, "Annual Address. Subject: The Geographical Work of the World in 1873," *Journal of the American Geographical Society of New York* 5 (1874): 49–94; see 53.

9 Rev. Joseph P. Thompson (AGS Vice President), "The Value of Geography to the Scholar, the Merchant, and the Philanthropist," *Journal of the American Geographical and Statistical Society* 1 (4, 1859): 98–107; James Wynne, "Benevolent Societies," *Journal of the American Geographical and Statistical Society* 1 (10, 1859): 298–303; Rev. Joseph P. Thompson, "The Physique of Different Nationalities," *Proceedings of the American Geographical and Statistical Society 1862–63*: 84–93. The status of U.S. gold and silver production appears in the same issue (93–117).

10 For useful examples see Charles Withers, *Geography, Science and National Identity: Scotland Since 1520* (Cambridge: Cambridge University Press, 2001); and Charles Withers, "A Partial Biography: The Formalization and Institutionalization of Geography in Britain since 1887," in *Geography: Discipline, Profession and Subject Since 1870*, ed. Gary Dunbar (Dordrecht, Netherlands: Kluwer Academic, 2001): 79–119.

11 T. Gregory Garvey, *Creating the Culture of Reform in Antebellum America* (Athens: University of Georgia Press, 2006); Cecelia Tichi, *Civic Passions: Seven Who Launched Progressive America (and what they teach us)* (Chapel Hill: University of North Carolina Press, 2009); Tyler Anbinder, *Five Points: The 19th-Century New York City Neighborhood that Invented Tap Dance, Stole Elections, and Became the World's Most Notorious Slum* (New York: The Free Press, 2001); Roy Lubove, *The Progressives and the Slums: Tenement House Reform in New York City, 1890–1917* (Pittsburgh: University of Pittsburgh Press, 1962); Steven L. Piott, *American Reformers, 1870–1920* (Lanham, MD: Rowman & Littlefield Publishers, 2006); and John T. Cumbler, *From Abolition to Rights for All* (Philadelphia: University of Pennsylvania Press, 2008).

12 Matthew Hannah, *Governmentality and the Mastery of Territory in Nineteenth-Century America* (Cambridge: Cambridge University Press, 2000): 53–55; Dana Nelson, *National Manhood: Capitalist Citizenship and the Imagined Fraternity of White Men* (Durham: Duke University Press, 1998): 103; quote is from E. Anthony Rotundo, *American Manhood: Transformations in Masculinity from the Revolution to the Modern Era* (New York: Basic Books): 219, also see 173, 252–253; Judy Hilkey, *Character is Capital: Success Manuals and Manhood in Gilded Age America* (Chapel Hill: University of North Carolina Press, 1997): 91–96.

13 Carol Smith-Rosenberg, *Disorderly Conduct: Visions of Gender in Victorian America* (New York: Oxford University Press, 1985); Catherine Hall, *White, Male and Middle Class: Explorations in Feminism and History* (New York: Routledge, 1988); Nancy Armstrong and Leonard Tennenhouse, eds. *The Ideology of Conduct: Essays in Literature and the History of Sexuality* (London: Methuen, 1987); and Peggy Pascoe, *Relations of Rescue: The Search for Female Moral Authority in the American West, 1874–1939* (New York: Oxford University Press, 1990).

14 Tichi, *Civic Passions*, 18–23.

15 Michael Heffernan, "The Cartography of the Fourth Estate: Mapping the New Imperialism in British and French Newspapers, 1875–1925," in *The Imperial Map: Cartography and the Mastery of Empire*, ed. James R. Akerman (Chicago: University

of Chicago Press, 2009): 261–299; Hy B. Turner, *When Giants Ruled: The Story of Park Row, New York's Great Newspaper Street* (New York: Fordham University Press, 1999); Richard Kluger, *The Paper: The Life and Death of the* New York Herald Tribune (New York: Vintage Books, 1986); John D. Stevens, *Sensationalism and the New York Press* (New York: Columbia University Press, 1991); and Leo Herschkowitz, "The Irish and the Emerging City: Settlement to 1844," in *The New York Irish*, eds. Ronald H. Bayor and Timothy J. Meagher (Baltimore: Johns Hopkins University Press, 1996): 11–34; see 24.

16 Stevens, ibid., 32–33, 41; Turner, ibid., 43. Even Karl Marx and Friedrich Engels contributed letters to the *Tribune* in the 1850s.

17 For instance, Joseph P. Thompson, AGS Vice President, in a letter to Daly in October of 1876, asked Daly to "use his influence through the press" (as well as with parliamentary bodies and in his social circles) to "arouse people's attention to [the] important question" – of a conference to establish a system of uniform laws, usages, and forms of bills of exchange. AGS Correspondence, Thompson to Daly, 6 October 1876.

18 Matthew Hale Smith, "Chief Justice Daly," *Successful People and How They Win* (New York, 1877).

19 Hammond, *Commoner's Judge*, 275; Thomas Carr, *New York Leader*, 1 May 1858; *The Hour*, 29 January 1881.

20 "Justice Daly Retires," *The Daily Telegraph*, 20 November 1885.

21 The "clean streets" article appeared in 1 June 1854, as quoted in Kluger, *The Paper*, 76. The *Tribune* justified the actions of the police in the Astor Place case for the same reason Daly did: to "maintain law and order." Greeley disagreed with Daly's decision in the Southern Privateering case, for instance.

22 Wright, *Geography in the Making*, 3. Bennett, for instance, asked Daly to arbitrate in print the 1895 dispute between Great Britain and Venezuela, regarding the boundary between Venezuela and British Guiana. These statistics are from Kluger, *The Paper*, 92. Bennett's son and namesake continued the elder Bennett's interest in geography after his father's death, albeit from Paris.

23 Charles P. Daly, *Want of a Botanical Garden in New York: Remarks of Ex-Chief Justice Chas. P. Daly, Meeting held May 19, 1891, To Take Action Under the Law Enacted by the Legislature for the Establishment of a Botanical Garden in the City of New York.* Original 12-page pamphlet, Box 9, Daly Papers, NYPL.

24 For example, "For the Botanical Garden," *New York Times*, 13 June 1895, and "Botanical Garden Fund: Institution Gets Principal of Ex-Chief Justice Daly's Bequest," *New York Times*, 2 August 1925. *New York Tribune*, 7 January 1894. Julian Hawthorne, "An American Kew," *Lippincott's Magazine*, February 1891, 252–260. Julian Hawthorne was Nathanial Hawthorne's son.

25 Daly, *Want of a Botanical Garden*, 10.

26 Richard Drayton, *Nature's Government: Science, Imperial Britain, and the "Improvement" of the World* (New Haven: Yale University Press, 2000): 180.

27 Ibid., 188.

28 "Transactions of the Society, January–February 1900," *Journal of the American Geographical Society of New York* 32 (1, 1900): 98–99.

29 Charles P. Daly, "Annual Address. Subject: The Geographical Work of the World in 1874," *Journal of the American Geographical Society of New York* 6 (1874): 53–92; see 60. The keyword "botany" garners almost 500 "hits" in AGS journals from 1850–1900.

30 Hammond, *Commoner's Judge*, 375–377, 433. See also Box 11, Daly Papers (Maria L. Daly Papers), NYPL. In addition to work on behalf of the botanical garden, Mrs. Daly's main philanthropic work was care of orphans of soldiers who died in the Civil War.

31 When Daly spoke at the 50th anniversary celebration of the Hebrew Benevolent and Orphan Asylum Society in 1883, "he was received with such warmth that he could not speak for five minutes after being introduced" (Hammond, *Commoner's Judge*, 253). The *New York Times*, 15 December 1893 covered Daly's election as honorary member of the Jewish Historical Society. See Charles P. Daly, *The Settlement of the Jews in North America*, Max Kohler, ed. (New York: Philip Cowan, 1893). Daly serialized his *Settlement of the Jews* and other works in the *Jewish Times* in 1872 and 1875; as well as in the *American Hebrew* as "The Jews of New York." Also see Charles P. Daly, "Notes on the History of the Jews in England and the American Colonies," *The Jewish Messenger*, New York, 4 January 1884.

32 Max Kohler, pamphlet, *Chas. P. Daly: A Tribute to His Memory* (New York: *The American Hebrew*, 1899): 10. Hammond, *Commoner's Judge*, 19–22, outlines Daly's teenage years based on his interviews with Daly's niece. He provides very little factual detail of Daly's early life, however, which Daly himself apparently preferred to keep private and "mysterious."

33 Kohler, ibid., 7–8.

34 Hammond, *Commoner's Judge*, 109; *The Asmonean*, 20 February 1852.

35 Kohler, *Chas. P. Daly Tribute*, 3.

36 Hasia R. Diner, "'The Most Irish City in the Union': The Era of the Great Migration, 1844–1877," in *The New York Irish*, 87–106; immigrant statistics appear on 91.

37 Charles P. Daly, "Annual Address. Subject: The Geographical Work of the World in 1872," *Journal of the American Geographical Society of New York* 4 (1873): 63–118; see 90–91.

38 See "Distress in Ireland," *New York Herald*, 1 January 1880. Daly chaired a funds committee of the Irish Relief Society. Also see a number of newspaper articles in Vols. 2 and 3, Daly Papers, NYPL, which discuss the history of the relief movement. Hammond, *Commoner's Judge*, 294, 297, also discusses Daly's participation in the Friendly Sons and the Fenian Brotherhood. The Friendly Sons of St. Patrick was the oldest Irish organization in the United States. See *New York Times*, 18 March 1870, on the 86th anniversary meeting of the society.

39 See Box 9, Daly Papers, NYPL, for "Address Upon [Irish] Famine … 1863," for minutes of Irish society meetings, and a manuscript, "Notes on New York Taverns." *The World*, the *New York Herald*, *The Sun*, the *New York Daily Tribune*, and the *New York Times*, all 17 March 1879 and 18 March 1879 cover the St. Patrick's parades and dinners. A dinner to raise money for the Irish famine covered in the *New York Times* 18 March 1880; for similar articles see the same papers, 18 March 1883.

40 The *Boston Herald*, 30 April 1863. See Hammond, *Commoner's Judge*, 254, 338; and an interview with Daly, "Home Rule for Ireland," *New York Times*, 15 November 1885 (Vol. 11, 5–7, Daly Papers, NYPL).

41 "Irish Home Rule," *New York Herald*, 24 January 1886. See David Brundage, "'In Time of Peace, Prepare for War': Key Themes in the Social Thought of New York's Irish Nationalists, 1890–1916," in *The New York Irish*, 305, for an explanation of Gladstone's liberal government in England and its effect on the New York labor movement. "Sons of Liberty: America's Successful Revolutionists and Ireland's Struggling Patriots," *New York Herald*, 23 May 1887.

42 Sally Marston, "Public Rituals and Community Power: St. Patrick's Day Parades in Lowell, Massachusetts, 1841–1874," *Political Geography Quarterly* 8 (3, 1989): 255–269. Brundage, "In Time of Peace," cites Ernest Gellner's term on 321. For Daly's war-time activities see Hammond, *Diary of a Union Lady*, 23 April 1861 (and others).

43 Herschkowitz, "Irish and Emerging City," 20.

44 Hoyt Interview, 24.

45 See "Freedom of Worship Bill," *New York Herald*, 16 February 1885, and "In and About the City: The House of Refuge, Judge Daly's Resignation from the Board of Managers," *New York Times*, 10 March 1885.

46 Hammond, *Diary of a Union Lady*, xliv–xlviii. Maria's parents were against the marriage, although they finally acquiesced. Maria nonetheless felt cheated out of her full inheritance.

47 Leo Herschkowitz, *Tweed's New York: Another Look* (New York: Anchor Press, 1977).

48 See *The Sun*, 10 September 1871 about Tammany's support for Daly despite Tweed's opposition; Hammond, *Commoner's Judge*, 139, 215, 237, 346. Daly's views on direct aid to the poor were clearly influenced by the social-political context of Tammany corruption. The *New York Times* quoted Daly as arguing that the "great evil which rendered public charity inefficient in this country was its subjection to political domination." "To Strike at Pauperism," *New York Times*, 8 December 1883. Also see Hammond, ibid., 336–37, note 29.

49 "Home Rule for Ireland," *New York Times*.

50 Iver Bernstein, *The New York City Draft Riots: Their Significance for American Society and Politics in the Age of the Civil War* (New York: Oxford University Press, 1990); Diner, "Most Irish City," 98; Edward K. Spann, "Union Green: The Irish Community and the Civil War," in *The New York Irish*, 193–212; see 204–205; Hammond, *Commoner's Judge*, 131. Meanwhile Irish women were taking over domestic work formerly done by African-American women.

51 Graham Hodges, "'Desirable Companions and Lovers': Irish and African Americans in the Sixth Ward, 1830–1870," in *The New York Irish*, 107–124.

52 Hoyt Interview, 25. Bernstein, *New York City Draft Riots*, 53–54.

53 Hammond, *Diary of a Union Lady*, 14–15 July 1863. Maria despised abolitionists Lyman Beecher, Henry Ward Beecher, Harriet Beecher Stowe, and Julia Ward Howe.

54 Hammond, *Commoner's Judge*, 148, 159.

55 Lawrence Veiller, *Tenement House Reform in New York, 1834–1900. Prepared for the Tenement House Commission of 1900* (New York: The *Evening Post* Job Printing House, 1900): 21.

56 F. Dekker Watson, *The Charity Organization Movement in the United States: A Study in American Philanthropy* (New York: Macmillan, 1922): 290; Hershkowitz, "Irish and Emerging City," 11–34, quote is from 20. Also see Anbinder, *Five Points*.

57 "Report, Tenement House Committee, May 31, 1879," Box 5, Charles P. Daly Papers, NYPL. Also see Hammond, *Commoner's Judge*, 291.

58 Veiller, *Tenement House Reform*, 6.

59 Jon A. Peterson, "The Impact of Sanitary Reform upon American Urban Planning, 1840–1890," *Journal of Social History* 13 (1, 1979): 83–103; Jon A. Peterson, *The Birth of City Planning in the United Stated, 1840–1917* (Baltimore: The Johns Hopkins University Press, 2003), see especially 29–54, quote on 37–38.

60 Veiller, *Tenement House Reform*, 25; Anbinder, *Five Points*, 343–361.

61 A.N. Bell, ed. *The Sanitarian: A Monthly Magazine Devoted to the Preservation of Health, Mental and Physical Culture* (New York: A.N. Bell, M.D., 1881): 125.

62 Watson, *Charity Organization*, 290.

63 Bell, *The Sanitarian*, 125–127; Veiller, *Tenement House Reform*, 24.

64 Bell, ibid., 128, 129.

65 "First Annual Meeting of the New York Sanitary Society," *New York Herald*, 19 November 1880; "The Sanitary Reform Society," *New York Times*, 19 November 1880; "Views from the Rostrum, Discussing the Evils of Tenement-House Life," *New York Times*, 19 November 1880; "City Sanitary Reform," *The World*, 19 November 1880; "Urging Sanitary Reform," *New York Daily Tribune*, 19 November 1880. Also see earlier articles on the work of the committee: "The Sanitary Reform Society: A Conference with the Board of Health," *New York Times*, 11 January 1880, and "Tenement Reform," *New York Herald*, 11 January 1880.

66 "Up in Arms!" *New York Herald*, 19 March 1881.

67 "Last Night's Meeting," The *Evening Telegram*, 19 March 1881. Also see, "How to Clean the Streets," *The World*, 19 March 1881, and the *Evening Mail*, 17 March 1881.

68 "The Street Cleaning Question," *New York Times*, 12 April 1881; "The Streets of New York Must Be Cleaned," *The Sun*, 15 April 1881; "The People and the Caucus," *New York Times*, 12 April 1881. Also see "New York's Bosses, Another Speech on the Citizens' Street Cleaning Bill," *New York Herald*, 12 April 1881; "Perish Patronage," *New York Herald*, 13 April 1881.

69 J.W. Pryor, "The Greater New York Charter: The Formation of the Charter," *Annals of the American Academy of Political and Social Science* 10 (1897): 20–32; Hammond, *Commoner's Judge*, 323.

70 Diner, "Most Irish City," 95.

71 Hammond, *Diary of a Union Lady*, 222, 283–84, 317, 323. Charles Daly also presided at a number of meetings of the Ladies' Health and Protective Association.

72 Hammond, *Commoner's Judge*, 214. John Stuart Mill, in his *The Subjection of Women* (1869) advocated for the emancipation of women and amelioration of conditions of the working classes.

73 *New York Daily News*, 22 March 1864; *New York Herald*, 22 March 1864; and *New York Sun*, 22 March 1864. *New York Times*, 15 December 1893. See Vol. 14, Daly Papers, NYPL.

74 "Judge Daly's Address," *Home Journal*, 8 November 1862.

75 Hoyt Interview, 43.

76 See *The Sanitarian*, 1881, 129. As something of a response to the growing feminization of the reform movement in the later nineteenth century – when the charitable work of the reform societies became a principal means for women to participate in work outside the home – male reformers and philanthropists were susceptible to being accused of effeminacy. Perhaps as a response, men tended to reify such paternalistic behaviors and ideologies; see Rotundo, *American Manhood*, 270–272.

77 Daly's diaries are primarily about his travels in Europe with his wife. Vol. 22, Daly Papers, NYPL. The first diary covers 4–25 July 1864.

78 I thank Mike Heffernan for this observation, and both him and Charlie Withers for their advice on this chapter more generally.

79 See for instance, Bruce Harvey, *American Geographics: U.S. National Narratives and the Representation of the Non-European World, 1830–1865* (Stanford: Stanford University Press, 2001).

80 Wright, *Geography in the Making*, 128, notes that Daly refused to send AGS representatives to a teachers' convention that was to devote a day to geography. William A. Koelsch, "Academic Geography, American Style: An Institutional Perspective," in *Geography: Discipline, Profession and Subject Since 1870*, 245–279 provides a good overview of school and university geography in the nineteenth century.

81 Daly spoke at the RGS on a number of occasions. John K. Wright, "British Geography and the American Geographical Society, 1851–1951," *Geographical Journal* 118 (1952, 2): 153–167; Kohler, *Chas. P. Daly Tribute*, 5; also see "The International Geographical Congress," London *Times*, 26 July 1895 and (under the same headline) 29 July 1895.

82 Peterson, "Impact of Sanitary Reform," 83.

83 Withers' example of churchman Thomas Chalmers' geographical civic consciousness in nineteenth-century Scotland provides a useful counterpart; see *Geography, Science and National Identity*, 158–172. Withers argues that Chalmers saw geography as a means of ameliorating urban deprivation through the geographical project of dividing the city into districts for better access of social reformers. See also, Stephen V. Ward, *Planning and Urban Change*, 2nd ed. (London: Sage, 2004): 9–17.

Chapter 4
Transporting American Empire: Rails, Canals, and the Politics of the "Geo-Personal"

Introduction

Charles P. Daly began life in poverty and died a wealthy man.[1] He amassed a personal fortune through investments in real estate properties and other stocks, frontier land speculation (primarily in Minnesota and Wisconsin), and through a law practice he established after retiring as judge. Daly was almost 40 when he married Maria Lydig in 1856, and this partnership also considerably increased his wealth. Maria was daughter of David Lydig, an affluent New York flour mill and bakery merchant. Maria retained a significant fortune of her own, occasionally discussing stock losses or gains in her diary, as well as reflecting on how much more Charles could have made in legal practice or through a more aspirant political or judicial career.[2] A point that should not be overlooked when considering Daly's geographical work – through as well as outside of the American Geographical Society's formal platforms, speakers, and events – is that these all were a piece of both his vision for transforming space as well as for making money. Daly's and the AGS's extensive involvement with the development of western American railroads, and with plans for building a canal across the Central American Isthmus, offer two good examples of how such spatial and financial civic "missions" were linked. Both represented colossal physical and social engineering projects of nineteenth-century America, and as such were key ingredients and agents of American continental expansion and "commercial empire" building.

Growth of U.S. political, military, economic, and cultural power and influence was aimed not at territorial control of distant colonies that would require administration, but rather with developing trading markets that suited the needs of American corporations. American foreign policy itself was about creating "ordinary commercial transactions" that enabled the making and selling of commodities and the expansion of markets for them, as much as it was about political or military domination. This distinctive shape of the American commercial empire was made possible in the nineteenth century by rapid advancements in manufacturing and communication technologies and, perhaps most fundamentally, by development of transportation technologies and networks, primarily in railroads and shipping.[3]

One of Charles Daly's most important legacies, as civic leader, diplomat, and AGS President, was in advancing American commercial expansion, within the borders of the United States and outside of them. He served as an "agent of empire" by normalizing or naturalizing the role that mundane, everyday geographical knowledge and activities would play in American expansionism. This chapter takes up Daly's civic role in influencing American commercial expansion via promotion, acceptance, and development of large-scale American transportation systems. Particularly as geographical President Daly's authoritative voice and seasoned knowledge carried a great deal of weight within debates over the selection of competing rail and water transportation routes in the nineteenth-century heyday of big schemes – and the enormous "empire of wealth" to be created by them.[4] Such debates centered upon numerous physical geography, political, economic, technological, and social questions and concerns, particularly about the "best" routes to be developed. This chapter focuses specifically on two of Daly's own pet schemes: his associations with the Northern Pacific Railway Company (NPR) in the western United States, and with the Nicaragua Canal Company (a.k.a. Maritime Canal Company), an entity that competed for, but ultimately lost, the rights to build a shipping canal across Central America at Nicaragua.

During and after Reconstruction the American Geographical Society's developing geographical mission "at home" in North America principally focused in three areas: exploration of western resources, especially precious metals and water routes; development of the railroad and telegraph lines; and the impact of explosive population growth on associated agricultural output. As such, the AGS's agenda for American advancement was principally economic in nature; the society's discussions were absent of, for the most part, any rhetoric about American "manifest destiny" to bring about God's or Christianity's divine mission to uplift savages or create a garden from the wilderness, as was that of many expansionists of the time. AGS men supported American expansionism, but rather than making "big pronouncements" about the ideological framework behind it, they simply went about it through their day-to-day mundane and ordinary activities. As a geographical society comprised largely of businessmen, AGS men rather explicitly and unapologetically sided with American expansionists interested in markets, goods, and resources and with national legislation and policies that supported their development. If a political or military question arose, rationale for strategic military bases and so on were themselves to secure trade and access. These were profit-oriented actors.[5]

Charles Daly served as an important link between American national interests and geographical questions of the day. One might even say that Daly's expansionist vision for transforming American space was opportunistically nationalistic as well as commercially grounded. Moreover, reaffirming "American" interests writ large, as I discuss below, tended to obscure the fantastic personal financial gains that Daly and other private investors would make through the transportation networks they helped establish.

Daly functioned in a number of diplomatic capacities at the national level while simultaneously serving as AGS President, thus embodying a central node of communication between public geographical knowledge and the work of various departments of the federal government. He was frequently called upon to advise President Lincoln during the Civil War (most famously perhaps with his advice to Lincoln to not treat captured Confederate naval officers and seamen as "pirates"); he frequently appeared before the Washington Congress testifying on matters of national interest; and he also helped solidify connections between geography and Washington by keeping the public and AGS members abreast of western explorations and surveys sponsored by the federal government. Such knowledge was disseminated principally through Daly's annual addresses, which were widely covered in newspapers in New York and beyond. Daly also brought the "Washington Letters" to AGS publications later in his life, perhaps as compensation for discontinuing after 1880 the comprehensive annual addresses on the "geographical work of the world" for each year (he presented only one such annual summary after that, in 1888, although the annual addresses themselves continued). These Washington Letters, published from 1887–1900, outlined federal government activities of special interest to geographers (and vice versa), such as census data and the status of government-sponsored surveys.[6]

In this chapter I examine in some detail Daly's role in advancing particular western railroad and inter-oceanic canal interests, primarily via his geographical efforts but also through legal and diplomatic means. By way of an overview, there were more papers presented on railroad development during the first two decades of the American Geographical Society's existence than on any other single topic. Development of the railroad was closely tied to Daly's efforts in soliciting potential immigrants from Germany on land bought and sold from the Northern Pacific Railway, a company of whom he was a major stockholder. In turn, the western routes of the Northern Pacific were researched, debated, and published by the American Geographical Society – a nexus of interests that explicitly tied personal gains, civic duties and responsibilities, and American national growth and expansion with geographical knowledge and practices of the day. Daly's real estate ventures via his connection with the NPR lasted for decades. When he retired from his more than 40 years as a judge in the New York Common Pleas Court, he returned to private law practice. In his legal, diplomatic, and geographical capacities, Daly also fought for a federal charter to build a canal in Nicaragua linking the Atlantic and Pacific oceans; the route that was favored by the U.S. government at the time. He provided legal counsel for the Nicaragua Canal Company, became its Vice President and major stockholder, and advocated its case before Congress. In turn, the AGS was the primary venue in the United States for discussions of the proposed ship canal, offering its resources in the form of meetings, publications, and lobbying of governments, within what they argued was a "fair minded, scientifically-based" discussion of the proposed routes. Daly, of course, never knew that "his" canal route was never selected. At the time of his death in 1899 debates continued over where the canal ought to be sited, with two main contenders remaining, the Nicaragua and Panama routes.

The railroad and canal stories are foundational scenes in Daly's life and career, and are useful in illuminating connections between the power of geography – as discipline, knowledge, and practice – and the power of the state in the second half of the nineteenth century. Simultaneously they illustrate the close connection between the production of the national space of empire and the production of private wealth. There are also a number of resonances (and dissonances) in these two case studies with Daly's overall civic agenda, for instance with the reformist ideology and practices he deployed in helping settle German immigrants via his connections with the NPR, and the repercussions of such efforts on Native American land dispossession. Development of the western railroad necessarily resulted in the displacement of Native peoples from western regions. Notwithstanding the resonances with Daly's larger reform project and its connections to geographical practice (Chapter 3), in this chapter I turn to mainly focus on the capitalist agenda that lay behind Daly's efforts at transforming space.

Geographies of U.S. Expansionism I: The Northern Pacific Railway

"Humboldt said to me in 1851," Daly announced in his 1873 annual address, that "I do not know that your countrymen appreciate it, but your great scientific monument hereafter will be your coast-survey."[7] As if inspired by von Humboldt's observation, in 1873 the AGS made an official pronouncement – covered in *The Overland Monthly* magazine – "to devote more attention to American exploration, and to become the active agent in collecting and diffusing geographical information of a domestic character." AGS men promised to focus particularly on the Far West, arguing that, "nothing would conduce more to the unity, stability, and future greatness of our country, than the exploration and exposition of the resources of the great region which lies between the Mississippi and the Pacific." Daly used the platform to ask that naval and military officers, civilians engaged in exploration, and "gentlemen prominent in scientific and educational circles" send the AGS information, especially of the Pacific coast. Such formed the society's basic commercial discourse on the resource-rich western territories, with publications throughout the 1870s and 1880s commonly devoted to such topics as "North-Western North America: Its Resources and Its Inhabitants," and "Winter Grazing in the Rocky Mountains."[8] Statistical tables enumerating resources awaiting extraction often accompanied such articles. Possessing and disseminating such geographical knowledge, while also possessing the personal wealth or wherewithal to direct others' wealth, combined for AGS men into a powerful tool of American empire building.

Substantial portions of Daly's annual addresses themselves were comprised of results from western American surveys and expeditions – their locations, progress, and findings. As David Livingstone argues, such surveys contributed a "visualization" of America as a "coherent geographical entity, imaginable, mapable, and therefore substantial."[9] The geography of the continent Daly helped his listeners and readers visualize – this "science in service of the state" – was specific and substantive; he described in detail the surveys and expeditions

Figure 4.1 Fellow's ticket, Meeting of the American Geographical Society featuring Prof. Francis (Ferdinand) V. Hayden, 15 April 1874

Source: Collection of the American Geographical Society.

sponsored by the U.S. Coast Survey, the U.S. Army Corps of Engineers, the United States Geological Survey (USGS), the Smithsonian Institution, the Navy, and the Department of the Interior. From 1872 to 1880 Daly annually reported on the progress of a number of specific expeditions including Ferdinand Hayden's explorations of the territories of Utah, Idaho, and Montana; Clarence King's geological survey of the 40th parallel;[10] George Wheeler's survey west of the 100th meridian; John Wesley Powell's explorations of the Colorado River and vicinity; as well as a number of spin-off explorations of regions throughout the West.

In these speeches Daly communicated an array of physical geographical, geological, climatic, archeological, and ethnographical findings supplied by the expedition leaders. Information too detailed to be spoken was added as footnotes to the published versions of his reports, such as the 1877 description of the triangulation method used in coast surveys on both the Atlantic and Pacific coasts, provided by the J.E. Hilgard, then superintendent of the Coast Survey. In that same speech Daly outlined the vast mineral potential of Nevada's Comstock mine, which he declared "contains the richest mines of gold and silver of which the world to-day has any knowledge."[11] He thanked Hayden, Wheeler, and others who responded to his request to supply him with details for his reports, meanwhile also noting that he collated data supplied by various departments of the federal government, such as from Land Office atlases.[12] A number of the expedition leaders named in Daly's speeches delivered lectures about the Far West to AGS meetings in New York as well: Ferdinand Hayden (in 1874), George Wheeler (1874), Alvan Southworth (1875), and Frederick Dellenbaugh (1887), among others.[13]

Daly's annual reports, widely relayed in detail to both AGS members and the public, served as an important conduit in public education relating to western exploration and development. It is worth emphasizing that the government-sponsored expedition leaders themselves seem to have largely controlled the content – if not the significance – of the "western imaginary" that Daly's created for his various audiences. In 1880 Daly's claims for how the arid western regions surveyed by John Wesley Powell ought to be handled read as if the explorer himself had uttered them:

> what must be done by legislation to redeem a great part of this now worthless region, which cannot be accomplished simply by the efforts of individuals ... requires the adoption by the government of a general land system, organized pasturage and irrigation districts, with provisions regulating water-rights connected with the land and the manner in which the waters are to be used to accomplish the general purposes of irrigation.[14]

Such were not simply explanatory scripts but would become advocacy papers for future legislation on the Far West.

Daly also cited the reports of newspapermen accompanying various expeditions as valuable sources of information, thus furthering his symbiotic relationship with the *New York Herald*, the *New York Times*, and other papers that would, in turn, support his reputation, judicial decisions, and civic agendas.[15] Yet Daly was always one to craft an important role for "the public" in directing the American (not to mention his own) civic agenda. We see this rhetorical device at play in 1875 when Daly reiterated his view that it was the power of public opinion that directed American exploration in the West: "the reasons for ascertaining what is unknown respecting the globe are the same as they were in the time of Columbus. They are not now as then dependent upon the will of sovereigns, but upon an enlightened public opinion which stimulates individuals and acts upon nations." (While a useful sentiment for generating public activism perhaps, this vague reference begs many questions, particularly because Daly's published work on Columbus does not indicate any evidence that the explorer was driven by the will of public opinion rather than by that of sovereigns.[16])

In any case, a crucially important component of Daly's and the AGS's larger discourse about western exploration was the development and progress of the railroads. The railroad was the most powerful technological symbol of western dominance, serving what Michael Adas refers to as the "measure of man" in both the British colonial regimes and American commercial empires.[17] In the United States, as many scholars have observed, the railroads determined both the pace and direction of American frontier expansion; they were the pivotal integrator of the national space-economy between 1870 and 1910 when the extent of American railroad mileage increased almost five-fold (from 52,922 to 249,902 miles). Many expansionists "masked" their ultimate goal of control of the Europe-Asia trade across North America with claims that the railroads were a necessary part of domestic economic development.[18] With a number of foreign and domestic tensions at play the railroads proceeded apace to knit together – or break up – local and regional markets into increasingly integrated national ones, for instance by bringing goods from farther away to undercut local prices and by bringing raw materials from distant locations to feed industrial manufacturing, particularly in the American northeast. Cities and towns sprang up along the railroad lines – they "midwifed" cities into existence. Moreover the railroads required enormous amounts of industrial goods to be built, and the drive by entrepreneurs to supply them arguably drove the industrial revolution more than any other single force. The railroads stimulated manufacturing, mining, travel, and commerce; the western extractive industry expanded greatly with the railroads, as without them, commercial agriculture, most mining, and cattle and timber production for national markets remained unprofitable.[19]

The AGS functioned as promoter of capitalism and empire through what I have termed its mostly mundane or ordinary day-to-day work, such as by collating, analyzing, and disseminating knowledge on the western railroads. The society hosted scores of lectures and published dozens of papers on western American railroads and on those under construction in Arabia, Uganda, Australia, China, Scandinavia, Peru, and Alaska. The route for the first transcontinental railway was the subject of the first paper presented before the society, by Asa Whitney in 1851 (who hoped to build a national railroad), and AGS men contributed extensively to deliberations about it over the next 20 years. As already noted, there were more papers on railroad development during the society's first two decades than on any other single topic, with statistical tables and maps outlining the extent of the railroad by state, region, or country comprising the most basic data on offer. The AGS describes its efforts as having "supported projects, serv[ing] as a neutral forum for information on all routes, and ultimately compil[ing] the most complete map of its time, which was used for comparing the five candidate transcontinental routes." This map was presumably the one displayed by Henry Poor, AGS councilor and editor of the *American Railroad Journal*, at various meetings and lectures from 1854–1859. Poor referred his audience to the "magnificent map, one of the first labors of our infant society, which although unfinished, is by far the most complete of the kind yet executed of the western portion of the territory of the United States." The map, 26 feet long and 16 feet tall, was never published, likely due, according to Wright, to the comprehensive cartographic work then being undertaken by the government.[20] Nonetheless such efforts at mapping empire would serve AGS constituents in explicit ways, none of them "neutral" to the advance of the American commercial empire.

Many railroad executives served as AGS councilors; and in addition to them, expedition leaders, governors, topographic engineers, and newspapermen addressed the society on railroad development, used society offices to consult maps of the Far West, and published papers in the society's journals. In addition to Henry Poor these included the *New York Tribune*'s Horace Greeley (see Chapter 3) and John C. Fremont, surveyor of the central railroad route through Colorado, who joined the AGS Council and was elected Vice President. Among the most notable railroad executives who served as AGS councilors were Henry Hammond, President of the Indiana & Illinois Central Railroad, from 1877–1887 and Harlow Hoyt, executive of the Louisiana, Arkansas, & Mississippi Railroad Company from 1875–1880. During Charles Daly's AGS presidency a number of individuals delivered lectures specifically about U.S. railroad development. Daniel Gilman in 1873 discussed the Northern Pacific Railway (NPR), and James Douglas covered the "Historical and Geographical Features of the Rocky Mountains Railroads" in 1885.[21] Douglas' commentary provided an overview of all of the American railroads at the time, their routes, lengths, elevations, and problems in construction.

Overall, Daly himself discussed or mentioned railroad development in nine of his annual reports between 1870 and 1888.[22] With the exception of celebrating the advance of the Northern Pacific Railroad (below), most of his discourse was matter-of-fact rather than valedictory. He was interested in conveying measurements and other mundane facts and indicators of progress, and in that sense his discourse can be characterized as American "capitalist vanguard writing" of the nineteenth century.[23] In his presidential address of 1880, for instance, Daly outlined "Railroad Increase in the United States." His observation was that in 1878 and 1879, 7,346 miles of railroad were added in the United States, bringing the total in the country to 86,263 – "nearly one-half of the entire railroad mileage of the world."[24]

Such attention to railroad development should be framed by the fact that Daly was a major stockholder in the Northern Pacific Railroad, in the north central region of the United States, as well as in other railroad companies. He was, moreover, involved in plans to attract Dutch, German, and other northern European settlers to the middle and western United States, buying railroad land and reselling it to them. It was a common practice at the time for railroad companies to send agents to open "colonization offices" in Europe to secure immigrants to settle along its (government-granted) land. This was a "speculator's frontier," with land bought by speculators resold to settlers to both subsidize the extremely capital-intensive railroads and earn profits for the companies.

The Northern Pacific Railway was the first proposed and last built of the American railroads, with the company obtaining a charter in 1864 and construction lasting from 1870 to 1883. Daly reported on its specific advancement from his presidential podium, for instance in his 1873 annual address noting the exact length (450 miles) and exact location of the railroad to date (it had been "extended from Moorhead on the Red River of the North, to the Missouri River, opposite the mouth of the Heart River"), and applauding the "energy and celerity with which this great work has been carried on." Daly went on to identify a number of surveys undertaken in 1872 in the areas of the Missouri River, Rocky Mountains, and in the Pacific slope region and Cascade Mountains. He enumerated railroad and other surveys between latitudes 45 and 49 N, covering 3,843 miles, which "add[ed] greatly to our geographical knowledge of this most important and interesting region." The published version of Daly's speech also included a four-page single-spaced footnote containing a communication from "General Roberts" (General

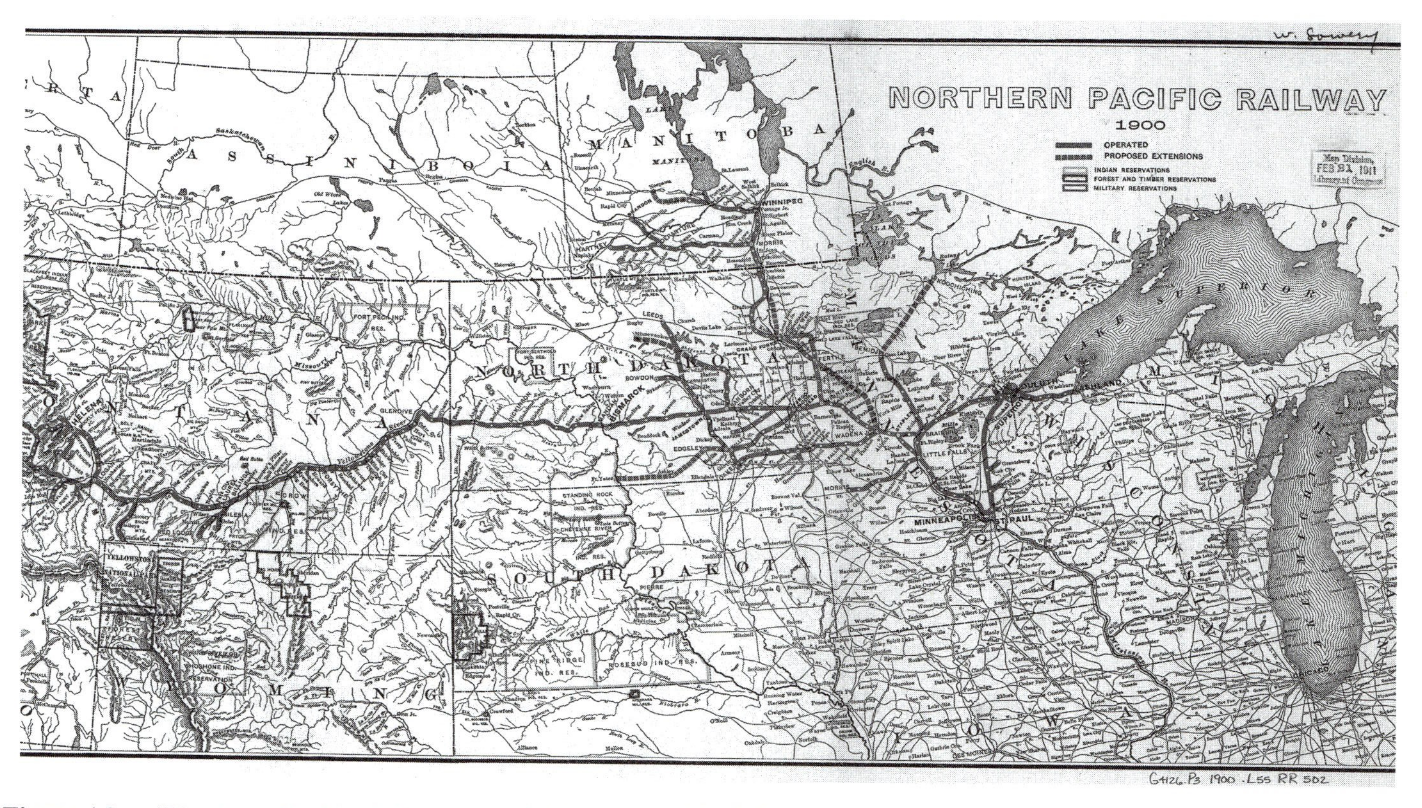

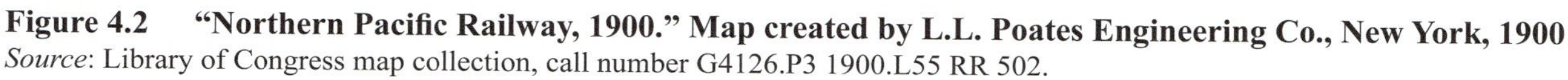

Figure 4.2 **"Northern Pacific Railway, 1900." Map created by L.L. Poates Engineering Co., New York, 1900**

Source: Library of Congress map collection, call number G4126.P3 1900.L55 RR 502.

William Roberts, one of the NPR's chief engineers), detailing what the NPR Company accomplished in 1872. Roberts' report included verbatim discussion of points Daly publicly included in his speech, thus identifying their source, as well as additional specifics on survey locations and results.[25]

Through the years statistical and physical geographical information on proposed routes was supplied to Daly through the NPR's financial agent and promoter, Jay Cooke & Company. In a letter dated 2 April 1870 H.D. Cooke, brother of Jay Cooke, wrote to Daly thanking him for the interest shown in their enterprise and offering help with his upcoming address. Jay Cooke, he noted, had accumulated "an immense mass of information, statistical, official and otherwise, in reference to that section of the country through which the road passes any portion of which he will be happy to place at your service, in the preparation of your proposed address."[26] Such letters offer a window into the quite obvious link between what Charles Daly constructed as "geographical knowledge" of the Far West and investors' personal bank accounts. Providing detailed plans of the NPR development via AGS venues would, of course, have aided the railroad company in attracting necessary stockholders. Again, one of the main features of the society's *Journal* throughout the nineteenth century was in providing statistical tables detailing population, minerals, manufactures, agriculture, climate, cities, farm land, and soils of Minnesota and Wisconsin as well as the other states, regions, and locales world wide – of interest to potential entrepreneurs and businessmen.[27] The use of a geographical society's lecture halls and publications, and its associated links to government and other influential individuals, for such wealth accumulation strategies aligns well with commercial geography's civic mission of capitalist and expansionist development of land, resources, and people; notably also serving the personal aims of the principals involved. Such also demonstrates clear connections between mundane geographical information, ordinary commercial transactions, and the making of empire.

Like many men of means at the time, Daly was a speculator in land and people, making (and losing) money through investments with Jay Cooke & Company. In the 1850s and 1860s returns could be reaped at 30 to 120 percent, but profits and losses varied wildly. High-risk speculation ventures and over-extension associated with the NPR brought the collapse of Jay Cooke in 1873, which led to the stock market crash and bankruptcy of the NPR itself. (The railroad eventually resumed operations in 1878.) Daly's investments with the company entitled him to purchase lands along the right of way of the NPR route from St. Paul, Minnesota to Portland, Oregon, which would transect and serve the district where he made investments in town development. His western lands in 1870 were worth approximately $21,000.[28] Archived letters testify to his numerous land and property transactions, with a host of partners and representatives – Thomas French, John F. Clapp, M.B. Maclay, Mr. Wright, Robert Pinkerton, and D.A. Robertson. Robertson in particular partnered with Daly in speculative transactions for a number of years, and at Robertson's urging Daly induced his German friend Baron Louis Tellkampf to join him into speculative activities. For 30 years of his life Daly developed such land investments in Wisconsin and Minnesota (and Daly and Robertson would work together well into the 1880s and 1890s, developing real estate in New York City[29]). Daly took trips west in 1855 and again in 1880 to inspect railroad routes and their "influence upon commerce." His most valuable western property was in Superior, Wisconsin; he helped plan and at one time owned about one-third of the original township – one might consider this Daly's personal "German colony."[30]

Daly's Superior Township was established in close association with Baron Friedrich von Gerolt, von Humboldt protégé in Mexico who served as Prussian Minister to Mexico and who later became President Lincoln's minister to the United States during the Civil War. Gerolt and Daly (who likely met through Baron Tellkampf) become close friends and frequent guests at one another's homes – Daly's was a "second home" for Gerolt, and there is much in Maria Daly's diary about Gerolt, his family, and their frequent visits with one another.[31] Letters, other correspondence, and receipts testify to a great many transactions between Daly and Gerolt, primarily about such land investments in Wisconsin and Minnesota. In the 1850s Daly and Robertson bought land and improved farms for Gerolt. In one 1857 letter to Daly, Gerolt requested 13 land warrants at 160 acres each, and asked to invest $3,000 in localities "that seemed advisable."[32] Meanwhile Robertson went to Europe in 1858 to invite German farmers to take advantage of rich lands in Minnesota and Wisconsin, and letters from Daly and Gerolt to the agent request protection for German immigrants at sea. Even though the railroad was yet to be constructed, housing was unavailable, and conditions would be unlikely to support them, efforts to bring settlers into the region and extend plans for railroad lines into the territory proceeded apace. Daly managed such ventures partly through his extensive contacts with government officials, for example discussing the transplanting of a large number of immigrants in Minnesota with its governor.[33]

Charles Daly nurtured his civic interest in German immigration in more broadly social ways as well. According to his niece Daly had "a great many German friends, when they all came over during 1848.... During the revolution, a great many of those men came to him."[34] Daly's re-election as judge to the Court of Common Pleas for over 40 years owed greatly to Irish supporters. But he liked to emphasize that other minority populations in New York favored him as well, such as the German Democratic Club. Daly's wife's family was of German descent, and Daly maintained close ties with New York's German Society (an organization Maria's grandfather helped found), dedicated as it was to "encouraging emigration from Germany, protecting indigent emigrants and furthering useful knowledge among Germans" in the United States.[35] Daly was an invited speaker to the society's centenary. Although his work among the Irish was more noteworthy – an observation he himself made at this anniversary celebration – the experiences and spaces of European immigrants were of general concern to him. And yet, Daly's work on behalf of German immigrants is intensely given to possible repercussions. Daly's "German colony" in Wisconsin and others like it necessarily involved the displacement of Native peoples from the area.

Native Americans: (Not) Geography of Social Reform

The archives reveal only glimpses of what Daly might have thought about Native peoples displaced by western immigrants, the railroad, or other U.S. expansionist projects supported by the AGS, though a number of AGS lectures and papers discuss Native American ethnographies.[36] The Oneida and other Native groups from Minnesota and Wisconsin specifically receive no coverage in any of Daly's speeches (or AGS publications) – they were not among his Jewish, Irish, and other "objects of reform" (Chapter 3). But because the situation of Native peoples was one of the foremost reform causes of the day (particularly important to Daly's close associate and AGS patron Peter Cooper), those whose plight was discussed in New York civic venues did draw Daly's attention. His scrapbooks contain two sets of newspaper articles about meetings that Daly chaired; one dealing with the Oglala Sioux in 1870, when Chief Red Cloud of the Pine Ridge Agency in Nebraska, embattled signatory to the 1868 Treaty of Fort Laramie, stopped in New York City on his lecture tour about the unjustifiable American take-over of the Black Hills of South Dakota; and the another from meetings of the Indian Rights Association in 1886, at which was discussed federal plans for Native land to be held in severalty.[37]

Chief Red Cloud, accompanied by Red Dog, spoke to "immense crowds" at the Cooper Union at the 1870 meeting, an event widely covered by the New York newspapers. Transcripts of Red Dog's and Red Cloud's speeches appear in the *New York Times*, *The World*, and others. The *New York Times* declared that the meeting was about "imploring simple justice," with Peter Cooper charging Congress to ensure that Indians were properly compensated for their lands. Daly declined to offer extensive comment on the issue, and in fact *The World*'s reporter made reference to Daly being "guarded and careful of speech."[38] He refrained from making any extended personal remarks, simply noting that the "warriors" and "orators" came to plead their cause in their own person and that the body present should not see these "original owners of the country wronged … every feeling of justice, every impulse of humanity, should urge that they be treated fairly."[39]

Throughout the 1870s Daly reported on the situation in the Black Hills in his annual addresses, with rhetoric caught between entreaties for justice and fairness for Indians, and the seductions of extensive gold and other mining opportunities and the "impressive" physical geography of the area. In his 1874 annual address Daly detailed General Custer's military expedition in the Black Hills (via a report from a Captain Ludlow), describing the region as "admirably adapted for settlement, abounding in timber and luxuriant grass and pure, cold water, valleys ready for the plow, [with a] profusion of flowers and fruits, cooler than the climate of the plains, not subject to drouth." In 1875 his report featured the discovery of gold in the region and miners flooding in. While Daly acknowledged that the region "was reserved by Treaty to the Sioux," he lamented the miners being unable to effect purchase of the region because the Indians "asked an exorbitant sum." Meanwhile

Daly reiterated the potential of the area in mining opportunities, cattle grazing, and general habitation, noting its "unsurpassed beauty." He concluded with the implausible and illogical view of a *New York Herald* reporter who asserted that "[t]here was no evidence that the Indians had ever lived in these hills, owing to the great prevalence of thunder storms and frequency of trees being struck by lightning."[40] By 1877 the region became for him an area of "the hostile Sioux, in the land of the turbulent Dacotahs."[41]

The following decade Daly presided over two well-publicized, well-attended meetings of the Indian Rights Association. These meetings publicly aired "the Indian Question" before 1,000 or more attendees, attempting to determine public opinion on the proper treatment and rights of Native peoples. The April 1886 meeting was widely covered by the *New York Times*, *The Sun*, and the *New York Tribune*, the latter which quoted Daly dispassionately observing that: "we have not improved their condition nor the conditions of the settlers whom they harass … the instinct of the Anglo-Saxon race with regard to the Indians has been to push them further westward and keep them outside instead of within the pale of civilization."[42] Other speakers urged that it was an obligation to civilize the Indians, lamented wrongs done to them, and recommended their citizenship rights. Speakers from the Hamilton and Carlisle schools described the "sameness" of Indians with other ethnic groups such as the Irish and Italians, and thus the similar potential assimilation of them into white American culture. The meeting ended with Daly summarizing the will of the group, which was to support land in severalty and recommend as much to U.S. President Cleveland.

In his public life Daly adopted the language of some reformers of the day – agreeing that Native people could, by imitating white people, avoid extinction – but the connection between his own participation in United States expansionism and the desperate condition of Native people seems to have eluded him. His was not a reform ethic focused on exposing the duplicity of the American government and settlers towards Native Americans; and indeed their land's commercial potential constituted Daly's main geographic interest in them. Charles Daly, like many of the white, Christian reformers of his day, selectively ignored the indirect though no less consequential effects of certain of his efforts – via the NPR and the AGS especially – that benefitted selected immigrants but that led to the usurpation of the rights and justice for others. His commercial geography clearly trumped his ethnic of reform, which is not to say also that the issue for him boiled down to a racial (or racist) one per se. Daly in fact nurtured his friendships with Inuit men and women, for instance, and those who visited his home greatly swayed his opinions on geographical knowledge of Arctic regions (Chapter 5).

What is obvious in all of this is that Charles Daly's civic motivations and goals complemented his personal ones, and these in turn produced a set of geographical practices and associated knowledges. Daly's and the AGS's support and promotion of western exploration, railroad development, and accompanying settlements – the western commercial empire – produced some of the most influential geographical knowledge of the western United States of the time. Meanwhile, such activities also greatly improved Daly's own financial profile; he was part of one of the most notorious land grabs in U.S. history, helping move huge sectors of public lands – indeed, Native American lands – into the hands of a small number of Gilded Age industrial giants.[43]

Geographies of U.S. Expansionism II: The Nicaragua Canal Company

Throughout the twentieth century and into the twenty-first, the American Geographical Society's direct field work overseas has been most closely tied to Latin America, evidenced most famously by the Millionth Map of South America produced under Isaiah Bowman during the inter-war years, and more recently, its controversial mappings of indigenous land in Oaxaca, Mexico, from 2005–2008 (the "Mexico Indigena" Project).[44] In the mid-nineteenth century though, the AGS took relatively little interest in one of the main political debates about the region of the period – whether, as some expansionists argued after the 1848 U.S. invasion of Mexico, American territory ought to be extended to the full of Mexico and into Cuba and beyond. Decades later not much had changed with respect to the Latin American or Pacific theaters; at the close of the nineteenth century AGS publications covered U.S. colonial interventions in the Philippines to a much lesser extent than did the *National Geographic*, and only a dozen or so articles appeared in AGS publications on U.S. occupation of Cuba, and the annexation of Puerto Rico, the Philippines, and Guam.[45] This latter absence is perhaps best explained by the fact that these government interventions elicited very little in the way of commercial advantages for American business.[46]

Rather than engaging in matters strictly geo-political, the AGS's primary focus in nineteenth-century Latin America was one more of a geo-commercial nature –the siting of the inter-oceanic isthmus canal. The society published a couple of papers on Central American canal projects as early as 1854, but beginning in 1879 and into the 1880s and early 1890s, its members became seriously engaged in – literally financially invested in – the geographical, governmental, and legal debates about the best route for a proposed ship canal that would link the Atlantic and Pacific Oceans, a canal eventually opened for business in Panama in 1914.

The idea of a canal connecting oceans and opening another "passage to India" had intrigued explorers, statesmen, and scientists centuries before it became a technological possibility in the latter nineteenth century. Nothing in U.S. history would approach in scale the monumental technological achievement, foreign market potential, as well as symbolic cultural value that an isthmus canal promised. The region's independence from Spain in 1821 combined with the mid-century ethos of the Monroe Doctrine provided American expansionists the rationale needed to push ahead for increased economic expansion through an area they considered neither quite foreign nor domestic.[47] The discovery of gold in California in 1848 had created a tremendous volume of American trans-isthmian business already, mostly overland by railroad beginning in 1855. Meanwhile French, American, and

British expeditions sought for decades a suitable location for a shipping route. To make short a long, intriguing story – American interests were thwarted when the French acquired a concession from Columbia to build a canal in Panama in 1878, though a host of public and private entities continued for decades to explore, finance, and promote a number of other plausible routes from Tehuantepec, Mexico to the Isthmus of Darien at the Columbian border.

Americans acting in a private entrepreneurial capacity, such as Cornelius Vanderbilt, sought rights to build the canal through Nicaragua beginning as early as 1849 (see below). The U.S. federal government, under President Grant, created an Inter-oceanic Canal Commission that sponsored seven expeditions throughout the region beginning with the 1870 Darien Expedition.[48] The results of these were inconclusive if not controversial, with U.S. naval officers themselves coming to different conclusions as to the best potential routes (Admiral Daniel Ammen and Commander T.O. Selfridge among the best known adversaries, with the former favoring the Nicaragua route and the latter, the Panama route). Grant himself determined that U.S. business and government would be best served by supporting the Nicaraguan route; among other perceived advantages it was closest to the U.S., was least expensive, and already contained navigable lakes and rivers (and not incidentally, it was the route previously advocated by the great Alexander von Humboldt). In 1880 Grant approved an agreement between the U.S. government and an entity called the Nicaragua Canal Company, the latter which would handle negotiations with the Nicaraguan government (a concession was signed that same year), as well as the planning, financing, and building of the canal.

Meanwhile French governmental, financial, and geographical interests united around their own plan to build a canal through Panama. Ferdinand de Lesseps – glorified builder of the Suez Canal two decades earlier – headed the project. De Lesseps aimed for official international approval of the French plan and so organized the "Interoceanic Canal Congress" in May 1879, with 136 international delegates in attendance (73 of whom were French), including 11 Americans. Among these were President Grant's naval officers and two councilors from the American Geographical Society.[49] The French plan passed by vote, although the outcome elicited strong differences of opinion, particularly between the U.S. supporters of the Nicaraguan route and the French supporters of the Panama route.

The site selection process and eventual building of the Panama Canal presents a complex and multi-layered story of labor struggles and loss of life, with a host of geo-political, diplomatic, legal, and engineering tensions and dimensions. So many aspects of the canal story are worthy of consideration by historical geographers, not least of which include the French "failure" to build the canal from 1882–1889. De Lesseps' construction project lasted for years until his company went financially bankrupt in 1889, adding to the tremendous moral bankruptcy it faced with the deaths of 20,000 workers from accidents and diseases such as malaria. Historical geographers also have much to contribute to analysis of American attempts to acquire land rights to build the canal, both by the federal government and private entrepreneurs, a process that culminated with Theodore Roosevelt's seizure of Panama when it gained independence from Columbia in 1902 in order to clear the way for the American resumption of the French project. My intention is not to revisit these and other big issues to do with the site selection and building of the canal, as scores of scholars have done so.[50] Rather, in what follows I dissect a small slice of the bigger story that relates geographical knowledge and practices advanced by AGS to the diplomatic negotiations and legal battles with which they engaged over competing routes – those everyday, mundane actions and knowledges – that posed a potential financial windfall had the Nicaragua route been selected. The AGS and Charles Daly were actively involved with the site selection process, and examination of their efforts reveals, like the railroad example above, important but as yet unexplored connections between the power of geography and the power of the state in nineteenth-century America. Such an examination also reveals how Charles Daly's – and thus American geography's – spatial and financial "civic missions" were closely linked in the sphere of Central America.

Geography's Civic Mission: The Nicaragua Canal

When the American contingent returned from de Lesseps' Paris conference mostly dissatisfied – whether because the Panama plan was not backed by sound engineering surveys or for more commercial or political reasons – the AGS declared that it would give the issue "a full airing." Several months later, in December 1879, the society held a large, well-publicized inter-oceanic canal meeting with a number of smaller meetings to follow.[51] John Wright convincingly describes the published account of these proceedings as "185 pages of what must be among the most fascinating records in print of a complex interplay of conflicting motives, personalities, and opinions concerning the great project in engineering and applied geography."[52] Charles Daly opened the meeting stating that an international sanction for the canal route selected was as yet still needed. He alleged that the discussion at the Paris Congress "was hardly a discussion," and that because the United States had completed more surveys and explorations of the isthmus than any other country, "we are naturally, therefore, not very much impressed – I say it in no spirit of discourtesy – with the action of the body coming together in Paris."[53] (Despite such strong words, the AGS was to later cordially host and entertain de Lesseps when he visited New York the following year, an event widely covered in New York newspapers. De Lesseps visited the offices of American Geographical Society on West 29th Street, and was honored with receptions and dinners. Daly welcomed him to the AGS "with great earnestness and sincerity," amidst packed houses of people "clamoring to meet the great de Lesseps." De Lesseps spoke briefly and to the point: "a lock canal is out of the question, I stake my reputation on it, [a canal at Panama] will succeed."[54])

At the 1879 meeting Daly argued that the AGS was both the proper venue for discussion of the canal and the appropriate party to acquire and diffuse information about it. "This duty seems especially to devolve upon us more than any other institution," he asserted, "[since] we have greater facilities than any other body in the

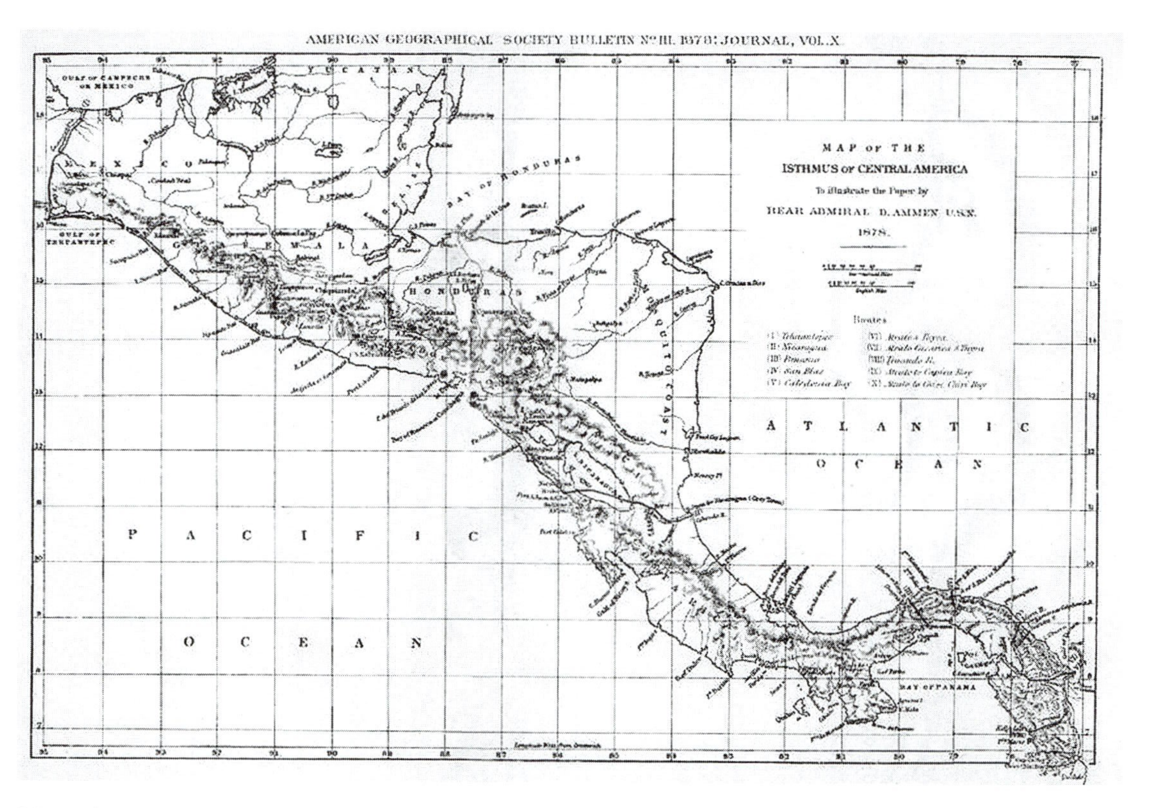

Figure 4.3 Map of the Isthmus of Central America to Illustrate the Paper by Rear Admiral D. Ammen, U.S.N., 1878

Source: *Journal of the American Geographical Society of New York*, Vol. 10 (1878): foldout after p. 162.

country, with perhaps the exception of the Smithsonian Institution, for disseminating throughout the world the information elicited by such an investigation." Daly went on to say that a full investigation of competing routes was necessary: "this is a question for physical geographers and civil engineers, not for congresses." Daly's claim that the AGS would be the appropriate scientific venue to discuss competing routes, outside the polluted realm of politics and national competition – much like the arguments made about the railroad discussions – masked the inherently political nature of AGS discourse and the vested interests of its protagonists.

Although Wright argues that the society did not favor any particular route, evidence from several sources points to their long-standing support, both direct and indirect, of the Nicaraguan. Papers solicited and read for the 1879 meeting seemed to overwhelming back the Nicaraguan route, although support for the "San Blas," Panama, and others, from AGS fellows or councilors, also appears in the proceedings. (A map accompanied the published version of the meeting, showing these various routes.) Nonetheless the centerpiece of the 1879 meeting was the lengthy disposition of Navy Admiral Ammen, President Grant's expedition leader (who favored the Nicaraguan route), and indeed the preponderance of the meeting was devoted to Ammen's views and responses to technical questions they elicited, answered by his like-minded civil engineer, A.G. Menocal. Ammen called the Nicaraguan route the only one "actually possible, and … relatively economical," and minced no words referring to the Paris conference as a charade that produced a rushed decision by uninformed participants.[55] Economic, physical geography, and civil engineering arguments were aired at the meeting: the logistics, relative costs, and practicality of constructing a sea-level canal without locks (de Lesseps' vision) versus the necessity of one with locks and/or tunnels, as well as the overall climatic, vegetative, geological and other physical conditions present at the respective sites. Because the American use of the canal would be two or three times that of any other country, Ammen argued, "their" American (Nicaraguan) route ought to be favored.

As convener and chair of the meeting, Charles Daly served his official capacity in the mode of (seemingly) neutral scientist – framing the issue, gathering information, and asking questions. He posed a question to Menocal about potential earthquakes in Nicaragua, who replied that although Nicaragua was indeed subject to slight shocks, their effects would be far less than those at the Panama site. And so on. At the meeting's conclusion Daly refuted a claim made by de Lesseps that Napoleon III had favored the Panama route; according to an AGS Fellow who studied the issue, Napoleon favored the route through Nicaragua. Daly's final comment foreshadowed much of what was to come for him personally: "when all the information that can be gathered is obtained and duly weighed, commercial sagacity will determine whether the canal should be built, and where it should be built, and if it is to be, commercial enterprise will, in my judgment, find the means of doing it."[56] To Daly it would be the neutral (mundane) facts of informed geographical knowledge that would serve the national interest of commercial development.

Several dozen related articles and reports appeared in AGS publications *ca.* 1870s–1890s, on topics ranging from "The Isthmus of Darien and the Valley of the Atrato Considered [etc.]," to "The Nicaragua Canal," to "The Commercial Geography of the American Inter-Oceanic Canal."[57] Given the wide-ranging subjects of these papers, and the varied backgrounds of their authors, no simple conclusions about a "collective" AGS position on the preferred canal route can be drawn from them specifically. And yet, documentation from other sources points to a collective AGS preference for the Nicaraguan route, as well as a persistent championing of the AGS as the appropriate body to study the question. Society and councilor meetings offer one indication. In 1870 the councilors determined that the "Nicaraguan route was the only practical one, the Darien gives no hope." In 1874 they went to the trouble of passing a resolution that noted their important role in the canal issue. In 1879, subsequent to the December meeting, they passed a motion stating that, "the rooms of the Society be opened on evenings to be named hereafter, for the further discussion of the Inter-oceanic Ship Canal Subject." And in 1886 their minutes indicate "the consistent record of the Society with regard to [the Nicaraguan Route] of interoceanic communication."[58]

If the society's published papers overall presented something more of a neutral envisage of the AGS perspective, Charles Daly's defense of the Nicaraguan route is unambiguous, including before the 1879 meeting. Daly steadily kept the society and the public updated on the status of the canal in most of his annual addresses, beginning in 1870 when he praised de Lesseps' work on the Suez Canal.[59] In 1873 he covered the U.S. Darien Expedition, noting that, "the results of the Nicaraguan survey … will prove [it] to be the most practicable."[60] His 1874 address focused on physical geography features of several routes based on reports from various expeditions.[61] By 1876, Daly announced that all the surveys had been completed, and in an uncharacteristically passive voice, declared that "although all the reports have not yet been published, it is understood that the result of the surveys shows that the Nicaragua route is the most practicable … the Department of State, it is said, is now in correspondence with various friendly powers for the negotiation of treaties guaranteeing the neutrality of [this site]."[62] The following year found Daly refuting the logic of de Lesseps' expectations about water flows at the Panama site.[63] And again in 1880 he reviewed de Lesseps' plans to construct a dam and divert water by rising flows of water rather than by locks, simply concluding that there was nothing more for him to comment on the matter, that the society was in the process of publishing the results of its 1879 meeting.[64]

Daly's "geographical" perspective on the canal – the knowledge that he constructed and disseminated about it through the venue provided by the AGS – should be framed within the larger scope of his legal and diplomatic career. As with his rhetorical talents trained on other geographical topics, Daly's discourse on the shipping canal always emphasized the "evidence," thus recalling his career as a judge and lawyer and those manly traits of reason, impartiality, and so on most valued in those professions. Like the ministry, the legal profession required, according to Rotundo, "a master of precedent and tradition; they demanded a

Figure 4.4 The Nicaragua Canal – Sailing of the steamship "Alvena," with the construction corps machinery, and supplies, from New York, 25th May. Charles Daly (third from left) appears with other backers of the Nicaragua project

Source: *Frank Leslie's Illustrated Magazine*, 8 June 1889.

cultivated faculty of reason, even as they obliged a man to master the less rational arts of persuasion."[65] Daly's exceptional facility with reason and persuasion worked well for him in his battles for the Nicaragua Canal, both as geographical President and as Vice President and legal counsel for the company that was set to build it.

Though Charles Daly had no formal education in the law, throughout his career as judge he lectured on the law at Columbia, and when he retired from the Court of Common Pleas in 1885 he returned to law practice, establishing the law firm of Daly, Hoyt, and Mason with his niece's husband as one of his partners. The firm opened its doors for business in 1886 at 44 Wall Street, and prospered throughout the last 14 years of Daly's life, principally by taking on many well-publicized corporate-interest cases. In 1886 Daly defended the New York Arcade Railway Company, a company for which he was, not incidentally, director and later President. As legal counsel Daly claimed to be "helping his friends save their investments" by fighting (and winning) a case brought by local property owners to restrain the company from building an underground railway (subway). He won the case but the District Court of Appeals later overturned the decision. His firm also defended the North River Sugar Refining Company and other similar interests.[66] The web of powerful relationships that such activities entailed in developing the urban-industrial fabric would be similar to those required for imperial relationships further afield.

Daly also served as legal counsel for the Maritime Canal Company (a.k.a. Nicaragua Canal Company), incorporated by the federal government in 1881 to build the Nicaragua Canal; he was among the original incorporators of the company, served as its Vice President, and was a principal investor.[67] In 1885, when a canal treaty with Nicaragua was pending before the U.S. Senate, (the new) U.S. President Cleveland called for private interest to take over the enterprise, rather than the government.[68] Daly solicited Francis Aquila Stout, AGS Councilor and Vice President (from 1872 until his death in 1892), to become the company's President,[69] and together they devised a plan to solicit investments from other businessmen and financiers. In 1888, as lead legal counsel for the company, Daly appeared before the U.S. House of Representatives' Committee on Commerce to urge granting of a federal charter to the company for building the canal.[70] By that time, he argued, the company had already spent $200,000 on the project and had eight working parties in the field. The Senate had passed the charter, but the bill stalled in the House. (Meanwhile, the company also sought a charter from the state of Vermont, which would have technically allowed them to proceed with the project, albeit without the benefits supplied by a federal charter.)

Daly absorbed some "bad press" when testifying before the House. Newspapers reported a great deal of name-calling and attempted character assassination, with Representative Francis Spinola accusing Daly of lobbying for his own company. The *New York Times* led off with a headline that screeched, "Is Spinola a Bone Hunter: His Opposition to the Nicaragua Canal Bill. He Assails Judge Daly as a Lobbyist."[71] The *New York Herald* interviewed Daly on the matter, introducing him as the "attorney for the American Company." Daly defended himself by stating that the group sought the Vermont charter owing to the great delay of Congress in incorporating the company, and time limitations of the concession: "We simply desired a national charter because the construction of this canal uniting the Atlantic and Pacific oceans, through Nicaragua, was a national enterprise which would benefit the whole of this country more than it would any other, and which ought to be in the hands of American citizens and under American control."

Daly explained in the interview that the provisions added to the House bill "would render it impossible for us or for any others to accomplish anything under it," referring both to provisions securing federal bonds for the project and those allowing the federal government to regulate tolls at the canal, "without," Daly argued, "having given anything for the enterprise."[72] Daly maintained that a private group of American citizens ought to be given a charter for a project that they would finance at their own expense; to do otherwise was to *de facto* sanction the French scheme at Panama. Daly's argument thus pivoted on the vulnerability of "American" interests, when in actuality the benefits to his scheme would accrue to only a few stockholders.[73]

In 1889 Daly's company faced another snag. The American Atlantic and Pacific Ship Canal Company (AAPSC, originally incorporated as Vanderbilt's Accessory Transit Company, above) filed a restraining order with the Supreme Court against Daly's company. They asserted that their 1849 charter with the Nicaraguan government gave them exclusive rights to construct a canal across Nicaragua. Daly again served as legal counsel for his company in the case, arguing that the AAPSC charter was annulled by later agreements, and that because they had neither commenced building of the canal, nor completed it within the 12-year period stipulated in the last standing agreement, their claims were void as were their arguments to protections under the Clayton-Bulwer Treaty.[74]

Daly's wife Maria meanwhile kept track in her diary of Charles being "up to his ears" in work on the canal, noting that he made 14 visits to Washington, D.C. in the six months preceding May 1889. Although admitting to having "made no previous mention of the great enterprise that the Judge is so much interested and busy in, the Nicaragua Canal, of which he is leading counsel," she declared in the same breath that "the firm of Daly, Hoyt, and Mason has been very prosperous. The Judge seems to like practicing law with his young associates." Moreover, the canal project had brought them into contact "with some charming navy men."[75]

When the French project collapsed in 1889 and de Lesseps resigned, scores of political figures, newspapermen, and other notables demanded that Congress charter the Nicaragua Company, suggesting that this "American" venture was the only one liable to succeed. That year the Maritime Canal Company was granted a charter to build the canal (assuming the charter originally granted in 1887 to the Nicaragua Canal Association). The issue played out contentiously in the papers, with *Frank Leslie's Illustrated Newspaper* coming out in favor of the Nicaragua plan but others, such as *The Sun*, reporting that Daly's company had secured a national charter by "revolutionary government in Central America."[76] *The Sun* seems to have been on to something, although the revolutionary act of government occurred more within the U.S. Congress, courts, and media than in Central America.

Work actually commenced on the Nicaragua canal and continued until 1893 under the direction of A.G. Menocal as chief engineer. Several miles of the future canal were dredged during those years, and construction completed on a pier, wharves, and warehouses for the reception of supplies. The project had (temporarily) succeeded by the efforts of many men, not least of whom included the Chairman of the Senate Committee on Interoceanic Canals, John Tyler Morgan of Alabama, whom Charles Daly would also encounter in Senate hearings on the Congo (Chapter 6).[77]

The Maritime Canal Company eventually collapsed with the Wall Street panic of 1893, proving that private capital alone would not be able to sustain such a monumental construction project. In 1894 Charles Daly fought one final legal battle for the company. In-fighting among the stockholders had divided the company when it attempted to reorganize, and the U.S. Circuit Court heard a fierce, well-publicized battle among principals. Daly defended the company against a small group of stockholders who sued to have the company's books opened, claiming that there was no consensus about reorganization, and that money had been misappropriated. Daly's opposition claimed that $2,400,000 had been wrongfully disposed, and that one-half of the company's $12,000,000 capital had been issued to persons composing the Nicaragua Canal Association, in return for only $300,000 provided by them for obtaining the concession from Nicaragua. "Members of the New York Bar ought to be neutral and not fight against stockholders of a company," the opposing lawyer contended. As with other such legal battles, one of Daly's principal legal strategies was to claim that his opponents were serving the interests of those who supported the Panama Canal site. While it would be too late to save the company, the opposition finally withdrew its complaint, stating that "the fact of the matter is we have found [the other faction] too strongly intrenched for us. They are fortified with money, influence and power. We do not see that we are gaining anything by continuing a hopeless fight. So for the present we will remain passive spectators of their plan of reorganization."[78]

As this last legal clash amply illustrates, American investments in the Nicaragua canal site generated great sums of money for those backing the enterprise. The close connection between the geo-political and the "geo-personal" should not be missed here. Geographical knowledge disseminated from the AGS about the various canal sites was closely tied to Daly's and others' personal vested interests in the success of the Nicaragua canal. In his efforts to see the canal built at Nicaragua, Charles Daly placed on the line both professional and personal investments – his judicial reputation, law practice, diplomatic connections – and especially his position and reputation as geographical President. A careful examination of the "evidence" – both legal and geographical – made by an influential, authoritative figure within judicial and geographical circles, served Daly well in arguing – shall we say in lobbying – for the Nicaraguan site. Such evidence would be widely dispersed among AGS members, business communities, and politicians set to make important legislative decisions. In this respect Daly's friends themselves saw the value in his connection to the AGS.[79]

If Daly's efforts served in mutually constituting legal, geographical, and political knowledges and discourses, in the U.S. and abroad, they also served to consolidate financial organizations and personal investments, and ultimately, began the transformation of material space at the Nicaragua site. Conventions and commissions continued studying and promoting the site until 1902, when, three years after Charles Daly's death, the U.S. expectation was still that the isthmanian canal would be built across Nicaragua. Ultimately though lobbyists for the Panama site succeeded in (erroneously) convincing the 1902 U.S. Congress that the Nicaragua site was subject to destructive earthquakes, and because the price was then right, the decision passed Congress by a slim margin to take over the French project at Panama. The fact that "his" canal was never constructed is, importantly, beside the point of what the Nicaragua canal story tells us about Charles Daly's production of geographical knowledge for political, commercial, and personal ends.

Conclusion

This chapter has barely scratched the surface of Charles Daly's many political and diplomatic connections with the U.S. federal government. His biographer identifies others of these, particularly of those influential during the Civil War when Daly advised men like William H. Seward, Secretary of State under President Lincoln and an avid American expansionist, on a variety of legal matters between North and South.[80] Daly and Seward met frequently throughout the 1860s, and at least one "geographical" consequence of such meetings was the U.S. purchase of Alaska Territory in 1867. As Daly noted in his annual address for the AGS a few years later,

> As the Society took a very active part in urging the negotiation … for the purchase of Alaska … it is gratifying to be able to state that the income now derived by the Government from this territory, after payment of all expenses, is greater than that from any other territory, and will in twenty years extinguish the debt. The southern portion of Alaska has a comparatively mild climate, and is capable of maintaining a large population. Potatoes, barley, rye, and probably oats, can be cultivated … It is an immense timber region, with great facilities for transportation, and it will continue for a long time to supply the products of fur-bearing animals.[81]

Alaska, like other western regions Daly brought into the geographical imagination of his many audiences, was a space of resource potential, to be acquired and developed for American commercial enterprise. Such resonates as well with the ways he cast American benefits to the development of the western railroad and Central American canal.

Daly's expansionist vision for transforming American space via the transportation networks he helped establish was commercially grounded as well as opportunistically nationalistic, particularly with respect to the Nicaragua canal. Reaffirming federal government arguments that the Nicaraguan site was the "American" one, for instance, was useful in advancing Daly's own investments in the project. At the same time Daly's assertions that the canal should be in the hands of "American citizens" rather than the government obscured the tremendous financial gains that these private investors were set to make by controlling and taxing the commercial traffic through the canal. He seems to have played the "American" card when it suited his purposes and those of American business and commerce.

My purpose in this chapter has not been to determine whether the Northern Pacific Railway or the Nicaragua Canal themselves were epic human achievements or disastrous human follies in terms of the American empire they helped create – they were both. Rather my purpose has been to show how mundane, everyday geographical knowledge and practice related to them was put to legal, political, and financial ends, and indeed, how legal, political, and financial ends themselves helped construct what we think of as geographical knowledge and practice. Such vested interests need to be made obvious as they tell us about the nature and origins of geography in the nineteenth century, and how influential figures portrayed and enacted their civic agendas and responsibilities through use of the "geographical," as well as helped create an American commercial empire in the continental U.S. and abroad. In the end Charles Daly and other AGS men succeeded in naturalizing and normalizing both what was produced *as* geographical knowledge, and the fact *of* American empire building that would proceed apace, supported by the knowledge and practices they put forward. In the details of his geographical, legal, and diplomatic career, Charles Daly did his part to carefully craft an acceptance of empire, at least in part to advance his personal financial stake in it.

While this chapter has focused on Charles Daly's very "American" experience and work in railroad and canal building, it should be kept in mind that Daly's geographical (and other) sensibilities were oftentimes more transnational than national – in addition to advocating for things like Irish home rule (Chapter 3) he did not particularly care who made it to the North Pole first, either (Chapter 5). Recognizing that the ethos of the individual many considered the leading American geographer of the day was more transnational than national allows for an important appraisal of how ideas generated from geographical work traveled into civic work, and vice versa, within this particular historical milieu. Daly's own immigrant, ethnic, and class background combined into an intense sense of upward mobility that hinged on his own personal commercial and other successes. Writ large, his support of American expansionism was above all, too, of a commercial impulse. As I have noted previously, it is not surprising that elite men such as Charles Daly who invested heavily in a successful American economic empire were primarily free-marketers fixated on their own returns, making no particular distinctions between "customers" of their end products. As Mona Domosh puts it, doing business for them "required a flexible view of world order … in the more commercial worldview that characterized American international companies, foreign nations as potential consumers were considered similar in kind, if not in fact, to each other and to the United States."[82]

My point here is not to cast Charles Daly's civic work and agenda as merely or simply self-serving; his generosity was widely acknowledged, for instance in the considerable sum of his estate that he willed to the AGS upon his death.[83] However it must be kept in mind that American businessmen required their own investments in space and place, and thus the geographical knowledge and practice they put forward were in line with their investment goals as they envisioned them.

Endnotes

1 Harold E. Hammond, *A Commoner's Judge: The Life and Times of Charles Patrick Daly* (Boston: Christopher, 1954): 376. According to Daly's niece, Daly mainly made money through real estate ventures, not through his job as judge, the latter which paid

approximately $5,000 annually. Mrs. Henry Hoyt, Transcribed Interview, 2 November 1947, 14. Box 10, Charles P. Daly Correspondence and Papers, Manuscripts and Archives Division, New York Public Library (NYPL), New York.

2 Maria's statements regarding her aspirations for Charles, her frustrated hopes and efforts towards securing him a governorship of New York or justice of the U.S. Supreme Court, are taken from the original text of her diary; they were deleted from the published version, Harold E. Hammond, ed. *Maria Lydig Daly, Diary of a Union Lady, 1861–1865* (Lincoln: University of Nebraska Press, 1962; rpt. 2000). Original diary, Vols. 25, 26, 27, 28 (Maria L. Daly Correspondence and Papers), Daly Papers, NYPL. While Maria's parents resisted their daughter's marriage to Charles Daly, her dowry included a new house and $20,000 (though "no great sum" according to her mother). From undated 1856 letter from Catherine Lydig to Charles Daly, Box 2, Daly Papers, NYPL. Daly's worth amounted to $69,000 in 1856, prior to his marriage, and by 1870 totaled $124,000. They died multi-millionaires by today's standards, employing three servants and maintaining homes in New York and on Long Island. Hoyt Interview, 46.

3 For two examples among many, see John Agnew, *Hegemony: The New Shape of Global Power* (Philadelphia: Temple University Press, 2005); Mona Domosh, *American Commodities in an Age of Empire* (New York: Routledge, 2006): 6–22.

4 The phrase comes from John Steele Gordon's, *An Empire of Wealth: The Epic History of American Economic Power* (New York: Harper Collins, 2004).

5 Alexander Missal, *Seaway to the Future: American Social Visions and the Construction of the Panama Canal* (Madison: University of Wisconsin Press, 2008): 26–27. Robert Wiebe, *The Search for Order, 1877–1920* (New York: Hill and Wang, 1967) distinguishes between profit-oriented and power-oriented actors among expansionists at the time. Also see Amy Greenberg, *Manifest Manhood and the Antebellum American Empire* (Cambridge: Cambridge University Press, 2005).

6 "Transactions of the Society, January–March, 1895," *Journal of the American Geographical Society of New York* 27 (1, 1895): 124, documents Mr. Henry Morrison's comments about Daly's service to the nation in December of 1861, when he appeared before the Cabinet at Washington and "clearly demonstrated the illegality of the seizure and transfer of the Confederate envoys, Messrs. Mason and Slidell, from the British Mail Steamer *Trent* to the United States war-vessel *Jacinto*." The published "Washington Letters" were compiled by the society's secretary George C. Hurlbut and signed simply "H." These reports collate a wide range of topics in very short order, from legislative action relevant to the AGS such as on boundary disputes and the status of government-sponsored expeditions; to international conferences, such as on tariff agreements; to miscellaneous information provided the AGS from its government sources, such as a pronunciation key to the Malay language. See, for some of the more lengthy examples, American Geographical Society, "Transactions," *Journal of the American Geographical Society of New York* 21 (1): 137–147; 21 (2): 270–286; 21 (3): 438–458; and 21 (4): 647–671.

7 While it is unclear to whom the "your" in von Humboldt's remark refers, coast surveys, which define coastlines, bays, harbors, and landmarks, are fundamentally required for commercial navigation. Charles P. Daly, "Annual Address: The Geographical Work

of the World in 1873," *Journal of the American Geographical Society of New York* 5 (1874): 49–94; quote on 54.

8 "Contributions to Physical Geography," *Overland Monthly* 11 (5 November 1873): 474–475. Arthur A. Brooks, *Index to the Bulletin of the American Geographical Society 1852–1915* (New York: The American Geographical Society, 1918): v–vi, outlines noteworthy articles and proceedings on western explorations. J.T. Rothrock, "North-Western North America: Its Resources and Its Inhabitants," *Journal of the American Geographical Society of New York* 4 (1873): 393–415 and Benjamin Alvord, "Winter Grazing in the Rocky Mountains," *Journal of the American Geographical Society of New York* 15 (1883): 257–288.

9 David N. Livingstone, *Putting Science in its Place: Geographies of Scientific Knowledge* (Chicago: University of Chicago Press, 2003): 126.

10 Daly's biographer describes Clarence King, first director of the USGS, as an intimate friend of Daly's. No mention of Daly, though, is made in Martha Sandweiss's, *Passing Strange: A Gilded Age Tale of Love and Deception Across the Color Line* (New York: Penguin, 2009), which offers a stunning historical exposé on the double life King led passing as the African-American porter James Todd. The AGS closely followed the work of the USGS throughout the 1870s and 1880s, providing a context for discussion of these explorations and serving as a repository for data (a collection of Powell's letters, for example, is currently housed at the AGS). See also Susan Schulten, *The Geographical Imagination in America, 1880–1950* (Chicago: University of Chicago Press, 2001).

11 Charles P. Daly, "Annual Address: Geographical Work of the World in 1877," *Journal of the American Geographical Society of New York* 10 (1878): 1–76; see 17–19.

12 Charles P. Daly, "Annual Address. Subject: the Geographical Work of the World in 1872," *Journal of the American Geographical Society of New York* 4 (1873): 63–188, American Explorations and Surveys on 65–79; Daly, "Annual Address" 5 (1874): 53–62; Daly, "Annual Address: The Geographical Work of the World in 1876," *Journal of the American Geographical Society of New York* 8 (1876): 54–64.

13 American Geographical Society, "Lectures Delivered before the American Geographical Society, Vol. 1, 1865–1892." AGS Archives, New York City.

14 Charles P. Daly, "Annual Address: Geographical Work of the World in 1878 & 1879," *Journal of the American Geographical Society of New York* 12 (1880): 41–50. The Powell quote on 48 is almost verbatim what the explorer himself states: John Wesley Powell, *Report of the Lands of the Arid Regions* (Washington, D.C.: Government Printing Office, 1879).

15 Daly cites a *New York Herald* reporter on the Black Hills in his "Annual Address: The Geographical Work of the World for 1875," *Journal of the American Geographical Society of New York* 7 (1875): 31–92; see 43; a *New York Times* reporter on the Wheeler expedition in his "Annual Address. Subject: The Geographical Work of the World in 1874," *Journal of the American Geographical Society of New York* 6 (1874): 53–92; see 60; and those of a correspondent for the St. Louis *Republican* on the extensive ruins on the Gila River, ibid., 69.

16 Daly, "Annual Address," 7 (1875): 92. Charles P. Daly, "Have We a Portrait of Columbus? Annual Address, January 9, 1893," *Journal of the American Geographical Society of New York* 25 (1893): 1–63.

17 Michael Adas, *Machines as the Measure of Men: Science, Technology, and Ideologies of Western Dominance* (Ithaca: NY: Cornell University Press, 1989): 221.

18 Ernesto E. Ruiz, *Geography and Diplomacy: The American Geographical Society and the "Geopolitical" Background of American Foreign Policy, 1848–1861* (PhD dissertation, Northern Illinois University, 1975): 92–96.

19 Robert D. Mitchell, "The North American Past: Retrospect and Prospect," in *North America: The Historical Geography of a Changing Continent*, eds. Robert D. Mitchell and Paul A. Groves (Savage, MD: Rowman & Littlefield Publishers, 1990): 3–21; David R. Meyer, "The National Integration of Regional Economies, 1860–1920," ibid., 321–346; also see Hugh Clout, *Agriculture in France on the Eve of the Railway Age* (London: Croom Helm, 1980); Gordon, *Empire of Wealth*, 148–149; Domosh, *American Commodities*, 22; and William Cronon, *Nature's Metropolis: Chicago and the Great West* (New York: W.W. Norton, 1991).

20 Asa Whitney's lecture before a closed meeting of the society on 8 November 1851 was never published; John K. Wright, *Geography in the Making: The American Geographical Society 1851–1951* (New York: American Geographical Society, 1952): 25. The AGS website describes the map (last accessed January 2008), as does Wright on 27; also see AGS, Society Meeting Minutes, 10 January 1854 for the resolution authorizing its production. Early papers on the railroads include Henry V. Poor, "Proposed Pacific Railroad," *Proceedings of the American Geographical and Statistical Society*, 1863–1864: 30–40; Henry V. Poor, "Railroad to the Pacific: Five Routes Proposed," *Bulletin of the American Geographical and Statistical Society* Vol. 1, Part III, 1854, 81–100.

21 Daniel C. Gilman, "Annual Address. Subject: Geographical Work in the United States during 1871," *Journal of the American Geographical Society of New York* 4 (1873): 119–144; James Douglas, "Historical and Geographical Features of the Rocky Mountain Railroads," *Journal of the American Geographical Society of New York* 17 (1885): 299–342.

22 These are annual addresses of 1870, 1872, 1873, 1874, 1875, 1876, 1877, 1878–1879, and 1888.

23 See an example of "capitalist vanguard writing" about British railways in Mexico, Karen M. Morin, *Frontiers of Femininity: A New Historical Geography of the Nineteenth-Century American West* (Syracuse: Syracuse University Press, 2008): 115–137.

24 Daly, "Annual Address" 12 (1880): 50.

25 Daly, "Annual Address" 4 (1873): 80; footnote appears on 79–83.

26 Hammond, *Commoner's Judge*, 6, 67, 104, 121–122, 231, 270, 305. Letter to Daly from H.D. Cooke, Box 5, Daly Papers, NYPL. The letter went on to discuss the work accomplished by Samuel Wilkerson, secretary of the railroad, and a letter of introduction to Wilkerson for Daly, promising information about his properties. See also Richard White, *"It's Your Misfortune and None of My Own": A History of the American West* (Norman: University of Oklahoma Press, 1991). Charles and Maria took a five-week

trip through the West in the summer of 1880, with Maria documenting the trip from St. Paul, Minnesota to the Colorado Rockies in her diary.

27 Dopp, "Geographical Influences in the Development of Wisconsin," Mary Dopp, "Geographical Influences in the Development of Wisconsin. Chapter III. The Settlement of Wisconsin," *Bulletin of the American Geographical Society* 45 (8, 1913): 585–609, details settlement patterns, railroad development, and agricultural and other statistical information in 1873 and 1880; 601–602.

28 Letters and stock purchase agreements from Jay Cooke & Company, dated 6 June, 1 July and 2 August 1870, Box 4 and Box 5, Daly Papers, NYPL. A letter dated 9 March 1871 informed Daly that he was not allowed to dispose of bonds for which he had paid. A letter dated March 1873 (Box 5), urgently requested that Daly send by express at the company's expense, the "Northern coupons" that he held, that they "may be replaced with registered bonds of like amount." The letter explained that "unauthorized offerings of original subscription bonds on the market at low rate" had injured the company's loan negotiations and impaired the confidence of investors. Daly's cooperation was urgently begged. Hammond, *Commoner's Judge*, also discusses these transactions and land purchases in Minnesota and Wisconsin on the NPR right-of-way (103–106, 122, 231–233, 270, 410), as does Daly's wife Maria in her diary (Vol. 27, Daly Papers, NYPL, see especially entry for 8 February 1874).

29 Letters to Daly from Robertson Real Estate and Mortgage Brokers, dated July–August 1882, 1886, and January 1893 explain (and seem to defend) Robertson's real estate maneuvers; Box 6, Daly Papers, NYPL. Daly still owned stocks in the Superior Consolidated Land Company in June of 1896; see letter from G. Mason (1894–1897), Box 7, Daly Papers, NYPL.

30 Daly's 1870 investments in western lands amounted to $8,000 in St. Paul; $2,100 in the town of Chestnut; $3,000 in Superior; in Pine County $3,000; and farm property in Changwahana worth $5,000. Daly also owned stock in the Lake Superior and Puget Sound Company; see letter from the company dated 1 January 1872 (Box 5, NYPL). Related correspondence in Box 2 (1849–1856), Box 4 (1870), Box 5 (1873), Daly Papers; and Box 11, Maria L. Daly Papers, NYPL (see especially that of 1856, and a circular to AGS fellows, dated 1876). The peak years for German immigration to Wisconsin were 1846–1854 and 1881–1884. See Dopp, "Geographical Influences in Development of Wisconsin," 598.

31 Gerolt's first correspondence to the AGS was published (*Bulletin of the American Geographical and Statistical Society* Vol. II, 1856, dated 11 March 1856); he acknowledges the request to exchange information between the AGS and Prussian government, and the receipt of AGS documents sent to him. A number of subsequent mentions are made about Gerolt in AGS publications from 1859–1890. It was at Gerolt's home in Washington, D.C. where Daly became acquainted with influential politicians and military men during the Civil War, and it was Gerolt who provided Daly with introductions on his trips to Europe.

32 Letter from Gerolt, 27 May 1857. This order was to a company called Riggs & Co. with the agent Robertson. Gerolt letters 1856–1859, Box 2, Daly Papers, NYPL. Also see Hammond, *Commoner's Judge*, 123–126, 253, 412.

33 Hammond, ibid., 124.

34 Hoyt Interview, 8.

35 "One Hundred Years Old: The German Society Celebrates its Centennial with Much Enthusiasm," *New York Herald*, 5 October 1884.

36 For instance, lectures and papers by pioneering anthropologist Franz Boaz; "Census and Reservations of the Kwakiutl Nation," *Journal of the American Geographical Society of New York* 19 (2, 1887): 225–232 and Boaz, "A Year Among the Eskimo," *Journal of the American Geographical Society of New York* 19 (4, 1887): 383–402.

37 See Vol. 5, Daly Papers, NYPL. "The Last Appeal of Red Cloud," *New York Times*, 17 June 1870; "Our Occidental Visitors," (newspaper unknown), 17 June 1870; "The Indians: Red Cloud and Red Dog on the Wrongs of the Red Men – Immense Crowds at Cooper Institute to Hear the Aboriginal Orators," *New York Herald*, 17 June 1870; "The Cooper Institute Pow Wow," *The World*, 17 June 1870; "To Civilize the Indians," *New York Times*, 3 April 1886; other articles covering the 1886 meeting include those from *The Sun*, 3 April 1886 and the *New York Tribune*, 3 April 1886. Also see Maria's diary (Vol. 26, Daly Papers, NYPL, for instance on 27 February 1866), where she discusses the chief of the Six Indian Nations, Dr. Wilson, having dinner at the Daly home with the British minister. "Land in severalty" refers to the 1887 *General Allotment [Dawes] Act*, which prescribed that reservation lands be divided and allocated into 160-acre sections to individual families, with the so-called "surplus" lands sold off to generate income. This process decimated Native peoples' land base throughout North America.

38 *New York Times*, 1886, ibid. Peter Cooper was New York alderman, industrialist, and Indian reformer, as well as a close ally of the American Geographical Society (as was his son-in-law Abram Hewitt).

39 "Cooper Pow Wow," *The World*, 17 June 1870.

40 Daly, "Annual Address" 6 (1874): 58–64; "Annual Address" 7 (1875): 42–44.

41 Daly, "Annual Address" 10 (1878): 20–26. He described the savagery of various tribes as reported by expedition leaders, for instance of the Arickarees in Montana's Big Horn River area, who have "no formal form of worship" and whose language is crude, the "word for man is also the word for [the number] 20 … They are very brave, gross in their appetites, and have a sort of rude eloquence."

42 "To Civilize," *New York Times*, 3 April 1886.

43 The significance of the railroad for American geography would continue well into the twentieth century. The next AGS President, Archer Huntington, scion of another railroad dynasty, funded the building of the New York headquarters and 1912 Transcontinental Excursion.

44 Neil Smith, *American Empire: Roosevelt's Geographer and the Prelude to Globalization* (Berkeley: University of California Press, 2003); Alastair W. Pearson and Michael Heffernan, "The American Geographical Society's Map of Hispanic America: Million-Scale Mapping Between the Wars," *Imago Mundi* 61 (2, 2009): 215–243. AGS President Jerome Dobson and colleagues were accused by a local NGO in Mexico, and subsequently by members of the Association of American Geographers (AAG), of not revealing to indigenous peoples of Oaxaca, Mexico, that their GIS project mapping of communally held land was funded by the U.S. Department of Defense and the results

of which were to be turned over to the U.S. Army. See the AGS response, Jerome E. Dobson, "Let the Indigenous People of Oaxaca Speak for Themselves," *Ubique* 29 (1, 2009). At the time of this writing the issue remains unresolved. (See www.indymedia.org/or/2009/04/923343.shtml; last accessed 5 December 2010.)

45 Wright, *Geography in the Making*, 181.

46 While these geo-political events are outside the purview of this chapter in any case, it is worth acknowledging that Charles Daly himself published a series of articles about Cuba decades earlier, in 1851, based on a few weeks' travel there: a rare example of Daly's published "travel writing." Charles P. Daly (signed "D"), "Letters on Cuba," *New York Chronicle*, 22 September 1851. See Chapter 3 for more on Daly's views on slavery; also see Hammond, *Commoner's Judge*, 99–100. In these letters Daly confirms that he is not opposed to the U.S. annexation of Cuba – that would inevitably happen in a matter of time – but as a Union Democrat he did oppose the sectional interest of the South in doing so; he condemned the "insane," "delusional" attempts of the South to expand U.S. slave territory there. He also feared liberation of slaves in Cuba would threaten slavery in the United States.

47 Missal, *Seaway to the Future*, 9–23.

48 In 1849 Cornelius Vanderbilt signed a contract with the Nicaraguan government giving his company, the Accessory Transit Company, the right to build the canal within 12 years, but a civil war in Nicaragua and invasion by freebooter William Walker intervened. Interest in the route was an important factor in the negotiation of the Clayton-Bulwer Treaty of 1850, as well as in the subsequent legal disputes with Daly's company. David McCullough, *The Path Between the Seas: The Creation of the Panama Canal 1870–1914* (New York: Simon and Schuster, 1977).

49 AGS Councilors William E. Johnston and Nathan Appleton attended the Paris conference, Appleton in his official capacity as representative of the U.S. Chamber of Commerce.

50 Julie Green, *The Canal Builders: Making America's Empire at the Panama Canal* (New York: Penguin Press, 2009); Matthew Parker, *Panama Fever: The Epic Story of One of the Greatest Human Achievements in All Time* (New York: Doubleday, 2007); Alfred C. Richard, Jr., *The Panama Canal in American National Consciousness, 1870–1999* (New York: Garland, 1990); J. Michael Hogan, *The Panama Canal in American Politics: Domestic Advocacy and the Evolution of Policy* (Carbondale: Southern Illinois University Press, 1986); and Herbert Knapp and Mary Knapp, *Red, White and Blue Paradise: The American Canal Zone in Panama* (San Diego: Harcourt Brace Jovanovich, 1984). A few notable works by historical geographers include Christian Brannstrom, "Almost a Canal: Visions of Interoceanic Communication across Southern Nicaragua," *Ecumene* 2 (1, 1995): 65–87; Stephen Frenkel, "Jungle Stories: American Representations of Tropical Panama," *Geographical Review* 86 (1996): 317–333; and Stephen Frenkel, "Geographical Representations of the 'Other': the Landscape of the Panama Canal Zone," *Journal of Historical Geography* 28 (1, 2002): 85–99.

51 American Geographical Society, "The Interoceanic Ship Canal. Meeting at Chickering Hall, December 9, 1879," *Journal of the American Geographical Society of New York*

11 (1879): 113–152. "The Isthmus Canal," *New York Herald*, 29 May 1879; "The Nicaraguan Canal," *The World*, 4 December 1879.

52 Wright, *Geography in the Making*, 98–101; quote on 99.

53 AGS, "Interoceanic Ship Canal Meeting" (1879): 151–152.

54 "M. De Lesseps at Panama," *The World*, 1 January 1880; "A Busy Day for De Lesseps," *New York Tribune*, 28 February 1880; "M De Lesseps at Dinner" and "Dinner at Delmonico's," *New York Times*, 29 February 1880 (also covered by the *Tribune*, 29 February 1880). Despite the different topographies, De Lesseps planned to build in Panama a sea-level canal without locks, like the Suez.

55 Wright, *Geography in the Making*, 100. Frederick Kelly, a well-known Wall Street canal booster, wrote to Daly on 4 December 1879 in support of the San Blas route. AGS Correspondence, New York. Nathan Appleton, along with W.W. Evans, supported de Lesseps's plan. Ammen, "Interoceanic Ship Canal Meeting" (1879): 134. A representative from Nicaragua, a Signore de Franco, attended this AGS meeting, although he is not recorded as having spoken.

56 Daly, "Interoceanic Ship Canal Meeting" (1879): 146–148; quote on 152.

57 Frederick Collins, "The Isthmus of Darien and the Valley of the Atrato Considered with Reference to the Practicability of an Interoceanic Ship-Canal," *Journal of the American Geographical Society of New York* 5 (1874): 138–165; H.C. Taylor, "The Nicaragua Canal," *Journal of the American Geographical Society of New York* 18 (1886): 95–97; Charles H. Stockton, "The Commercial Geography of the American Inter-Oceanic Canal," *Journal of the American Geographical Society of New York* 20 (1888): 75–93.

58 AGS, "Transactions of the Society for 1870," *Journal of the American Geographical Society of New York* 3 (1872): 35–53, quote on 41; "Transactions of the Society for 1873," *Journal of the American Geographical Society of New York* 5 (1874): 35–45, quote on 40; "Transactions of the Society for 1879," *Journal of the American Geographical Society of New York* 11 (1879): xlix–liv; quote on liv; "Transactions of the Society for 1886," *Journal of the American Geographical Society of New York* 18 (1886): lix–lxvi; quote on lxiv.

59 Daly, "Annual Address" 2 (2) (1870): lxxxvii–xci.

60 Daly, "Annual Address" 4 (1873): 83–84.

61 Daly, "Annual Address" 5 (1874): 70; "Annual Address," 6 (also 1874): 92.

62 Daly, "Annual Address" 8 (1876): 71.

63 Daly, "Annual Address" 10 (1878): 32–33.

64 Daly, "Annual Address" 12 (1880): 52.

65 E. Anthony Rotundo, *American Manhood: Transformations in Masculinity from the Revolution to the Modern Era* (New York: Basic Books, 1993): 170–172, 212. Rotundo adds that the courtroom itself was a masculine world, centered on a patriarchal figure cloaked in a robe.

66 This case received a great deal of press, particularly when Daly was called before a hearing to disclose the names of his clients, which he refused to do. After losing the case the law firm's findings were influential in passing the Transit Act, which began the vast New York subway system. "The Arcade Railway Scheme: Prominent New Yorkers Before the Senate Railroad Committee," *New York Herald*, 17 March 1886;

"The Broadway Arcade Road: Answering the Objections to its Construction," *New York Times*, 18 April 1886; "Railway Scheme," *New York Times*, 18 April 1886; and "The Arcade Bill Signed," *New York Herald*, 12 May 1886. Also see Daly Papers, NYPL, Vol. 13 (18–22).

67 Nicaragua Canal Construction Company, *The Inter-Oceanic Canal of Nicaragua: Its History, Physical Condition, Plans and Prospect* (New York: New York Print Company, 1891): 13, 15. Daly's personal financial stake in the company is outlined in Hammond, *Commoner's Judge*, 313, 366–71, 392.

68 "The Interoceanic Canal Question," *New York Herald*, 1 April 1884. Two treaties had been previously signed with Nicaragua and Columbia in 1867 and 1869 to ensure transit across a future canal, but the latter was never ratified.

69 Ehrman S. Nadal, John M. Read, Henry C. Taylor, *Francis Aquila Stout* (New York, 1894). Stout represented the society at two International Geographical congresses, in Antwerp and Berne.

70 See Hammond, *Commoner's Judge*, 313, 369. Maria L. Daly (Vol. 28, Daly Papers, NYPL), 9 May 1889, 20 June 1889, and 17 February 1891.

71 "Sunset Sunshine for Daly: The Nicaragua Bill Stirs Up the House of Representatives," *The World*, 15 December 1888; "Is Spinola a Bone Hunter: His Opposition to the Nicaragua Canal Bill. He Assails Judge Daly as a Lobbyist," *New York Times*, 15 December 1888; "Judge Daly Explains," *New York Herald*, 15 December 1888.

72 Daly did not believe the House bill would support the funds needed, arguing that at least $100,000,000 needed to be raised by "bonded indebtedness secured upon the work as it progressed, with one loan contracted for as one undertaking." *New York Herald*, 12 December 1888. Also see, "Uncle Sam, How About France? Our National Legislators Unanimously Opposed to Allowing Foreign Ownership of the Panama Canal" and "Dig that Ditch: the Interests of the Country Demand that Congress Charter the Nicaragua Canal Company, Let France Stand Aside," *New York Herald*, 12 December 1888.

73 Correspondence among many of the principals attest to the nature of the deals attempted; Box 6, Daly Papers, NYPL. These include letters from Stout (1886); Kalb letters dealing with reorganization of the company (1893); a letter from Ammen dated 17 July 1891, in which he wrote: "I would like to know what you think [of the plan to] secure the control of the canal to the government without prejudice to those who have actually secured the government against a foreign exception. The credit of the government through 3 percent bonds, without a dollar's outlay would, at say 15 years from date, make it two-thirds owner of the canal … As matters now stand without some such provision I would feel disposed to decline the proposed amendment to the Act of Incorporation and fall back to that of Vermont." One Thomas Atkins sent to Daly on 4 June 1897 notice of a special meeting of the Maritime Canal Company stockholders, called for 18 June 1897, to approve the issuing of the company's bonds of $150,000,000 to a trustee, payable 1 July 1996. Another letter from Atkins, 28 August 1893, marked "confidential," asked for the stockholders themselves to provide the means ($300,000) to protect their interests or the company was to go into the ruinous hands of a receiver.

74 Daly's legal response was published as "Answer of the Nicaragua Canal Association of the Protest of the Alleged American Atlantic and Pacific Ship Canal Company"

(Nicaragua Maritime Canal Company, Charles P. Daly counsel. New York, 1888). See Hammond, *Commoner's Judge*, 368–371. Also see "Opinion of Counsel as to the Constitutionality of the Bill to Incorporate the Maritime Canal Company of Nicaragua" (unknown binding); "The Nicaragua Canal: Legal Status of the Canal Concessions," The *Evening Post*, 23 July 1888.

75 Maria L. Daly (Vol. 28, Daly Papers, NYPL), 9 May and 20 June 1889.

76 "The Nicaragua Canal Scheme," *The Sun*, 24 February 1889; W. Nephew King, Jr., "The Nicaragua Canal," *Frank Leslie's Illustrated Newspaper*, 8 June 1889; "Change of the Panama Canal Level," *New York Herald*, 1 March 1886; "Canal Diggers at Odds," *New York Herald*, 24 April 1889; "Panama Canal Swindle," The *Evening Post*, 3 July 1888; "The Bubble Bursts: M. de Lesseps' Pet Scheme Threatened with Bankruptcy," *New York Herald*, 14 December 1888; "De Lesseps Resigns," *New York Herald*, 15 December 1888; "To Avert a Panic," *The Star*, 15 December 1888. These papers principally addressed the financial problems faced by the French, whether the Monroe Doctrine should inhere in the decision to site the canal, and what might happen if the desperate French seized control of the Panama coastline.

77 McCullough, *Path Between the Seas*, 240, 260, argues that Morgan had his "southern" reasons for supporting the Nicaraguan route, principally that it was closer to U.S. southern ports.

78 "Nicaragua Canal Fight: Opposing Stockholders Want to Examine the Books," *New York Times*, 28 January 1894. "The Struggle is Ended: Nicaragua Reorganization Can Now Go On Unimpeded," *New York Tribune*, 3 March 1894.

79 Nicaragua Canal Construction Company, *The Inter-Oceanic Canal of Nicaragua*, 13.

80 Hammond, *Commoner's Judge*; also see Hammond, ed., *Diary of a Union Lady*.

81 Daly, "Annual Address" 6 (1874): 67.

82 Domosh, *American Commodities*, 23.

83 Hammond, *Commoner's Judge*, 363, does not give figures, but does note that Daly donated 677 books, 1,401 pamphlets, 87 atlases, and 36 maps to the AGS library.

Chapter 5
Arctic Science and the "Jurist-Geographer"

> No expedition, in my opinion, ever depended so largely on the heroism and intelligence of its leader as [Lieut. Greely's]. I am glad that by his own account his expedition is not to be confounded with other expeditions to discover the Pole. It is my official opinion as a geographer that the only expeditions that should be sent out are those for physical observation at fixed points about the Arctic Circle. For this reason Lieutenant Greely's expedition should be separated from all others. His was a purely scientific expedition, not one of wild discovery.

Charles P. Daly, *New York Tribune*, 17 January 1886[1]

> We are indebted to Chief Justice Daly (Applause). Some of us know right well, and all of us ought to know, that there is a very small risk of any geographical discovery, in any part of the globe, escaping his notice. Every man who makes a discovery is very sure to come within reach of his voice or his pen. How many distinguished men have we welcomed to this platform! May the Judge's shadow never be less! (Applause).

Dr. Roswell D. Hitchcock, 1884, AGS Reception for Lieut. Greely[2]

Introduction

The arena of the Arctic and North Pole played a prominent, central role in establishing American geography as a knowledge field and practice in the mid- to late-nineteenth century. While exploration of America's Far West created some of the most important geographical knowledge recognized as such in the nineteenth century (Chapter 4), the Arctic provided a "happy distraction" from the geo-politics of American expansionism and the tensions of war (both the Civil War and war with Mexico) associated with it. Even though debates proliferated about the superfluousness of Arctic exploration in the face of more pressing national concerns, the region provided relief for the American geographical imagination; it was a place, as Michael Robinson puts it, that "could be explored without being administered, a place to flex imperial muscle without having to do the heavy lifting required by a colonial empire."[3] While Americans learned about the Arctic principally through the explorers themselves – from their books, lecture tours, and newspaper coverage – scientific organizations played an important role in mediating the relationship between explorers and the public, particularly in framing the results of Arctic expeditions for a consuming public. In this way the American Geographical Society, in addition to its principal objective of serving New York business interests, also served an important role as purveyor of Arctic science in the nineteenth century – it was the "unofficial headquarters of U.S. Arctic exploration" and the "heartland of Arctic patronage."[4]

In Chapter 2 I argued that the gender dynamics of the Arctic and North Pole "field" offered AGS men personal authority, credibility, and masculine cultural capital through their associations with returning Arctic heroes. The staging of dramatic Arctic meetings featuring expedition leaders and their crews, and disseminating findings from the expeditions, were some of the most important and influential work of the AGS in the nineteenth century. In this chapter I want to flesh out in greater detail the social impacts of these ventures on geographical knowledge and practice, particularly as Charles Daly was arguably New York's – and as AGS President, one of America's – most influential "access points" to the Arctic in the later decades of the nineteenth century. Daly mediated relationships among a host of Arctic "actors" – the explorers themselves, their patrons, the federal government, the press, and the public. Of Daly's many geographical interests he followed explorations in the Arctic most closely,[5] and devoted more actual text to it in his annual speeches than anywhere else. This influential New York judge and civic leader weighed in as an "official geographer" almost exclusively when it came to questions of the Arctic, evidenced for example in the first epigraph above, at a dinner honoring the return of Lieut. Adolphus Greely from his disastrous attempt in 1881 to establish an American Arctic research colony, which followed, as Daly explained to the *New York Tribune*, "the largest and most enthusiastic reception it ever tendered to any geographic hero."

Unlike that supporting exploration of its Far West, no American federal bureaucracy existed for Arctic exploration, although "friends" of the Arctic could be found in the U.S. Coast Survey, Signal Service, Naval Observatory (many of whose staff were AGS fellows), and Smithsonian Institution; as well as in other private entities such as the American Philosophical Society. From 1850–1910 approximately two dozen American Arctic expeditions were dispatched, most privately funded by wealthy East-Coast patrons such as Henry Grinnell and William Bennett. Most of these were under the official auspices of the federal government nonetheless, and were military in organization and command (under the Army or Navy). The federal government sought to usefully employ military officers in times of peace; in turn, agencies such as the Smithsonian collected and published official expedition results. Like explorations of North America and beyond, debates within the U.S. federal government would center on national and commercial objectives in the Arctic, while serving as a basic patron of Arctic "science."

Within this context the American Geographical Society and the federal government were closely linked, with the AGS working primarily as a private "pressure group" upon the government. The AGS proposed and endorsed specific surveys and expeditions; served as patrons to various expeditions, offering financial assistance or "in kind" help in obtaining funds; provided expeditionary equipment, training, and expertise as well as cartographic support; helped interpret expedition results; offered venues for debating travel routes and physical geography questions;

and helped develop the infrastructure necessary for Arctic exploration. Perhaps most influentially, though, the AGS widely diffused and popularized the results of Arctic explorations to its members and to the public.

The AGS was very busy in the second half of the nineteenth century with Arctic and North Pole exploration, even if its peak years for the hosting of lectures and receptions for explorers would come later, 1900–1915.[6] The AGS's first two decades have been referred to as the Grinnell Epoch, after the shipping magnate Henry Grinnell, elected first President of the society but not serving until as its third (1861–1864, immediately preceding Charles Daly). Grinnell had made a fortune in his whaling and shipping business, and indeed was one of the wealthiest merchants in New York City. AGS traditional lore has it that Grinnell responded to Lady Jane Franklin's pleas for help in finding the lost expedition of her husband, British Admiral Sir John Franklin, and it was a "humanitarian" response to her request that led to the establishment of the society itself in 1851.[7] Franklin had been lost in the Arctic for four years, and European rescue missions were already underway. Grinnell's personal stake in the whaling industry led him to privately support, in the name of the society, two attempts to find the Franklin expedition in the 1850s; the first was a U.S. Navy expedition led by Edwin De Haven (1850), the second by "polar idol" of the time, Elisha Kent Kane (1853), whose expedition established what became known as the "American route" to the North Pole.[8] (This was a route via Smith Sound and the strait formed between Greenland on the east and Baffin and Ellesmere Islands on the west.) De Haven, Kane, Isaac Hayes, and Charles Hall stand out as the American Arctic explorers in the mid-nineteenth century; all received support from the AGS, and Kane, Hayes, and Hall were frequent presenters at society meetings.[9]

As my discussion below elucidates, Arctic and polar exploration during the period of Charles Daly's AGS presidency (1864–1899) fused along a number of coordinates and goals. The searches for Franklin's lost expedition were linked either implicitly or explicitly to hopes of discovering new commercial fisheries or continuing the search for a trade route across the Arctic Circle (the North-West or North-East Passage). As the decades drew on maps of the region were gradually filled in with coastlines, islands, and ice sheets, and the discovery of the North Pole took on greater importance – for some, as a nationalist goal in itself, for the scientific benefits that would accompany its discovery, and as a link in finding the hoped-for water passage that could provide a short-cut for trade between Europe/North America and Asia.

While the AGS closely associated itself with the explorations of De Haven, Kane, and Hayes in the 1850s and 1860s, more prominent under Charles Daly were those later voyages of Charles Hall (1871), Frederick Schwatka (1878–1880), Greely (1881), and Robert Peary (1893–1895). The most well-publicized and well-attended Arctic meetings hosted by the AGS under Daly included the 1874 celebration for the survivors of Hall's *Polaris* expedition; the 1878 showcasing of the "Howgate Plan" to establish a permanent American polar research station (which led to Greely's expedition); the 1880 honor to Schwatka's 11-month overland (sledge) expedition, the so-called "final search" for Franklin remains; the 1884 reception for the returning survivors of the Greely Expedition, the "Ghosts of Cape Sabine";[10] and various meetings devoted to the expeditions of future AGS President Robert E. Peary (1903–1907), recipient of much of Daly's patronage for his Greenland expeditions in the 1890s (and disputed discoverer of the North Pole in 1909).

Charles Daly "staged" these expeditions, and Arctic geography more generally, in shrewdly calculated ways. Daly's professional credentialing as judge, lawyer, and geographer allowed him to present himself as authoritative "jurist-geographer" when maneuvering through public, business, and scientific communities in order to secure Arctic exploration as a valuable civic and commercial enterprise.[11] Through many venues – his public addresses, published articles, celebrated public Arctic meetings, dinners and receptions, newspaper coverage, diplomatic efforts in Washington, as well as private meetings with explorers in his home[12] – Daly shaped the cognitive content of the north for his many audiences and thus "disciplined" American Arctic geographical thought and practice in numerous ways. This became especially important when he weighed in on scientific questions of the day, convincingly "holding court" as armchair geographer on physical geography debates such as on the Open Polar Sea theory, for which he, of course, had no first-hand experience.

In what follows I trace Charles Daly's imaginative geographies of the Arctic, and examine how he processed them into a popular brand of American geographical knowledge and practice. Various projects, events, patronage, and discourses intersected in Daly's and the AGS's armchair geographies of Arctic spaces. Although science and Arctic exploration were closely linked in the 1850s and 1860s, significant cultural shifts occurred such that the sensationalism of Arctic exploration would come to eclipse its scientific value in later decades. This owed, among other things, to a new age of journalism (Chapter 3). Thus I revisit in the next section the important role the emerging newspaper industry played in creating what was constituted *as* geographical knowledge of the Arctic within Daly's milieu, and his attempts to capitalize on this sensationalism while emphasizing the scientific value of Arctic exploration for the national prestige and rank within the international scientific community that such would offer.

Within broader cultural shifts Charles Daly's greatest impact would be in promoting a type of what Richard Powell has called "scientific sovereignty" over Arctic space, where cultures of science intersected with powerful nationalist tensions.[13] Daly's was a popular geography, but not a geography of competitive "firsts" that is so often constituted substantially as *the* geographical tradition in the nineteenth century. As I discuss later in the chapter, Daly's insistence on the scientific benefits to Arctic exploration informed geography as a practical science of coastal surveys, hydrology, magnetism, and meteorology, with ends that would nonetheless mediate and delimit Arctic commerce, national and multi-national diplomatic relations, and race relations with Inuit. Thus my interest in drawing out Daly's relationships with a number of explorers, including Frederick Schwatka,

Robert Peary, and Joe Ebierbing, is also to examine the important colonialist understandings of racial difference he and the AGS advanced with respect to the far north. Daly's understanding of the public culture of scientific travel and exploration gives us a picture that was, among other things, shrewd in its cross-cultural politics. Daly's enthusiasm for Arctic research would ultimately pay off in a number of ways, not least of which was that Arctic spaces would come to directly bear the imprint of his name – "Cape Daly" in Eastern Greenland, for example, so named for him by the German Association for Polar Exploration (among others).[14]

Arctic Publicity and the New York Press

One of Charles Daly's greatest contributions to the American Geographical Society was arguably his "public advocacy" of its cause, and this, on no clearer subject of interest than the Arctic.[15] A captivating storyteller, Daly could "electrify" his audiences with human suffering and survival stories.[16] As with his attempts to elicit public support for infrastructural improvements in New York City (Chapter 3), Daly often reiterated in his speeches the importance of "the public" attending AGS-sponsored Arctic meetings, a sentiment met often with exuberant applause. Such public meetings had, since the 1830s, become a widespread form of public education and entertainment; and as AGS meetings were open to members and nonmembers alike, audiences could include diverse groups of people, including members' wives and daughters, city residents, and even passers-by.[17]

At the 1874 Arctic meeting honoring Hall's returning *Polaris* expedition, the standing-room only auditorium held 3,000 spectators, with "many more turned away unable to obtain seats." Daly's insistence on public audiences for such events owed, he claimed, to its "interest to the whole country," and to the fact that the survivors deserved public acknowledgment and sympathy for their extraordinary escape ("at least the escape of a large portion of them"; their leader Charles Hall himself had died on the expedition).[18] At such meetings Daly also took on the civil servant mantle of public educator. At the 1884 meeting honoring the survivors of the Greely Expedition, for instance (also reportedly attended by thousands), he began by requesting that the AGS secretary direct the audience's attention to the large map in the hall that showed the different expeditions that had preceded Greely's, "in order that [they] may have this portion of the Arctic fully in [their] minds throughout the evening."[19] Maps, artifacts, and stereopticon images provided important staged "specimens" at these meetings, as did the bodies of the explorers themselves: Inuit men and women providing the most spectacular objects of interest (below), but (white) captains and crews as well, on both their departures for or arrivals from their famed expeditions. The 1892 meeting debating the logic of an expedition to the northern magnetic pole featured William H. Gilder, *New York Herald* star reporter-turned explorer who would lead the expedition.[20] In closing the meeting Daly announced: "Ladies and Gentlemen … before we depart,

I will introduce Colonel Gilder. He is not a speaker, but probably you would like to see him."

Such details of Daly's modus operandi are important as their effect was to draw the New York press ever more to his Arctic subjects, which in turn galvanized civic interest in them. Daly's every utterance on Arctic matters seems to have become "news," helping the press create, as Riffenburgh argues, public interest through "hero worship" and "myth-making" of explorers. Chapter 3 traces the development of sensationalist news and its relationships to geography: newspapers, hungry to increase their circulation, created news around intrepid and daring explorers who persevered and triumphed over obstacles in the name of science, the flag, or mankind; the more difficult the journey, the more heroic the explorer and the more papers that sold. Newspapers paid large sums of money to sponsor reporters who accompanied various expeditions, eventually sponsoring expeditions themselves – with, of course, exclusive rights to the stories that would unfold dramatically in print.

The *New York Herald*'s James Gordon Bennett, Jr., is known to have most notoriously created – as opposed to merely reporting – geographical news, first by employing Henry Morton Stanley to "rescue" Scottish missionary David Livingstone in Africa. According to Riffenburgh, Bennett "believed that the descriptions of the areas from which the stories emanated were as important to the readers as anything that might be happening there; he therefore began to send reporters to cover not only events in strange places but the places themselves."[21] Bennett's geographical sensibilities (and egotism) led him to most famously perhaps directly fund and outfit George De Long's 1879 North Pole attempt (via the Bering Strait) in the *Jeannette*. Daly maintained steady attention to the progress of the *Jeannette* in his annual geographical addresses; in 1880 noting that the expedition's results seemed promising.[22] When the ship subsequently disappeared, Daly's appeal to U.S. President Hayes to send a relief effort was read to Congress and published at length in the *Herald*, resulting in "the entire New York press be[coming] aroused by the issue."[23] Daly's voice prevailed and a relief vessel was immediately dispatched to rescue the *Jeannette* – only to find it crushed in the ice, with its captain and crew dead.[24]

One cannot overstate the foundational role the news media played in creating and diffusing geographical knowledge to the public within this milieu, nor ignore how the corporate agenda of news organizations was often disguised as American nationalistic fervor.[25] Bennett's reporters would be allowed to accompany those Arctic expeditions the *Herald* directly outfitted, and they would in turn provide eye-witness accounts of the expeditions' progress. Bennett's reporter William Gilder announced the geographical "firsts" of the Schwatka expedition (below), and as such, simultaneously created both the "news" and "geographical knowledge" of the type most widely accepted as such in the period (being the first to find a route or draw a map, going the longest or farthest, or collecting the most). Gilder's accounts in the *Herald* often took up an entire page of a 12–16-page daily newspaper. Thus we see an unprecedented marriage between news organizations and geographical patrons working in tandem to create geographical

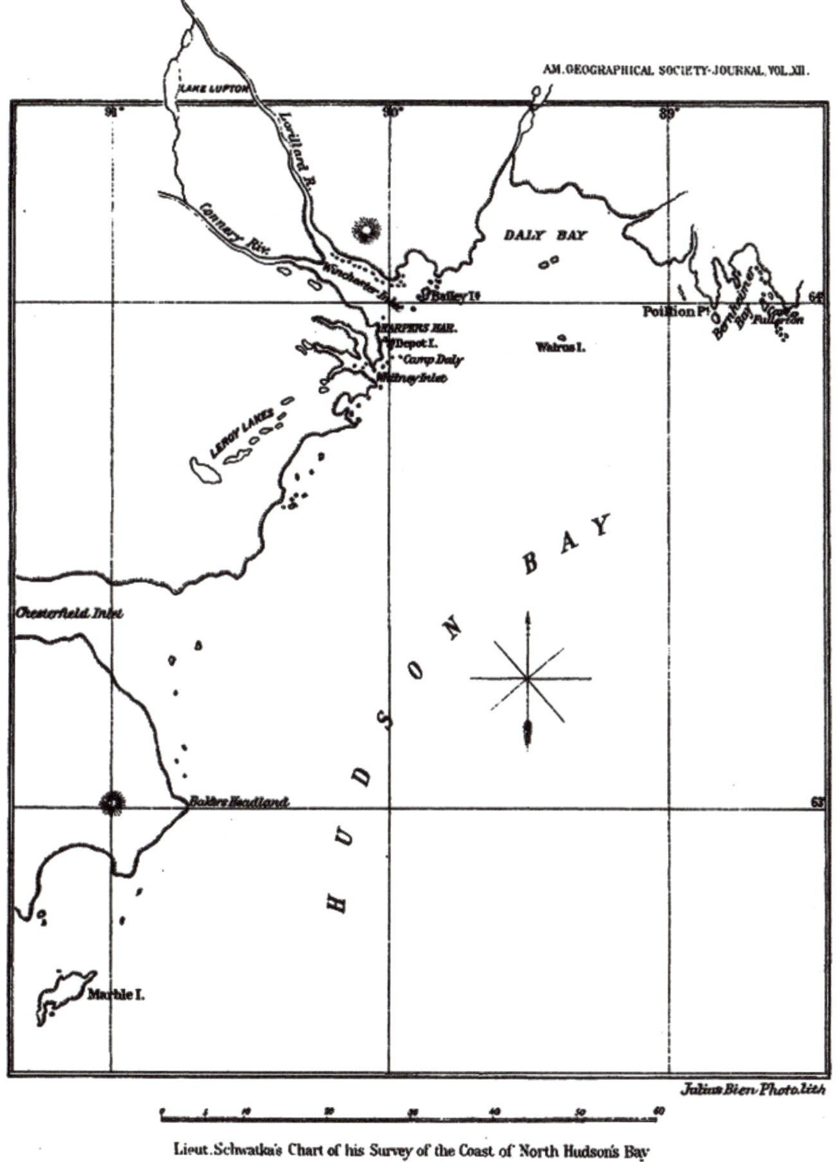

Figure 5.1 **Lieut. Schwatka's Chart of his Survey of the Coast of North Hudson's Bay, Franklin Search Expedition. Map locates "Daly Bay" and "Camp Daly"**

Source: *Journal of the American Geographical Society of New York* 12 (1880): 1–2.

firsts – and even if such firsts were not firsts at all.[26] This symbiotic and sometimes contentious relationship between explorers, their patrons, and the news media was manifested in a number of such ways. For instance, explorers, in needing to repay their patrons, oftentimes did so by naming places they explored after them. This ensured that the patrons would continue supporting them, and also that the patrons would, in turn, publicly "advertise" explorations that featured the places so named. The Arctic spaces "Cape Daly," "Daly Bay," "Lake Daly," and "Camp Daly" all provide relevant examples.

Meanwhile, as President of a geographical society whose speeches and works were closely followed by an eager press, Daly himself had a great deal of power to articulate (and promote and manipulate) that which would become newsworthy – new routes, measurements, and findings; the heroic stature of explorers and images of new lands; but also the commercial advantages or scientific merit of various expeditions.[27] As armchair explorer Daly certainly made use of a sensationalist press for the benefits that would accrue to male masculinity (Chapter 2), however his ends were far more nuanced than sensationalism ala Bennett, in his positioning Arctic geography as a commercial, scientific, and national civic enterprise; themes to which I now turn.

Limits to American "Commercial Geography" in the Arctic

One of the more interesting questions that arises with respect to the historical AGS is how one might connect its interest in Arctic and North Pole exploration to its explicit commercial geography and efforts to advance an American "commercial empire." The resource-rich North and Central Americas would seem obviously appealing to AGS men (Chapter 4), but the Arctic and poles? AGS meeting notes from the mid- to late-nineteenth century demonstrate that support of Arctic or polar expeditions always rested on their presumed "practical" use, and lacking practicality, many projects failed to receive support. Generally, "practicality" was understood broadly as containing either a humanitarian logic or serving a commercial purpose.[28] But how does a commercial- or business-oriented geographical society construct a geography that requires explicit practical use of research findings of the Arctic regions and North Pole, spaces seemingly devoid of commercial potential in their cold, dark expanse of snow and ice?

While it was the humanitarian efforts of the Franklin search parties that technically brought the Americans into Arctic exploration in the first place, there were, of course, many potential commercial benefits to polar exploration for them as well. In fact, the original *raison d'être* of polar exploration was commercial or mercantilist in nature, if not in attempting to directly acquire resources and goods to trade – most notably in the whaling industry – then in attempting to find a route through which to trade them. Two valued components of whales, train oil and baleen (whalebone), were widely sought for their use in a range of commercial products.[29] Throughout northern Europe whaling profits subsidized the financing of many private (non-government-sponsored) expeditions from the late seventeenth century onwards. The period 1770–1830 saw the creation of systematic, coordinated, maritime surveys on a global scale, alongside major investments in technologies for construction of better ships, harbors, docks, ports, and processing and distribution centers in cities such as Amsterdam and Hamburg. Meanwhile American whalers had been in Arctic or sub-Arctic areas such as Hudson's Bay and the Bering Sea since the early nineteenth century, seeking whales for their oil and bone, as well as seal and otter furs and various minerals.[30] Amidst these mercantilist and early capitalist endeavors in the fishing industry were concerted attempts to discover a navigable North-West or North-East Passage. Infused with the commercial logic of finding a practical shipping route between Europe/America and Asia (China and Japan) through waters of the Arctic circle, this was an aspiration more or less dependent upon, and hopeful of, finding a short-cut from the Atlantic to the Pacific via open water at the North Pole itself.

This brief survey of a type of "commercial empire" in the Arctic is one to which Henry Grinnell's patronage of AGS expeditions is most obviously linked. Some have argued that Grinnell's expeditions purporting to search for Franklin were in fact "thinly disguised" attempts to locate the North-West Passage or the purported Open Polar Sea.[31] In addition, a great deal of nationalist sentiment accompanied Grinnell's efforts. At the 1874 *Polaris* meeting, Charles Daly theatrically produced the flag that Grinnell had sent out with De Haven, Kane, Hayes, Hall, and Charles Wilkes (to Antarctica), noting that it had traveled farther north and farther south than any other country's flag: "Grinnell requests me to say he is ready to send it again if there is any American fitted out for the discovery of the Pole, but not for any other purpose."[32] On Grinnell's death later that year, as if to seal the "patron's deal" discussed above, Daly summarized Grinnell's devotion to both the AGS and to Arctic exploration: "That long line of coast known as Grinnell Land [beginning in Smith's Sound] ... will remain forever a monument to his inspiring spirit, the benevolent feeling, [and] the broad and generous aspiration of an American merchant."[33]

With the important exception of Grinnell (and Robert Peary, below), few overtly commercial links seem to have existed between the Arctic and AGS men of Charles Daly's milieu. Nonetheless, as with explorations of other parts of the globe, Daly dutifully relayed commercial findings from leaders of Arctic expeditions when they were supplied to him, for instance in 1873 when outlining a North-West trade route proposed from the findings of E.H. Johannsen's sailing around Nova Zembia: "a staunch steamer could pass from the Scandinavian coast through the Arctic Ocean to Behring Strait and return the same summer." He noted that a Swedish colony was being established in Spitsbergen, "the object being mercantile – the obtaining of phosphates for [the manufacture of] artificial manure."[34] Findings from Otto Nordenskjold's (Swedish) explorations in the region of the Kara Sea found their way into a number of Daly's annual addresses as well, noting fish, vegetation, and potentially viable transportation routes (and dismissing others). Daly's commercial logic appeared as findings of both "presences" and "absences" from voyages of discovery. In 1880, for instance, Nordenskjold's findings from Cape Chelyuskin, the northernmost point of Asia, indicated that:

> [Some of the plains] were nearly bare, while others were clothed with vegetation, consisting of grass, moss or lichens. The strata of the rocks were upright, devoid of fossils, and on the outer promontory there was a strata of slate crossed by large veins of quartz. Animal life was scarce; a few birds were seen … vegetable life was equally meager. In the sea about them they saw walrus, a few seals, two shoals of white whales.[35]

While such findings appear occasionally in Daly's depictions of Arctic space, he did not cast them as of primary civic importance. Rather, most of his professional discourse on the Arctic was more "disinterestedly" scientific, especially focused on advances in physical geography. In that sense, his Arctic lacked the explicit nod to humanitarian or commercial practicality so frequently admonished by AGS men in support of various expeditions or researches. Daly's civil service in the Arctic would be in advancing the scientific benefits of polar exploration, and helping develop the infrastructure necessary for it. Particularly lacking the obvious ulterior motives of mercantilism, either personal or professional, Daly's interest in the Arctic aligns with those scientific practitioners whose very disinterest could be called into question for their underlying commercial motives or geo-political, foreign policy, or nationalistic impulses.[36] His geography harbored an American scientific sovereignty that often underlay debates about the costs versus benefits of polar and Arctic exploration, yet his sensibilities were cast as – perhaps "disguised as" is a better term – progressively multi-national. It is to such issues I turn in the remainder of the chapter, beginning with Daly's role as judicious arbitrator in the Open Polar Sea question, continuing with a discussion of the "race to the pole," and finishing with some reflections on what this meant for U.S.-Inuit relations.

The Open Polar Sea and Armchair Explorer Revisited

Charles Daly derived a great deal of authority to speak on issues for which he had no first-hand knowledge by associating himself with those in the field who did. This tension between the explorer in the field who could claim first-hand experience and knowledge, and the careful scholar at home studying his maps and books, had a great deal of relevance for how Daly authoritatively constructed geographical knowledge and practice in the Arctic. While direct experience of the eye-witness offered one type of legitimacy needed to debate Arctic geography and science, the armchair explorer, particularly one with extensive resources at his disposal, had the advantage of studying the bigger picture offered by maps and atlases, reports from diverse sources, the scientific literature of the day, and so on. Daly's story resonates closely with that of British estate manager James MacQueen, whose early nineteenth-century armchair speculations about the course and terminus of the River Niger turned out to be correct – without MacQueen ever visiting the African continent.[37] As David Livingstone points out, the study or laboratory offered a perspective the traveler in the field lacked:

> [The fieldworker] quickly traversed territory and viewed many things in a sequence [and thus] observations of the fieldworker were "broken and fleeting." By contrast, the bench-tied student … had the time to spread out samples, to collate and analyze them, and thereby to come to reliable conclusions. The laboratory naturalist occupied a kind of hyperspace: because creation in all its dazzling diversity passed across the workbench, it afforded the opportunity to rearrange the natural order and grasp it as a whole. By patient comparison and correlation, the armchair naturalist could easily triumph over the fragmentary and precarious claims of the fieldworker.… Only in the study could one roam the Cosmos.[38]

As Dorinda Outram further argues, the field offered one set of epistemological assurances, such as instantaneous, precise, and direct observation; while the study offered another set – mastery and comprehension provided through an opposite kind of gaze, the distant: "true knowledge of the order of nature comes not from the whole-body experience of crossing the terrain, but from the very fact of the observer's *distance* from the actuality of nature. True observation of nature depends on *not* being there."[39] Of course the explorer in the field also relied on "science" to interpret that field, primarily via extensive scientific instrumentation and technology – especially true perhaps for otherwise physically demanding or inaccessible spaces such as the deep or frozen oceans.[40] And yet the Arctic explorer's ability to authoritatively and credibly speak about the field once back at home nonetheless derived principally from his recounting embodied experiences, particularly those of extreme hardships withstood. The real "currency" of Arctic exploration, according to Robinson, was explorers' stories, and even as these shifted from the rational, scientifically-based stories of early explorers such as Kane to those more heroically "muscular" in the later decades of the nineteenth century.[41] And again, as I think Charles Daly succeeded in personally aligning himself in the public eye with explorers returning from the field through his spectacular public Arctic meetings, he could simultaneously turn attention to his professional distance from the field, through his careful, judicious, bench-tied study of the scientific issues at hand; ultimately all his bases would be covered. Rhetorically his approach was not unlike that of writing a legal brief. To wit: in the debate over the Open Polar Sea.

The Open Polar Sea was a legendary body of free-flowing water at the North Pole that explorers and others had sought from the eighteenth century. The hope of finding free-flowing (warm) water at the pole was primarily a commercially motivated one, aimed at finding a navigable trade route across the Arctic Circle or North Pole. While a controversial theory at the time – both widely accepted and widely disparaged – the American Arctic explorers, particularly Elisha Kane and Isaac Hayes, exploited their close affiliation with the AGS to advocate its existence via lectures and in print.[42] Kane and Hayes based their arguments on their first-hand "sightings" of the open waters, as well as on the ideas of the "father of American oceanography" Matthew Maury (AGS Vice President and councilor in the 1850s), European geographer August Petermann, and outspoken American naval captain and oceanographer Silas Bent, among others. Such proponents based their theory on a number of inductive assertions, such as those about the length and direction of the warm ocean currents (the Gulf Stream and Japanese current) meeting at the pole, as well as on the migration patterns of birds, fish, and whales. (Maury theorized that warmer waters must exist at the pole in order for whales to travel from the Atlantic to Pacific, as heat from equatorial waters would have killed them.) Numerous eye-witness accounts of free flowing water at the pole and warm water flowing south from it bolstered such arguments.[43]

AGS members actively debated the issue throughout the 1850s and 1860s. Though Daly was a friend and advocate of Isaac Hayes throughout the latter's career (he once referred to Hayes as the AGS's "most competent member") – Daly was one of the people voting against Hayes' project in 1860 to take up where Kane left off in finding the Open Polar Sea – "there could be no practical result from the expedition," he reasoned. The AGS ultimately endorsed Hayes' voyage and helped raise the necessary funds for it, although Hayes returned in 1861 not having found the open sea but his belief in it "unshaken."[44] Hayes subsequently claimed to have seen it, "extending as far as the eye could see."[45]

Using a type of distinguished "rational license," Daly maintained over the course of his career that logic and scientific evidence proved contrary to such first-hand reports. Over two-thirds of Daly's 1870 annual address (31 single-spaced published pages) was devoted to Arctic and Polar expeditions and in refuting the existence of the Open Polar Sea. As per his annual "accounting" of the geographical work of the world for each year, he collated a breathtaking volume of material for his report on expeditions occurring in the 1850s and 1860s: degrees longitude reached, means of transport and routes taken, the nature of the ice and other obstacles encountered, and a panoply of geological, botanical, zoological, and meteorological findings, as well as comparisons with previous explorations and researches in applicable areas. He concluded that from 1553 to 1870, the world had witnessed a total of 113 polar expeditions.

As to the Open Polar Sea, Daly began his 1870 colloquy by refreshing his audience's memory of this "old theory" and using a range of rhetorical devices, countered the "evidence" supporting it, with frequent reference to his extensive supply of supporting documents and sources close at hand. He referred to his detailed comparisons of a number of atlases, for instance, which were not in agreement about northern areas (such as about the coastline of Norway), and therefore about the path of the Gulf Stream. Daly summed up what was then known about the path and velocity of the Gulf Stream, supported by a letter from G.W. Blunt, "one of the oldest members of the society" and publisher of mariner charts, who argued that it was too weakened by the time it reached the far north to create a warm sea. (Blunt's letter was published with Daly's address, along with letters from others at the U.S. Coast Survey.)

Daly refuted the theory of the Open Polar Sea based on such physical geography evidence as well as on that of a more social nature. He noted simply that if the sea existed, more people would have seen it. Two and a half centuries of expeditions, along with the lucrative Dutch, English, Scotch, Spanish, and American fishing industry, with at some points 12,000 people and as many as 130 vessels in the seas in some years – surely more people would have registered sightings of open water, he reasoned, particularly as it would have benefitted them to do so: "In short, they ransacked every portion of these seas, until … they fished them out; It is not unreasonable to suppose [that] these hardy, experienced, and adventurous mariners would have failed to find it." He further discussed an AGS lecture and subsequent correspondence with Captain Silas Bent, charging him with careless and contradictory research, confusion of facts, and misinterpretation of seamen's eye-witness accounts. He noted further that Hadley's quadrant was not invented until 1731 and that the astrolabe previously in use [by such seamen] could not be depended upon. Daly bolstered this range of rhetorical strategies by frequent reference to his reputation and experience as a judge, impressing upon his audience that,

> Those who, like myself, have passed years in the daily occupation of sifting and weighing testimony, know that little or no value whatever is to be attached to [the] memory of witnesses [who] after a lapse of time cannot be depended upon in matters of detail, even in affairs in which they have been actors.[46]

In others of his speeches he displayed little tolerance for what he called the "imaginary geography" of explorers such as Charles Hall who "startled" Daly in his belief in the Symmes Hole, pursuit of which, along with the open sea, inspired Hall's third Arctic voyage. "I mention these circumstances to show that even in this scientific age, theories are seriously advanced with about as much to support them as the crudities advocated during the middle ages."[47]

The content of Daly's Arctic reports (speeches, interviews, and written reports) was constituted primarily of scientific advancements – for instance from the *Polaris* voyage was gained magnetic observations, a survey of 700 miles of coastline, and knowledge of ocean physics, gravity, and astronomy – and even if he also told harrowing stories of human endurance for other ends.[48] Daly gave particular credit to any expedition that promised to shed light on the past physical geography of the earth, and in fact cast discovery of the North Pole itself as a scientific objective, a position widely quoted verbatim by the *New York Times*, *New York Herald*, *The World*, and *New York Tribune*:

> [T]here is no portion of the earth's surface where observations in respect to scientific matters affecting the whole globe – every part of it – are so important as in the polar basin or its vicinity. The tremendous forces there … are physical phenomena most important to observe and study. They have to do with the winds, ocean currents, magnetic influences and numerous other questions … There, and only there, in all probability, will the key be found to unlock these mysteries, especially in respect to the laws of one of the most important and universal of them, at least as it affects our globe – magnetism.[49]

His view of the scientific importance of the North Pole, articulated in 1878, had been percolating for years. At the end of his 1870 speech Daly had stated that "[i]t had been [his] intention to give the reasons why, in a geographical and scientific point of view, the discovery of the Pole was of great importance; but my limits forbid." Instead, he offered a footnote: such reasons would be "elaborately set forth by M. Gustave Lambert" in the *Paris Geographical Society Bulletin*. In this way he shifted the weight of his arguments towards European scientist(s). A review of Lambert's geography reveals him to have been supportive of the Open Polar Sea, yet Lambert also argued in the *Paris Bulletin* that "the scientific conquest of the Pole would fecundate all the sciences."[50] Daly's participation in the "race to the

Figure 5.2 Meeting of the American Geographical Society at Chickering Hall, for the Reception of Earl Dufferin and the Consideration of the Howgate Plan for the Exploration of the Arctic[51]

Source: Lithograph, *The Daily Graphic*, New York, 5 February 1878.

pole," if it can be called that, was based on scientific views closely aligned with, if not identical to, those of his French colleague.

And though never explicitly stated as such, his views were also closely aligned with those of Austro-Hungarian army officer Karl Weyprecht, architect of the first (1882) International Polar Year.[52] At the 1879 International Polar Conference in Hamburg Weyprecht had laid out his idea for a multi-national ring of scientific research stations in the Arctic, arguing that such research should be the only justification for costly Arctic expeditions – and not the search for a North-West passage, commercial gain, personal glory, the nonexistent Open Polar Sea, or to plant the national flag farther than any other expedition. To Weyprecht, scientific research was "better achieved by nations in concert rather than in rivalry."[53] Such ideas led, in 1882, to 11 countries setting up 12 Arctic stations for a year of observation, with the AGS offering support of various description for the American station.

While the U.S. War department, Signal Corps, and U.S. Congress chose to avoid such "foreign entanglements," U.S. Army Captain William Howgate (another supporter of the Open Polar Sea) was interested in Weyprecht's plan. Howgate initiated an expedition to establish an American Arctic research station, the northernmost one, on Ellesmere Island. Howgate presented his plans before the American Geographical Society in January 1878.[54] Called the "Lady Franklin Bay Expedition," led by Howgate's good friend U.S. Army Lieut. Greely, this mission would receive widespread news coverage before, during, and after it ended in disaster. Greely had received vague orders, little government support, and an ostensibly "scientific" crew only half of whom had any scientific training.[55] Stories of the expedition's purported scientific mission were overcast by its bold attempt to reach the North Pole. Supplies, recruits, and replacements failed to arrive, and titillating stories told of three winter ordeals, conflict among the crew, starvation, scurvy, an execution, suicide, insanity, death, and cannibalism. The "Horrors of Cape Sabine" were widely covered by the *New York Times*, *New York Herald*, *New York Tribune*, the *Chicago Tribune*, and *Washington Post*, among others.[56] Such reportage marked a transitional shift in American Arctic discovery from a focus on "science" to that of "sensationalism." While Greely's was the most scientific of American polar expeditions to date – he "brought back the most comprehensive and systematic set of observations ever produced by Americans in the Arctic" – the expedition's controversies and scandals eclipsed all else. As this coincided with a period of increasing competition among newspapers to create and sell news, as well as the cultural pressures of urban men to shore up and prove their masculinity in new ways, Greely in the end was praised more for his manly character than for his science.[57]

Charles Daly, meantime, had criticized the science of the Open Polar Sea throughout his career, but the issue came once again to a head at the 1884 AGS Arctic Meeting celebrating the return of Greely's expedition – though only six of the crew of 25 had survived (including Greely). Seemingly intent on avoiding scandal above all else, Daly began the meeting announcing a "heroes' welcome" to the crew, who were received with "long continued rounds of applause." In his opening remarks Daly reminded his audience of the scientific benefits to such expeditions: "I have never had any faith in the finding of an open Polar sea, but I have profound faith in the value of such expeditions … we shall never know the laws of the currents of the air and of the ocean until we know what is periodically taking place in the great Arctic basin."[58] While Greely's experiences would receive a great deal of news coverage on their own, Daly's broaching of the Polar Sea issue also drew media attention. A writer for the *New York Tribune* covering the meeting sarcastically complained that "whenever an explorer ascertained the existence of certain geographical facts by personal observation, some *library geographer* was certain to come forward with a paper discrediting those findings" [italics mine]. The *Tribune* editorial went on to say that:

> Kane and Hayes believed in the open polar sea … Greely confirmed their opinion, and some of his men narrowly escaped drifting into [it]. But Chief Justice Daly, whose Arctic travels have been made chiefly in the rooms of the American Geographical Society, has undertaken to show a priori argument that what these explorers have seen cannot exist.[59]

While the armchair explorer would be susceptible to such attacks, Daly did not appear much affected by them, sustained as he was by his comfortable reputation as reliable jurist-geographer; and he was, of course, subsequently proved correct. And despite such attacks Daly's allegiance to men in the field also would be manifestly sustained; he went on to cordially review Greely's book in the *Herald*.[60] And when subsequently interviewed by the *New York Herald* about the Greely expedition, Daly admonished,

> During the many years I have been president of the American Geographical Society, I have never urged the fitting out of an expedition merely for the discovery of the North Pole. The interest felt in this country for such an expedition owed chiefly to the late Lt. Maury's theory of an open polar sea, to which the late Dr. Kane and Dr. Hayes became converts … I called attention, more than twenty years ago in one of my annual addresses before the Society, to the fact that there was no trace of warm currents at the Poles … There is now no ground for assuming the discovery of the North Pole. [Its discovery will be] nothing but a geographical feat that will confer distinction upon the navigator.[61]

Daly's dismissal of the North Pole discovery for its own sake, or for the sake of individual fame, is instructive, particularly as it was bound so closely to his scientific denunciation of the Open Polar Sea – which itself was both the most contentious scientific issue with which he "held court" and became embroiled, as well as one that gave him the most credibility as geographer. Daly's rejection of the "pole for the pole's sake" serves as a useful entrée into what would become his signature "contribution" to Arctic exploration, advancing a scientific, yet no less nationalistic, mission for American claims to it.

8

The further geographical work was
an exploration to Grinnell Land,
conducted by Lieut Greely himself,
which has added largely to our
geographical knowledge. The journey—
over 250 miles—was made in 12 days
which compares favorably with
McClintock's extraordinary journeys.
It embraced the discovery of "an im=
mense ice-bound lake", Lake Hazen
and the fact that in the interior
of Grinnell Land there are valleys
which, in the brief Arctic Summer
are covered with—~~for that high~~
latitude—luxuriant vegetation,
affording pasturage for considerable
game.
Another discovery was a frozen sea
stretching 85 miles across Grinnell
Land—Mer de glace Agassiz—which
with its vertical front, 150 feet high,
and the glacial ice of the United
States mountains, constitutes the
"wonderful boundaries of the
extraordinary "fertile belt of Grinnell
Land." How far this Mer de glace
extends southward, was not ascertained.
Lieut Greely devotes a portion of the

Figure 5.3 Excerpt from Charles Daly's hand-written review of *Three Years of Arctic Service* by Lieut. A.W. Greeley (published version appeared in the *New York Herald*, February 1886)

Source: Charles P. Daly Papers, Box 9. Manuscripts and Archives Division, The New York Public Library, Astor, Lenox and Tilden Foundations.

International Diplomacy and the Race to the Pole

As AGS President Charles Daly served an important role as American "diplomat" to Arctic affairs, keeping close ties to Washington's Arctic program – such as it was. Soliciting funds and providing a range of cartographic and other equipment and advice for U.S. expeditions often took place quietly and as a matter of course; but when lobbying Congress the AGS role became considerably more public. Daly publicly lobbied Congress to support the funding of a number of expeditions, Charles Hall's *Polaris* expedition, the *Jeanette* relief expedition, and Schwatka's search for Franklin relics. (Both Isaac Hayes and Charles Hall applied to the U.S. President to lead the *Polaris* expedition, while also advocating their cases at Daly's home.[62]) Meanwhile Daly also positioned himself as a sort of American foreign affairs diplomat by publicly praising other nations' Arctic triumphs, and was just as apt to note the shortcomings of U.S. efforts. Just to take one example from among many, in his 1874 annual address Daly lavished distinct praise on Weyprecht's 1873 *Tegethoff* expedition in Franz Josef Land, declaring that "this expedition, in the difficulties it encountered, the perseverance displayed, the discipline maintained, and the success achieved is about as heroic as anything that has occurred in the history of Arctic exploration [and] contrasts strongly with the vacillation, petty squabbles and ineffective discipline on board the *Polaris* on our own expedition."[63]

When it comes to the Arctic, as numerous scholars have observed, the element of nationalism is "unusually powerful."[64] Competition for discovery of the North Pole especially brought out nationalistic aspirations, and yet Daly, atypically perhaps, liked to go on record claiming that he did not particularly care who made it to the North Pole first, even while complaining that the U.S. government was doing little to reach the North Pole: "to do anything effectually, it must be done by our Government."[65] His occasional flag-waving towards the North Pole seemed mostly aimed at speaking the floridly patriotic language of politicians, attempting to motivate conflicted U.S. Congresses to fund various projects. He admonished the Congress in 1870 to awaken to what is due America, "in this emulous strife of nations it would be a proud distinction for us, and a noble vindication of a marked feature in our national character, should the flag which bears as its emblem the stars that guide the mariner, be the first to wave over this pivot of the globe."[66] Such statements should be read against Daly's other constant admonitions, that discovery of the pole would serve primarily in the acquisition of important scientific data. When the subject of the North Pole contest came up Daly resolutely maintained that the pole ought to be achieved "for science," and logistically, via ship then sledge through the American route first attempted by Kane and Hayes. "That the pole will be ultimately reached I entertain no doubt," he stated, "but the better method [to reaching it] is to go prepared also for sledge boat explorations upon the land when the farthest point by water has been reached."

Most competition for reaching the North Pole, and for Arctic achievements more generally during this milieu, implicitly had their basis in political or territorial claims that were in tension with the more explicit and seemingly "purer" quotidian purpose of scientific advancement. Arguments suggesting that winning the pole for neutral, disinterested science had at their core highly nationalistic ends portrayed as anything but that. As Michael Bravo argues, "science and sovereignty have a history of [such] entanglements": scientific knowledge is never acquired simply for its own sake, but serves rather as an instrument of nationalism, demonstrating, at the very least, the nation's prestige and rank within the scientific community, if not containing more covert political or economic ends.[67] To Bravo, the research station in particular, as exceptional, ostensibly non-political space, serves as an "iconic technology" in matters of Arctic sovereignty and national identity; it enacts on behalf of sovereign states "certain rituals of possession," exerting a national presence while at the same time disavowing them.[68]

Daly's and the AGS's alignment with Weyprecht's plan for a multi-national ring of Arctic stations illustrates this type of "scientific sovereignty" to which Bravo (and Powell) refer. The political discourse of international sharing and collaborating in science – of "international benefits" of science for all that rise above the interests of individual nations – emerged most clearly in the period 1860–1914 and indeed gave rise to the first International Polar Year. Daly's aspirations for Arctic science clearly resonated with such internationalist or multi-nationalist ideals, especially obvious in his decades-long argument that the best route to the North Pole was the American one – whichever nation should choose to take it.

Daly demonstratively supported the British government when it decided to outfit what became its final attempt at the North Pole, an 1875 expedition led by Sir George Nares, that was to take the American route to the pole: "Great hopes are entertained that it will succeed in reaching the Pole either by water or by sledging," Daly stated in his annual speech, "but whether or not, the scientific researches will entirely warrant sending it out." He quoted RGS men who affirmed England's gratitude "to her American cousins who had cleared the way by successful operations through Smith Sound."[69] Daly's support for the British attempt at the pole via this "peculiarly American" route was quoted in the *Herald*; he advised that "the world is interested only in the fact that Pole should be discovered, and it is immaterial by what nation." The *Herald* commended Daly on his "liberal and enlightened views, without exhibiting jealousy of any other country."[70] Such a position must have made an impact on public perception of America's equananimous role in Arctic exploration.

On Nares' return, however, events took a complicated turn for Daly. In his 1876 annual address he praised Nares for the scientific and geographical successes of the journey (reaching as it did by sledge the farthest point north of any previous expedition), and reiterating the practical scientific value of the expedition:

> To reach the Pole [is] not the main object in an Arctic expedition; that was a mere geographical feature, to which necessarily great *éclat* would be attached; but that the real object of such an expedition was to explore the Arctic region in every direction; as far as possible to obtain scientific information of … great practical importance. This object has been to a considerable degree advanced by the English expedition. All this was accomplished in the face of the greatest obstacles and in the most trying circumstances with a cheerfulness, courage and perseverance on the part of both officers and men which is beyond all praise.

And yet Daly's multi-national ethos had its limits. He went on to complain in the speech that Nares did not give proper credit to preceding American explorers:

> I regret to say that I cannot pass, without animadversion, certain matters in [Nares'] report to the RGS … Nares did not have the courtesy and kindliness which almost uniformally explorers especially of the Arctic give to labors and discoveries of their predecessors … not only did Nares not do this, but he spoke unfavorably of Kane and Hayes in his report. I feel called upon to say something upon the subject.

In his report Nares had dismissed as useless the inferior and inaccurate maps drawn by the American explorers Kane and Hayes, which were to have directed his expedition. Daly defended the heroic efforts of Kane and Hayes in some detail, noting their achievements despite being outfitted privately, with small sums of money, in small frail vessels, inadequate equipment, and without maps. They were young and experienced (like America itself perhaps?) Daly reminded his audience, not trained naval officers such as those who traveled with Nares. As if to take the opportunity to resolve an old feud meanwhile, Daly further reminded his audience of the "well known fact" that the English had replaced their own names for Grinnell Land on their maps: something Kane and Hayes would never have done and which Daly brought up "simply to suggest the application of the homely proverb indicating what those should avoid who live in glass houses."[71]

I relate these portions of Daly's speeches and interviews to illustrate the limits, as it were, to his explicit multi-national aspirations in the Arctic. Eventually Daly's hopes for an American scientific sovereignty in the Arctic would, in the first decade of the twentieth century, be obliterated by the sensationalized Peary-Cook controversy and each's individualistic and baldly patriotic claims to the North Pole. Whether at bottom Daly's rhetoric of global cooperation in advancing Arctic science served American nationalistic claims to the North Pole or not, the manner and content of his public education of the Arctic advanced a more cooperative, universalist conception of the role of geography and geographical exploration than the overtly grandiose, chauvinistic American claims to the North Pole made later, especially by Robert Peary. Such should be kept in mind as characterizing a unique moment in nineteenth-century American geography. Meanwhile though, American claims to a "presence" in the Arctic would continue to be marked and validated in the latter two decades of the nineteenth century via Charles Daly's and the AGS's relations with Inuit, a subject I turn to in the final section of the chapter.

Arctic Patronage and Colonial Race Relations

As noted earlier, the only Arctic expedition directly funded by the AGS as an organization during Charles Daly's presidential term was that led by Frederick Schwatka in 1878–1880. This was a pet project of Daly's for which he personally solicited funds from AGS fellows, six of whom eventually paid for it (including himself) in the name of the society. Schwatka's expedition would become known as the "final search" for relics of the perished Franklin expedition. The humanitarian logic of this expedition was tied closely to its mercantilist agenda, as it went out as part of a whaling venture in Hudson's Bay under the auspices of the shipping firm of Morison and Brown (both AGS fellows) – although the expedition was so unsuccessful that it led to the firm's collapse. Schwatka's would nonetheless become the longest sledge journey on record, planting, as the *New York Herald* proudly announced, a U.S. flag nearer the pole than in any previous attempt.[72]

My interest in this expedition lies in the fact that it was Inuit ("Eskimo") testimony that inspired jurist-geographer Charles Daly to organize it. The AGS was directly involved with Inuit people in a number of such ways, ranging from Inuit supplying information to explorers or patrons; serving as guides on expeditions; enabling the "public consumption" of their stories and experiences by appearances at Arctic meetings; and by receiving personal financial support post-expedition. Daly would come to deal deftly with Inuit "witnesses" when he met them, when he weighed their evidence, and also in the ways that he was willing to stage them at AGS events. His understanding of the public culture of scientific travel and exploration gives a picture of a geographer shrewd in cross-cultural politics.

When Daly publicly explained the origins of the Schwatka expedition he noted that he was initially exhorted by AGS Fellow John Morison to undertake it.[73] Morison had collected evidence from one of his ship's officers, Thomas Barry, who had spoken to "Netchelli" (Netsilik or Netsilik-region) people about the existence of Franklin relics at Repulse Bay, claiming most provocatively that Franklin's logbook could be retrieved. Daly consulted with Joe Ebierbing – an Inuit man with close ties to the AGS – to question him about the reliability of Barry's testimony.[74] Ebierbing convinced Daly that Barry could speak Esquimaux sufficiently that his information could justify sending out another search for the Franklin relics. Meanwhile Daly asked Joe Ebierbing to join the expedition. The search party included 12 Inuit men in addition to Ebierbing (who would serve as interpreter, hunter, and guide), the illustrator and surveyor Heinrich Klutschak, and *New York Herald* reporter William Gilder.[75]

Schwatka's expedition left New York Harbor in June 1878, with newspapers reporting the "lusty cheers" that went out for each of the principals in turn, especially Joe Ebierbing.[76] By early August the party had set up their base camp

Figure 5.4 "Joe" Ebierbing (Ipirvik Taqulittuq), Inuit explorer, 1860–1880
Source: Original appeared in J.E. Nourse, ed. *Narrative of the Second Arctic Expedition Made by Charles F. Hall: His Voyage to Repulse Bay, Sledge Journeys to the Straits of Fury and Hecla and to King William's Land, and Residence Among the Eskimoes During the Years 1864–1869* (1879).

Figure 5.5 "Winter-Quarters at Camp Daly. The American Franklin Search Expedition," from "Sketches Taken on the Spot by Henry W. Klutschak"

Source: *Harper's Weekly*, 4 December 1880.

on the northwestern shore of Hudson's Bay, a camp they named "Camp Daly," on a lake they named "Lake Daly." Like Charles Hall before them, the crew learned Inuit ways and lived in igloos. They did not find any of Franklin's written records. As it turned out, of the two Inuit men who had given information to Barry about such records, one turned out to be dead and the other "knew only of the Franklin expedition by hearsay." Thus the expedition completely failed in its intended purpose, as Schwatka informed Daly by letter: "From all the information which I can obtain here, I find it utterly impossible to confirm, even in part, the story on which the present Franklin Search Party is based. In fact, I am thoroughly convinced there is nothing whatsoever in it."[77] He recommended that, "if anything can be accomplished," the party instead perform new surveys of King William's Land. Ultimately the expedition made the longest overland Arctic sledge journey on record, 2,819 miles over 11 months. Much was done to save face for the expedition's efforts, such as Schwatka reporting that it was the first such expedition undertaken during an Arctic winter, recording one 43-day blizzard and the coldest temperatures endured by white men in the field (-71 degrees F). Klutschak's sketches of the camp, environs, Franklin graves, and Inuit people were widely circulated in several New York and London newspapers, including the *London Illustrated News* and *Harper's Weekly*.[78]

The crew and their findings were presented to the public at the AGS Arctic meeting of 1880. Newspapers reported a "hurricane of applause" that greeted Schwatka. The *New York Herald* noted the spectacle of national pride in Daly's remarks as he pointed to the organ keyboard draped with an American flag, proclaiming it had been "hoisted at a point two degrees nearer the north magnetic

Figure 5.6 Lieut. Frederick Schwatka showing Inuit a copy of *The Illustrated London News*, from "Sketches Taken on the Spot by Henry W. Klutschak"

Source: *Harper's Weekly*, 4 December 1880.

pole than had ever been reached by any other party … [a] circumstance not lessened by the fact that the flag was hoisted on the Fourth of July." Daly read quotes from the London *Times* in his opening remarks, emphasizing the specter of the particular hardships endured in an overland journey:

> None who have not braved an Arctic winter can rightly understand the mere meaning of a temperature 100 degrees below the freezing point. How human frames endured such an ordeal, it is hard to imagine. Only the human sense of power to bear what others have borne and the instinct of an obligation ... could have sustained this little company of dauntless sailors amid the warning evidences of polar remorselessness.[79]

Schwatka amplified the successes of the expedition and white men's ability to withstand the "peculiarly depressing" Arctic landscape and long sledge journey: "It was the first expedition," he explained, "wherein the white men of a party lived solely upon the same diet, *voluntarily assumed*, as its native allies." In much of his speech Schwatka reinforced ideologies of inherent (hierarchical) racial differences between white explorers and Arctic Natives, yet in his letters to Daly from the field, during the journey itself, he had also represented Inuit men and Joe Ebierbing in particular as equals and as essential to the success of the expedition. He supported his own decisions with statements such as "and Joe believes," thus connecting his own knowledge and authority to that of Natives'.

Joe Ebierbing and his wife Tookoolito had had a long association with the AGS and particularly with the explorations of Charles Hall; they were staged with Hall at AGS Arctic meetings and throughout the U.S. East Coast and Europe in the 1860s. While Hall was never one to diminish the important role they played on his expeditions, he was also careful not to undermine their "savage" appeal with American audiences. Though they wore western clothing in everyday life, for instance, Hall requested them to appear on stage in sealskin suits, carrying bows and arrows, fish spears, and with barking dogs in full harness. "Only after this dramatic introduction did Tookoolito and Ebierbing demonstrate their less 'savage' side, bantering with surprised audiences in British English."[80] Charles Daly and Joe Ebierbing had been close associates for years. Daly referred to Ebierbing and Tookoolito as his "old friends." At the 1874 Arctic meeting honoring the return of the *Polaris*, they were publicly credited with keeping the crew alive on the ice floe.[81] Ebierbing was also a guest at Daly's house on several occasions, and Maria Daly wrote about one such visit in her diary, describing Ebierbing as "much more civilized and more of a natural gentleman than many calling himself such."[82] At these dinners Joe Ebierbing must have shared his knowledge of Arctic geography with Daly. At the Schwatka celebration the most Daly would announce publicly though was that the expedition had "cleared the reputation of a harmless people from an undeserved reproach." He was referring, evidently, to Joe Ebierbing's advice to him about the reliability of Thomas Barry's failed "translation" of Inuit testimony that led to the expedition in the first place.

As he did on many other such occasions, Joe Ebierbing provided the spectacle of a live Native "curiosity" on stage at the Schwatka celebration. Though he apparently did not address the audience directly, he wrote a statement explaining what he told Daly prior to the expedition, which was published in the AGS *Journal* along with the other speeches delivered that evening. His letter mostly reiterated his view that Thomas Barry was knowledgeable of the Inuit language and thus should have been considered by Daly to be a reliable source of information. Ebierbing wrote, "I know Thomas F. Barry … I have talked a good deal with him in Esquimaux. I can always understand him and he always understands me." Ebierbing's letter provided a plausible cross-cultural interpretation of why Schwatka would have been unsuccessful in obtaining information from Inuit informants about Franklin's remains: "The [Natives]," Ebierbing explained, "are not willing to tell much, because they think the white man believes that they killed the white men and might punish them. They might, therefore, fool the white man when talking to them."[83]

This tiny piece of archival evidence illustrates something important about AGS-Inuit relations. Whether Inuit eye-witness accounts of Franklin's notebooks etc. were "true" or falsified for Schwatka we may likely never know. But what is equally important is the public dramatization of Daly judiciously weighing the veracity of the "translation," via his detailed explanation of events and Joe Ebierbing's published letter. Ebierbing's public interpretation is significant because, as Shari Huhndorf argues, prevailing white discourse about Inuit men, while acknowledging that they were indispensable guides and hunters, for instance, also depicted them as simple, childish, and happy-go-lucky, feminized in relation to white men, serving as the object of a masculine fantasy of domination.[84] Clearly the AGS relationship to Ebierbing offered something a good deal more nuanced, as does Schwatka's and Hall's public statements that white men would need to emulate the Inuit in order to survive in the Arctic. (Interestingly, white Arctic explorers such as Schwatka, while trying to impress upon their audiences the horrors and difficulties of survival in the north, at the same time had to concede that Natives survived there perfectly well, even making it seem easy to do so: they hunted, knew the tricks for survival, knew what resources were required for keeping warm, and so on.[85])

Such appears then to be a rather nuanced but shrewdly civic-minded appreciation for Inuit ways on the part of AGS men – that is, until Robert Peary appeared on the scene. Most of the more infamous events of Peary's career occurred after Daly's death (in 1899), though in the last decade of Daly's life it was Peary's explorations that most attracted him to the Arctic. (Socially as well, Daly and Peary, and their wives, were good friends who spent a great deal of time together.[86]) Daly enlisted AGS help in funding Peary's expeditions to Greenland in 1891–1892 and two Peary rescue efforts, in 1895 and 1899. Peary's appeals brought out strong differences of opinion among AGS men, however, with the council finally agreeing to donate (only) $1,000 towards the efforts (and the same amount towards two Peary polar expeditions).[87] Just before his death Daly was made an executive member of the exclusive Peary Arctic Club, and by 1902, an AGS gold medal had been established in Daly's name, with Peary as its first recipient (Peary had already received the society's first Cullum Medal in 1896).

Much has been made of the controversy surrounding Peary's North Pole attempt, including that he likely faked his results.[88] More relevant for my purposes is that Peary subsequently came under severe attack for his racism – both in neglecting to give credit to Matthew Henson, the African-American who accompanied him on his North Pole attempt; as well as his patronizing and cruel treatment of Inuit men and women. While some explorers such as Charles Hall and Frederick Schwatka openly praised the skills and knowledge of their Inuit guides, others such as Peary treated Arctic peoples as "children," if not servants. By the end of the nineteenth century Peary would come to epitomize the sensationalism associated with Arctic exploration, oftentimes by amplifying Native primitiveness. Peary controlled all of the trade in the polar region for a time, claiming at an 1895 reception honoring him that the "children of the North" – upon whom he had so obviously depended upon for his own survival – were "raised to a condition of affluence" with the knives, guns, wood, harpoons, and better clothing that he had exchanged for their services. While some have argued that Inuit "did Peary's bidding" simply because he was cruel, this likely had more to do with economics – despite the cruelty rather than because of it.[89]

At the 1895 reception for Peary, Daly praised the explorer's career and accomplishments; Peary in turn, in his typical self-promoting style, likewise praised his own leadership abilities and masculine vitality: "Every individual in the party represents a drain upon the vital magnetism and force of the leader … when day after day of arduous struggle, of cold, of hunger, and discouragement, have reduced the powers, both physical and mental, the infusion of fresh courage into a desponding one requires [a] tangible transfer of the leader's stamina and nerve force."[90] That an individual whose reputation embodied the quintessential hyper-masculine explorer would subsequently assume the AGS presidency suggests the benefits Charles Daly enjoyed in cultivating the relationship, particularly owing perhaps to Daly's own declining "nerve force." And as Riffenburgh reminds us, Peary never contributed to any ethnographic or scientific advances, contrary to his hypocritical claims to have done so.[91]

Particularly due to his association with U.S. President Theodore Roosevelt, Peary's chief advocate, Peary's self-image would come to play a pivotal role in American self-identity as a world power when American expansionism abroad would become for a time more official foreign policy. Such "demanded" racial hierarchies of the type deployed by Peary, who used Inuit relationships as tokens of American presence, if not outright conquest in the Arctic region. Thus in the end, despite the sharp contrast with the scientific sovereignty Charles Daly had advocated for American presence in the Arctic, and his civic minded and judicious relationships with "credible" Inuit men and women in earlier decades, Daly's close association with Peary implicates him in this racist strategy for claims to the Arctic at the end of his career.

Conclusion

Robert Peary and the AGS Council would come to disagree over many things, including the relative value of reaching the North Pole. In time the South Pole would come to take on greater significance in AGS publications, transactions, and meetings, although celebrations for Peary's successes would continue well into the twentieth century (and even though the AGS Council declined taking an "official" position on the Peary-Cook controversy[92]). Robert Peary perhaps more so than any other figure affiliated with the AGS embodied the masculinist exploratory tradition of firsts. American expansion in the Arctic, to Charles Daly, departed considerably from this geographical tradition; his was a practical geography whose civic agenda was that of scientific advancement, yet which was at the same time dependent on a news cycle promoting those same sensationalistic firsts.

Analysis of the dramatic narratives of Arctic exploration is well-tread area for popular and scholarly attention, although intellectual histories of Arctic science and knowledge are only beginning to receive adequate attention.[93] Just in terms of narrative structure and language, in his *Arctic Dreams*, Barry Lopez outlines a number of ways that men and women within different eras and with different backgrounds and agendas have described the Arctic: as a place full or bereft of life; as enemy to be conquered or as benign place to love; as wild place that sagacious and incessantly tough men are meant to subdue, to survive in; and as a place with economic promise; among others.[94] Charles Daly's civic vision for the Arctic rested in between so many of these divides – between spaces of nationalism and multi-nationalism; between those of racial inclusiveness and racial hierarchies; and between those of the manly field explorer and the armchair "jurist-geographer."

This chapter offers ways of thinking about relationships among geographical societies, geographical knowledge, and American national civic enterprise in nineteenth-century Arctic space. Through newspapers, public Arctic meetings, and a host of other rhetorical and material strategies the AGS became associated in the public eye with heroic explorers in the field. Charles Daly and his cohorts staged events featuring the arrival and departures of glorified explorers and Inuit "witnesses" in carefully calculated ways. Yet, Daly's professional roles as judge, lawyer, and geographer effectively combined to match this focus with both a (limited) commercial approach to the Arctic and especially a scientific one. Daly's weighing the evidence on scientific issues of the day, and his frequent reference to his credentials to do so, was similar in strategy to that he put into play when arguing for the most "logical" location of the Isthmus Canal (Chapter 4), among so many others of his projects. His perspective seems to have been that developing infrastructure itself was part of building civic life – as he did in New York City, the American West, Central America, and in Africa – which is what likely gave him an appreciation for the sciences and polar research stations in particular.

In all of these ways Daly exerted a powerful influence over press coverage and thus the public culture of Arctic exploration more generally, and indeed, conveyed through such efforts his understanding of the importance of Arctic geography as a valuable civic and national enterprise. Though Daly's and the AGS's "commercial geography" more generally lacked a strong nationalistic component, underlying his civic agenda for Arctic exploration had a highly nationalistic end, casting polar research as disinterested science that would ensure national prestige and rank within the scientific community.

Endnotes

1 "A Dinner to Lieut. Greely," *New York Tribune*, 17 January 1886.
2 A.W. Greely, "Arctic Meeting at Chickering Hall, November 21st, 1884. Reception of Lieut. A.W. Greely, U.S. Army, and His Surviving Companions in the Exploration of the Arctic," *Journal of the American Geographical Society of New York* 16 (1884): 311–344; quote on 335.
3 Michael Robinson, *The Coldest Crucible: Arctic Exploration and American Culture* (Chicago: University of Chicago Press, 2006): 12.
4 Ibid., 34, 59.
5 John K. Wright, *Geography in the Making: The American Geographical Society 1851–1951* (New York: American Geographical Society, 1952): 101.
6 Ibid., 154.
7 AGS archives hold a number of valuable Arctic-related treasures, including Henry Grinnell's scrapbooks from the Franklin expeditions, 1851–1860. It is also an important repository for Robert Peary materials.
8 Wright, *Geography in the Making*, 14–70; Ernesto Ruiz, *Geography and Diplomacy: The American Geographical Society and the 'Geopolitical' Background of American Foreign Policy, 1848–1861* (PhD dissertation, Northern Illinois University, 1975): 134, 143–170; W.G. Ross, "Nineteenth-Century Exploration of the Arctic," in *North American Exploration, Volume 3: A Continent Comprehended*, ed. John L. Allen (Lincoln: University of Nebraska Press, 1997): 298–299; David Chapin, *Exploring Other Worlds: Margaret Fox, Elisha Kent Kane, and the Antebellum Culture of Curiosity* (Amherst: University of Massachusetts Press, 2004); Pierre Berton, *The Arctic Grail* (London: Viking, 1988); Fergus Fleming, *Ninety Degrees North: The Quest for the North Pole* (New York: Grove Press, 2001); and Arthur A. Brooks, *Index to the Bulletin of the American Geographical Society 1851–1915* (New York: American Geographical Society, 1918): vi.
9 The North-West passage existed, but it was impassable most of the time. Glyndwr Williams, *Voyages of Delusion: the Northwest Passage in the Age of Reason* (London: Harper Collins, 2002). E.g. E.K. Kane, "Paper on Access to an Open Polar Sea Along a North American Meridian," *Bulletin of the American Geographical and Statistical Society* 1 (2, 1853): 85–103.
10 So aptly named by Leonard F. Guttridge, *Ghosts of Cape Sabine: The Harrowing True Story of the Greely Expedition* (New York: Putnam, 2000).
11 I thank Michael Bravo for his incisive observations on this point.

12 Harold E. Hammond, *A Commoner's Judge: The Life and Times of Charles Patrick Daly* (Boston: Christopher Publishing House, 1954), 255. Charles P. Daly Correspondence and Papers, Vol. 27, Maria L. Daly Correspondence and Papers, Manuscripts and Archives Division, New York Public Library (NYPL), New York; entry dated 31 January 1872.

13 Richard C. Powell, "Science, Sovereignty and Nation: Canada and the Legacy of the International Geophysical Year, 1957–1958," *Journal of Historical Geography* 34 (2008): 618–638.

14 Hammond, *Commoner's Judge*, 279.

15 Ibid., 362.

16 Ibid., 309; Charles P. Daly, "Annual Address. Geographical Work of the World in 1877," *Journal of the American Geographical Society of New York* 10 (1878): 1–76.

17 Robinson, *Coldest Crucible*, 38–39.

18 I.I. Hayes, J.O. Buddington, George E. Tyson, H.C. Chester and William Morton, "Proceedings of the Arctic Meeting in Relation to the Voyage of the *Polaris*," *Journal of the American Geographical Society of New York* 6 (1874): 93–115; quotes on 93–95.

19 A.W. Greely, "Arctic Meeting at Chickering Hall," 311.

20 Charles P. Daly and W.H. Gilder, "An Expedition to the Northern Magnetic Pole," *Journal of the American Geographical Society of New York* 24 (1892): 215–261, quote on 259. Beau Riffenburgh, *The Myth of the Explorer: The Press, Sensationalism, and Geographical Discovery* (London: Bellhaven Press, 1993): 111–112 explains that the proposed expedition never got off the ground. Gilder accompanied Schwatka on his search for Franklin remains in 1878–1880.

21 Riffenburgh, ibid., 57. Robinson, *Coldest Crucible*, 10–11, makes a similar argument.

22 Charles P. Daly, "Annual Address. Geographical Work of the World in 1878 & 1879," *Journal of the American Geographical Society of New York* 12 (1880): 1–107; see 32. Also see Leonard Guttridge, *Icebound* (New York: Paragon, 1988).

23 "The Jeannette: Judge Daly's Appeal for a Search Vessel," *New York Herald*, 27 January 1881. See Hammond, *Commoner's Judge*, 315–317, for a full account.

24 Daly's letter was published in the 27 January 1881 *New York Herald*, "Editorial: Relief of the Jeanette." Also see the *Herald*, same date, "The Jeanette: Judge Daly's Appeal for a Search Vessel"; "The Jeannette's Peculiar Ice Perils" and "Relief for the Jeanette: Prompt Action of the Senate Naval Committee," *New York Herald*, 3 February 1881; "Arctic Search Expedition: Passage of Mr. McPherson's Bill by the Senate," *New York Herald*, 5 February 1881.

25 Riffenburgh, *Myth of the Explorer*, 3, 19–22, 56.

26 Charles Hall was associated with Horace Greely's *Tribune*, and Schwatka himself later became a "professional adventurer" for the *New York Times*, *New York World*, and *New York Ledger*. The later Cook-Peary controversy also lined up behind these two main newspapers: *Herald* (Cook) and *Times* (Peary). Riffenburgh, *Myth of the Explorer*, 111, calls Schwatka one of the first "mercenaries" of exploration, a man who would travel anywhere if he had sufficient financial incentive. Also see Schwatka's biography in Jonathan Dore, *Encyclopedia of the Arctic* (London: Routledge, 2005): 1847–1849.

Gilder had ignored Rae's and Hall's, among others, extensive living among Native Inuit.

27 As Riffenburgh, ibid., 38, argues for the RGS's Sir Roderick Murchison, he "helped promote public interest in not only science and exploration, but in the images of new lands … he served as a creator of the heroic stature of the explorers, and as a mediator of their myths."

28 American Geographical Society, Society Meeting Minutes (1854–1915). Vol. 27. New York: AGS.

29 Richard Vaughan, *The Arctic: A History* (Dover, NH: Alan Sutton Publishing Inc, 1994), see especially 85–86, 120, 130–133, 244–254; and Michael Bravo, "Geographies of Exploration and Improvement: William Scoresby and Arctic Whaling, 1782–1822," *Journal of Historical Geography* 32 (2006): 512–538. Harvested train oil was used in soap manufacture; as an additive in leather and textiles; and provided energy for lighting of oil lamps, among others. Baleen or whalebone was used for hats, harps, furniture, and hair brushes. See Philip Steinberg, *The Social Construction of the Ocean* (Cambridge: Cambridge University Press, 2001) for a useful discussion of the transition from mercantilist to industrial capitalism in ocean space.

30 The fur trade in the non-Russian Arctic and sub-Arctic is mainly history of the Hudson's Bay Company and Royal Greenland Trading company; beaver as well as furs from seals and otters were sought, as was gold, coal, oil, gas, and fossil ivory. See Ross, "Nineteenth-Century Exploration of the Arctic," 311–316.

31 Vaughn, *The Arctic*, 170; Fleming, *Ninety Degrees North*, 9.

32 Hayes et al., "Proceedings of Arctic Meeting" (1874): 95.

33 Isaac I. Hayes and Paul Du Chaillu, "The Norse Meeting; Iceland and Lapland," *Journal of the American Geographical Society of New York* 6 (1874): 227–232; quote on 227–228.

34 Charles P. Daly, "Annual Address. Subject: The Geographical Work of the World in 1872," *Journal of the American Geographical Society of New York* 4 (1873): 63–188; see 92–94.

35 Daly, "Annual Address" 12 (1880): 35–39.

36 Bravo, "Geographies of Exploration and Improvement," 519, 522–525.

37 David Lambert, "'Taken Captive by the Mystery of the Great River': Towards an Historical Geography of British Geography and Atlantic Slavery," *Journal of Historical Geography* 35 (2009): 44–65.

38 David Livingstone, *Putting Science in Its Place: Geographies of Scientific Knowledge* (Chicago: University of Chicago Press, 2003): 40–41; his discussion is after Cuvier's analysis of Alexander von Humboldt.

39 Dorinda Outram, "New Spaces in Natural History," in *Cultures of Natural History*, eds. Nicholas Jardine, James A. Secord and Emma C. Spary (Cambridge: Cambridge University Press, 1996): 249–265; quote on 262.

40 Helen M. Rozwadowski and David K. Van Keuren, eds. *The Machine in Neptune's Garden: Historical Perspectives on Technology and the Marine Environment* (Sagamore Beach, MA: Watson Publishing International, 2004).

41 Robinson, *Coldest Crucible*, 4–6.

42 George Corner, *Doctor Kane of the Arctic Seas* (Philadelphia: Temple University Press, 1972); Oscar Villarejo, *Dr. Kane's Voyage to the Polar Lands* (Philadelphia: University of Philadelphia Press, 1965); Ruiz, *Geography and Diplomacy*, 152; Kane, "Access to Open Polar Sea"; "Transactions of the Society," *Bulletin of the American Geographical and Statistical Society* II (January 1857): 4.

43 See for instance, E. Tammiksaar, N.G. Sukhova, and I.R. Stone, "Hypothesis versus Fact: August Petermann and Polar Research," *Arctic* 52 (3, 1999): 237–244. Also see M.F. Maury, "Annual Address," *Bulletin of the American Geographical and Statistical Society* I (III, 1854): 3–31; Lieut. Bent, "The Japanese Gulf Stream," *Bulletin of the American Geographical and Statistical Society* II (1856): 203–213.

44 Ruiz, *Geography and Diplomacy*, 159 and Wright, *Geography in the Making*, 56. I.I. Hayes, *The Open Polar Sea: A Narrative of a Voyage of Discovery Towards the North Pole* (London, Sampson Low, Son and Marston, 1867). Hayes reference in Charles P. Daly, "Annual Address. Subject: Review of the Events of the Year, and Recent Explorations and Theories for Reaching the North Pole," *Journal of the American Geographical Society of New York* 2 (2, 1870): lxxxiii–cxxci; see ciii.

45 Hayes et al., "Proceedings of Arctic Meeting" (1874): 96.

46 Daly, "Annual Address" 2 (2, 1870): cxii–cxx.

47 Charles P. Daly, "Annual Address: The Geographical Work of the World for 1875," *Journal of the American Geographical Society of New York* 7 (1875): 31–92; see 59–60. John Symmes theorized that the earth was hollow and the North Pole offered a way into habitable space within.

48 Charles P. Daly, "Annual Address. Subject: The Geographical Work of the World in 1874," *Journal of the American Geographical Society of New York* 6 (1874): 53–92; see 76.

49 H.W. Howgate, "1878 Arctic Meeting at Chickering Hall. Plan for Exploration of the Arctic Regions," *Journal of the American Geographical Society of New York* 10 (1878): 276–298; see 277–278. The AGS subsequently sponsored a meeting on polar magnetism in 1892.

50 Daly, "Annual Address" 2 (2, 1870): cxxv, cxxci. M. Gustave Lambert, "L'expedition au Pole Nord: Assemblee Generale du 20 Decembre 1867," *Bulletin de la Societe de Geographie* (Paris: Au Siège de la Societe, 1868). Lambert argued that the pole would allow "accurate geodetic measurement of the precise shape of our globe, observations fixing the power of the pendulum to measure heights; the ascertaining the amount of solar heat received by the earth, and locating the point of greatest cold; solving the important problem of the circulation of the atmosphere and the currents of the sea; and the clearing up of many meteorological, magnetic, and botanical questions"; as quoted in T.B. Maury, "Polar Expeditions and its Hopes," *The Atlantic Monthly* 26 (Boston: Fields, Osgood & Co., 1870): 493; Vaughn, *The Arctic*, 187–188. Gustave Lambert also tried ballooning to the North Pole.

51 Howgate was not present at the meeting, so Wright's speculation, *Geography in Making*, 95, about the men shown in this image is likely incorrect: "On the platform from left to right: Lord Dufferin (speaking), Captain H.W. Howgate (?), Judge Daly, General Cullum (?), Dr I.I. Hayes." Greely, who read Howgate's paper, is likely the

figure on the far right. Howgate, "1878 Arctic Meeting," 276, notes that among the 20 "prominent gentlemen upon the stage were: Chief Justice Daly, Lord Dufferin, William Cullen Bryant, Paul B. Chailllu, Bayard Taylor, General George W. Cullum, Professor T. Sherry Hunt, Albert Bierstadt, Professor W. Wright Hawkes, Walton W. Evans, Francis A. Stout, Colonel C. Chaille Long (Bey), Chief Justice Curtis, Harlow M. Hoyt, Professor James T. Gardner, Luther R. Marsh, Samuel Sloan, William Remsen, Lieutenant Greeley, and Colonel William Ludlow, U.S.A."

52 Weyprecht only appears in Daly's reports for his explorations of Franz Josef Land; Daly, "Annual Address" 4 (1873): 95–96; "Annual Address" 6 (1874): 72–75; and "Annual Address" 7 (1875): 57.

53 Guttridge, *Ghosts of Cape Sabine*, 8–13.

54 Guttridge, ibid., 19–20, 25–26. Howgate's move to "win Congressional support" was the paper he read before the AGS, 31 January 1878. Box 1, Correspondence, AGS archives, New York, holds a thick file of letters from Howgate to Daly. At this point the plan was awaiting final action of the U.S. House of Representatives. Howgate was later accused of embezzling funds from the Signal Service, and after 13 years as fugitive served time in the Albany penitentiary. For news coverage of the Howgate meeting, see "The Geographical Society: Reception of the Earl of Dufferin at Chickering Hall" and "Arctic Exploration: Captain Howgate's Plan," both *New York Herald*, 1 February 1878; "The Geographical Society: Reception to Lord Dufferin," *New York Times*, 1 February 1878; "Lord Dufferin and the Geographical Society" and "Captain Howgate's Plan," both *The World*, 1 February 1878.

55 Barry Lopez, *Arctic Dreams* (New York: Vintage Books, 1986), 370, depicts the Greely expedition as "one of the most shameful episodes in American history," particularly owing to the disparagement heaped on Greely by the very politicians who would not underwrite a serious effort to rescue him; "heroic attempts did not account for much against unqualified success in America."

56 Riffenburgh, *Myth of the Explorer*, 103–106; Lopez, ibid., 368. Greely was also looking for survivors of De Long's *Jeanette* expedition.

57 Robinson, *Coldest Crucible*, 84–85.

58 Greely, "Arctic Meeting," 312.

59 "Judge Daly's Beliefs and Reception to Lieut. Greely," *New York Tribune*, 22 November 1884. Also see, "The Open Polar Sea: Chief Justice Believes it Does Not Exist," *New York Herald*, 21 July 1884; "Reception to Lieut. Greely," *The World*, 22 November 1884; "Lieutenant Greely Feted," *New York Herald*, 17 January 1886. The writer was evidently quoting Henry Morton Stanley in his complaints.

60 Charles P. Daly, review, "Of Three Years of Arctic Service by Lt. A.W. Greeley," *New York Herald*, 14 February 1886. Daly's original hand-written review, Daly Papers, Box 9, NYPL. Also see Hammond, *Commoner's Judge*, 359.

61 "Open Polar Sea," *New York Herald*, 21 July 1884; also see Hammond, ibid., 357.

62 "The Arctic Expedition," *New York Herald*, 16 October 1872.

63 Daly, "Annual Address," 6 (1874): 72–74.

64 Bravo and Sorlin, *Narrating the Arctic*, 7.

65 While demanding government action in Arctic exploration, Daly was a free-market, private enterprise ideologue when it came to other large-scale technological projects, such as with building the Nicaragua Canal (Chapter 4). Quite obviously personal commercial gains were at stake with the latter, but not the former.

66 Daly, "Annual Address," 2 (2, 1870): cxxci. And again in 1873 he expressed hope that the U.S. government would not allow "another nation to accomplish what we have done so much to attain; but that … this great geographical achievement will be the reward of American enterprise, and that the first flag which floats over the pole will be our national ensign." "Annual Address" 6 (1874): 67–68.

67 Michael Bravo, "Preface: Legacies of Polar Science," in *Legacies and Change in Polar Sciences: Historical, Legal and Political Reflections on the International Polar Year*, eds. Jessica M. Shadian and Monica Tennberg (Farnham: Ashgate, 2009): xiii–xvi; see xvi.

68 Michael T. Bravo, "Arctic Science, Nation Building and Citizenship," in *Northern Exposure: Peoples, Powers and Prospects in Canada's North*, eds. Frances Abele, Thomas J. Courchene, F. Leslie Seidle and France St.-Hilaire (Montreal: The Institute for Research on Public Policy, 2009): 141–168; see 141–142, 149–151; Powell, "Science, Sovereignty and Nation," 633–638.

69 Charles P. Daly, "Annual Address: The Geographical Work of the World for 1875," *Journal of the American Geographical Society of New York* 7 (1875): 31–92; see 52–53.

70 "Shall We Have a North Pole Expedition? An Appeal to Congress," and "The Polar Mystery: An Appropriation for Its Exploration to be Made by Congress," *New York Herald*, 1 March 1875.

71 Charles P. Daly, "Annual Address. The Geographical Work of the World in 1876," *Journal of the American Geographical Society of New York* 8 (1876): 45–95; see 64–69, 76.

72 "Arctic Meeting of Chickering Hall, October 28th, 1880. Reception for Lieut. Frederick Schwatka and his Associates of the Franklin Search Party of 1878, 1879 and 1880," *Journal of the American Geographical Society of New York* 12 (1880): 237–296; patrons are listed on 240; Morison and Brown's fate discussed on 241–242. Bennett supplied astronomical instruments, several merchants of the city supplied stores, and "Messrs. Brevoort, Herrman, Bernheimer and [Daly] made up a sum of money to pay the main part of the cost of the outfit." Hammond, *Commoner's Judge*, n13, 427, notes "replies to Daly's solicitations for funds" among AGS correspondence. "Honor to Schwatka," *New York Herald*, 29 October 1880.

73 "Arctic Meeting of 1880," 237–243, includes published speeches or written statements by Admiral McClintock, Frederick Schwatka, Isaac I. Hayes, Thomas Barry, Joseph Eberling [sic], and others of the British Admiralty. The Franklin search had hitherto been ended in 1859 when McClintock found artifacts, human remains, and written records of the expedition on the shores of King William Island that confirmed the fate of the missing men. *Oxford Companion to Canadian History* 45: 606.

74 Joe and Hannah Ebierbing (as they were known in English) had been living in New Bedford, Connecticut at the time, in the home purchased for them by Charles Hall. Joe had become a carpenter and farmhand, and Hannah a seamstress of furs. Their child

Punna died in 1875 at age 11 (as well as another of their children), and Hannah a year later, at age 38.

75 See, among others, William H. Gilder, *Schwatka's Search: Sledging in the Arctic in Quest of the Franklin Records* (1881).

76 "Seeing the Eothen Sail," *New York Sun*, 20 June 1878; "The Franklin Search Party," *New York Herald*, 20 June 1878; "Good-By to the Eothen," *The World*, 20 June 1878.

77 Daly, "Annual Address" 12 (1880): 39. Schwatka's letter to Daly, ibid., 107.

78 "Arctic Meeting 1880," 256. Also see "The American Franklin Search Expedition," *The Illustrated London News*, 1 January 1881 and under the same title, *Harper's Weekly*, 4 December 1880. H. Klutschak, *Overland to Starvation Cove: With the Inuit in Search of Franklin 1878–1880* (Toronto: University of Toronto Press, with translation and editing by William Barr of Als Eskimo unter den Eskimos, 1987).

79 "Honor to Schwatka," *New York Herald*, 29 October 1880; The London *Times*, 17 October 1879 as quoted in "Arctic Meeting of 1880," 242; ibid., 256.

80 Robinson, *Coldest Crucible*, 73–74; Untitled article, *New York Herald*, 6 November 1862; and Loomis, *Weird and Tragic Shores*, 149–152.

81 See for instance, Sheila Nickerson, *Midnight to the North: The Untold Story of the Inuit Woman Who Saved the Polaris Expedition* (New York: Putnam, 2002) and H.G. Jones, "Teaching the Explorers: Some Inuit Contributions to Arctic Discoveries," *Polar Geography* 26 (1, 2002): 4–20.

82 Daly Papers, Maria L. Daly Correspondence and Papers, NYPL, Vol. 27, diary entry for 13 June 1870. Also see Hammond, *Commoner's Judge*, 207.

83 "Arctic Meeting 1880," 279–281.

84 Shari M. Huhndorf, "Nanook and His Contemporaries: Imagining Eskimos in American Culture, 1897–1922," *Critical Inquiry* 27 (1, 2000): 122–148; Native men provided a counterpoint to western masculine ideals, but also embodied them when placed alongside Native women.

85 Nickerson, *Midnight to the North.*

86 Hammond, *Commoner's Judge*, 361–362.

87 AGS Council Minutes indicate controversial discussions over the amount of funds to devote to Peary's expeditions in February and March 1891; see for instance minutes from 6 March 1891. Also see Lyle Dick, "Peary, Robert," *Encyclopedia of the Arctic* (London: Routledge, 2005): 1600–1601.

88 Lisa Bloom, *Gender on Ice* (Minneapolis: University of Minnesota Press, 1993). Both Peary and Frederick Cook claimed to have discovered the Pole in 1909. "A polling of the AGS was made soon after Cook's claim, to decide how they might respond to the counter claim of their former President and councilman … The council decided to remain impartial" (Wright, *Geography in the Making*, 176). Also see Neil Smith, *American Empire: Roosevelt's Geographer and the Prelude to Globalization* (Berkeley: University of California Press, 2003): 83–110; and Wally Herbert, *The Noose of Laurels* (London: Hodder & Stroughton, 1989).

89 R.E. Peary, "The Reception of Mr. Peary," *Journal of the American Geographical Society of New York* 27 (4, 1895): 373–384; see 379–380. Huhndorf, "Nanook and His Contemporaries," 122–137.

90 "Reception of Mr. Peary," 373, 381. Among scores of other Peary studies Bloom, *Gender on Ice,* provides a useful analysis of his troubled gender and race relationships.
91 Riffenburgh, *Myth of the Explorer*, 168–169.
92 E.g., Smith, *American Empire*, 83–110.
93 Bloom, *Gender on Ice*; Michael Bravo, "Ethnological Encounters," in *Cultures of Natural History*, 339–357; David Chapin, *Exploring Other Worlds;* Bruce Henderson, *Fatal North: Adventure and Survival Aboard the USS* Polaris (New York: Signet, 2001); Richard Parry, *Trial by Ice: The True Story of Murder and Survival on the 1871* Polaris *Expedition* (New York: Ballentine Books, 2001); W.G. Ross, "Nineteenth-Century Exploration of the Arctic"; John Wiley, "Earthly Poles: The Antarctic Voyages of Scott and Amundsen," in *Postcolonial Geographies*, eds. Alison Blunt and Cheryl McEwan (New York: Continuum, 2002): 169–183; Michael Bravo and Sverker Sorlin, eds. *Narrating the Arctic: A Cultural History of Nordic Scientific Practices* (Canton, MA: Science History Publications, 2002); Robinson, *Coldest Crucible*.
94 Lopez, *Arctic Dreams*, 373.

Chapter 6
"Geographical Exploration is Commercial Progress": In the Congo

Introduction

Not unlike many men of his professional milieu, but also unlike the more peripatetic AGS Presidents after him, Charles Daly himself never set foot in most of the places about which he studied, lectured, and became an authoritative expert. This was true for the far-flung and distant such as the Arctic and North Pole, as well as locations relatively closer to New York City such as Central America. In this chapter I turn to Daly's influential armchair explorations of distant Africa in the nineteenth century. The chapter revolves around an issue largely ignored or simply off the map of most histories of American geography – the role of geographical knowledge and practice complicit with colonization of Central Africa's Congo region. While many scholars have examined representations of Africa in popular nineteenth-century American geographical media such as textbooks, maps, and magazines; and/or have studied the relative insignificance, especially of Central Africa, to American consumers of geography until the early twentieth century;[1] this chapter outlines a more concrete, if you will, diplomatic and business relationship between the AGS and Central African exploration, colonization, and development decades earlier.

From its beginning AGS men took a keen interest in Africa, closely tracking the whereabouts of European explorers and filling in their maps with ethnographic detail and resource availability supplied by them. Topics finding their way into AGS lecture rooms and publications in the second half of the nineteenth century ranged widely, from "A Description of Natal" in 1854; to "The Soudan and the Valley of the White Nile" in 1874; to "The Resources of Central Africa [and] Their Development by a Railway" in 1881; to "Districts Where White Men May Live" in 1897.[2] In all, I count over 80 (very roughly about a sixth) of the society's substantive journal articles to be about Africa during Charles Daly's presidential tenure, primarily in the form of reports of physical geography descriptions, maps, and tables of resource availability.[3] As AGS President, Charles Daly amply and systematically reported on explorations throughout the African continent in all of his annual addresses from 1869 to 1888, distinguished by region – North, South, East, West, and Central Africa – and/or by nation originating the expeditions. He also explicitly promoted a type of commercial colonization of Central Africa, by both Europe and the U.S., in a number of lectures and meetings. To the mid-1870s Daly primarily relayed explorers' findings, albeit with an eye towards stimulating interest in that continent among his many constituents. From 1876 onwards, though, he became much more of an active participant in developments in the Congo. This chapter thus takes as a focal point a little-acknowledged fact that the United States, via the work of Daly and his AGS colleagues, actively participated in the colonization of the Congo region in the later nineteenth century.[4]

Belgian King Leopold II's ruthless colonization of the African Congo (subsequently called Zaire, and today the Democratic Republic of the Congo) is a familiar subject of academic inquiry as well as more popular scrutiny. Among geographers, for instance, Felix Driver describes the "militant geography" involved in the nineteenth-century explorations of Central Africa by Henry Morton Stanley in his capacity as Leopold's man on the ground. Popular writers such as Adam Hochschild in his *King Leopold's Ghost* (1998) also have brought to a wide public audience the story of Leopold's countless atrocities, including 10 million deaths in his attempt to establish what amounted to his own private colony in 1885 and the personal fortune he hoped to make from harvest of its wild rubber and ivory. Leopold left arguably the worst legacy of all European colonial regimes in the late nineteenth-century Africa,[5] though what is far less often understood is U.S. participation in his scheme.

In this chapter I examine Charles Daly's "African geography" generally; and then specifically with respect to his ties to Leopold, Leopold's men, and explorers of Africa, particularly Henry Morton Stanley and Paul Belloni du Chaillu. Stanley's reputation is well known. Daly's close relationship with Franco-American explorer Du Chaillu especially deserves scrutiny as he received a great deal of personal patronage from Daly and his wife Maria, and in fact came to live with Charles after Maria's death. Both Stanley and Du Chaillu undoubtedly influenced Daly's opinions on Africa.

As with his imaginative geographies of other global destinations, the New York Press closely followed Daly's lectures, reports, and events relating to Africa, particularly during 1870s and 1880s. The Belgian king heavily recruited Daly's support and in turn Daly, along with the help of other principals such as Henry S. Sanford, one-time U.S. minister to Belgium, provided the influential American arm of Leopold's organization (developed below). Daly provided the platform for American support of Leopold's plan via AGS meetings, his own substantial lectures, the hosting of explorers, through AGS publications, and via lobbying of the New York business community and U.S. government. Daly and Sanford effectively won the approbation of the mercantile community in New York by lobbying the Chamber of Commerce, for instance; and won U.S. recognition for Leopold's plan in Washington by lobbying the Congress and President.

Though they did not materialize as expected, the commercial advantages Leopold promised to American businessmen played an important role in Daly's African geography. Key moments in the narrative surround the resolutions passed by the U.S. Congress that Daly helped write, as well as the deals struck among the American mercantile community at the 1886 Berlin conference. Also relevant were the close ties between the "Congo question" and the "Negro question" in the

U.S. following the Civil War. U.S. race relations in the era of Reconstruction were unfolding on many complex levels, and Leopold's plan (among others) seemed to offer a "safety value" solution to the problem of freed slaves, popular especially among southern legislators.

Was Charles Daly simply seduced by the charms and notoriety of famous explorers and a European king who would raise him to the status of a "player" in nineteenth-century international relations rather than a mere observer of the action? Why did this gentle judge align himself so enthusiastically with Leopold and the likes of Henry Morton Stanley, a controversial figure regarded with suspicion if not outright disdain by some geographers of the day, most notably some influential RGS men? To answer such questions my discussion below begins by outlining general AGS exploratory interest in African geography for its first couple of decades, then moving on to the shift of interest towards Central Africa, the slave trade, and mercantilist and commercial geographies that came into play *ca.* 1876 when Leopold approached Daly with his colonization plan.

The AGS's African Geography

Scholars have generalized the period 1851–1878 as the "golden age" of European exploration of Africa, one that would quickly usher in the subsequently ruthless "scramble" for colonial or imperial control of Africa from 1884–1891.[6] Taking the long view, the relationship of the American Geographical Society to Africa maps roughly onto this division. The society's interest in Africa began mid-century with general lectures and published articles about European explorers' physical geography findings and mappings of lakes and rivers, particularly of East and Central Africa, and then gravitated from the late 1870s onwards towards a much sharper focus on African colonization, resource potential, and the slave trade of the same region (practiced for centuries prior by Portuguese from the West Coast and Swahili "Arabs" from Tanzania). Such a path might seem surprising for an American geographical society with no explicit or "official" ties to African exploration or colonization in the nineteenth century, unlike its ties to other parts of the globe and also unlike that of its British, French, and other European counterparts. Moreover, formal U.S. federal government ties to Africa during Reconstruction was also limited primarily to attempts to develop a colony in Liberia for freed American slaves (a process that would lend support to the geographical projects of the AGS). Of course, American economic and political ties to Africa predated such interests for centuries, particularly with respect to the slave trade but also with crop and mineral trade and resource extraction.[7] In what follows I carve out a small piece of that story to illuminate the development and nature of American geographical knowledge of primarily Central Africa in the later nineteenth century, and its increasingly close ties to U.S. trade, commerce, and politics.

In its early years some of the AGS's most noteworthy published commentary on Africa featured the letters from Scottish explorer and missionary David Livingstone, tracing his search for the source of the Nile River and eventual entry into the Congo River basin. Letters from Livingstone were written directly into the society's meeting minutes, and in fact the first (1852) issue of the *Journal* includes a letter from Livingstone written from the "Banks of the Zonga, October, 1851."[8] A number of other letters from Livingstone appeared in the *Journal* until his death in 1873. Livingstone was evidently well aware of the circulation of his works in America, and took seriously his role as elected AGS corresponding member, writing to the society periodically about his travels and findings.[9] Livingstone's explorations were to find their way into the American popular imagination when *New York Herald* publisher (and AGS fellow) James Gordon Bennett created his acclaimed media stunt by sending Henry Morton Stanley to rescue Livingstone from the "dark continent" in 1869–1871. The AGS offered its formal credibility to the venture. While in 1870 Charles Daly had reported having received "official communication from Dr. Livingstone, under his own hand, putting at rest all questions of his safety"; by 1872 Daly appeared as keen as any of his contemporaries to express his pride in Stanley's "energy, intrepidity, and capacity" in locating Livingstone.[10] (Bennett had also bankrolled De Long's *Jeanette* attempt at the North Pole in 1879; see Chapter 5.)

The Africa sections of Charles Daly's annual addresses up to 1876 basically summarized the findings of German, British, Dutch, Portuguese, Italian, and French explorers, and such findings were also often published verbatim in the society's *Journal* as letters or reprinted lectures. Central Africa would become the centerpiece of Daly's African discourse, but reports from all parts of Africa were systematically if briefly treated in his annual addresses, presumably when such were supplied to him. Thus in 1872 African exploration appeared under such specific headings as "Dr. Schweinfurth's Explorations West of the White Nile," "M. Grandidier's Explorations in Madagascar," and "Ancient Ruins Discovered by Karl Mauch," in eastern Africa.[11] In 1873 Daly reported on French explorations in Algeria, Morocco, and in the Sahara; tribal tensions in West Africa; and German expeditions in Gaboon [sic], locating trading outposts along the coasts and interior.[12]

But it was the play or replay of the British explorations of John Speke, Richard Burton, James Grant, David Livingstone, V.L. Cameron, Samuel Baker and others whose mappings of the great hydrological systems of Central Africa that stimulated Daly's popular and business geographical imagination most – those invested in locating the source of the Nile, identifying the number of large lakes and their coastlines, and determining the length, depth, and networks of the large river systems as they crossed the continent, especially of the Congo and the Nile. The Africa section of Daly's 1874 annual address was devoted to Livingstone's one-time assistant, British naval officer Verney L. Cameron's journeys around the waterways of Lake Tanganyika and attempts to connect the Lualaba with the Congo: "If [Cameron] should be successful," Daly declared,

> we may next hear of his returning through the Congo to the western coast; and, if he effects this, it will be one of the most important geographical achievements that has been accomplished in Africa, and place his name in the very front rank of African explorers.

Cameron did "discover" the Lualaba as the main stream of the Congo River, and became the first European to cross equatorial Africa, although it would be Henry Morton Stanley who accomplished this via the Congo River route.

Although relaying reports supplied by European explorers from their work in North, South, East, and West Africa (identified as such) gave the AGS something of a connection to Africa, it was Daly's and other AGS men's own research, studies of the society's map collection, and independent calculations – identifying and mapping the length, depth, direction, connections, and flows of the rivers and lakes of Africa – that would give them more of a credentialed foothold in the continent, akin to James MacQueen's armchair discovery of the Niger River system illustrated by David Lambert.[13] With a great deal of knowledge about maps from antiquity, for instance, one of Daly's conclusions about the lakes of Central Africa in 1875 was that contemporary explorers were re-discovering what geographers such as Ptolemy knew centuries earlier:

> [Several years ago] after the discovery of the Victoria Niyanza by Speke, and of the Albert Niyanza by Baker, you may remember that I expressed the belief that these lakes were merely re-discoveries … The view I then expressed was not at first very favorably received, which led me to investigate further, and I found that these two lakes were not only known to Ptolemy, or to his cartographer Agathodaemon, but that the Arabian geographers from the ninth to the eleventh centuries, represented on their maps as the source of the Nile a large lake upon the equator, in exactly the same position as the Victoria Niyanza.[14]

Daly's interest and study of such topics helped create a collegial and spirited atmosphere of geographical inquiry at the AGS. Other members, such as Archibald Russell, weighed in on similar topics. Russell deduced that Livingstone had erroneously concluded that the Congo and Nile rivers connected to form a large lake, before this had been proven in the field. Russell's correct calculations appeared in the *Journal* for 1876, advancing the theory that the Lualaba represented the upper Congo.[15]

While such physical geography questions primarily occupied Daly and AGS men during this "golden age" of mapping Africa, Daly would gradually shift attention to Africa's commercial potential, and to the slave trade. This move coincided with general shifts in the post-Civil War American economic landscape, beginning in the 1870s, when profits from eastern manufacturing industries began to decline and unemployment increased. Commercial expansion abroad – the search for resources and markets abroad in which to directly invest – was seen as the way of both increasing trade and the returns on investments. American expansionism in the later decades of the nineteenth century would be characterized by such direct foreign economic intervention; a desire to expand the American economy beyond its territorial boundaries, but without military or political conquest of colonial outposts that would require administration.[16] Daly's African geography resonated well with this model.

"Exploration leads to cultivation," he observed in 1874: "What exploration has accomplished in Africa may be judged by a single fact. In 1850 the area of cultivated land in Egypt was 2,000,000 of acres, in 1874 it was 5,000,000."[17] He described Central Africa in 1875 as "remarkable for the sublimity of its scenery, the picturesqueness of its valley and plains, its many rivers, its great fertility, and for its salubrity, being one of the healthiest parts of Africa."[18] Cameron's progress by 1876 indicated to Daly the commercial and mercantile advantages of the lake region and valleys of the Congo, Lualaba, and Zambesi rivers, ubiquitous with large copper mines, coal, cinnabar, tin resources, cultivated crops of sugar cane, rice growing in "wild luxuriance," wheat, cotton, and hemp. Daly emphasized Cameron's observation that "the whole country, however, was at present a vast slave-field."[19] Thus while the potential of mineral and agricultural production would become the principal entrée for AGS, and state-sponsored American, involvement in Africa, it would also be one intimately if only ostensibly connected to the trade in human lives. I take up this subject in detail below. For now I would simply point out that AGS men argued that "geography" would be the science to morally uplift Africa out of the depths of slavery, because it would lead to commercial development and organized trade. Daly concluded his 1877 annual address stating that, "the world is now fully awake to the importance of this [geographical] work, and pervaded by the sentiment that there are no people too remote or too degraded to feel the influence and benefit by the results of geographical inquiry."[20]

Seductive Geographies: Getting Established in the Congo

Charles Daly first broached the topic of the African slave trade with his geographical audiences in 1872, asserting that "the opening of the large region of Central Africa to civilization – a country the great value of which is now becoming apparent – depends more upon the suppression of this infamous debasing traffic than upon anything else."[21] The development of Daly's discourse on African slavery, and how he managed the geographical knowledge associated with it, sits rather ambivalently alongside his anti-abolition, more instrumentalist view of slave holding in the United States. Daly's opposition to the African slave trade was cast in moral and "developmental" arguments. Yet with respect to slavery in the U.S., like many elite American northerners (Democrats and Republicans alike), Daly opposed slavery on different grounds – on the overtly political grounds of keeping the Union together during the Civil War, which itself was based, if obliquely, on protecting northern economic interests and expansion. His opposition to the abolition movement was also in line with his personal devotion to the Irish cause in New York as freed slaves were the bane of Irish laborers (see Chapter 3). Yet the desire to help abolish the trade in slaves was the ostensible basis for Daly's affiliation with King Leopold's colonization plan for the Congo.

King Leopold II of Belgium was a monarch obsessed with a desire for his own colony, and Africa in the mid-1870s was a good place to look for one.[22] In 1876 Leopold called an international conference of leading African explorers, several eminent geographers, and heads of geographical societies in Great Britain, France, Germany, Italy, Russia, and the United States, to meet in Brussels to establish the International African Association (or AIA), superficially devoted to extending "civilization" into the heart of Africa to suppress or eradicate the slave trade. This organization, disguised as a philanthropic and scientific one, was the veneer covering Leopold's plan for profits and power that would be enabled only through subterfuge and bald manipulation of the international community as well as his own Belgian people.

As AGS President Charles Daly was invited to attend the Brussels meeting, but owing to his judicial duties, declined the invitation. The following month the King's assistant hand-delivered a letter to Daly in New York, asking him to form and head an American branch of Leopold's organization, to cooperate in establishing colonies in Africa.[23] Leopold wanted to first establish a permanent station in the East Coast of Africa, from which a chain of stations would be gradually extended into the interior. Deeply flattered by the attention of a European King, Daly enthusiastically responded to Leopold in a seven-page letter dated 28 November 1876, in which he wrote,

> I accept with great pleasure … [and] I look forward to more comprehensive, practical, and important results from the scheme which your Majesty has inaugurated, and if it shall have the success which I anticipate, your Majesty will be remembered hereafter, with Prince Henry and others, as among the benefactors of mankind.[24]

For the remainder of his life Daly enthusiastically supported Leopold's plans, through letter-writing, his annual addresses, published articles, special AGS meetings, and lectures to other institutions such as the New York Chamber of Commerce and U.S. Congress. Daly's role in Leopold's enterprise would be, ultimately, to publicly support and lobby for it, with the business community and federal government.

In his 1876 annual address Daly declared that, "I cannot speak in terms too eulogistic of the example set by this enlightened monarch in inaugurating this important movement."[25] Daly's address outlined the conclusions of the 1876 Brussels meeting, explaining the structure of Leopold's organization and its project for building posts across Central Africa. Daly reported that the King was made President of the organization, and himself, as geographical President, a member of the international committee, the "International Society for the Exploration and Civilization of Africa." This organization would be comprised of crown princes,

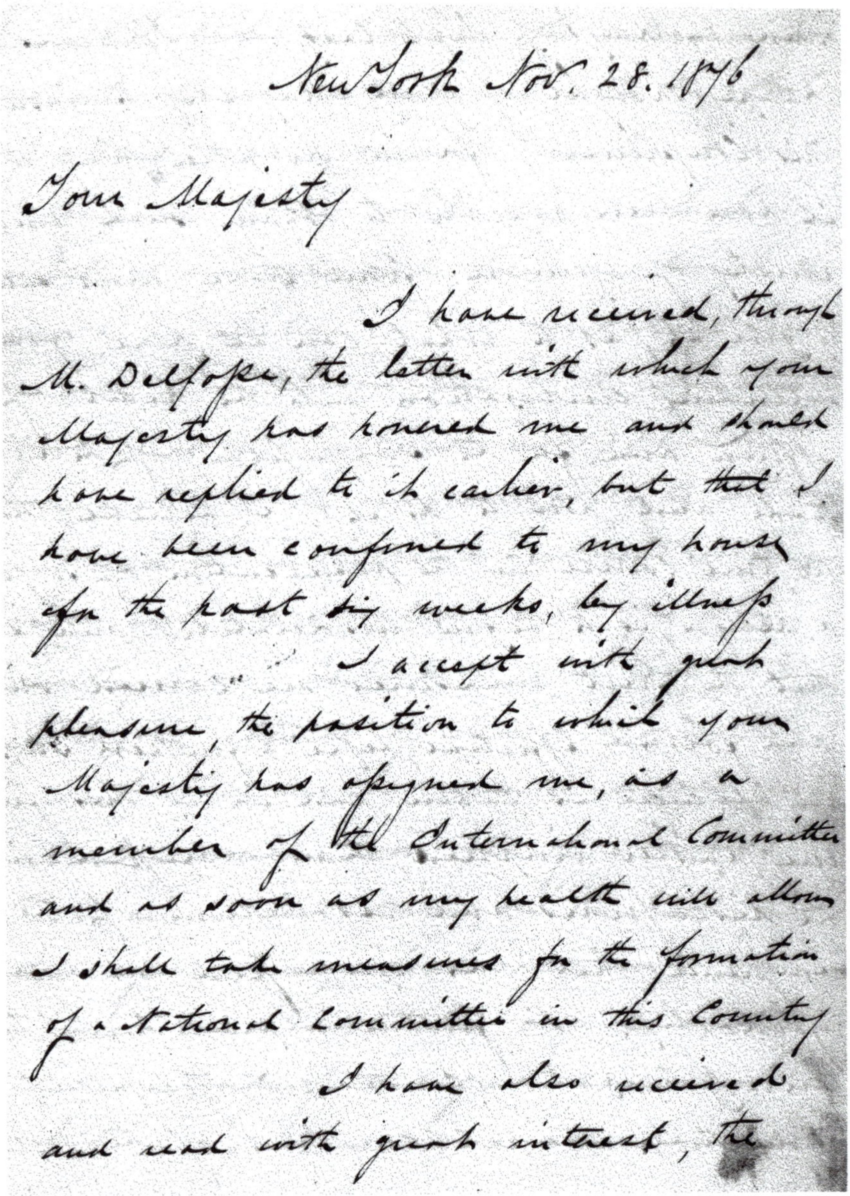

New York Nov. 28. 1876

Your Majesty

I have received, through
M. Delfosse, the letter with which your
Majesty has honored me and should
have replied to it earlier, but that I
have been confined to my house
for the past six weeks, by illness.
I accept with great
pleasure, the position to which your
Majesty has assigned me, as a
member of the International Committee
and as soon as my health will allow
I shall take measures for the formation
of a National Committee in this Country.
I have also received
and read with great interest, the

Figure 6.1 First page of Charles Daly's letter to King Leopold II of Belgium, 28 November 1876, accepting the King's request to head the American branch of the International African Association

Source: Charles P. Daly Papers, Box 5. Manuscripts and Archives Division, The New York Public Library, Astor, Lenox and Tilden Foundations.

geographers, and explorers, and with a name purposefully to be confused with others of Leopold's African organizations.[26] Daly explained also that he had complied with the King's request to form an American national committee of the international one. (Most such national committees never got off the ground, but the American one did.)[27] Daly received many positive responses from men he invited to join the American committee, mostly those with potential commercial interests in the Congo.[28]

Daly subsequently spent much of the first half of 1877 organizing the American branch of the association. He called an AGS meeting in May 1877 to explain in detail Leopold's plans. Present and speaking in favor of establishing the American branch were men such as Arnold Guyot, Paul Du Chaillu, and the abolitionist and African-American missionary to Liberia, Rev. Alexander Crummell. Leopold as well as those present expected Daly to become President of the American National committee, but he declined owing to his other duties. Instead, John Latrobe, a Baltimore lawyer and longtime President of the American Colonization Society (a group that "aided" free blacks in emigrating to Africa), accepted Daly's request to become President.[29] All spoke at the meeting in fervent support of Leopold's plan.

This meeting began with Daly's assessment of the geographical "obstacles" to commercial development in Africa, in comparison to America – its lack of harbors and bays, obstructed rivers, swamps, as well as its beasts of prey and dreaded diseases. And yet, owing to the discoveries of various "martyrs" in the cause of geographical inquiry, Daly laid out the great commercial potential of Africa: parts of the continent are healthy, well watered, productive, and fertile, he told his listeners; they represented undeveloped wealth and "healthy, intellectual and vigorous native races," if aided by civilized men who would be led by Leopold to eradicate the slave trade. To Daly, to civilize Africa was to realize its commercial potential, "not only for its benefit, but for the advantages which civilized, and especially commercial, nations will derive from the development of its mighty resources." The commercial potential of Africa would be realized by the King's plan to inspire the African people "to industry and by instructing them in the mechanical arts and agriculture; promoting peace and harmony between different tribes; securing them in their homes; and connecting lines of communication across the breadth of the continent." Daly concluded the speech by underlining his personal role in the process: "I have already expressed my hearty approval of the whole plan, both in reply to communications addressed to me by His Majesty and in my last annual address."

Other speakers at the meeting echoed Daly's position. Rev. Crummell asserted that "Greed … is *the* grand characteristic of the native African"; every chief or king is a merchant at bottom. Mercantilism and Christianity went hand in hand for Crummell; he outlined in detail the commodities coming out of Africa – among others, palm oil, palm kernels, camwood, ebony, ivory, ground nuts, gum, barwood, beeswax, India-rubber, copal, and cotton – and provided via statistical tables, the total costs for each item. Steamships were carrying such export items to England,

Figure 6.2 Henry S. Sanford of Florida, U.S. diplomat to Belgium and supporter of King Leopold II

Source: Brady-Handy Photograph Collection, Prints & Photographs Division, Library of Congress, LC-BH82-4937A.

he warned, and Americans must step into the action.[30] John Latrobe spoke about the potential benefits of Leopold's plan "for colored people of America," among those hoping for a Pan-African movement that would embrace, and be embraced by, freed American slaves.[31] Paul Du Chaillu also spoke at the meeting, for his part warning that the success of Leopold's venture would depend on those chosen to take charge of the stations. The *New York Times* covered this meeting, and Leopold's plan, in some detail.[32]

Meanwhile Henry S. Sanford of Florida, wealthy American aristocrat and former American minister to Belgium with close connections to Leopold (and investments in Brussels) was one of two men selected to attend Leopold's subsequent meeting in June 1877 as an AGS delegate.[33] The *New York Times* reported that AGS gentlemen witnessed the departure of Sanford for the Brussels conference, noting that, "it is expected that the Congress will have considerable geographical significance."[34] Sanford and Daly kept in close communication throughout 1877. A number of letters attest to Daly's admonitions to Sanford about the role and content of the colonial stations to be established.[35] For instance in a letter dated 3 June 1877, Daly argued for their military protection:

> The posts should have all the efficiency of a police; not only for the protection of those connected with them, but of the people of the country where they are situated. This will involve something of a military organization, I mean the possession of arms & the ability to use them … What the African will respect in these permanent establishments is the ability to use force, and its use only to protect him from being carried off by the slave trader, & to preserve to him the fruits of his industry, by preventing his fields from being ravaged by plundering chiefs & their followers … Do not understand my suggestion … as countenancing conquest of the country, the displacement of the authority & the government of the chiefs & taking their places. That has hitherto been the English plan, and it is, in my opinion, a very bad one.[36]

Whether Daly acknowledged Leopold's colonialist aspirations in the Congo or not – those that could not have in any case been accomplished without his own and Sanford's help – this passage makes clear that Daly's own aspiration in the Congo was, importantly, a non-territorial one (and was perhaps more similar to mid-century, non-territorial British imperialism than Daly allows). His aim was to protect African "industry," for itself and from raiding slave traders, and ultimately would be to lay the groundwork for American commercial interests.

Sanford's report from the 1877 Brussels Congress was published alongside the speeches of the 1877 AGS meeting.[37] Sanford misled his audience (and annoyed Daly) by implying that he had attended Leopold's first (1876) meeting in Brussels as an AGS delegate (no Americans had attended, nor was Sanford even an AGS member at the time).[38] Other than this, his report principally outlined the location and content of Leopold's posts; he noted the considerable disagreement at the Congress as to the character of the stations to be established, but that the views of the "learned President of the American Geographical Society of New York, expressed in private letters, harmonized" and were accepted by the executive committee in charge. "It was decided that the posts should be both hospitable and scientific" he explained; he detailed the meteorological, geological, botanical, and cartographic mission they would purportedly support.

Meanwhile Sanford claimed that abolition of the slave-trade was one of the ulterior objects of Leopold's 1876 Congress, but he admitted that it held a "less aggressive or rather less prominent place" by 1877. Archival letters also attest to this shift in emphasis. Nonetheless he reiterated that the "enlightening influence of commerce" would bring about the end of slaving most expeditiously. Sanford ended his report declaring that Americans have a special interest in Africa, as "5,000,000 of our people are of the African race."[39] As it developed, Daly and Sanford became leaders in the American work for an enterprise that was indeed soon diverted from the slave trade problem to the cultivation of trading outposts.

Meanwhile Henry Morton Stanley would come to serve as Leopold's "man on the ground" in Africa for five years (1878–1883), and was also in close communication with Charles Daly and the AGS during these years. Like many in the U.S. press, business community, and government, Daly closely followed, disseminated, praised, and advocated Stanley's movements in Central Africa even before his association with Leopold. Daly followed Stanley's movements with some obsession, and the AGS council celebrated Stanley as "the discoverer of Livingstone" in 1872, holding a special meeting in his honor. Insinuating health problems, Stanley did not attend the meeting, although he did manage a miraculous recuperation in time to attend a banquet held in his honor the following evening at New York's Delmonico's restaurant.[40] The *Herald*, the *New York Times*, and other newspapers covered the meeting and the banquet, emphasizing Stanley's "burning desire to end the terrible traffic in slavery … the frightful cruelties he had seen under his eyes."[41]

Stanley's explorations in Central Africa appeared frequently in Daly speeches throughout the 1870s and 1880s. Daly praised Stanley's "verification of Ptolemy's geography" in 1875, for instance.[42] Of Stanley's travels along the southern and eastern shores of Victoria Niyanza in 1875, and against "gratuitous and ungenerous" British detractors of Stanley's claims to have discovered the source of the Nile, Daly cast Stanley as a reliable and knowledgeable explorer (and personal acquaintance): "the last time Mr. Stanley was at my house he spent the whole evening in reading all that could be found about this region of Eastern Africa." (To the British geographical establishment, by contrast, Stanley – even though his ambitions were originally for a British Congo – was a crude amateur trespassing on British African exploration; a mercenary "hacking his way through the African jungle for a journalistic scoop."[43])

In his 1877 Annual Address Daly called Stanley's 1876 exploration of the Congo "the great event of the year." Stanley was the first European[44] to cross the African continent east to west, via the Congo River system. This 7,000- mile trek took over two and half years, with a company that included 365 African men, women, and

Figure 6.3 "Stanley on His Way to the Coast"
Source: Originally published in *Harper's Weekly: A Journal of Civilization* (New York: Harper's Weekly Co., 1857–1916). Picture Collection, The New York Public Library, Astor, Lenox and Tilden Foundations.

children – only 115 of whom survived. Stanley proved to be a savage taskmaster, using corporeal punishment as his means to an end; what Felix Driver has referred to as "geography militant": Stanley's "methods of exploration seem to blur so profoundly the distinction between geography and warfare as to make it almost unrecognizable … every one of his expeditions were 'invasions' … designed to overcome resistance, whether from the terrain or from its inhabitants, and to come back with a trophy."[45] Charles Daly was impressed though; he provided a detailed description of each of Stanley's movements up the Lualaba (part of Congo River), presenting not a ruthless taskmaster but an inspiring leader to a discouraged crew. He relayed Stanley's descriptions of "treacherous" and "gloomy" forests; physical geography impediments such as cliffs and rapids; heat, rain, mud, and quicksand; scarce food and starvation; insects and diseases; and the fierce and warlike cannibals that mercilessly attacked the expedition. Through all of this, Stanley heroically persevered and accomplished his mission in reaching the sea. "Finally," Daly enthused, "a great problem was solved, the Lualaba of Livingstone and the Congo were the same river"; and given Stanley's physical geographical findings, the Congo would prove invaluable for commerce.[46] Daly concluded that, "It may be truthfully said that no one man [besides Stanley] has ever, in explorations upon the land, done so much for the acquisition of geographical information."

Twelve letters of Stanley's published in the *New York Herald* were reprinted in the American Geographical Society's *Journal* in 1875.[47] Given the adoration Daly himself received from New York (and other) newspapers and journalists, his effusive support for Stanley must have owed at least partly to Stanley's close connection to the press – he was originally in Africa as a roving correspondent for Bennett's *Herald*. In fact, Daly dubbed Stanley's 1876 cross-continent exploration of the Congo, financed by the *New York Herald* and London's *Daily Telegraph*, no less than "an era in journalism; for by the results obtained it has placed the whole world under obligation to the proprietors of these two great newspapers."[48] And it was, not incidentally, through the *Daily Telegraph* that Leopold learned about Stanley's explorations in Africa.

As Central Africa was as yet officially "unclaimed" by any European colonial power, Leopold saw his golden opportunity in the Congo with Stanley. From 1879–1884 Leopold hired Stanley to help build his colony along the Congo, with H.S. Sanford as go-between. Though Daly provided his geographical audiences with the more general picture of European African exploration during these years – noting for instance that 32 expeditions in Africa alone occurred during 1878–1879 – he mostly followed Stanley's specific "labors on the Congo" in his annual addresses.[49] Stanley officially worked for the Comité d'Etudie du Haut Congo, a bankrupt Dutch company that Leopold bought out and used as a financial smokescreen for his unilateral operations. Stanley would help Leopold, at a cost of $10,000,000, to establish the minimum infrastructure for five colonial outposts along the Congo, employing 150 European and American officials and supplied by four steamers. Stanley had effectively established *de facto* administration in the Congo, while Leopold formed the International Association of the Congo (AIC) for administering it. Five hundred nominal "treaties" were signed with Native chiefs, who ceded their land (and trading monopoly) to Leopold by X or thumb print. Revised by Leopold's heavy editorial hand, Stanley published an account of his work in *The Congo and the Founding of its Free State: A Story of Work and Exploration* (1885) – a volume that undoubtedly influenced Daly's own account of the years of Stanley's "wonderful" work there in his later addresses.[50]

Geographical Enterprise and American Commerce in the Congo

Leopold's claims to his aspiring empire in the Congo came to a head in 1883–1884. The complex series of events and actors, not least of which involved African resistance to Leopold and beyond, will not be rehearsed here (see Nzongola-Ntalaja's 2002 *The Congo From Leopold to Kabila: A People's History*). I recall simply the American response to Leopold's plan. Briefly, as French, Portuguese, British, and German competition for Congo land and resources stiffened in the late 1870s and early 1880s, Leopold determined to make an "end-run" around this European competition by seeking full American diplomatic recognition of his claim to the Congo. He successfully did so, principally through the lobbying efforts of Henry S. Sanford and Sanford's many associates, including Charles Daly.

Sanford, though at this point ex-Belgian minister, retained his status as a well-connected Washington diplomat as well as executive committee member of Leopold's African International Association (AIA) – a useful combination for serving Leopold's interests in the United States. Sanford began in 1883 heavily lobbying for Leopold in America, and gained the enthusiastic support of Charles Daly and the AGS, members of the U.S. Congress, many among the northeast business community, and the press. According to Hochschild, Sanford made Leopold's organization sound like "travelers' aid," something akin to the International Red Cross. He promised golden American business opportunities in the Congo, settlements that would be welcoming to travelers along the Congo River, land available for purchase, an attractive destination for freed American slaves, and perhaps most problematically for him later, that American goods would be free of customs duties in Central Africa. Though Sanford would be betrayed by Leopold in the end, his elaborate wining and dining efforts arguably represented "the most sophisticated piece of Washington lobbying on behalf of a foreign ruler in the nineteenth century," bearing fruit with official American recognition of Leopold's claim in 1884.[51]

Archival evidence from the AGS, NYPL, and Sanford Museum archives in Sanford, Florida, indicates a great deal of correspondence between Charles Daly and Sanford during the years 1876–1878 and 1884–1885.[52] As early as 1879 Sanford had been pressuring Daly, as respected geographical President, to help him secure U.S. government approval of Leopold's plan and create a situation in the Congo amenable to American business interests. He wrote to Daly in 1879 arguing that "while we (the United States) are apathetic or quiescent, all Europe is a stir with expeditions to Central Africa … and I want to see American merchants and philanthropists and enterprise having their share in the rich mine which is opening up there."[53] Numbers of businessmen applied to Daly for information about prospects of trade in the Congo, including the exporting company of Carleton and Moffat, and Sanford directly induced New England's largest textile mills to evaluate the African market by sending out cotton and woolen samples.[54]

In 1884 Daly in New York and Sanford in Washington carried on a campaign to obtain U.S. recognition of the regime and flag of the International African Association (again, a deliberately misleading cover for Leopold's privately-controlled AIC).[55] The AGS participated in this campaign, lending its lecture platform and pages of its periodical to discuss the issues involved. Daly personally advocated for Leopold in two widely publicized speeches in 1884, one to the New York Chamber of Commerce and the other to his AGS audiences. Daly's own views on the Congo had evolved considerably from his 1877 position – that Leopold's colonization plan was primarily one for the suppression of the slave trade (albeit through the "civilizing forces of commerce"; above). Nonetheless by 1884 Daly's goals stridently shifted towards American commercial benefits to Congolese investments.

Daly addressed the New York Chamber of Commerce in January 1884 with a lecture entitled, "On the Importance of Africa and the Free Navigation of the Congo" (a lecture that, not incidentally, sounded very similar to Stanley's inaugural address to the Manchester Geographical Society in 1885).[56] The Chamber was then considering resolutions supporting Leopold's supposed "neutral" control over the Congo River and its basin. A.A. Low, in introducing Daly to the Chamber, impressed upon his audience that to recognize the International African organization, which by that time had established its flag over 22 stations along the Congo River, was to "secure American commercial intercourse along the river and through the various settlements established by the association." The *New York Herald*'s story covering the meeting was sub-headed, "Judge Daly's Address – The King of Belgium and His Neutrality Project."[57] When Daly took the lectern he first established his authority to speak on the topic both by reminding the Chamber – as he reminded many of his audiences – that he was the *only* American honored by an invitation to the Belgian King's initial conference on Central Africa, and also by displaying his ample geographical knowledge of the African continent. Thus he focused part of his lecture on the limits to the continent's bays, harbors, and river flows, but complemented these by then illustrating the vast potential wealth in the heart of Africa – a territory of six million square miles with a potentially limitless supply of cotton, coffee, pepper, nutmeg, India rubber, and other mineral and agricultural produce – corn, wheat, rice, sweet potatoes, ivory, iron, and copper – while also noting the "friendly tribes" found throughout the region. The *New York Herald* reported that:

> Judge Daly began by saying that … he felt very much as a gentleman might [have] in 1620 [going] before a body of merchants in London to impress them with the importance of a settlement which had just been established in the wilds of North America at a place called Plymouth … The possibilities which might come from the opening to commerce of the rich valley of the Congo were so great that if anything he might say was wild and extravagant he would have to ask the merchants present to remember the precedent he had quoted.[58]

Meanwhile Daly scoffed at the Portuguese attempts to block Leopold's claims to the Congo River (backed by a treaty with Great Britain), claiming sovereignty over land on either side of the river. Daly maintained that control of the region belonged in the hands of the Belgian king's International African Association because only it could remain neutral and protect American interests.

Correspondence between Daly and Sanford indicate that Daly drafted and redrafted the resolutions that were ultimately adopted by the Chamber of Commerce and forwarded on to U.S. President Chester Arthur. For instance, on 9 January Daly wrote to Sanford,

CENTRAL AFRICA.

Chief Justice Daly's Address Before the American Geographical Society.

WONDERS OF THE CONGO.

A Plea for American Protest Against Portuguese Assumption.

Chief Justice Daly, president of the American Geographical Society, last night delivered his annual address to the society and its guests at Chickering Hall. Heretofore the President has, with a single exception, reviewed annually the geographical work of the world, but this year its details were so great that he doubted if a review of the kind would prove interesting, and so he selected from the rich field of discovery and research before him a single topic, "The Recent Developments in Central Africa and the Valley of the Congo." After tracing in general terms the history of Africa during the present generation in its relation to geographical science, he referred in detail to the journeys of Barth, Nachtigal, Rohlfs and Schweinfurth in the north and through the deserts, and the explorations for thirty years of Livingstone (1843–1873) from Cape Colony to near the Equator, and from the Indian Ocean to the Atlantic, comprising about one-third of the whole continent; to Du Chaillu's journeys, of 8,000 miles, from the West Coast in the region of the Equator (1856 and 1865); Burton's, Speke's, Grant's and Baker's

Figure 6.4 Charles Daly in the news. "Central Africa: Chief Justice Daly's Address before the American Geographical Society: Wonders of the Congo"

Source: *New York Herald*, 1 April 1884.

> I have drawn, in accordance with your request, a reconstruction of the 2nd resolution, a copy of which I sent you; and have sent it today to Mr. Low, as a substitute for the others … The previous resolutions were drawn after a conference with him, as embodying what he was willing to offer, which recommended a course, on the part of our government, that, if complied with, would practically I think amount to recognition. He wrote me yesterday, after receiving your letter, that he thought the present resolution had gone far enough … I have complied with your request, by framing a resolution embodying your idea, as nearly as I could.[59]

These resolutions were printed in full in the *New York Herald*. The first resolution asserted that the United States government should inform the Portuguese government that it had no territorial right to the river or to the countries upon its banks. The second, that "the United States recognizes the flag of the International African Association … under the rights ceded to it by African chiefs of independent territories, in exercising rule and authority … in protection of life and liberty, extinguishment of the slave trade, and facilitating commercial intercourse and other attributes of sovereignty." The resolution went on to recommend that the U.S. President send an agent "to secure to American citizens free commercial intercourse along the course of that river, and through the various settlements or stations established by the association."[60] The Chamber unanimously passed these resolutions and forwarded them on to President Arthur. Moreover the resolutions that the U.S. Congress itself would subsequently endorse read almost verbatim with those crafted by Daly and Sanford.[61]

Sanford meanwhile wrote to Daly requesting him to urge businessmen to follow up on the matter, and asked Daly to dispatch a letter to the U.S. Secretary of State Frederick Frelinghuysen – "the first act in the program – and don't mention my name for awhile." Frelinghuysen wrote back to Daly, thanking him for his valuable suggestions for increasing American commerce on the Congo.[62] Daly informed Sanford of his work:

> I wrote a long letter to Secretary Frelinghuysen, and sent it before the President's message last week. I said nothing about you in it, but only my own views of the necessity of immediate action, and what action should be taken in the official recognition of our government, giving the reasons for it, & how it could be done. The passage in the President's message, on the Congo, is all that was necessary to begin the movement, and I will follow it up here.[63]

Daly's friends at the State Department indeed "saw his fingermarks" in the decision. John Latrobe, who himself had appeared before the U.S. Senate subcommittee considering Leopold's plan, wrote to Daly thanking him for his address before the New York Chamber of Commerce and declaring that,

> you have done more to attract attention to [the Congo] before an audience especially interested in its truth than has yet been done. You have got all the *merchants* – my audiences have been the philanthropists … I am still busy on *my side* of the Dark Continent … you know it was the nibbling of the mouse at the edge of the net of the lion that freed the animal. I am glad to say that colonization is alive and in good condition [his italics].[64]

By late January, President Arthur, as if to validate his position by emphasizing that "a citizen of the United States [is] the chief executive officer" of the King of Belgium's organization (i.e. his good friend H.S. Sanford), argued before the Congress that the United States "cannot be indifferent to this work nor to the interests of their citizens involved in it." He urged that "large tracts of territory have been ceded to [Leopold's] association by native chiefs, roads have been opened, steamboats placed on the river … [the association] does not aim at permanent political control, but seeks the neutrality of the valley." Sanford had delivered a letter to Arthur from Leopold, again promising U.S. complete freedom of tariffs on all American goods exported to the Congo, and moreover, that the constitution of the Free State he hoped to establish would be modeled on the U.S. constitution. Now also on board with Leopold's plan, Arthur instructed the Senate Committee on Foreign Relations, led by Senator John T. Morgan of Alabama, to study the issue and determine what could be done by the U.S. government to promote American commercial interests in the Congo.[65]

Back at the American Geographical Society in New York, Daly abided Sanford's request to urge American businessmen to seek opportunities in the Congo, and used the AGS venue to do so. In April 1884, in lieu of his customary review of the "geographical work of the world" for the year, Daly chose "Recent Developments in Central Africa and the Valley of the Congo" as his subject. This topic resonated well, he argued, with the society's maxim, "Geographical Exploration is Commercial Progress." In the speech (subsequently published, as all the others, in the society's *Journal*), Daly repeated much of his Chamber of Commerce speech but emphasizing that the topic should be of interest to an AGS audience both for its geographical content and its commercial bearing.[66] After tracing the course of major explorations of the African continent during the nineteenth century, Daly talked at equal length of the Congo. The *New York Herald*, *New York Times*, and other newspapers covered the "interesting and instructive" speech.[67] Leopold's design was not, Daly asserted, "to [personally] engage in any commercial operations, but in those which are purely scientific, geographical, and philanthropical." Leopold's *de facto* standing in the Congo should be recognized, he argued; Leopold was an example of "enlightened munificence in forwarding geographical exploration." To the brief attention Daly directed towards the people of Central Africa, he asserted that they were "a very superior race of savages who are handsomely formed, exceedingly vigorous, industrious, and who exhibit, for savages, considerable skill in handicraft and agriculture." Daly returned as well to the claims made by Portugal to the Congo River, decisively deriding their claims as "preposterous and absurd"; "we will certainly not, as a great commercial nation, assent to any such claim. We are called upon now to enter our protest and to enforce it … not only as a commercial nation, but as the home of a population descended from the natives of Africa." To Daly, no doubts should remain about whether the resources of Africa were worth all the trouble: "there is a future in Central Africa."

Late in April 1884 recognition of Leopold's claims to the Congo came up for vote in the U.S. Congress. Senator Morgan of Alabama introduced the Sanford/Daly resolutions to the Senate, with support from R.L. Gibson of Louisiana. These men aimed their pro-Leopold arguments on the availability of lands and favorable trade agreements to African-Americans who would be induced by them to migrate "back" to Africa. Capitalizing on fears of a growing number of freed American slaves, such southern legislators in particular invoked the "send them back to

Africa" refrain, arguing that the "American Negro would be more acceptable to the African as a civilizing influence" than the white man. Morgan stated on the Senate floor that Africa "was prepared for the Negro as certainly as the Garden of Eden was prepared for Adam and Eve … In the Congo basin we find the best type of the Negro race, and the American Negro … can find here the field for his efforts."[68]

The Senate Committee on Foreign Relations concluded that the Leopold's AIA had already a *de jure* and certainly a *de facto* standing on the Congo and thus should be entitled to the recognition of the U.S. and other countries.[69] The *Herald* reported that the action of this committee "accords with the views expressed by Chief Justice Daly in his annual address before the American Geographical Society." Though described (unsurprisingly) by some as an "incoherent debate" on the Senate floor, on 22 April 1884 Morgan's resolution passed.[70] The case for the International Association as the governing authority on the Congo was helped along by the timely public dispatches, likely planted by Sanford himself, reporting that Europeans were attacked by natives at Nokki on the lower Congo, and that Leopold's Association offered help and mediation.[71] The U.S. Congress, "having decided that the cessions by native chiefs were lawful," recognized the International Association of the Congo as a sovereign, independent state under the title of "Congo Free State." The resolutions passed, and Sanford wrote to Daly: "You did the thing as you do all you undertake – admirably."[72]

The United States was the first country to recognize Leopold's claim to the Congo. Their example was followed by ten leading European nations. This American action, coincident with the conflicts that erupted over Portugal's claims respecting transit by land on both sides of the Congo River, hastened discussions that brought about the Berlin Conference in 1885, at which the independence of the new Congo Free State was formally established and placed under the personal suzerainty of Leopold II. Events at this conference have been termed the European "scramble" for and partition of Africa, but as many scholars have argued, the real scramble happened later, with effective occupation of large territories principly by Germany, France, and Britain. The Berlin conference involved complex concessions and maneuvers by American representatives (lobbyists) Sanford and Henry Morton Stanley, and other representatives of the U.S. and European countries who ultimately ensured Leopold's control over a vague portion of Central Africa, and promises of free trade through it. Even if some representatives to the conference disdained Leopold the man, they approved of his control over the Congo, believing that a free trade zone would be more likely supported through a "weak little country" like Belgium rather than another major European power.[73] Among a host of other machinations, in June 1886 Leopold acceded to Sanford's modest request for the right to launch a small company to undertake commercial operations in the Upper Congo, the "Sanford Exploring Expedition," which sent out two steamers in the interest of trade in ivory and rubber. Sanford, though not averse to seeking personal investment opportunities in the Congo, believed that he was paving the way for American enterprise through such efforts. He was greatly disappointed that he received no response from American business interests in his Congo project, though, nor help from Leopold's agents and employees on the ground.[74] The Sanford Exploring Expedition was liquidated in 1888 and in its place a purely commercial Belgian company was established.

Leopold meanwhile, from 1895–1900, became desperate for money to build the expensive infrastructure needed to exploit Congo resources; the building of forts, roads, railways, and so on. To do this he manipulated the growing international concern over the slave trade and organized the "Brussels Anti-Slavery Conference" in 1889, at which he proposed measures allegedly intended to stop the slave trade but which were aimed at collecting personal funds. To the shock of all those who had signed on to his Congo Free State, Leopold now requested conference delegates to authorize him to levy customs' duties on goods imported into the region – in effect, amending the Berlin agreement which had guaranteed free trade. Suddenly, Leopold was asking for 10 percent customs' duties on imported American goods.[75] Sanford, who had been sent as U.S. "Plenipotentiary and Envoy Extraordinary" to this conference, felt betrayed for all the work he had done to convince Americans to support Leopold in exchange for promises of free trade. Sanford died in 1891 bitterly disillusioned with Leopold and deeply in debt.[76]

Leopold, maintaining the façade of humanitarian, continued to control the Congo as a private enterprise from 1885–1908, contracting land deals, railroad development, and sale of ivory and rubber. Beginning in 1889, however, reports of his atrocities and crimes against humanity began to surface, including from Americans such as journalist-historian George Washington Williams in his *An Open Letter to His Serene Majesty Leopold II* (1890), as well as Franco-British journalist E.D. Morel, in his *The Congo Slave State* (1903).[77] Williams, Morel, and others discovered Leopold directly encouraging slave raids, deriving his wealth from rubber and ivory via forced labor, subjecting villagers to daily quotas and torturing, maiming, raping, and murdering those who did not acquiesce. The American praise that had greeted his project was replaced later by denunciation of the abuses inflicted on the inhabitants of the Congo; in 1908 Leopold's personal colony was annexed by the Belgium parliament.[78]

Discussion

Despite Leopold's downfall, or more likely, because of it (below), the Congo Free State remained of intense interest to Americans business. For its part, the AGS continued support of Leopold through the 1880s and 1890s, most notably through Charles Daly's annual address to the society in 1888. (Daly also delivered an address on Africa to the International Geographical Congress meeting in Chicago, an auxiliary of the Columbian Exposition, in 1893).[79] In his 1888 annual address Daly noted that, "in the past few years Africa has been the part of the globe in which geographical exploration has been the most extensive and the most important." While he described explorations throughout the African continent (especially those involving German colonization in East Africa), the centerpiece of his address was the Congo Free State and the three years of "wonderful" work that Leopold had accomplished there. Undoubtedly influenced by Stanley's 1885 book he declared,

> The greater part of the valley of this great river … is full of streams and capable of extensive cultivation. Along the river many stations have been founded, which are likely to grow into extensive centres of civilization … The effort of the King of the Belgians in maintaining the organization and the keeping up of a central route as a means of communication from the west to the east coast, has added greatly to our information of the extensive region through which the Congo flows. Steamers now run on the upper Congo from Stanley Pool to Yellala Falls, where the lower Congo begins. For 230 miles this great river is unavailable for the purposes of navigation … Over this unavailable space for navigation a railway is now contemplated, and when this is accomplished a great change in the whole of Central Africa will follow.[80]

Daly clearly never lost hope in American enterprise in the Congo, although he did regret the adulation he conferred on Leopold.[81] Although he did not live to see them materialize, the mercantilist seeds he planted in the closing decades of the nineteenth century began to pay off for American business in the Congo in the first decade of the twentieth century. The emerging globalization of capitalist exploitation and Leopold's own interest in maintaining good relations with the major powers did provide an entry to the vast riches of the Congo for wealthy bureaucrats of imperialist countries. Given the time it takes to build railroads, harbors, and mining facilities, the economic role of most investments yielded dividends only in the post-Leopoldian era, well into the twentieth century.[82]

Scholars such as Jerome Sternstein and David Gibbs argue that when the "Congo Reform Movement" began to turn Leopold into an international pariah, the monarch skillfully sought a select handful of American businessmen to invest in the Congo and thereby "outmaneuver and immobilize" any group against him – a strategy that was well adapted to an American foreign policy "peculiarly sensitive to such entrepreneurial interests."[83] When the U.S. Senate Foreign Relations Committee was considering action against Leopold's atrocities and an investigation was pending under the Roosevelt administration in 1906, Leopold began a "second line of defense" by directly courting American capitalists with influential political ties. The syndicate that emerged was headed by Wall Street magnate Thomas Fortune Ryan and Republican Senator Nelson Aldrich of Rhode Island (one of the most influential U.S. senators of his time); and involving John D. Rockefeller, Daniel and Solomon Guggenheim, and financial speculator Bernard Baruch.[84] In a 1906 deal these men obtained practically exclusive concessionary rights to the rubber and mineral riches of more than nine-tenths of the Congo Free State. To Leopold these men's investments would neutralize the political effectiveness of Congo reformers in the U.S., to slow its momentum and dissipate pressures being put upon the state department from reformers. And while it ultimately turned out that these men's investments in rubber would require more extensive outlays of capital, labor, and time than they were willing to invest (and some stockholders started to divest by 1911), the Guggenheims' infamous Forminière enterprise eventually found the concessions to be worth millions in diamonds.[85]

It is beyond the scope of this chapter to address in detail American business ventures sought and won by Leopold. It is worth underlining, however, the close connection between the AGS and many of the Gilded Age industrial giants and politicos who helped bring about Leopold's successes, and thus his atrocities, in the Congo. As noted in previous chapters, the names Vanderbilt, Rockefeller, Cabot Lodge, and Astor frequently appeared in AGS membership logs. The New York financier and multi-millionaire Thomas F. Ryan, for instance, who sailed to Brussels to directly negotiate with Leopold for his company's concessions in 1906 (above), was elected Fellow of the AGS in December 1889.[86] Along with other of New York's most influential businessmen, Ryan likely attended AGS meetings and events, in addition to likely rubbing shoulders with Charles Daly via Tammany Hall (Chapter 3; both men were Roman Catholic Democrats). If it is befitting that, as Meyer argues, "everybody who had been involved in promoting Leopold's schemes … was in some degree guilty by association,"[87] the fact is that the geographical knowledge advanced through the AGS lectern, publications, and so on aided the brutal colonization of Central Africa; albeit for the commercial advantages to be accrued to American business interests.

Not unlike many Americans, Charles Daly was susceptible to the personal charms and mystique of royalty.[88] Time and again Daly reminded his audiences of the honors bestowed on him personally by the European monarch. Leopold frequently employed flattery as a strategic mechanism, particularly with Americans. Moreover in his capacity as geographical President, Daly was offered a potentially significant role to play in the civilization and reform of a distant land, a region also of increasing interest to his counterparts in Europe. In short, Leopold offered Daly the opportunity to become a "player" in international affairs in ways not otherwise open to Daly. And, as if to counteract his personal stake in the matter, Daly also often spoke of the importance of "geographical inquiry" in the civilization of Africa.

Seductions aside, it is also important to keep in mind that Daly's views on Leopold's Congo scheme evolved through the decades. In 1877 he expressed hopes of a humanitarian effort to end the slave trade, and made clear to Sanford that he opposed British-style conquest and control of Congolese trading stations: recall Daly arguing that authority in the region should remain in the hands and government of local chiefs. By 1884 however, Daly was much more attuned to the potential of American business ventures in Africa. The leitmotif of the American Geographical Society had always been, since its inception, the support of a commercial or business geography, and Daly reminding his audiences of the society's maxim that "Geographical Exploration is Commercial Progress" resonated well with the knowledge of Africa that it disseminated. Geographical knowledge

Figure 6.5 Franco-American Explorer Paul Belloni Du Chaillu, Charles P. Daly's close friend and associate

Source: Print Collection, Miriam and Ira D. Wallach Division of Art, Prints and Photographs, The New York Public Library, Astor, Lenox and Tilden Foundations.

discovered, discussed, and disseminated by the AGS links to an extensive number of American commercial ventures; though unlike Daly's personal financial stake in developments in the American West and Central America that linked closely to his work at the AGS (Chapter 4), as far as I know he did not personally own stock in any Congo ventures. This again, though, likely owes primarily to the fact that Leopold did not seek or offer American financial backing in the Congo until the decade after Daly's death (even if American commercial interests in Africa predated Leopold). Daly's contribution to Leopold's enterprise was much more in establishing the commercial potential of the Congo River basin in the imaginations of his many geographical and business audiences.

It might also be said that because Leopold so successfully confused his various organizations – their names, purposes, and structures – American supporters of his "humanitarian" plans, including Daly and perhaps Henry Sanford himself, did not know precisely what they were ultimately backing – if nothing else they believed they were helping establish some sort of free trade zone across Central Africa, protecting it against individualist claims made by other European nations. Daly claimed in 1884 that Leopold's various organizations were virtually the same, aimed towards "scientific, geographical, and philanthropical" results. His colleague in the American branch of Leopold's organization, John Latrobe, despite his facility with the French language, wrote to Sanford in April 1884 asking, "What, in good plain English, do the words, 'Comité d'Etudes du Haut Congo' *mean*?"[89]

If there is any closure than can be placed on Daly's and the AGS's involvement in Africa in the nineteenth century, it might be that the close personal (to his biographer, "intimate") relationship Charles Daly cultivated with the Franco-American African explorer Paul Du Chaillu could offer some insight. Du Chaillu, a contemporary of Burton and Speke who was the controversial discover of the gorilla and the "Pygmies" in the 1850s and 1860s West Africa, may have influenced Daly's views on Africa more so than anyone else.[90] Du Chaillu was a constant presence at the Daly household, and Daly's wife Maria served as Du Chaillu's financial patron throughout his career (at her death she bequeathed $20,000 to Du Chaillu). Du Chaillu wrote to Maria in June 1894:

> I will be so very glad to get a line from you and to hear how you are and the Judge. I often think of you and of all your kindnesses to me. You and the Judge are the best friends I ever had and I need not tell you that I love you dearly.[91]

After Maria's death Du Chaillu came to live with Charles, and the two men attended many family and other social gatherings together. The two also took a trip to Europe together in the summer of 1895. Du Chaillu also seems to have found a "home" at the American Geographical Society. He occupied a regular place at the society; often mentioned in society and councilor meeting minutes and in the *Journal*, as lecturer, knowledgeable commentator on a range of topics, benefactor, and award winner. He was named honorary secretary of the AGS in 1871, and elected councilor in 1876.[92] When discussions of Leopold's plans for the Congo arose at the AGS, Du Chaillu went on record as avid supporter of the "noble" and "good hearted" Leopold, and considered his plan practical and advantageous. He asserted that the African is a "great trader," but also must be convinced that trading in products other than slaves is better and more profitable: "this will be promoted by the chain of stations contemplated in the plan of the King of the Belgians."[93]

A number of scholars have described Du Chaillu's dis-comfortable position within the wider geographical and scientific community and his contested contributions to geographical knowledge (primarily focusing on his writings of the 1860s). Briefly, Du Chaillu enjoyed a great deal of popular celebrity in London, Paris, and New York as a field collector of African artifacts, bringing back skins and skeletons of gorillas, hundreds of bird specimens, and stories of dramatic encounters with cannibals and jungle savages.[94] While his personal biography remains vague, scholars have documented a youth spent in the Gabon among a family of traders, of possibly mixed race heritage.[95] Du Chaillu's lack of pedigree, along with his sometimes inconsistent, fabricated, "unscientific," and sensationalist accounts of his African discoveries, drew contempt from some "gentlemanly" British natural history circles, such that Du Chaillu was never fully accepted as credible explorer.

Charles Daly, however, often discussed – and defended – Du Chaillu's travels and findings in his annual addresses before the AGS, for instance in defending Du Chaillu against the French explorer Pierre de Brazza, who, Daly claimed, had mis-read Du Chaillu's writings about the "cannibals" (Fans) of Central Africa. Daly noted that "this is not the first time that the accuracy of Mr. du Chaillu's statements has been called in question … In every instance, however, Mr. du Chaillu's statements have been verified, including about his discoveries of the gorilla."[96] One of Daly's last public geographical lectures, delivered in 1892, was also one devoted to Du Chaillu, a lecture titled, "Who Discovered the Pygmies?" Daly availed himself of the occasion to expose Henry Morton Stanley's false and self-aggrandizing claims to have discovered the diminutive people, publicly siding with his friend Du Chaillu.[97] As Daly told it,

> [Du Chaillu] was not himself aware of the full value of his important discovery until I told him, after reading his account. "You have not only, Mr. Du Chaillu, in your previous journey, found in the gorilla the wild hairy men that the Carthaginian navigator Hanno saw on the west coast of Africa, but you have now, in this last journey, found the Pygmies of Herodotus; two important discoveries with which your name will always hereafter be connected."[98]

As Stuart McCook argues, Du Chaillu's reliability rested on who made a good scientist, rather than what constituted good scientific theory.[99] Though I do not have the space here to develop the issue in full, suffice it to say that it is interesting that an African explorer many considered a "charlatan" was legitimated and wholly embraced by Daly and other AGS men. They apparently enjoyed rather than disdained some of Du Chaillu's theatrics, such as his dressing in the costumes of Natives when lecturing before the society. Perhaps Daly felt a particular kinship with Du Chaillu's class background, lack of advanced education, and so on as these were similar to Daly's own story (see Chapters 1 and 3). Ultimately, one could easily speculate that given Du Chaillu's extensive personal experience and travels in Africa, his views would come to count for much in Charles Daly's own developing views on Leopold II and the Congo.

Endnotes

1 See for instance, Bruce A. Harvey, *American Geographics: U.S. National Narratives and the Representation of the Non-European World, 1830–1865* (Stanford: Stanford University Press, 2001) and Susan Schulten, *The Geographical Imagination in America, 1880–1950* (Chicago: The University of Chicago Press, 2001).

2 Rev. H.A. Wilder, "A Description of Natal," *Bulletin of the American Geographical and Statistical Society* Vol. 1, Part III (1854): 45–61; Alvan S. Southworth, "The Soudan

and the Valley of the White Nile," *Journal of the American Geographical Society of New York* 5 (1874): 95–111; M. Channebot and Egbert L. Viele, "The Resources of Central Africa: M. Channebot's Project for Their Development by a Railway," *Journal of the American Geographical Society of New York* 13 (1881): 165–195; and Anon, "Record of Geographical Progress: Districts in Tropical Africa Where White Men May Live and Work," *Journal of the American Geographical Society of New York* 29 (1, 1897): 74.

3 As the *Journal* was not reconstituted as such until 1870, six years after Charles Daly became AGS President, this number includes only those articles with Africa as a subject from 1870–1899.

4 This chapter focuses on the AGS and American commercial interests in the Congo only. There is a bigger story about American commercial influence in Central (sub-Saharan) Africa historically, especially of East Africa via Zanzibar. See, for instance, Jeremy Prestholdt, *Domesticating the World: East African Consumerism and the Genealogies of Globalization* (Berkeley: University of California Press, 2008).

5 Adam Hochschild, *King Leopold's Ghost: A Story of Greed, Terror, and Heroism in Colonial Africa* (New York: Houghton Mifflin, 1998); Felix Driver, *Geography Militant: Cultures of Exploration and Empire* (London: Blackwell Publishers, 2001): 117–145.

6 I problematize the designation "scramble" below. Driver, ibid., 125; Georges Nzongola-Ntalaja, *The Congo from Leopold to Kabila: A People's History* (London: Zed Books, 2002); David N. Gibbs, *The Political Economy of Third World Intervention: Mines, Money, and U.S. Policy in the Congo Crisis* (Chicago: University of Chicago Press, 1991); Thomas Pakenham, *The Scramble for Africa: White Man's Conquest of the Dark Continent from 1876 to 1912* (New York: Avon Books, 1992); Ernesto E. Ruiz, *Geography and Diplomacy: The American Geographical Society and the 'Geopolitical' Background of American Foreign Policy, 1848–1861* (PhD dissertation, Northern Illinois University, 1975): 220. Also see Michael Heffernan, "The Cartography of the Fourth Estate: Mapping the New Imperialism in British and French Newspapers, 1875–1925," in *The Imperial Map: Cartography and the Mastery of Empire*, ed. James R. Akerman (Chicago: University of Chicago Press, 2009): 261–299.

7 Just to take two examples; Howard Zinn, *A People's History of the United States 1492–Present*, 20th ed. (New York: HarperCollins, 1999) and Judith A. Carney and Richard Nicholas Rosomoff, *In the Shadow of Slavery: Africa's Botanical Legacy in the Atlantic World* (Berkeley: University of California Press, 2009). Legal and regularized trade in Africans to the United States dated from the mid-seventeenth century, as labor for southern tobacco and cotton plantations. By 1860, approximately four million African-Americans were enslaved in the United States.

8 American Geographical Society, "Discoveries in South Africa," *Bulletin of the American Geographical and Statistical Society* Vol. 1 (1, 1852): 47–60. The letter was sent to the AGS from Livingstone's brother; it was believed to have been written on the banks of the Zambesi River.

9 In the published version of a letter Livingstone wrote from "Tette, Zambesi, February 22, 1859" he said he hoped it would prove interesting to AGS members as well as show

his good will to perform a corresponding member's duty. *Bulletin of the American Geographical and Statistical Society* Vol. II (1, 1860): 64. Livingstone's work synopsized by RGS President Sir Roderick Murchison appeared in *Proceedings of the American Geographical and Statistical Society*, 1862–1863 (dated 2 October 1862) and included a map, the "Lake Region of Tropical Africa." According to Felix Driver (personal correspondence, 21 June 2010), Livingstone was keenly aware that his works were reviewed, published, and pirated in North America.

10 Charles P. Daly, "Annual Address. Subject: Review of the Events of the Year, and Recent Explorations and Theories for Reaching the North Pole," *Journal of the American Geographical Society of New York* 2 (2, 1870): lxxxiii–cxxvi; see xci.

11 Charles P. Daly, "Annual Address. Subject: The Geographical Work of the World in 1872, *Journal of the American Geographical Society of New York* 4 (1873): 63–188; quote on 108. These and other expeditions discussed on 109–115.

12 Charles P. Daly, "Annual Address. Subject: The Geographical Work of the World in 1873," *Journal of the American Geographical Society of New York* 5 (1874): 49–94; quote on 90.

13 David Lambert, "'Taken Captive by the Mystery of the Great River': Towards an Historical Geography of British Geography and Atlantic Slavery," *Journal of Historical Geography* 35 (2009): 44–65.

14 Charles P. Daly, "Remarks on Stanley's Verification of Ptolemy's Geography," *Journal of the American Geographical Society of New York* 7 (1875): 290–295; quote on 292. Daly had expressed this same logical conclusion in 1870: "Annual Address," 2 (2, 1870): xci. He notes four centuries of confusion that there were three rather than two lakes in question.

15 A.J. Russell, "Livingstone's Nile. What is It?" *Journal of the American Geographical Society of New York* 6 (1874): 288–301.

16 John Agnew, *Hegemony: The New Shape of Global Power* (Philadelphia: Temple University Press, 2005): 82–90; Mona Domosh, *American Commodities in an Age of Empire* (New York: Routledge, 2006).

17 Charles P. Daly, "Annual Address. The Geographical Work of the World for 1875," *Journal of the American Geographical Society of New York* 7 (1875): 31–92; quote on 36.

18 Charles P. Daly and Bayard Taylor, "Meeting of the American Geographical Society, November 15, 1875. Remarks on Explorations in Central Africa," *Journal of the American Geographical Society of New York* 7 (1875): 296–304; quote from 297.

19 Charles P. Daly, "Annual Address. Geographical Work of the World in 1876," *Journal of the American Geographical Society of New York* 8 (1876): 45–95; Cameron's journey on 86.

20 Charles P. Daly, "Annual Address. Subject: The Geographical Work of the World in 1874," *Journal of the American Geographical Society of New York* 6 (1874): 53–92; quotes on 83, 92.

21 Daly, "Annual Address," *Journal* 4 (1873): 113–114.

22 Hochschild, *King Leopold's Ghost*, 38–42, describes Leopold's obsessive desire for colonial power as an emotional substitute for a loveless childhood and marriage. He

was brother to Carlota, briefly Empress of Mexico alongside Maximilian, and first cousin to England's Queen Victoria.

23 Hochschild, ibid., 46.

24 Leopold's letter to Daly and Daly's letter to Leopold, Charles P. Daly Correspondence and Papers, Box 5, Manuscripts and Archives Division, New York Public Library (NYPL), New York. The King's letter, asking Daly's cooperation in establishing colonies in Africa, was hand-delivered to Daly by a Mr. Delfosse (a Belgian minister). It also offered Daly hospitality while in Brussels. See also Maria L. Daly diary, Charles P. Daly Papers, NYPL, Vol. 27, entry dated 13 July 1876. In his response to Leopold Daly added that he was not sure the United States could give pecuniary aid to Leopold, but "we are very liberal in aiding public enterprise of every description during periods of public prosperity."

25 Daly, "Annual Address," *Journal* 8 (1876): 80. Also see Ruiz, *Geography and Diplomacy*, 219; Maria Daly's diary, ibid., entries for 13 July 1876; 23 October 1876; and diary Vol. 28, entry dated 14 March 1879; and John K. Wright, *Geography in the Making: The American Geographical Society 1851–1951* (New York: American Geographical Society, 1952): 95–96. Also see Sanford H. Bederman, "The 1876 Brussels Geographical Conference and the Charade of European Cooperation in African Exploration," *Terrae Incognitae* 21 (1989): 63–73, for a discussion of American interests at the Brussels Conference.

26 Hochschild, *King Leopold's Ghost*, 65.

27 Daly, "Annual Address," *Journal* 8 (1876): 79–80.

28 Letters from some of the men who were invited to become members of Daly's association include J. Berrien Lindsley of Nashville and Joseph Jackson of Detroit, letters dated 2 May 1877 and 10 August 1873, respectively. Charles P. Daly Correspondence, Box 1, 1859–1879, AGS Archives, New York. Also see letter from Joseph Moore of Philadelphia dated 23 January 1884, Daly Papers, Box 6, NYPL.

29 Charles P. Daly and Alexander Crummell, "The Plan of the King of Belgium for the Civilization of Central Africa, and the Suppression of the Slave Trade," *Journal of the American Geographical Society of New York* 9 (1877): 88–103; list of men who had attended the Brussels meeting on 92. Wright, *Geography in the Making*, 96. The AGS archives contain numerous letters from Latrobe to Daly, Daly Correspondence, Boxes 1 and 2, letters dated 21 September, 11 October, 29 October 1877; 6 July, 7 September 1878; 10 February, 21 July 1879; 20 February 1884; and 9 August 1885. Several letters from 1877 refer to Sanford's report. Latrobe was President of the American Colonization Society, a group that in 1821–1822 helped freed American slaves found and colonize Liberia, on the contentious premise that they would have greater freedom and equality there. Support for Leopold's plan in the U.S. Congress rested on similar logic (below).

30 Daly and Crummell, "Plan of the King of Belgium," *Journal* 9 (1877); quotes on 91, 93, 97.

31 Ibid., 100–103.

32 "The Interior of Africa," *New York Times*, 23 May 1877. Also see "The Civilization of Africa," *New York Times*, 3 June 1877. They reported that two expeditions would be organized immediately, with 1,500 men each.

33 During the Civil War Sanford was the minister in charge of the secret service in Belgium. He inherited a fortune and invested it heavily in Florida orchards, railroads in Minnesota, and other real estate schemes; most of it he lost.

34 "The Civilization of Africa," *New York Times*, 3 June 1877.

35 The AGS archives contain numerous letters from Sanford to Daly, Daly Correspondence, Box 1, including those dated 22 June, 15 August, 22 October 1877; 25 April, 16 December 1879. Also see, Harold E. Hammond, *A Commoner's Judge: The Life and Times of Charles Patrick Daly* (Boston: The Christopher Publishing House, 1954): 430, 525.

36 Charles P. Daly to Henry Sanford, 3 June 1877. Box 24, Folder 8, Sanford Museum, Sanford, Florida.

37 Henry Shelton Sanford, "Report on the Annual Meeting of the African International Association, in Brussels, in June, 1877," *Journal of the American Geographical Society of New York* 9 (1877): 103–108.

38 Sanford went to the second Brussels meeting the following year. Lysle E. Meyer, "Henry S. Sanford and the Congo: A Reassessment," *African Historical Studies* 4 (1, 1971): 19–39, see 22, n. 16. Sanford did not appear on the AGS membership roles until 1877.

39 The original text to Hammond's *A Commoner's Judge* differs from the published version on Daly's involvement in the Congo. To wit: he states in the original manuscript: "The work of the American Auxiliary Society seems to have been done principally in 1884, but it is sufficient to say now that Daly and Sanford were the leaders in the American work and that the object of the enterprise was soon diverted from the slave trade problem to the cultivation of trading outposts." (Original typescript, p. 365, Box 9, Daly Papers, NYPL). Compare to the published version: "The work of the American Auxiliary Society seems to have been done principally in 1884, but it will suffice here to say that Daly and Sanford were its leaders and that abolishing the slave trade and establishing trading posts became the Society's objective" (p. 289). Letters cited in both accounts, AGS Correspondence, Boxes 1 and 2, H.S. Sanford to Charles Daly, 25 April and 16 December 1879, and 3 December 1884. Note the subtle but significant change of emphasis. Sanford, "Report on Annual Meeting," *Journal* 9 (1877): 104–108.

40 "Transactions of the Society, for the Years 1870, 1871 and 1872," *Journal of the American Geographical Society of New York* 3 (1872): 51. Charles P. Daly and David Livingstone, "Report of the Reception Tendered by the American Geographical Society to Henry M. Stanley, Esq., on His Return from Central Africa," *Journal of the American Geographical Society of New York* 4 (1873): 453–468. Daly emphasized Stanley's heroism in finding Livingstone and how much Livingstone appreciated Stanley, entrusting his diary to Stanley (455–456).

41 "The Stanley Reception: Meeting of the American Geographical Society at the Cooper Institute Last Night – A Large and Fashionable Attendance," *New York Herald*, 27 November 1872; "Stanley Banquet of the Geographical Society at Delmonico's," *New York Herald*, 28 November 1872. Also see "African Explorations," *New York Times*, 14 December 1875; "Dr. Livingstone," *Harper's Weekly*, 27 July 1872; "Stanley's Discoveries," *New York Herald*, 14 December 1875.

42 Daly, "Remarks on Stanley's Verification," *Journal* 7 (1875): 290–295.

43 Jon Hegglund, "Empire's Second Take: Projecting America in Stanley and Livingstone," in *Nineteenth-Century Geographies: The Transformation of Space from the Victorian Age to the American Century*, eds. Helena Michie and Ronald Thomas (New Brunswick, NJ: Rutgers University Press, 2003): 268; Driver, *Geography Militant*; Hochschild, *King Leopold's Ghost*.

44 Actually Stanley was Welsh, passing himself off as American; Hegglund, ibid., 265–277.

45 Driver, *Geography Militant*, 144–145.

46 Charles P. Daly, "Annual Address. Geographical Work of the World in 1877," *Journal of the American Geographical Society of New York* 10 (1878): 1–76; quotes on 53, 60. "A Year's Explorations," *New York Herald*, 28 February 1878 and *New York Times*, 28 February 1878.

47 Daly and Taylor, "Remarks on Explorations in Central Africa," *Journal* 7 (1875): 299. Henry M. Stanley, "Explorations of Central Africa," *Journal of the American Geographical Society of New York* 7 (1875): 174–282. Also see William Schneider, *An Empire for the Masses: The French Popular Image of Africa, 1870–1900* (Westport: Greenwood Press, 1982) and Beau Riffenburgh, *The Myth of the Explorer: The Press, Sensationalism, and Geographical Discovery* (London: Bellhaven Press, 1993).

48 Daly and Bayard, "Remarks on Explorations," *Journal* 7 (1875): 302.

49 Charles P. Daly, "Annual Address. Geographical Work of the World in 1878 & 1879," *Journal of the American Geographical Society of New York* 12 (1880): 1–107; see 73.

50 Hochschild, *King Leopold's Ghost*, 81; Nzongola-Ntalaja, *Congo from Leopold to Kabila*. Colonel Maximilien Strauch was Leopold's financial henchman, President of the Committee for Studies of the Upper Congo, another of Leopold's front organizations that supplied Stanley's payments. AGS Correspondence, Box 2, Strauch to Daly, 24 September 1884, also another dated Janvier 1884. See Hochschild, *King Leopold's Ghost*, 64–65.

51 Hochschild, ibid., 66, 80.

52 In addition to the approximately 25 letters from Sanford to Daly and Latrobe to Daly held at the AGS, the Sanford Museum archives in Sanford, Florida, holds 11 letters Daly wrote to Sanford, and 29 Latrobe wrote to Sanford. According to its archivist, the most significant correspondents for the African part of the Sanford papers are: H.P. Bailey, Chatrobe Bateman, James G. Blaine, Cambier, F.F. Carter, F. DeWinton, Frederick T. Frelinghuysen, Baron Greindl, George Grenfell, E.J. Glave, Cam Janssen, John A. Kasson, J.B. Latrobe, Amos A. Lawrence, Leopold II (through the agency of Barons Borchgrave, E. Beyens, and DeVaux), Jules Levita, Montefiore-Levi, John Tyler Morgan, W.G. Parmenter, Capt. Popelin, A. Rabaud, Henry Morton Stanley, Col. M. Strauch, A.B. Swinburne, E.H. Taunt, Edwin Terrell, Capt. Albert Thys, W.P. Tisdel, A.J. Wauters, and T. Wauters. The museum holds 5,000 items dealing with Sanford's activities in Africa.

53 AGS Correspondence, Box 1, H.S. Sanford to Judge Daly, 25 April 1879.

54 AGS Correspondence, Box 2, Carleton and Moffat (to Charles Daly, 23 January 1884), asked about protection for life and property were they to establish a trading station in

the Congo. A second Moffat letter (Box 6, NYPL), dated 28 January 1884, argues that Americans were being taxed 30–40 percent more than the Portuguese on the West Coast of Africa. Moffat was following up on a request from Daly to consider the potential for profitable business in Africa, relaying back to Daly information they collected from other merchants. On Sanford's and Morgan's views of America's "color problem," see Meyer, "Henry S. Sanford and the Congo," 27–29.

55 Daly himself referred to it as the "Congo Committee or Association" active in establishing communication between the upper and lower Congo. Daly, "Annual Address," *Journal* 16 (1884): 99–100, explained that the Comité and the International African Association, "though distinct organizations, are, in effect, practically the same: they both aim to accomplish one object, in different parts of this great line of communication, which they mutually carry on under one general flag, which they have adopted as the symbol of the combined organizations. Their design is not to engage in any commercial operations, but in those which are purely scientific, geographical and philanthropic."

56 The original hand-written speech (untitled), Box 9, NYPL. Charles P. Daly, *The Commercial Importance of Central Africa and the Free Navigation of the Congo. Address before the Chamber of Commerce of the State of New York, January 10, 1884, in Favor of Resolutions Presented to the Chamber by A.A. Low, Esq., and Adopted by that Body* (New York: H. Bessey, 1884). Driver, *Geography Militant*, 126, discusses Stanley's lectures to geographical societies and chambers of commerce on the economic opportunities created by the work of exploration. Driver muses (personal correspondence, 21 June 2010) that perhaps Stanley plagiarized Daly in his Manchester lecture.

57 "The Valley of the Congo, Practical Steps Toward the Opening to Trade of a Rich Territory, Action of the Chamber of Commerce, Judge Daly's Address – the King of Belgium and His Neutrality Project," *New York Herald*, 11 January 1884 and "American Interests Abroad," *New York Times*, 11 January 1884.

58 "Valley of the Congo," *New York Herald*, 11 January 1884.

59 Daly to Sanford, 2 January, 3 January, 5 January, 5 January (two letters that day), 9 January, 11 February, 22 March 1884. Box 24, Folder 8, Sanford Museum. In his letter dated 11 February 1884 Daly added, "I scarcely know what to advise" with respect to Portugal; it "will do little for the country."

60 "Valley of the Congo," *New York Herald*, 11 January 1884.

61 AGS Correspondence, Sanford to Daly, 15 January 1884.

62 AGS Correspondence, Sanford to Daly, 30 January, 9 February, and 1 April 1884; Frelinghuyson to Daly, 19 January 1884.

63 Daly to Sanford, 5 December 1883, Box 24, Folder 8, Sanford Museum.

64 Hammond, *Commoner's Judge*, 343. AGS Correspondence, letter from John H.B. Latrobe to Charles P. Daly, dated 20 February 1884.

65 Pakenham, *Scramble for Africa*, 243; "Commercial Importance of the Valley of the Congo," *New York Herald*, 22 January 1884.

66 Charles P. Daly, "Recent Developments in Central Africa and the Valley of the Congo," *Journal of the American Geographical Society of New York* 16 (1884): 89–159. Charles

Daly to H.S. Sanford, 22 March 1884, Sanford papers, Box 24, Folder 8, Daly wrote: "I am to deliver an address before the Society on the Congo next Monday evening, but I have been so occupied with my duties that I think I will not be able to add much to what has been said before the Chamber of Commerce." Relevant passages quoted here on 100, 102, 107, 112, 116–117, 121–122.

67 "Central Africa: Chief Justice Daly's Address Before the American Geographical Society, Wonders of the Congo, A Plea for American Protest Against Portuguese Assumption," *New York Herald*, 1 April 1884. Also see, "The Anglo-Portuguese Congo Treaty" and "Congo Politics: Protest Against the Treaty Between Great Britain and Portugal," *New York Herald*, 1 April 1884; and "Civilization in Central Africa," *New York Times*, 1 April 1884.

68 Hochschild, *King Leopold's Ghost*, 79; Pakenham, *Scramble for Africa*, 243–246; Meyer, "Henry S. Sanford and the Congo," 28.

69 AGS Correspondence, H.S. Sanford to Charles Daly, letters dated 8 February, 14 February, 4 March, 5 March, 30 April 1884.

70 Nzongola-Ntalaja, *Congo from Leopold to Kabila*, 15–24; quote on 16 from John Reader, *Africa: A Biography of a Continent* (New York: A.A. Knopf, 1998), 540. Morgan's resolution read: "Resolved … that the committee on foreign relations be instructed to inquire into the subject of settlement and trade and trading posts now being made and established in the valley of the Congo River … and report as to any action that may be properly taken by Congress or the Executive in the furtherance of our commerce in that quarter, and that said committee report by bill or otherwise." Pakenham, *Scramble for Africa*, 242. The resolutions appeared in full in the *New York Herald*, 22 January 1884 "The Congo Valley Trading Posts."

71 As Hochschild points out, *King Leopold's Ghost*, 80, one of Sanford's strategies was to quietly pay newspapers to publicize favorable accounts of Leopold's work. "The Congo: A Battle on the River – Protection Afforded by the International Society," *New York Herald*, 3 April 1884. The paper quoted a letter by "Parminter, Chief of Vivi" stating that, "The events of the last few days and the efficacious and prompt protection which the association gave to the factories at Noki, and the sending of two hundred and fifty armed men under the command of a dozen Europeans to repel aggressions upon commercial houses, have augmented the prestige and influence of the association, not alone in the eyes of the native but of Europeans also … The natives have agreed to give the International Association possession of the coast from latitude 2 degrees south to latitude 4 deg. 40 min. south."

72 AGS Correspondence, H.S. Sanford to Charles Daly, 16 July 1884.

73 Nzongola-Ntalaja, *Congo from Leopold to Kabila*, 18. Sanford and Stanley spent the winter in Berlin working with the United States Minister, John A. Kasson, to provide technical support and to secure concessions from the European powers.

74 Meyer, "Henry S. Sanford and the Congo," 32–33.

75 Hochschild, *King Leopold's Ghost*, 91–94.

76 Pakenham, *Scramble for Africa*, 398.

77 The full title to Williams' 1890 exposé of Leopold's cruelties is *An Open Letter to His Serene Majesty Leopold II, King of the Belgians and Sovereign of the Independent*

State of Congo, by Colonel the Honorable Geo. W. Williams, of the United States of America. He also wrote *A Report upon the Congo-State and Country to the President of the Republic of the United States of America* in 1890. See Hochschild, *King Leopold's Ghost*, 101–114.

78 Though I have not called attention to it here, Henry Morton Stanley's many abuses in Africa were certainly also called into question; see Driver's chapter, "Exploration by Warfare," in *Geography Militant*, 117–145, for a comprehensive treatment.

79 See Hammond, *Commoner's Judge*, 364 and 432, n. 22. Also see AGS Council meeting minutes, 5 March and 7 May 1892; and under Projects, 4 March and 20 May 1893. Lecture invitation, letter dated 8 October 1892, Box 6, Daly papers, NYPL.

80 Charles P. Daly, "Annual Address. Recent Geographical Work of the World," *Journal of the American Geographical Society of New York* 20 (1888): 1–38; quotes from 14, 17–19.

81 Bederman, "1876 Brussels Geographical Conference," 72–73.

82 Nzongola-Ntalaja, *Congo from Leopold to Kabila*, 14–41; Gibbs, *Political Economy of Third World Intervention*, 37–76.

83 Jerome Sternstein, "King Leopold II, Senator Nelson W. Aldrich, and the Strange Beginnings of American Economic Penetration of the Congo," *African Historical Studies* 2 (2, 1969): 189–204; Gibbs, ibid., 47–48. The anti-Leopold movement was based in Britain, led by Liverpool traders who had their own economic incentives for discrediting Leopold.

84 Sternstein, ibid., 190–197, 203. Banker J.P. Morgan served as "Leopold's fiscal agent in America." For further details of the "Ryan Congo Concessions," *New York Times*, 14 December 1906; and Ryan's partnership with King Leopold II, *New York Times*, 24 November 1928.

85 Sternstein, ibid.; Gibbs, *Political Economy of Third World Intervention*, 44–60.

86 "Transactions of the Society for 1889," *Journal of the American Geographical Society of New York* 21 (1889): lxxi–lxxvii; see lxxvi.

87 Meyer, "Henry S. Sanford and the Congo," 37.

88 Sternstein, "King Leopold II," 191.

89 John Latrobe to H.S. Sanford, Box 25, Folder 8, Sanford Museum. Lengthy correspondences between the two men are held in these archives, particularly covering the years 1884–1889.

90 Miklos Pinther, personal correspondence, 15 June 2004. Paul Belloni Du Chaillu, *Explorations and Adventures in Equatorial Africa* (New York: Harper & Brothers, 1861) and *A Journey to Ashango-land, and Further Penetration into Equatorial Africa* (London: John Murray, 1867). He also wrote about Scandinavia, *Land of the Midnight Sun* (New York: Harper & Brothers, 1882) and Russia.

91 Du Chaillu is mentioned in Hammond's *Commoner's Judge* more than any other explorer of Africa (20 mentions); see 202, 376, 387–390. Also see Maria Daly's diary, entry dated 19 June 1894, Vol. 28, Charles P. Daly Papers, NYPL. Box 7, NYPL, many letters from Du Chaillu to Daly.

92 See for instance, "Transactions," *Journal of the American Geographical Society of New York* 2 (2, 1870): li, lxxiii; "Transactions," *Journal* 3 (1872): 68; "Transactions," *Journal* 4 (1873): 41; and "Transactions," *Journal* 8 (1876): 28.

93 "Remarks of Paul B. Du Chaillu," Daly and Crummell, "The Plan of the King of Belgium," *Journal* 9 (1877): 102–103.

94 Stuart McCook, "'It May Be Truth, But It Is Not Evidence': Paul du Chaillu and the Legitimation of Evidence in the Field Sciences," *Osiris* 2nd series 11 (1996): 177–197; Mary Louise Pratt, *Imperial Eyes: Travel Writing and Transculturation* (London: Routledge, 1992): 208–213.

95 McCook, ibid., 190.

96 Daly, "Annual Address," 12 (1880): 72. De Brazza and Stanley were contemporaries feuding over space and treaties in the Congo; see Hochschild, *King Leopold's Ghost*, 70.

97 Charles P. Daly, "Who Discovered the Pygmies?" *Journal of the American Geographical Society of New York* 24 (1892): 18–22.

98 Ibid., 21.

99 McCook, "It May Be Truth," 178.

Chapter 7
Postscript: Reclaiming Charles P. Daly, Prospects and Problems

Introduction

It is something of a truism that archival-based historical research is tedious and time-consuming, with published results slow to come. In consulting the extensive archives available on Charles P. Daly at the American Geographical Society and at the New York Public Library over a number of years, I have had plenty of time to wonder how such a one-time prominent public figure as Charles Daly – this very public intellectual – could drift into almost total obscurity today, within the geographical community but also within histories of New York City as well as those of the legal profession.[1] True, Daly had something of a self-deprecating manner that led him to resist certain positions of power and authority. He resisted attempts to be recruited as mayor or governor of New York, or Supreme Court justice, for example, and also opposed the erection of a statue of himself in New York's Central Park. Yet Daly was a renowned New York judge, community leader, and geographer, appearing hundreds of times in newspapers of his day and before immense public crowds. His disappearance today is interesting not only because he was such a notable figure within his milieu, but also because he went to such great lengths to carefully collect and store extensive records of both his personal and professional lives for, presumably, future generations.[2] As far as I know, though, only one other individual has consulted the Daly papers to any great extent, Daly's biographer Harold Hammond, whose 1954 book I relied upon a great deal throughout my research.[3]

Charles Daly is clearly a neglected figure in historiographies of American geography today. No entries appear on Daly in Susan Schulten's study of geography in America from 1880–1950, or in earlier works such as that by Geoffrey Martin and Preston James; nor was there an entry on Daly in *Geographers Biobibliographical Studies* until my own submission.[4] Daly's absence in such works seems to mirror the relative absence of studies of the nineteenth-century AGS itself in historiographies of American geography. Very few secondary works are available on the nineteenth-century AGS,[5] and in fact when I began research on Daly I was the first person to check out of my university library its copy of John K. Wright's *Geography in the Making: The American Geographical Society, 1851–1951* (1952), the only book-length institutional history of the AGS (produced in-house). That lonely book sat

Figure 7.1 Charles Patrick Daly, President of the American Geographical Society, 5 May 1864–18 September 1899. Oil painting by Harper Pennington purchased for the AGS in 1899

in the library unread for over 50 years; it had never been loaned out, nor seemingly ever even opened – its pages were still perfectly smooth, slick and unruffled – a very unpopular book indeed.

This relative lack of interest in the nineteenth-century AGS has always seemed rather peculiar to me, especially as compared to the rich critical histories of other Anglophone (European and American) geographical organizations.[6] The fact that the nineteenth-century AGS has not been of much interest to geographers has a number of plausible explanations. In historical geography circles in the U.S., there simply has not been the same level of interest in the history of American geography like that found in places such as Britain. No doubt the reasons for this are complicated and multi-dimensional, but certainly in the British case, the intense interest in Empire has given critical historical geography itself a big boost over the last several decades that we just do not see in the U.S. case. There is a lot of work to be done in making connections between geography and nineteenth-century American empire building.

While it is outside the scope of this chapter to directly examine the relative lack of scholarly interest in the nineteenth-century AGS, the question driving my discussion is related to it: why did such a prolific and influential figure as Judge Charles P. Daly fade from public (and academic) consciousness, interest, and scrutiny? In this chapter I address this question, and reflect on the process of attempting to recover his archived life and what I have termed his "civic geography" for today's audiences. My intervention suggests a number of inter-related social processes at work in Daly's case, both during his lifetime and today. These include the type of geography he practiced – his intellectual contribution to the discipline – as well as the care and preservation of his archived papers. Ultimately it is a useful and necessary exercise to trace the neglect of Charles P. Daly within histories of geography and recapture him for today's audiences, not only because of his influences upon American geography and American empire, but also because his story can shed additional light on how "disciplinary remembering" functions in geography.[7] It is also worth considering the power and privilege exercised by researchers such as myself in reclaiming lost, invisible, or forgotten lives in the archives, and I conclude with a brief discussion of some of the issues involved in that process.

Popular Geographer to Unpopular Archives

Charles Daly's relative neglect within the annals of American geography likely has most to do with the type of geography he practiced. I would underline that I do not claim that some "injustice" has been enacted upon Charles Daly via his current invisibility. Rather, my interest is to reflect and comment upon Daly as a particular type of popular public geographer within his own milieu, and his subsequent containment within the archive, both of which prefigured his "unpopularity" and dismissal among geographical audiences of today. Recent debates about popular geography and archival reason help in analyzing how certain criteria come to have value and importance in constructing histories of geography itself.

I frame my discussion around the question of how an archived life might become socially "popular" versus "unpopular." Ascribing the term unpopular to Daly and his archived life will undoubtedly be contested, especially because I do *not* use the term to refer to active distaste or disapproval of an individual; nor conversely do I use popular to mean widely liked, admired, or appreciated. Rather, I use the term unpopular in its second, less-used sense, to refer to archived lives that have been forgotten, neglected, or dismissed as unimportant; something more akin to "not widely known" by the people at large, or unfashionable. I draw on David Bogen and Michael Lynch's term "popular archive" – as that with a mass audience – and Alastair Bonnett's term "popular geography" – as that with a large public audience outside of academia – to trace Daly's move from a popular geographer in his day to one simply "not sought after" today (by either the public or specialist researchers).[8]

It is tempting to say that Charles Daly is not well known or studied within geography today simply because he was "just a minor figure." But such an appellation would beg the question of how we understand the "making" of the history of geography in the first place and subsequently come to label our precursors as important or unimportant to that process. A substantial body of critical scholarship has amply documented the extent to which histories and historiographies of geography *produce* the realm or limits of geography as much as they reflect some pre-existing condition of it as a coherent, mutually agreed upon body of knowledge, with particular protagonists central to the narratives.[9] Who becomes a major and minor figure, who has the authority to speak, what kind of knowledge and skills make for dominant traditions within our discipline, and so on are important questions about the social construction of geographical knowledge and the "worlding" of its creators. This, of course, has most relevance to those legions of under-represented and under-recognized groups of people left out of dominant narratives and traditions, recovered now especially through feminist and postcolonial research. In short, though, declaring Daly (or anyone else) a minor figure before analysis of his life, contributions, or the processes surrounding the preservation and retrieval of his papers in effect precludes study of exactly that which demands it.

The "politics of the archives" has drawn a great of deal of scholarly attention from historians, sociologists of science, as well as from geographers.[10] Such scholars raise questions about whose voices are heard, and whose are not? Who controls, establishes, and maintains the archive, and how do they do so? Which materials are preserved in the archive and which are excluded? How do classification systems and structures include, exclude, foreground, or marginalize certain voices? To what extent do the logical hierarchies for classification and arrangement reflect social or political hierarchies?[11] The question of authority to create and maintain an archive and present it to the public is basic to all of these questions, and thus a sort of sociology of power pervades the work. And of course, no straightforward outcome is guaranteed with archival research either; it is never simply a matter of revealing a given truth that is waiting to be found in the archive, so it would be a mistake to think that there could be an archive without a politics of the archive.

As just noted, the recovery of voices heretofore buried or silenced in the archive has become the project of many critical historical geographers and archivists in recent years.[12] This retrieval of formerly silenced voices has allowed geographers to meaningfully challenge the connection or identification of the "unpopular" with the powerless: such scholars have, in a sense, popularized the powerless and thus empowered new voices to speak for the past. But my research subject Charles Daly – he might be unpopular but he certainly was not powerless, in speaking for himself or for geography, as the previous chapters attest. To recapture Daly's "silenced" voice, then, would not be to somehow democratically redress some past violence enacted against him. He was a well known and well regarded figure in his own time and place; he was not denied agency or marginalized, was in fact well published and effectively represented himself through many venues. Rather, Daly's unpopularity seems mostly to do with views of him as uninteresting or irrelevant to geographers today. Thus silenced can mean many things. Some events and people are silenced or forgotten on purpose, an effacement of violent acts of the past rather forgotten.[13] Others are silenced by powerful regimes covering their tracks. Still others, though, are silenced because they are considered mundane, commonplace, of no consequence: i.e. unpopular.

David Bogen first applied the term "popular" to archives; to him they were those available on the Web or widely available through mass media. Such media turned a body of documentary evidence into a popular archive when it was subject to mass visitation, reproduction, and dissemination.[14] Bogen set popular archives in opposition to what he termed "academic" archives, those available only to a privileged few. Using televised court proceedings as an example, he argued that the public in such cases actually have better access to archival information than do the "privileged" sequestered jurors in the trials. Likewise, Lynch's "popular archive" is one whose use has proliferated through electronic media, particularly the Internet, and as against the exclusiveness of material accessed through more "scholarly" means.[15]

These works raise a number of questions, including those about the relationship between popularity and privilege – both the privileged sites of stored documents and the privileged people who have access to them. Other studies call attention to the "arbitrariness" of the archive, that quality of haphazardness, disorder, and serendipity that characterizes the material that finds its way into the archive, the manner by which it does so, and the meanings that will be read from those stored documents.[16] Charles Withers writes that he does not see the archive as a "straightforward expression of power. It is, at least in [his] experience, the result of contingency, of the haphazard accumulation of 'stuff'."[17] Others note how important the collection development phase is in archival work: who makes the decisions as to what is and what is not collected? What is merely stored but not catalogued (and hence made intellectually accessible), and what is thrown away? Brown and Davis-Brown ask, "should [the archivist] focus on canons and traditions, or strive for diversity? What constitutes a canon anyway other than to constitute one through such documentation?"[18] Collection can be driven by ideological ends, but can also be "demand-driven," from the outside. Yet because demand is itself a social construction, one must ask how demand or desire for certain archival materials arises in the first place.

All of these issues are relevant to the archived life of Charles Daly, perhaps most basically the issue of the handling and "containment" of Daly in the archives at the NYPL and AGS. At both sites, little attention has been paid to the upkeep or care of his papers; they are poorly maintained and difficult to access. The contents of the boxes, files, and scrapbooks in the extensive collection of Daly papers held within the Manuscripts and Archives Division of the NYPL are un-indexed and undocumented – all described only by dates on a list (e.g. "Box 1, 1829–1843"). This makes negotiating the material a tedious, time consuming, un-enticing process. One needs to essentially read everything to find anything of use and value. (These papers were donated to the NYPL by Daly's niece upon her death.)

The AGS's archives contain material dating back to 1851, including a comprehensive institutional record in the form of nearly complete sets of handwritten councilor and society meeting minutes, but also including an uneven assortment of other valuable documents and artifacts. At the time of this writing, most of the society papers at its current Wall Street headquarters are stuffed into a single, small storage room, with materials crammed into file cabinets and boxes stacked to the ceiling, and with a small path running through the room. Two boxes of Charles Daly's correspondence are held there. In the 1950s this material was indexed in a wooden card catalog box. Because sufficient resources have not been available for keeping the archives in any kind of working order, however, the numbers in this card catalog do not match up with documents in storage. Nor are procedures in place for accessing materials, due to the low demand. It appears that it is only by way of the part-time archivist's memory that particular documents can be located. (Happily this situation is about to change. In 2008 the AGS announced a new push to hire trained personnel to catalog and preserve their valuable archives, implying meanwhile that the present condition resulted at least in part from three moves in the last 25 years.)[19]

Thus one rather obvious observation one might be inclined to make is that because the Daly papers are poorly preserved – too difficult and time consuming to access – they are thus not worth the trouble and hence become unpopular. However this line of thinking sets up something of a tautology: these archives are in poor use because they are in poor condition. The funding question sets up a similar tautology: that is, if the Daly papers were considered more important, money would be there to better maintain them, and their use would increase. However, it might also be the case that the hard-to-access nature of some archives is what gives them renewed popularity.[20] It is also important not to overstate the extent to which the Daly papers have been "neglected," since it is the case that many major archival collections have substantial un-indexed components. Moreover, the "serendipity effect"– the possibility of finding surprise nuggets of useful information – is not necessarily a problem and can lead to some important revelations.[21] In the end poor containment of his papers might be more of a manifestation of Charles Daly's unpopularity than a cause of it; but certainly such handling has not appreciably enabled or enhanced study of the nineteenth-century AGS.

Another likely explanation for Daly's unpopularity today (at least among geographers) has to do with the type of geography he practiced and propagated via the AGS, what might be termed popular or public-oriented geography. A number of geographers have recently turned their focus to such geographies, those widely known to the public and set against those of more professional or academic men. Some have called for more histories of geography as popular or "ordinary" practice.[22] While Daly is not among the grass roots practitioners, such as school field instructors, studied by Hayden Lorimer[23] for instance; his geography was popular in its appeal among (principally) New York businessmen, other professionals, and the public. One of Daly's primary "contributions" to geography was the hold he had over the popular imagination about distant locations such as in the Arctic and Africa. He also exercised considerable power in civic and governmental circles and through them, affected geographies on the ground. Considering Daly's geographical practices allows an understanding of a particular moment in American geography's history when geography was produced as a popular practice while just emerging as an academic discipline, and how the popular side of that division has been oftentimes dismissed as having made few lasting contributions to the discipline.

The type of geography Daly practiced in his lifetime can be easily cast as popular – both in terms of its non-academic nature as well as its extensive reach to a broad audience. When Daly discussed American benefits from exploration they were typically cast as commercial or business in nature, which of course aligns well with the interests of the professional and mercantile class of men who established the society (Chapter 2). Daly's association with African exploration, for instance, was based on commercial links to be developed there (Chapter 6), yet I have also emphasized that his leadership in a number of social reform causes in New York City also resonated closely with his work as geographer (Chapter 3). Daly's interests and agenda fits well with Bonnett's definition of "popular geography": that which has a mass audience and is developed outside of the higher education academic community – a non-university geography influential in public culture.[24] Although a number of university professors served as AGS councilors in the later nineteenth century,[25] academic geography was tiny in the U.S. during Daly's most active and influential period (only a couple of college professors were teaching geography in 1874, for instance, Arnold Guyot at Princeton and Daniel Gilman at Yale). "Professional geographer" at the time mostly meant teacher; and meanwhile it was the federal government, in association with organizations such as the AGS, that sponsored most surveys, explorations, and other such work (see Chapters 4, 5, and 6). Near the end of

Daly's life (*ca.* 1895), this "geography as exploration" began to be challenged by many influential figures as a useful or appropriate definition of the subject. William Morris Davis, for instance, countered what he regarded as the populist understanding of geography propagated by the AGS (among others) in support of more "expert" and "scientific" work.[26] Thus by the end of Daly's tenure as AGS President the society did begin to adopt more of an educational slant.[27]

For his part Daly neither drew much upon nor influenced much the work of the emerging discipline as it was practiced at schools and universities. This might be particularly surprising with respect to school geography, as Daly in many other capacities strongly identified as a New York civic leader committed to developing an ethos of civic responsibility among his many constituents. Ultimately Daly's contribution was in popularizing field geography, advancing geo-commercial links at home and abroad, while laying the foundation for a successful geographical society that would go on after his death to make important contributions to academic geography.

The telling of geography's history has frequently revolved around such late nineteenth-century moves to secure the academic credibility of the subject in a way that has left out of the story popular geographers such as Charles Daly. Of course, there is no particular relation of necessity that Daly himself would disappear from histories of geography today owing to his brand of popular geography. This becomes especially obvious when considering that other popular nineteenth-century American geographers, such as leading men from the National Geographic Society, did not meet the same fate. It is outside the purview of this chapter to compare the relative histories and fortunes of the AGS and NGS, though quite obviously the latter has sustained an audience of millions around the world today while the former met with a number of unfortunate obstacles in the later twentieth century that damaged its stature within the geographical community and likely diminished the interest that future generations of geographers would have in it. Following the influential career of Isaiah Bowman in the mid-twentieth century, for reasons that are complicated and multi-dimensional, the AGS lost a building in Manhattan and was forced to outsource its library to the University of Wisconsin at Milwaukee.[28] Without a strong institutional presence in American geography circles, it is not surprising that people earlier associated with the institution might drift out of view. That is a given eventuality; however it is not the end of the story. As the researches into the lives of more "ordinary" geographers make clear,[29] the writing of geography's history is always a work in progress, as I hope the preceding chapters have made clear.

The Archive Revisited: Popularity and Privilege

> Geography's archive … is, simultaneously, something that pre-exists awaiting use … and something yet to be, brought into being by virtue of others' prompts.
>
> Ron Johnston and Charles Withers[30]

The question of who is included or excluded in the history of geography is an interesting and important question and one that has generated considerable debate within geography over the last couple of decades. Feminist historiographers of geography, for instance, have introduced challenging questions about how geography's history has been framed. From a feminist perspective, I would note that by focusing on Charles P. Daly I realize that I run the risk of reinforcing the "Great Man" tradition of geographical inquiry that Gillian Rose eloquently critiqued in her influential *Feminism and Geography: The Limits to Geographical Knowledge* (1993). In it Rose argued that David Livingstone's *The Geographical Tradition* offered a,

> paternal tradition [that] can be used as a kind of legitimation process, in which would-be great men cite men already-established-as-great in order to assert their own maturity: what might be described as the "dutiful son" model of academic masculinity.[31]

Other feminist geographers have likewise noted the paternalism, sexism, and masculinism inherent in histories and historiographies of geography – the gendering of geographers, of the knowledge and science they created, and of the social milieus within which they worked.[32] Such scholarship has forced us to question the origins of "dominant traditions" in geography, since their authors usually elide the fact that histories or historiographies of geography *produce* the realm or limits of geography as much as they reflect some pre-existing condition of it as a coherent, agreed upon body of knowledge. My focus here on the man Charles Daly is thus not without a certain amount of anxiety, particularly since Rose's admonitions have made relatively little impact on the most acclaimed of the subsequent histories of western geography in the last decade, although there are notable exceptions.[33] My purpose in studying Daly, though, has not been to inscribe yet another man or homo-social men's-club into the historiography of geography, though the work will inevitably do that. Rather, it is to highlight and better explore the *produced* nature of geography, geographical traditions, and geographical imaginations that feminist geographers and others have discussed.

Over the last couple of decades historiographers of geography have also emphasized the critical role played by geographical institutions and organizations historically in shaping and reinforcing state and commercial power and the building of empires.[34] With the present work I have attempted in a broad sense to direct critical attention to the "colonial science" of geography in the nineteenth-century American context, where geographers have been slower to take up this type of analysis. While other Anglo-oriented geographical societies, such as the Royal Geographical Society, the National Geographic Society, and the Royal Scottish Geographical Society, are now understood as having supported colonial or imperial relationships of power in the nineteenth century – such as by cataloguing data or mapping colonies for territorial acquisition or military control, extracting resources, or opening trade markets for home goods – we have not seen critical examinations of such processes with respect to American post-Civil War geography to a similar extent.[35] Thus my initial interest in this project began with the question of whether the *explicit* business and commercial orientation of the AGS produced for it a somewhat different set of programs than those for other geographical societies. While other geographical societies also carried strong commercial goals in the nineteenth century – most notably those in France, as well as some smaller, provincial societies throughout Britain (see Chapter 2) – study of the AGS's emplacement in New York City has allowed for a deepened understanding not only of the spatiality of knowledge production, but also has illustrated new links between geography and American social reform, commercial development, gender norms, and state power and competition in the nineteenth century.

One might say that Charles P. Daly's formerly popular geography now rests in currently unpopular archives – those exclusive, scholarly, academic archives available mainly to the privileged few who know how to access them and have the resources to do so. The relationship between Daly's popularity in his day and his invisibility at present is an important one, with respect to the man and his geographical contributions but also with respect to my own participation in situating the Daly archives as an important site of geographical knowledge. I have drawn attention to a mostly forgotten public intellectual from the geographical stable and have "marked" Charles Daly's contribution to geography. Though re-telling Daly's story is not entirely reducible to an arbitrary act of power and privilege on my part, it is worth keeping in mind that archives are sites of power: not least power to tell a particular story from a particular point of view.[36] Thus it is not only the power of the researcher to resuscitate forgotten figures prominent in their day that matters. How that task is carried out is equally important.

Critical archivists and geographers have comprehensively addressed this issue: almost two decades ago Felix Driver emphasized the important role of the researcher as intermediary between geography's past and present. Harriet Bradley, too, recognizes that stored documents "remain passive, inert in their meanings until read and written [about] by the researcher," underlining both the arbitrariness of meanings of those stored documents as well as the authority of the researcher to articulate them. Thomas Osborne further adds that "what is at stake … in fact, is a distinctive way of making visible the question of power itself."[37]

In one of Michel Foucault's lesser known works, *The Life of Infamous Men*, he wrote about what might be called mundane men, archives, and power. Foucault describes the archive – medical records, police reports, church documents, and so forth – as an effect of sovereignty.[38] Though Foucault focuses on the never-famous (monks, prisoners, workers), his useful observation for purposes here is that what is important about the archive today is that it requires a "re-animation" through the workings of another kind of sovereignty, which is that of the researcher. While Foucault was more interested in the power that assigned such lives to the archives in the first place – they "collided with power and provoked its forces" – his observations about researchers' function in re-animating lives contained in the archives is instructive. He brought into sharp relief the politics of invading lives, of drawing attention to them, of analyzing them in ways that suit our purposes – in short, the power to create *popularity*.

While legions of geographers are unlikely to clamor now for more information about Charles P. Daly from the AGS and NYPL archives, my drawing attention to Daly and (re)writing him into histories of geography will necessarily affect his "popularity rating." But again, it is not just *that* I have resuscitated an individual and organization from geography's past that is important, but also, *how* I have done so. I want to emphasize that my efforts have not been aimed at judging the current AGS organization by the actions and values of Charles Daly, nor the organization's activities in the nineteenth century according to the values, projects, and ethics of today. There are indeed, though, some overlaps. As one current councilor noted to me, the current AGS focus on regional studies, lecture tours on cruise ships and trains, efforts to host globe-signing events and honor distinguished explorers,

> seems to be directly linked to the work and vision of Daly and remain important parts of distinguishing the unique AGS identity among our discipline's professional organizations. In addition, our ongoing attempts to insure that AGS Council is made up today of one-third business people, one-third political leaders, and one-third academics also fits within the Daly model in many ways.[39]

It is important not only to contextualize Charles Daly's and the AGS's nineteenth-century work within their own milieu historically, but also to acknowledge links with current practice.

Quite obviously though my treatment of Charles Daly has not been an hagiographic "celebration" of his or the AGS's work historically, but neither has it suggested that individuals currently associated with the society should take personally the way I have attempted to understand the foundations, impulses, and effects of the geography constituted as such by the organization historically.[40] For instance, in Chapter 4 I argued that Daly's personal financial stake in developing North and Central American transportation systems became deeply intertwined with his geography. That power reproduces itself this way should come as no surprise to anyone, and of course this is true regardless of one's position on the political continuum. Today we have the likes of (former U.S. Vice President) Dick Cheney taking advantage of his position in the Enron and Halliburton corporations to inappropriately influence State Department operations abroad, but we also have the seemingly more transparent Al Gore (presidential candidate in 2000) fighting the political battle against global warming partially through his personal investments in companies advancing green energy technologies.[41] This is what people with power and financial resources *do*: they invest quite obviously for personal gain, but also in projects that resonate well with their ideological orientation. Of the two I find Gore's efforts immeasurably more justifiable, but that does not detract from the fact that we need to understand the powerlines in each's palace, to borrow Cheryl McEwan's phrase.[42]

Thus I think it is most important of all to pause and appreciate the layers of geographical knowledge and practice produced by Charles P. Daly. Throughout the 1870s, 1880s, and 1890s he was a prominent figure and popularizer of geography. His ability to garner wide support for geographical projects near and far, and whose ideas about distant people and places would measurably impact American commercial interventions in those places, deserves our attention. Daly's fastidious collection of a vast array of papers of and about himself; his alignment with a subsequently declining geographical society; the AGS's and NYPL's less than ideal means of storing his papers; and especially his popular brand of geography and savvy management of the New York press to draw attention to himself and his many causes; all potentially impact Daly's popularity within contemporary geography. These, combined with my own "sovereign power" to re-animate Daly's life and work, illuminates criteria that are often used in deciding who gets remembered in disciplinary histories.

Endnotes

1 Miklos Pinther, "Charles Patrick Daly 1816–1899," *Ubique: Notes from the American Geographical Society* 23 (2, 2003): 1–4.

2 And he exercised a pretty heavy hand when doing so; from what I can tell, Daly himself labeled and organized all of his own letters held at the NYPL, and inserted dates and other notations into the margins of his wife's diaries.

3 Harold E. Hammond, *A Commoner's Judge: The Life and Times of Charles Patrick Daly* (Boston: Christopher Publishing House, 1954). Hammond also edited *Maria Lydig Daly, Diary of a Union Lady 1861–1864* (1962; rpt. Lincoln: University of Nebraska Press, 2000). Charles Daly also appears in John K. Wright's institutional history of the AGS, *Geography in the Making: The American Geographical Society 1851–1951* (New York: American Geographical Society, 1952): 71–111; also see Wright, "British Geography and the American Geographical Society, 1851–1951," *Geographical Journal* 118 (2, 1952): 153–167; also see Pinther, ibid.

4 Susan Schulten, *The Geographical Imagination in America, 1880–1950* (Chicago: University of Chicago Press, 2001); Preston E. James and Geoffrey J. Martin, *All Possible Worlds: A History of Geographical Ideas*, 2nd ed. (New York: John Wiley, 1993); Karen M. Morin, "Charles Patrick Daly," *Geographers: Biobibliographical Studies* 28 (2009): 105–117; and Karen M. Morin, "Charles P. Daly's Gendered Geography, 1860–1890," *Annals of the Association of American Geographers* 98 (2008): 897–919.

5 Very few scholarly works are available on the AGS, for reasons beyond the purview of the present research. They include Wright, *Geography in the Making*, and Ernesto E. Ruiz, *Geography and Diplomacy: The American Geographical Society and the 'Geopolitical' Background of American Foreign Policy, 1848–1861* (PhD dissertation, Northern Illinois University, 1975). Neil Smith's *American Empire: Roosevelt's Geographer and the Prelude to Globalization* (Berkeley: University of California Press, 2003) focuses

on the influential twentieth-century AGS director, Isaiah Bowman, beginning *ca.* 1915; and several works detail women of the AGS, including Janice Monk, "Women's Worlds at the American Geographical Society," *Geographical Review* 93 (2, 2003): 237–257 and Douglas McMannis, "Leading Ladies at the AGS," *Geographical Review* 86 (1996): 270–277. Other works make only brief mention of the AGS: e.g. Schulten, *Geographical Imagination*, and Tim Inwin, *The Place of Geography* (New York: John Wiley & Sons, 1992).

6 Schulten, ibid.; Inwin, ibid., Martin and James, *All Possible Worlds*; Wright, *Geography in the Making*; Catherine Lutz and Jane Collins, *Reading National Geographic* (Chicago: University of Chicago Press, 1993); Tamar Y. Rothenberg, *Presenting America's World: Strategies of Innocence in National Geographical Magazine, 1888–1945* (Burlington: Ashgate Publishing, 2007); Julie Tuason, "The Ideology of Empire in National Geographic Magazine's Coverage of the Philippines, 1898–1908," *The Geographical Review* 89 (1999): 34–53; Roger M. Downs, "Popularization and Geography: An Inseparable Relationship," *Annals of the Association of American Geographers* 100 (2, 2010): 444–467 all discuss geographical societies functioning alongside the AGS in the nineteenth-century America. Of the plentiful texts on British geographical societies see, for example, Felix Driver, *Geography Militant* (London: Blackwell, 2001); Charles Withers, *Geography, Science and National Identity: Scotland Since 1520* (Cambridge: Cambridge University Press, 2001); Morag Bell and Cheryl McEwan, "The Admission of Women Fellows to the Royal Geographical Society, 1892–1914: The Controversy and the Outcome," *The Geographical Journal* 162 (1996): 295–312; among hundreds of others.

7 For instance, Hayden Lorimer, "Telling Small Stories: Spaces of Knowledge and the Practice of Geography," *Transactions of the Institute of British Geographers* 28 (2003): 197–217; Charles W. Withers, "History and Philosophy of Geography 2003–2004: Geography's Modern Histories? – International Dimensions, National Stories, Personal Accounts," *Progress in Human Geography* 30 (2006): 79–86; Avril Maddrell, "The 'Map Girls': British Women Geographers' War Work, Shifting Gender Boundaries and Reflections on the History of Geography," *Transactions of the Institute of British Geographers* 33 (2008): 127–148.

8 Michael Lynch and David Bogen, *The Spectacle of History: Speech, Text & Memory at the Iran-Contra Hearings* (Durham: Duke University Press, 1996); Alastair Bonnett, "Geography as the World Discipline: Connecting Popular and Academic Geographical Imaginations," *Area* 35 (2003): 55–63.

9 For instance, Felix Driver, "Geography's Empire: Histories of Geographical Knowledge," *Environment and Planning D: Society and Space* 10 (1992): 23–40; Gillian Rose, *Feminism and Geography: The Limits to Geographical Knowledge* (Minneapolis: University of Minnesota Press, 1993).

10 Thomas Osborne, "The Ordinariness of the Archive," *History of the Human Sciences* 12 (1999): 51–64; Harriet Bradley, "The Seductions of the Archive: Voices Lost and Found," *History of the Human Sciences* 12 (1999): 107–122; Charles W. Withers, "Constructing 'The Geographical Archive'," *Area* 34 (2002): 303–311; Hayden Lorimer and Nick Spedding, "Excavating Geography's Hidden Spaces," *Area* 34 (2002): 294–302; Kate

Boyer, "Feminist Geography in the Archive: Practice and Method," *Geography and Gender Reconsidered* (London: Women and Geography Study Group of the Institute of British Geographers, 2004).

11 And so on, after Richard Harvey Brown and Beth Davis-Brown, "The Making of Memory: The Politics of Archives, Libraries and Museums in the Construction of National Consciousness," *History of the Human Sciences* 11 (1998): 17–32; see 17.

12 For instance see Cheryl McEwan, "Building a Postcolonial Archive? Gender, Collective Memory and Citizenship in Post-Apartheid South Africa," *Journal of Southern African Studies* 29 (2003): 739–757; Maddrell, "The Map Girls"; among hundreds of others.

13 Kenneth E. Foote, "To Remember and Forget: Archives, Memory, and Culture," *American Archivist* 53 (1990): 378–392.

14 Lynch and Bogen, *Spectacle of History*, 51, 83.

15 Michael Lynch, "Archives in Formation: Privileged Spaces, Popular Archives and Paper Trails," *History of the Human Sciences* 12 (1999): 65–87.

16 Withers, "Constructing the Geographical Archive"; Bradley, "The Seductions of the Archive."

17 Withers, ibid., 305; after Carolyn Steedman, "The Space of Memory: In an Archive," *History of the Human Sciences* 11 (1998): 65–83.

18 Brown and Davis-Brown, "The Making of Memory," 20.

19 Peter Lewis, "AGS Archives in Limelight," *Ubique: Notes from the American Geographical Society* 28 (3, 2008): 11.

20 For instance, McEwan, "Building a Postcolonial Archive." Also see James Sidaway, "Postcolonial Geographies: An Exploratory Essay," *Progress in Human Geography* 24 (2000): 591–612.

21 Bradley, "Seductions of the Archive"; Withers, "Constructing the Geographical Archive."

22 Lorimer, "Telling Small Stories"; Lorimer and Spedding, "Excavating Geography's Hidden Spaces"; Bonnett, "Geography as World Discipline." Also see Downs, "Popularization and Geography."

23 Lorimer, "Telling Small Stories," 200.

24 Bonnett, "Geography as World Discipline," 56.

25 For example, "Transactions of the Society for 1872," *Journal of the American Geographical Society of New York* 4 (1873): 35–56; 51 mentions Daniel Gilman, President of the University of California; Professor William Newcomb and Professor Hartt of Cornell; and Rev. Mytton Maury of Fordham University.

26 Schulten, *Geographical Imagination in America*, 72–75; Rothenberg, *Presenting America's World*, 38–39.

27 Wright, *Geography in the Making*, 113, 120 discusses an aging and conservative AGS Council in the 1890s, and with the approaching end of Daly's tenure as President, more emphasis to be placed on professionalism and education. Among the many relevant works on school geographies see Bruce A. Harvey, *American Geographics: U.S. National Narratives and the Representation of the Non-European World, 1830–1865* (Stanford: Stanford University Press, 2001).

28 Among the many important works on Bowman and his era at the AGS see Smith, *American Empire*; and Alastair W. Pearson and Michael Heffernan, "The American Geographical Society's Map of Hispanic America: Million-Scale Mapping Between the Wars," *Imago Mundi* 61 (2, 2009): 215–243. The story of the deep financial difficulties the society faced in the 1970s, gross mismanagement, and the loss of the treasured library is a story I leave for someone else to tell.

29 For example, Lorimer and Spedding, "Excavating Geography's Hidden Spaces"; Lorimer, "Telling Small Stories"; Maddrell, "The Map Girls."

30 Ron J. Johnston and Charles Withers, "Knowing Our Own History? Geography Department Archives in the UK," *Area* 40 (1, 2008): 3–11; quote on 5.

31 Rose, *Feminism and Geography*, 414; see David Livingstone, *The Geographical Tradition* (London: Blackwell, 1992).

32 For instance see Cheryl McEwan, "Gender, Science and Physical Geography in Nineteenth-Century Britain," *Area* 30 (3, 1998): 215–223; Linda Peake, "Proper Words in Proper Places … or of Young Turks and Old Turkeys," *The Canadian Geographer* 38 (3, 1994): 204–206; Karen M. Morin, *Frontiers of Femininity: A New Historical Geography of the Nineteenth-Century American West* (Syracuse: Syracuse University Press, 2008); Jeanne Kay Guelke and Karen M. Morin, "Gender, Nature, Empire: Women Naturalists in Nineteenth-Century British Travel Literature," *Transactions of the Institute of British Geographers* 26 (2001): 306–326.

33 Driver, *Geography Militant*, is an important exception.

34 Smith, *American Empire*; Morag Bell, Robin A. Butlin, and Michael Heffernan, eds. *Geography and Imperialism, 1820–1940* (Manchester: Manchester University Press, 1995); Felix Driver, "Geography's Empire"; Anne Godlewska and Neil Smith, eds. *Geography and Empire* (Oxford: Blackwell, 1994); Clive Barnett, "Impure and Worldly Geography: The Africanist Discourse of the Royal Geographical Society, 1831–73," *Transactions of the Institute of British Geography* 23 (1998): 239–251; Withers, *Geography, Science and National Identity*.

35 But see works that take up such subjects at later periods, such as Tamar Rothenberg, "Voyeurs of Imperialism: *The National Geographic Magazine* before World War II," in *Geography and Empire*, ibid., 155–172; Tuason, "Ideology of Empire"; Lutz and Collins, *Reading National Geographic*.

36 Withers, "Constructing the Geographical Archive"; Antoinette Burton, ed. *Archive Stories: Facts, Fictions, and the Writing of History* (Durham: Duke University Press, 2005).

37 Driver, "Geography's Empire," 36; Bradley, "Seductions of the Archive," 113; Osborne, "Ordinariness of the Archive," 59.

38 Michel Foucault, "The Life of Infamous Men [La Vie des Hommes Infâmes]," *Les Cahiers du Chemin* 29 (1977): 12–29; rpt. *Michel Foucault: Power, Truth, Strategy* (Sydney: Feral Publications, 1979): 76–91; quotations from 76, 80–81.

39 Personal Correspondence, AGS Councilor Susan Hardwick, 7 July 2009.

40 Jerome Dobson, "Judge Charles P. Daly, AGS President (1864–1899)," *Ubique: Notes from the American Geographical Society* 29 (2, 2009): 1–3 seems to have done just that. "Recently, Karen Morin wrote an article about Judge Daly (2008). I won't review it

here because this column is not the proper venue. Instead, I'll simply encourage you to read her essay and my column or, better yet, Hammond's (1954) exhaustive biography of Judge Daly and decide for yourself if we can be talking about the same person. Yet, likely a whole new generation of geographers will know Daly more through her eyes than von Humboldt's, Hammond's, or mine." He went on to say that "if Judge Daly were alive today he would be called a feminist for his judicial opinions, a humanitarian for his personal commitment to orphans, and a social activist for his advocacy of minorities." Unfortunately, we learn very little about Charles Daly's geography from the article.

41 John Nichols, "Enron: What Dick Cheney Knew," *The Nation*, 15 April 2002; "Gore's Dual Role: Advocate and Investor," *New York Times*, 2 November 2009.

42 Cheryl McEwan, "Cutting Powerlines Within the Palace? Countering Paternity and Eurocentrism in the 'Geographical Tradition'," *Transactions of the Institute of British Geographers* 23 (3, 1998): 371–384.

Bibliography

Manuscript Sources

American Geographical Society, New York. Council Meeting Minutes (1854–1915), 16 volumes; Society Meeting Minutes (1851–1877), 7 volumes; Letters of Charles P. Daly, 2 boxes; also archived letters by author last name (various boxes, including approximately 25 letters from H.S. Sanford to Charles Daly and John Latrobe) and one box, Foreign Correspondence. Other AGS sources are published as the *Journal [Bulletin, Proceedings] of the American Geographical Society of New York* (1851–1915).

Henry S. Sanford Museum Archives, Sanford, Florida. Holdings include 11 letters from Charles P. Daly to H.S. Sanford, and 29 letters from John Latrobe to Sanford.

New York Public Library, Manuscripts and Archives Division, Charles P. Daly Correspondence and Papers, 12 boxes, 28 volumes, New York. Collection includes letters, writings, legal papers, diaries, notebooks, scrapbooks, account books, and personal papers, as well as the Maria Lydia Daly Correspondence and Papers.

Books, Scholarly Articles, and Newspaper Articles

Adas, Michael. *Machines as the Measure of Men: Science, Technology, and Ideologies of Western Dominance*. Ithaca, NY: Cornell University Press, 1989.

"African Explorations," *New York Times*, 14 December 1875.

Agnew, John. *Hegemony: The New Shape of Global Power*. Philadelphia: Temple University Press, 2005.

Alvord, Benjamin. "Winter Grazing in the Rocky Mountains," *Journal of the American Geographical Society of New York* 15 (1883): 257–288.

"American Franklin Search Expedition," *Harper's Weekly*, 4 December 1880.

"American Franklin Search Expedition," *The Illustrated London News*, 1 January 1881.

"American Interests Abroad" [Africa], *New York Times*, 11 January 1884.

Anbinder, Tyler. *Five Points: The 19th-Century New York City Neighborhood that Invented Tap Dance, Stole Elections, and Became the World's Most Notorious Slum*. New York: The Free Press, 2001.

"Anglo-Portuguese Congo Treaty," and "Congo Politics: Protest Against the Treaty Between Great Britain and Portugal," *New York Herald*, 1 April 1884.

"Arcade Bill Signed," *New York Herald*, 12 May 1886.

"Arcade Railway Scheme: Prominent New Yorkers Before the Senate Railroad Committee," *New York Herald*, 17 March 1886.

"Arctic Expedition," *New York Herald*, 16 October 1872.

"Arctic Meeting of Chickering Hall, October 28th, 1880. Reception for Lieut. Frederick Schwatka and his Associates of the Franklin Search Party of 1878, 1879 and 1880," *Journal of the American Geographical Society of New York* 12 (1880): 237–296.

"Arctic Search Expedition: Passage of Mr. McPherson's Bill by the Senate," *New York Herald*, 5 February 1881.

Armstrong, Nancy and Leonard Tennenhouse, eds. *The Ideology of Conduct: Essays in Literature and the History of Sexuality*. London: Methuen, 1987.

Asad, Talal. "Ethnographic Representation, Statistics, and Modern Power," *Social Research* 61 (1, 1994): 55–87.

Baker, Paula. "The Domestication of Politics: Women and American Political Society, 1780–1920." In *Unequal Sisters: A Multicultural Reader in U.S. Women's History*, edited by Vicki Ruiz and Ellen C. DuBois, 66–91. New York: Routledge, 1994.

Barnett, Clive. "Impure and Worldly Geography: The Africanist Discourse of the Royal Geographical Society, 1831–73," *Transactions of the Institute of British Geography* 23 (1998): 239–251.

Bayor, Ronald H. and Timothy J. Meagher, eds. *The New York Irish*. Baltimore: Johns Hopkins University Press, 1996.

Bederman, Gail. *Manliness & Civilization: A Cultural History of Gender and Race in the United States, 1880–1917*. Chicago: University of Chicago Press, 1995.

Bederman, Sanford H. "The 1876 Brussels Geographical Conference and the Charade of European Cooperation in African Exploration," *Terrae Incognitae* 21 (1989): 63–73.

Bell, A.N. ed. *The Sanitarian: A Monthly Magazine Devoted to the Preservation of Health, Mental and Physical Culture*. New York: A.N. Bell, M.D., 1881.

Bell, Morag and Cheryl McEwan. "The Admission of Women Fellows to the Royal Geographical Society, 1892–1914: The Controversy and the Outcome," *The Geographical Journal* 162 (1996): 295–312.

Bell, Morag, Robin A. Butlin, and Michael Heffernan, eds. *Geography and Imperialism, 1820–1940*. Manchester: Manchester University Press, 1995.

Bent, Lieut. "The Japanese Gulf Stream," *Bulletin of the American Geographical and Statistical Society* II (1856): 203–213.

Bernstein, Iver. *The New York City Draft Riots: Their Significance for American Society and Politics in the Age of the Civil War*. New York: Oxford University Press, 1990.

Berton, Pierre. *The Arctic Grail*. London: Viking, 1988.

Bloom, Lisa. *Gender on Ice: American Ideologies of Polar Expeditions*. Minneapolis: University of Minnesota Press, 1993.

Blouet, Brian W., ed. *The Origins of Academic Geography in the United States*. Hamden, CT: Archon Books, 1981.

Boaz, Franz. "Census and Reservations of the Kwakiutl Nation," *Journal of the American Geographical Society of New York* 19 (2, 1887): 225–232.

Boaz, Franz. "A Year Among the Eskimo," *Journal of the American Geographical Society of New York* 19 (4, 1887): 383–402.

Bonnett, Alastair. "Geography as the World Discipline: Connecting Popular and Academic Geographical Imaginations," *Area* 35 (2003): 55–63.

"Botanical Garden Fund: Institution Gets Principal of Ex-Chief Justice Daly's Bequest," *New York Times*, 2 August 1925.

Boyer, Kate. "Feminist Geography in the Archive: Practice and Method," *Geography and Gender Reconsidered*, 169–174. London: Women and Geography Study Group of the Institute of British Geographers, 2004.

Bradley, Harriet. "The Seductions of the Archive: Voices Lost and Found," *History of the Human Sciences* 12 (1999): 107–122.

Brannstrom, Christian. "Almost a Canal: Visions of Interoceanic Communication across Southern Nicaragua," *Ecumene* 2 (1, 1995): 65–87.

Bravo, Michael. "Ethnological Encounters." In *Cultures of Natural History*, edited by Nicholas Jardine, James A. Secord, and Emma C. Spary, 339–357. Cambridge: Cambridge University Press, 1996.

Bravo, Michael. "Geographies of Exploration and Improvement: William Scoresby and Arctic Whaling, 1782–1822," *Journal of Historical Geography* 32 (2006): 512–538.

Bravo, Michael. "Arctic Science, Nation Building and Citizenship." In *Northern Exposure: Peoples, Powers and Prospects in Canada's North*, edited by Frances Abele, Thomas J. Courchene, F. Leslie Seidle, and France St.-Hilaire, 141–168. Montreal: The Institute for Research on Public Policy, 2009.

Bravo, Michael. "Preface: Legacies of Polar Science." In *Legacies and Change in Polar Sciences: Historical, Legal and Political Reflections on the International Polar Year*, edited by Jessica M. Shadian and Monica Tennberg, xiii–xvi. Farnham: Ashgate, 2009.

Bravo, Michael and Sverker Sorlin, eds. *Narrating the Arctic: A Cultural History of Nordic Scientific Practices*. Canton, MA: Science History Publications, 2002.

"Broadway Arcade Road: Answering the Objections to its Construction," *New York Times*, 18 April 1886.

Brooks, Arthur A. *Index to the Bulletin of the American Geographical Society, 1852–1915*. New York: American Geographical Society, 1918.

Brown, Richard Harvey and Beth Davis-Brown, "The Making of Memory: The Politics of Archives, Libraries and Museums in the Construction of National Consciousness," *History of the Human Sciences* 11 (1998): 17–32.

Brundage, David. "'In Time of Peace, Prepare for War': Key Themes in the Social Thought of New York's Irish Nationalists, 1890–1916." In *The New York Irish*, edited by Ronald H. Bayor and Timothy J. Meagher, 321–336. Baltimore: Johns Hopkins University Press, 1996.

"Bubble Bursts: M. de Lesseps' Pet Scheme Threatened with Bankruptcy," *New York Herald,* 14 December 1888.

Burton, Antoinette, ed. *Archive Stories: Facts, Fictions, and the Writing of History*. Durham: Duke University Press, 2005.

"Busy Day for De Lesseps," *New York Tribune*, 28 February 1880.

"Canal Diggers at Odds," *New York Herald*, 24 April 1889.

Carney, Judith A. and Richard Nicholas Rosomoff. *In the Shadow of Slavery: Africa's Botanical Legacy in the Atlantic World.* Berkeley: University of California Press, 2009.

"Central Africa: Chief Justice Daly's Address Before the American Geographical Society, Wonders of the Congo, A Plea for American Protest Against Portuguese Assumption," *New York Herald*, 1 April 1884.

"Change of the Panama Canal Level," *New York Herald*, 1 March 1886.

Channebot, M. and Egbert L. Viele. "The Resources of Central Africa: M. Channebot's Project for Their Development by a Railway," *Journal of the American Geographical Society of New York* 13 (1881): 165–195.

Chapin, David. *Exploring Other Worlds: Margaret Fox, Elisha Kent Kane, and the Antebellum Culture of Curiosity*. Amherst: University of Massachusetts Press, 2004.

"Chief Justice Daly," *The Hour*, 29 January 1881.

"Chief Justice Daly," *New York Times*, 15 November 1885.

"Chief Justice-ship," *New York Herald*, 16 September 1873.

"City Sanitary Reform," *The World*, 19 November 1880.

"Civilization of Africa," *New York Times*, 3 June 1877.

"Civilization in Central Africa," *New York Times*, 1 April 1884.

Clout, Hugh. *Agriculture in France on the Eve of the Railway Age*. London: Croom Helm, 1980.

Colley, Linda. *The Ordeal of Elizabeth Marsh: A Woman in World History*. New York: Pantheon Books, 2007.

Collins, Frederick. "The Isthmus of Darien and the Valley of the Atrato Considered with Reference to the Practicability of an Interoceanic Ship-Canal," *Journal of the American Geographical Society of New York* 5 (1874): 138–165.

"Commercial Importance of the Valley of the Congo," *New York Herald*, 22 January 1884.

"Congo: A Battle on the River – Protection Afforded by the International Society," *New York Herald*, 3 April 1884.

"Congo Valley Trading Posts," *New York Herald*, 22 January 1884.

"Contributions to Physical Geography," *Overland Monthly* 11 (5 November 1873): 474–475.

"Cooper Institute Pow Wow," *The World*, 17 June 1870.

Corner, George. *Doctor Kane of the Arctic Seas*. Philadelphia: Temple University Press, 1972.

Crampton, Jeremy. "Cartographic Rationality and the Politics of Geosurveillance and Security," *Cartography and Geographic Information Science* 30 (2, 2003): 135–149.

Crampton, Jeremy and Stuart Elden. "Space, Politics, Calculation: An Introduction," *Social and Cultural Geography* 7 (5, 2006): 681–685.

Cronon, William. *Nature's Metropolis: Chicago and the Great West*. New York: W.W. Norton, 1991.

Cumbler, John T. *From Abolition to Rights for All*. Philadelphia: University of Pennsylvania Press, 2008.

Daly, Charles P. ["D."]. "Letters on Cuba," *New York Chronicle*, 22 September 1851.

Daly, Charles P. *Common Pleas for the City and County of New York, With an Account of the State and Its Tribunals, from the Time of Its Settlement by the Dutch in 1623 until the Adoption of the State Constitution in 1846*. New York: R. Delafield, 1855.

Daly, Charles P. *Naturalization: Embracing the Past History of the Subject, and the Present State of the Law in the United States [Etc.]* From the *New American Cyclopedia*. New York: John F. Trow Printer, 1860.

Daly, Charles P. "Annual Address. Subject: Review of the Events of the Year and Recent Explorations and Theories for Reaching the North Pole," *Journal of the American Geographical Society of New York* 2 (1870): lxxxiii–cxxvi.

Daly, Charles P. "Annual Address. Subject: The Geographical Work of the World in 1872," *Journal of the American Geographical Society of New York* 4 (1873): 63–118.

Daly, Charles P. "Annual Address. Subject: The Geographical Work of the World in 1873," *Journal of the American Geographical Society of New York* 5 (1874): 49–94.

Daly, Charles P. "Annual Address. Subject: The Geographical Work of the World in 1874," *Journal of the American Geographical Society of New York* 6 (1874): 53–92.

Daly, Charles P. "Annual Address: The Geographical Work of the World for 1875," *Journal of the American Geographical Society of New York* 7 (1875): 31–92.

Daly, Charles P. "Remarks on Stanley's Verification of Ptolemy's Geography," *Journal of the American Geographical Society of New York* 7 (1875): 290–295.

Daly, Charles P. "Annual Address: The Geographical Work of the World in 1876," *Journal of the American Geographical Society of New York* 8 (1876): 54–64.

Daly, Charles P. "Annual Address: Geographical Work of the World in 1877," *Journal of the American Geographical Society of New York* 10 (1878): 1–76.

Daly, Charles P. "Annual Address: Geographical Work of the World in 1878 and 1879," *Journal of the American Geographical Society of New York* 12 (1880): 1–107.

Daly, Charles P. "Editorial: Relief of the Jeanette," *New York Herald*, 27 January 1881.

Daly, Charles P. "Recent Developments in Central Africa and the Valley of the Congo," *Journal of the American Geographical Society of New York* 16 (1884): 89–159.

Daly, Charles P. "Notes on the History of the Jews in England and the American Colonies," *The Jewish Messenger*, New York, 4 January 1884.

Daly, Charles P. *The Commercial Importance of Central Africa and the Free Navigation of the Congo. Address before the Chamber of Commerce of the State of New York, January 10, 1884, in Favor of Resolutions Presented to the Chamber by A.A. Low, Esq., and Adopted by that Body*. New York: H. Bessey, 1884.

Daly, Charles P. Review, *Of Three Years of Arctic Service by Lt. A.W. Greeley*, *New York Herald*, 14 February 1886.

Daly, Charles P. "Annual Address: Recent Geographical Work of the World," *Journal of the American Geographical Society of New York* 20 (1888): 1–38.

Daly, Charles P. *Answer of the Nicaragua Canal Association of the Protest of the Alleged American Atlantic and Pacific Ship Canal Company*. New York: Nicaragua Maritime Canal Company, 1888.

Daly, Charles P. "Annual Address. On the History of Physical Geography," *Journal of the American Geographical Society of New York* 22 (1890): 1–55.

Daly, Charles P. *Want of a Botanical Garden in New York: Remarks of Ex-Chief Justice Chas. P. Daly, Meeting held May 19, 1891, To Take Action Under the Law Enacted by the Legislature for the Establishment of a Botanical Garden in the City of New York*. New York: 1891.

Daly, Charles P. "Who Discovered the Pygmies"? *Journal of the American Geographical Society of New York* 24 (1892): 18–22.

Daly, Charles P. *The Settlement of the Jews in North America*, edited by Max Kohler. New York: Philip Cowan, 1893.

Daly, Charles P. "Have We a Portrait of Columbus? Annual Address, January 9, 1893," *Journal of the American Geographical Society of New York* 25 (1893): 1–63.

Daly, Charles P. and Alexander Crummell. "The Plan of the King of Belgium for the Civilization of Central Africa, and the Suppression of the Slave Trade," *Journal of the American Geographical Society of New York* 9 (1877): 88–103.

Daly, Charles P. and Bayard Taylor. "Meeting of the American Geographical Society, November 15, 1875. Remarks on Explorations in Central Africa," *Journal of the American Geographical Society of New York* 7 (1875): 296–304.

Daly, Charles P. and David Livingstone. "Report of the Reception Tendered by the American Geographical Society to Henry M. Stanley, Esq., on His Return from Central Africa," *Journal of the American Geographical Society of New York* 4 (1873): 453–468.

Daly, Charles P. and W.H. Gilder. "An Expedition to the Northern Magnetic Pole," *Journal of the American Geographical Society of New York* 24 (1892): 215–261.

Davis, R.C. "The Beginnings of American Social Research." In *Nineteenth Century American Science*, edited by G. Daniels, 152–178. Evanston, IL: Northwestern University Press, 1972.

"De Lesseps Resigns," *New York Herald*, 15 December 1888.

DeRogatis, Amy. *Moral Geography: Maps, Missionaries and the American Frontier*. New York: Columbia University Press, 2003.

Dettlebach, Michael. "Humboldtian Science." In *Cultures of Natural History*, edited by Nicholas Jardine, James A. Secord, and Emma C. Spary, 287–304. Cambridge: Cambridge University Press, 1996.

Devlin, Athena. *Between Profits and Primitivism: Shaping White Middle-Class Masculinity in the U.S., 1880–1917*. New York: Routledge, 2005.

Dick, Lyle. "Peary, Robert," *Encyclopedia of the Arctic,* 1600–1601. London: Routledge, 2005.

Diner, Hasia R. "'The Most Irish City in the Union': The Era of the Great Migration, 1844–1877." In *The New York Irish*, edited by Ronald H. Bayor and Timothy J. Meagher, 87–106. Baltimore: Johns Hopkins University Press, 1996.

"Dinner to Lieut. Greely," *New York Tribune*, 17 January 1886.

"Discoveries in South Africa," *Bulletin of the American Geographical and Statistical Society* Vol. 1 (1, 1852): 47–60.

"Distress in Ireland," *New York Herald*, 1 January 1880.

Disturnell, John. *New York as it Was and as it Is* ... New York: Van Nostrand, 1876.

Dobson, Jerome E. "Let the Indigenous People of Oaxaca Speak for Themselves," *Ubique: Notes from the American Geographical Society* 29 (1, 2009).

Dobson, Jerome E. "Judge Charles P. Daly, AGS President (1864–1899)," *Ubique: Notes from the American Geographical Society* 29 (2, 2009): 1–3.

Domosh, Mona. *Invented Cities: The Creation of Landscape in 19th Century New York and Boston*. New Haven: Yale University Press, 1996.

Domosh, Mona. *American Commodities in an Age of Empire*. New York: Routledge, 2006.

Dopp, Mary. "Geographical Influences in the Development of Wisconsin. Chapter III. The Settlement of Wisconsin," *Bulletin of the American Geographical Society* 45 (8, 1913): 585–609.

Dore, Jonathan. *Encyclopedia of the Arctic*. London: Routledge, 2005.

Douglas, James. "Historical and Geographical Features of the Rocky Mountain Railroads," *Journal of the American Geographical Society of New York* 17 (1885): 299–342.

Downs, Roger M. "Popularization and Geography: An Inseparable Relationship," *Annals of the Association of American Geographers* 100 (2, 2010): 444–467.

"Dr. Livingstone," *Harper's Weekly*, 27 July 1872.

Drayton, Richard. *Nature's Government: Science, Imperial Britain, and the "Improvement" of the World*. New Haven: Yale University Press, 2000.

Driver, Felix. "Geography's Empire: Histories of Geographical Knowledge," *Environment and Planning D: Society and Space* 10 (1992): 23–40.

Driver, Felix. *Geography Militant: Cultures of Exploration and Empire*. London: Blackwell, 2001.

Du Chaillu, Paul Belloni. *Explorations and Adventures in Equatorial Africa.* New York: Harper & Brothers, 1861.

Du Chaillu, Paul Belloni, *A Journey to Ashango-land, and Further Penetration into Equatorial Africa.* London: John Murray, 1867.

Du Chaillu, Paul Belloni, *Land of the Midnight Sun*. New York: Harper & Brothers, 1882.

Dunbar, Gary, ed. *Geography: Discipline, Profession and Subject Since 1870* Dordrecht, Netherlands: Kluwer Academic, 2001.

Edney, Matthew. *Mapping an Empire: The Geographical Construction of British India, 1765–1843*. Chicago: University of Chicago Press, 1997.

"First Annual Meeting of the New York Sanitary Society," *New York Herald*, 19 November 1880.

Fleming, Fergus. *Ninety Degrees North: The Quest for the North Pole.* New York: Grove Press, 2001.

Foote, Kenneth E. "To Remember and Forget: Archives, Memory, and Culture," *American Archivist* 53 (1990): 378–392.

"For the Botanical Garden," *New York Times*, 13 June 1895.

"Forty-one Years a Judge: The Honorable Career of a Wise and Upright Jurist," *New York Times*, 15 November 1885.

Foucault, Michel. *The Archaeology of Knowledge and the Discourse on Language*. New York: Pantheon, 1972.

Foucault, Michel. "The Life of Infamous Men [La Vie des Hommes Infâmes]," *Les Cahiers du Chemin* 29 (1977): 12–29; rpt. *Michel Foucault: Power, Truth, Strategy*, 76–91. Sydney: Feral Publications, 1979.

Foucault, Michel. *The Order of Things: An Archaeology of the Human Sciences*. 1970; rpt. New York: Vintage, 1994.

"Franklin Search Party," *New York Herald*, 20 June 1878.

"Freedom of Worship Bill," *New York Herald*, 16 February 1885.

Frenkel, Stephen. "Jungle Stories: American Representations of Tropical Panama," *Geographical Review* 86 (1996): 317–333.

Frenkel, Stephen. "Geographical Representations of the 'Other': The Landscape of the Panama Canal Zone," *Journal of Historical Geography* 28 (1, 2002): 85–99.

Garvey, T. Gregory. *Creating the Culture of Reform in Antebellum America.* Athens: University of Georgia Press, 2006.

"Geographical Progress," *New York Times*, 28 February 1878.

"Geographical Society: Reception of the Earl of Dufferin at Chickering Hall" and "Arctic Exploration: Captain Howgate's Plan," *New York Herald*, 1 February 1878.

"Geographical Society: Reception to Lord Dufferin," *New York Times*, 1 February 1878.

Gibbs, David N. *The Political Economy of Third World Intervention: Mines, Money, and U.S. Policy in the Congo Crisis*. Chicago: University of Chicago Press, 1991.

Gilder, William H. *Schwatka's Search: Sledging in the Arctic in Quest of the Franklin Records*, 1881.

Gilman, Daniel C. "Annual Address. Subject: Geographical Work in the United States during 1871," *Journal of the American Geographical Society of New York* 4 (1873): 119–144.

Godlewska, Anne and Neil Smith, eds. *Geography and Empire*. Oxford: Blackwell, 1994.

Golinski, Jan. *Making Natural Knowledge: Constructivism and the History of Science*. Cambridge: Cambridge University Press, 1998.

"Good-By to the Eothen," *The World*, 20 June 1878.

Gordon, John Steele. *An Empire of Wealth: The Epic History of American Economic Power*. New York: Harper Collins, 2004.

"Gore's Dual Role: Advocate and Investor," *New York Times*, 2 November 2009.

Greely, A.W. "Arctic Meeting at Chickering Hall, November 21st, 1884. Reception of Lieut. A.W. Greely, U.S. Army, and His Surviving Companions in the Exploration of the Arctic," *Journal of the American Geographical Society of New York* 16 (1884): 311–344.

Green, Julie. *The Canal Builders: Making America's Empire at the Panama Canal*. New York: Penguin Press, 2009.

Greenberg, Amy. *Manifest Manhood and the Antebellum American Empire*. Cambridge: Cambridge University Press, 2005.

Guelke, Jeanne Kay and Karen M. Morin, "Gender, Nature, Empire: Women Naturalists in Nineteenth Century British Travel Literature," *Transactions of the Institute of British Geographers* 26 (2001): 306–326.

Guttridge, Leonard F. *Icebound*. New York: Paragon, 1988.

Guttridge, Leonard F. *Ghosts of Cape Sabine: The Harrowing True Story of the Greely Expedition*. New York: Putnam, 2000.

Habermas, Jurgen. *The Structural Formation of the Public Sphere: An Inquiry Into a Category of Bourgeois Society*. Cambridge MA: Cambridge University Press, 1989.

Hall, Catherine. *White, Male and Middle Class: Explorations in Feminism and History*. New York: Routledge, 1988.

Hallowell, Gerald, ed. *Oxford Companion to Canadian History*. London: Oxford University Press, 2006.

Hamilton, W.J. "Method of Geographical Observation," *Bulletin of the American Geographical and Statistical Society* 1 (1852): 77–79.

Hammond, Harold E. *A Commoner's Judge: The Life and Times of Charles Patrick Daly*. Boston: Christopher Publishing House, 1954.

Hammond, Harold E., ed. *Maria Lydig Daly, Diary of a Union Lady 1861–1865*. 1962; rpt. Lincoln: University of Nebraska Press, 2000.

Hannah, Matthew. *Governmentality and the Mastery of Territory in 19th Century America.* Cambridge, UK: Cambridge University Press, 2000.

Hannah, Matthew. "'In Full View Yet Invisible': On Neil Smith's American Empire," *Political Geography* 24 (2005): 240.

Haraway, Donna. "Situated Knowledges: The Science Question in Feminism and the Privilege of Partial Perspectives," *Feminist Studies* (1988): 575–599.

Harvey, Bruce. *American Geographics: U.S. National Narratives and the Representation of the Non-European World, 1830–1865.* Stanford: Stanford University Press, 2001.

Hawthorne, Julian. "An American Kew," *Lippincott's Magazine*, February 1891, 252–260.

Hayes, I.I. *The Open Polar Sea: A Narrative of a Voyage of Discovery Towards the North Pole*. London, Sampson Low, Son and Marston, 1867.

Hayes, I.I., J.O. Buddington, G.E. Tyson, H.C. Chester, and W. Morton, "Proceedings of the Arctic Meeting in Relation to the Voyage of the *Polaris*," *Journal of the American Geographical Society of New York* 6 (1874): 93–115.

Hayes, Isaac I. and Paul Du Chaillu, "The Norse Meeting; Iceland and Lapland," *Journal of the American Geographical Society of New York* 6 (1874): 227–232.

Heffernan, Michael. "The Science of Empire: The French Geographical Movement and the Forms of French Imperialism, 1870–1920." In *Geography and Empire*, edited by Anne Godlewska and Neil Smith, 92–114. Oxford: Blackwell, 1994.

Heffernan, Michael. "Geography, Empire and National Revolution in Vichy France," *Political Geography* 24 (2005): 731–758.

Heffernan, Michael. "The Cartography of the Fourth Estate: Mapping the New Imperialism in British and French Newspapers, 1875–1925." In *The Imperial Map: Cartography and the Mastery of Empire*, edited by James R. Akerman, 261–299. Chicago: University of Chicago Press, 2009.

Hegglund, Jon. "Empire's Second Take: Projecting America in Stanley and Livingstone." In *Nineteenth-Century Geographies: The Transformation of Space from the Victorian Age to the American Century*, edited by Helena Michie and Ronald Thomas, 265–278. New Brunswick, NJ: Rutgers University Press, 2003.

Henderson, Brian. *Fatal North: Adventure and Survival Aboard the USS* Polaris. New York: Signet, 2001.

Herbert, Wally. *The Noose of Laurels*. London: Hodder & Stoughton, 1989.

Herschkowitz, Leo. *Tweed's New York: Another Look*. New York: Anchor Press, 1977.

Herschkowitz, Leo. “The Irish and the Emerging City: Settlement to 1844.” In *The New York Irish*, edited by Ronald H. Bayor and Timothy J. Meagher, 11–34. Baltimore: Johns Hopkins University Press, 1996.

Hilkey, Judy. *Character is Capital: Success Manuals and Manhood in Gilded Age America*. Chapel Hill: University of North Carolina Press, 1997.

Hochschild, Adam. *King Leopold's Ghost: A Story of Greed, Terror, and Heroism in Colonial Africa*. New York: Houghton Mifflin, 1998.

Hodges, Graham. “‘Desirable Companions and Lovers’: Irish and African Americans in the Sixth Ward, 1830–1870.” In *The New York Irish*, edited by Ronald H. Bayor and Timothy J. Meagher, 107–124. Baltimore: Johns Hopkins University Press, 1996.

Hogan, J. Michael. *The Panama Canal in American Politics: Domestic Advocacy and the Evolution of Policy*. Carbondale: Southern Illinois University Press, 1986.

Hogason, Kristin L. *Fighting for American Manhood: How Gender Politics Provoked the Spanish-American and Philippine-American Wars*. New Haven: Yale University Press, 1998.

“Home Rule for Ireland,” *New York Times*, 15 November 1885.

“Honor to Schwatka,” *New York Herald*, 29 October 1880.

Howgate, H.W. “Arctic Meeting at Chickering Hall, Plan for Exploration of the Arctic Regions,” *Journal of the American Geographical Society of New York* 10 (1878): 276–298.

“How to Clean the Streets,” *The World*, 19 March 1881.

Huhndorf, Shari M. “Nanook and His Contemporaries: Imagining Eskimos in American Culture, 1897–1922,” *Critical Inquiry* 27 (1, 2000): 122–148.

“In and About the City: The House of Refuge, Judge Daly's Resignation from the Board of Managers,” *New York Times*, 10 March 1885.

“Indians. The: Red Cloud and Red Dog on the Wrongs of the Red Men – Immense Crowds at Cooper Institute to Hear the Aboriginal Orators,” *New York Herald*, 17 June 1870.

“Interior of Africa,” *New York Times*, 23 May 1877.

“International Geographical Congress,” London *Times*, 26 July 1895.

“Interoceanic Canal Question,” *New York Herald*, 1 April 1884.

“Interoceanic Ship Canal. Meeting at Chickering Hall, December 9, 1879,” *Journal of the American Geographical Society of New York* 11 (1879): 113–152.

Inwin, Tim. *The Place of Geography*. New York: John Wiley & Sons, 1992.

“Irish Home Rule,” *New York Herald*, 24 January 1886.

“Is Spinola a Bone Hunter: His Opposition to the Nicaragua Canal Bill. He Assails Judge Daly as a Lobbyist,” *New York Times*, 15 December 1888.

“Isthmus Canal,” *New York Herald*, 29 May 1879.

James, Preston E. and Geoffrey J. Martin. *All Possible Worlds: A History of Geographical Ideas*, 2nd ed. New York: John Wiley, 1993.

“Jeannette: Judge Daly's Appeal for a Search Vessel,” *New York Herald*, 27 January 1881.

"Jeannette's Peculiar Ice Perils" and "Relief for the Jeanette: Prompt Action of the Senate Naval Committee," *New York Herald*, 3 February 1881.

Johnston, Ron J. and Charles Withers. "Knowing Our Own History? Geography Department Archives in the UK," *Area* 40 (1, 2008): 3–11.

Jones, H.G. "Teaching the Explorers: Some Inuit Contributions to Arctic Discoveries," *Polar Geography* 26 (1, 2002): 4–20.

"Judge Daly's Address," *Home Journal*, 8 November 1862.

"Judge Daly's Beliefs" and "Reception to Lieut. Greely," *New York Tribune*, 22 November 1884.

"Judge Daly Explains" [Nicaragua Canal], *New York Herald*, 15 December 1888.

"Justice Daly Retires. An Affecting Scene Yesterday in the Court of Common Pleas: A Chat with the Judge," *The Daily Telegraph*, 20 November 1885.

Kalpagam, U. "The Colonial State and Statistical Knowledge," *History of the Human Sciences* 13 (2, 2000): 37–55.

Kane, E.K. "Paper on Access to an Open Polar Sea Along a North American Meridian," *Bulletin of the American Geographical and Statistical Society* 1 (2, 1853): 85–103.

Kimmel, Michael. *The History of Men: Essays on the History of American and British Masculinities.* Albany: State University of New York Press, 2005.

Kimmel, Michael. *Manhood in America: A Cultural History*, 2nd ed. New York: Oxford University Press, 2006.

King, W. Nephew, Jr. "The Nicaragua Canal," *Frank Leslie's Illustrated Newspaper*, 8 June 1889.

Kluger, Richard. *The Paper: The Life and Death of the* New York Herald Tribune. New York: Vintage Books, 1986.

Klutschak, H. *Overland to Starvation Cove: With the Inuit in Search of Franklin 1878–1880.* Toronto: University of Toronto Press, 1987.

Knapp, Herbert and Mary Knapp. *Red, White and Blue Paradise: The American Canal Zone in Panama.* San Diego: Harcourt Brace Jovanovich, 1984.

Knott, H.W.K. "Charles Patrick Daly," *Dictionary of American Biography* 5 (1973): 41–42.

Koelsch, William A. "Academic Geography, American Style: An Institutional Perspective." In *Geography: Discipline, Profession and Subject Since 1870*, edited by Gary Dunbar, 245–279. Dordrecht, Netherlands: Kluwer Academic, 2001.

Kohler, Max. *Chas. P. Daly: A Tribute to His Memory*. New York: *The American Hebrew*, 1899.

"Ladies Sit at the Tables," *New York Tribune*, 17 November 1885.

Lambert, David. "'Taken Captive by the Mystery of the Great River': Towards an Historical Geography of British Geography and Atlantic Slavery," *Journal of Historical Geography* 35 (2009): 44–65.

Lambert, M. Gustave. "L'expedition au Pole Nord: Assemblee Generale du 20 Decembre 1867," *Bulletin de la Societe de Geographie* (Paris: Au Siège de la Societe, 1868).

Lane, K. Maria D. *Geographies of Mars: Seeing and Knowing the Red Planet.* Chicago: University of Chicago Press, 2010.

"Last Appeal of Red Cloud," *New York Times*, 17 June 1870.

"Last Night's Meeting," The *Evening Telegram*, 19 March 1881.

Latour, Bruno. *Science in Action: How to Follow Scientists and Engineers Through Society*. Milton Keynes: Open University Press, 1987.

Lewis, Peter. "AGS Archives in Limelight," *Ubique: Notes from the American Geographical Society* 28 (3, 2008): 11.

"Lieutenant Greely Feted," *New York Herald*, 17 January 1886.

Livingstone, David L. *The Geographical Tradition: Episodes in the History of a Contested Enterprise*. London: Blackwell, 1992.

Livingstone, David N. *Nathaniel Southgate Shaler and the Culture of American Science*. Tuscaloosa, AL: University of Alabama Press, 1987.

Livingstone, David N. "Climate's Moral Economy: Science, Race and Place in Post-Darwinian British and American Geography." In *Geography and Empire*, edited by Anne Godlewska and Neil Smith, 132–154. Cambridge, MA: Blackwell, 1994.

Livingstone, David N. "The Spaces of Knowledge: Contributions Towards a Historical Geography of Science," *Environment and Planning D: Society and Space* 13 (1995): 5–34.

Livingstone, David N. *Putting Science in its Place: Geographies of Scientific Knowledge*. Chicago: University of Chicago Press, 2003.

Livingstone, David N. "Science, Site and Speech: Scientific Knowledge and the Spaces of Rhetoric," *History of the Human Sciences* 20 (2, 2007): 71–98.

Loomis, Chauncey. *Weird and Tragic Shores: The Story of Charles Francis Hall, Explorer*. New York: The Modern Library, 2002.

Lopez, Barry. *Arctic Dreams*. New York: Vintage Books, 1986.

"Lord Dufferin and the Geographical Society" and "Captain Howgate's Plan," *The World*, 1 February 1878.

Lorimer, Hayden. "Telling Small Stories: Spaces of Knowledge and the Practice of Geography," *Transactions of the Institute of British Geographers* 28 (2003): 197–217.

Lorimer, Hayden and Nick Spedding. "Excavating Geography's Hidden Spaces," *Area* 34 (2002): 294–302.

Lubove, Roy. *The Progressives and the Slums: Tenement House Reform in New York City, 1890–1917*. Pittsburgh: University of Pittsburgh Press, 1962.

Lutz, Catherine and Jane Collins. *Reading National Geographic*. Chicago: University of Chicago Press, 1993.

Lynch, Michael. "Archives in Formation: Privileged Spaces, Popular Archives and Paper Trails," *History of the Human Sciences* 12 (1999): 65–87.

Lynch, Michael and David Bogen. *The Spectacle of History: Speech, Text & Memory at the Iran-Contra Hearings*. Durham: Duke University Press, 1996.

"M. De Lesseps at Panama," *The World*, 1 January 1880.

"M. De Lesseps at Dinner" and "Dinner at Delmonico's," *New York Times*, 29 February 1880.

Maddrell, Avril. "The 'Map Girls': British Women Geographers' War Work, Shifting Gender Boundaries and Reflections on the History of Geography," *Transactions of the Institute of British Geographers* 33 (2008): 127–148.

Marston, Sally. "Public Rituals and Community Power: St. Patrick's Day Parades in Lowell, Massachusetts, 1841–1874," *Political Geography Quarterly* 8 (3, 1989): 255–269.

Maury, M.F. "Annual Address," *Bulletin of the American Geographical and Statistical Society* I (III, 1854): 3–31.

Maury, T.B. "Polar Expeditions and its Hopes," *The Atlantic Monthly* 26. Boston: Fields, Osgood & Co., 1870.

Mayhew, Robert J. "Materialist Hermeneutics, Textuality and the History of Geography: Print Spaces in British Geography, c. 1500–1900," *Journal of Historical Geography* 33 (2007): 466–488.

McCook, Stuart. "'It May Be Truth, But It Is Not Evidence': Paul du Chaillu and the Legitimation of Evidence in the Field Sciences," *Osiris* 2nd series 11 (1996): 177–197.

McCullough, David. *The Path Between the Seas: The Creation of the Panama Canal 1870–1914*. New York: Simon and Schuster, 1977.

McEwan, Cheryl. "Gender, Science and Physical Geography in Nineteenth-Century Britain," *Area* 30 (3, 1998): 215–223.

McEwan, Cheryl. "Cutting Powerlines within the Palace? Countering Paternity and Eurocentrism in the 'Geographical Tradition'," *Transactions of the Institute of British Geographers* 23 (3, 1998): 371–384.

McEwan, Cheryl. "Building a Postcolonial Archive? Gender, Collective Memory and Citizenship in Post-Apartheid South Africa," *Journal of Southern African Studies* 29 (2003): 739–757.

McMannis, Douglas. "Leading Ladies at the AGS," *Geographical Review* 86 (1996): 270–277.

Meyer, David R. "The National Integration of Regional Economies, 1860–1920." In *North America: The Historical Geography of a Changing Continent*, edited by Robert D. Mitchell and Paul A. Groves, 321–346. Savage, MD: Rowman & Littlefield Publishers, 1990.

Meyer, Lysle E. "Henry S. Sanford and the Congo: A Reassessment," *African Historical Studies* 4 (1, 1971): 19–39.

Michie, Helena and Ronald R. Thomas, eds. *Nineteenth-Century Geographies: the Transformation of Space from the Victorian Age to the American Century*. New Brunswick, NJ: Rutgers University Press, 2003.

Missal, Alexander. *Seaway to the Future: American Social Visions and the Construction of the Panama Canal*. Madison: University of Wisconsin Press, 2008.

Mitchell, Robert D. "The North American Past: Retrospect and Prospect." In *North America: The Historical Geography of a Changing Continent*, edited by Robert D. Mitchell and Paul A. Groves, 3–12. Savage, MD: Rowman & Littlefield Publishers, 1990.

Monk, Janice. "Women's Worlds at the American Geographical Society," *Geographical Review* 93 (2, 2003): 237–257.

Morin, Karen M. "Peak Practices: Englishwomen's 'Heroic' Adventures in the 19th Century American West," *Annals of the Association of American Geographers* 89 (1999): 489–514.

Morin, Karen M. *Frontiers of Femininity: A New Historical Geography of the Nineteenth-Century American West*. Syracuse: Syracuse University Press, 2008.

Morin, Karen M. "Charles P. Daly's Gendered Geography, 1860–1890," *Annals of the Association of American Geographers* 98 (2008): 897–919.

Morin, Karen M. "Charles Patrick Daly," *Geographers: Biobibliographical Studies* 28 (2009), 105–117.

Morin, Karen M. and Jeanne Kay Guelke, eds. *Women, Religion, & Space: Global Perspectives on Gender and Faith*. Syracuse: Syracuse University Press, 2007.

Nadal, Ehrman S., John M. Read, and Henry C. Taylor. *Francis Aquila Stout*. New York, 1894.

Nelson, Dana. *National Manhood: Capitalist Citizenship and the Imagined Fraternity of White Men*. Durham: Duke University Press, 1998.

"New York Celebrities, Chief Justice Daly," *The Sun*, 3 January 1885.

"New Yorker's Views on Spain," *New York Times*, 14 April 1882.

"New York's Bosses, Another Speech on the Citizens' Street Cleaning Bill," *New York Herald*, 12 April 1881.

"Nicaragua Canal: Legal Status of the Canal Concessions," The *Evening Post*, 23 July 1888.

Nicaragua Canal Construction Company, *The Inter-Oceanic Canal of Nicaragua: Its History, Physical Condition, Plans and Prospect*. New York: New York Print Company, 1891.

"Nicaragua Canal Fight: Opposing Stockholders Want to Examine the Books," *New York Times*, 28 January 1894.

"Nicaragua Canal Scheme," *The Sun*, 24 February 1888.

"Nicaraguan Canal," *The World*, 4 December 1879.

Nichols, John. "Enron: What Dick Cheney Knew," *The Nation*, 15 April 2002.

Nickerson, Sheila. *Midnight to the North: The Untold Story of the Inuit Woman Who Saved the* Polaris *Expedition*. New York: Putnam, 2002.

Nzongola-Ntalaja, Georges. *The Congo from Leopold to Kabila: A People's History*. London: Zed Books, 2002.

"Off-hand Portraits VIII: Charles P. Daly," *The Knickerbocker*, 15 June 1882.

Ogborn, Miles. *India Ink: Script and Print in the Making of the English East India Company*. Chicago: University of Chicago Press, 2007.

"One Hundred Years Old: The German Society Celebrates Its Centennial with Much Enthusiasm," *New York Herald*, 5 October 1884.

"Open Polar Sea: Chief Justice Believes it Does Not Exist," *New York Herald*, 21 July 1884.

Osborne, Thomas. "The Ordinariness of the Archive," *History of the Human Sciences* 12 (1999): 51–64.

Outram, Dorinda. "New Spaces in Natural History." In *Cultures of Natural History*, edited by Nicholas Jardine, James A. Secord, and Emma C. Spary, 249–265. Cambridge: Cambridge University Press, 1996.

Pakenham, Thomas. *The Scramble for Africa: White Man's Conquest of the Dark Continent from 1876 to 1912*. New York: Avon Books, 1992.

"Panama Canal Swindle," The *Evening Post*, 3 July 1888.

Parker, Matthew. *Panama Fever: The Epic Story of One of the Greatest Human Achievements in All Time*. New York: Doubleday, 2007.

Parry, Richard. *Trial by Ice: The True Story of Murder and Survival on the 1871* Polaris *Expedition*. New York: Ballentine Books, 2001.

Pascoe, Peggy. *Relations of Rescue: The Search for Female Moral Authority in the American West, 1874–1939*. New York: Oxford University Press, 1990.

Peake, Linda. "Proper Words in Proper Places … or of Young Turks and Old Turkeys," *The Canadian Geographer* 38 (3, 1994): 204–206.

Pearson, Alastair W. and Michael Heffernan, "The American Geographical Society's Map of Hispanic America: Million-Scale Mapping Between the Wars," *Imago Mundi* 61 (2, 2009): 215–243.

Peary, R.E. "The Reception of Mr. Peary," *Journal of the American Geographical Society of New York* 27 (4, 1895): 373–384.

"People and the Caucus," *New York Times*, 12 April 1881.

"Perish Patronage," *New York Herald*, 13 April 1881.

"Personal Reflections of Distinguished Statesmen and Politicians: Judge Charles P. Daly," *New York Leader*, 1 May 1858.

Peterson, Jon A. "The Impact of Sanitary Reform upon American Urban Planning, 1840–1890," *Journal of Social History* 13 (1, 1979): 83–103.

Peterson, Jon A. *The Birth of City Planning in the United States, 1840–1917*. Baltimore: Johns Hopkins University Press, 2003.

Phillips, Richard. *Mapping Men & Empire: A Geography of Adventure*. New York: Routledge, 1997.

Pinther, Miklos. "Charles Patrick Daly 1816–1899," *Ubique: Notes from the American Geographical Society* 23 (2, 2003): 1–4.

Piott, Steven L. *American Reformers, 1870–1920*. Lanham, MD: Rowman & Littlefield Publishers, 2006.

Poor, Henry V. "Railroad to the Pacific: Five Routes Proposed," *Bulletin of the American Geographical and Statistical Society* Vol. 1, Part III, 1854: 81–100.

Poor, Henry V. "Proposed Pacific Railroad," *Proceedings of the American Geographical and Statistical Society*, 1863–1864: 30–40.

Powell, John Wesley. *Report of the Lands of the Arid Regions*. Washington, D.C.: Government Printing Office, 1879.

Powell, Richard C. "Science, Sovereignty and Nation: Canada and the Legacy of the International Geophysical Year, 1957–1958," *Journal of Historical Geography* 34 (2008): 618–638.

Pratt, Mary Louise. *Imperial Eyes: Travel Writing and Transculturation*. London: Routledge, 1992.

Prestholdt, Jeremy. *Domesticating the World: East African Consumerism and the Genealogies of Globalization.* Berkeley: University of California Press, 2008.

Pryor, J.W. "The Greater New York Charter: The Formation of the Charter," *Annals of the American Academy of Political and Social Science* 10 (1897): 20–32.

"Railway Scheme," *New York Times*, 18 April 1886.

Reader, John. *Africa: A Biography of a Continent*. New York: A.A. Knopf, 1998.

"Reception to Lieut. Greely," *New York Tribune*, 22 November 1884.

"Reception to Lieut. Greely," *The World*, 22 November 1884.

"Record of Geographical Progress: Districts in Tropical Africa Where White Men May Live and Work," *Journal of the American Geographical Society of New York* 29 (1, 1897): 74.

"Retirement of Chief Justice Daly," *The Albany Law Journal*, 28 November 1885.

Richard, Alfred C. Jr., *The Panama Canal in American National Consciousness, 1870–1999*. New York: Garland, 1990.

Riffenburgh, Beau. *The Myth of the Explorer: The Press, Sensationalism, and Geographical Discovery*. London: Bellhaven Press, 1993.

Robinson, Michael. *The Coldest Crucible: Arctic Exploration and American Culture*. Chicago: University of Chicago Press, 2006.

Rose, Gillian. *Feminism and Geography: The Limits to Geographical Knowledge*. Minneapolis: University of Minnesota Press, 1993.

Ross, W.G. "Nineteenth-Century Exploration of the Arctic." In *North American Exploration, Volume 3: A Continent Comprehended*, edited by John L. Allen, 244–331. Lincoln: University of Nebraska Press, 1997.

Rothenberg, Tamar Y. "Voyeurs of Imperialism: *The National Geographic Magazine* before World War II." In *Geography and Empire*, edited by Anne Godlewska and Neil Smith, 155–172. Oxford: Blackwell, 1994.

Rothenberg, Tamar Y. *Presenting America's World: Strategies of Innocence in National Geographical Magazine, 1888–1945*. Burlington, VT: Ashgate Publishing, 2007.

Rothrock, J.T. "North-Western North America: Its Resources and Its Inhabitants," *Journal of the American Geographical Society of New York* 4 (1873): 393–415.

Rotundo, E. Anthony. *American Manhood: Transformations in Masculinity from the Revolution to the Modern Era*. New York: Basic Books, 1993.

"Royal Geographical Society," *Morning Post*, *Daily News*, the London *Times*, and *Daily Telegraph*, all 23 June 1874.

Rozwadowski, Helen M. and David K. Van Keuren, eds. *The Machine in Neptune's Garden: Historical Perspectives on Technology and the Marine Environment*. Sagamore Beach, MA: Watson Publishing International, 2004.

Ruiz, Ernesto. *Geography and Diplomacy: The American Geographical Society and the 'Geopolitical' Background of American Foreign Policy, 1848–1861*. PhD dissertation, Northern Illinois University, 1975.

Russell, A.J. "Livingstone's Nile. What is It?" *Journal of the American Geographical Society of New York* 6 (1874): 288–301.

Ryan, Barry. "Charles Patrick Daly." In *The American National Biography*, edited by John Garraty. Cary, N.C.: Oxford University Press, 1999.

"Ryan Congo Concessions," *New York Times*, 14 December 1906.

Said, Edward. *Orientalism: Western Conceptions of the Orient*. London: Kegan Paul, 1978.

Said, Edward. *Culture and Imperialism*. New York: Alfred A. Knopf, 1993.

Sandweiss, Martha. *Passing Strange: A Gilded Age Tale of Love and Deception Across the Color Line*. New York: Penguin, 2009.

Sanford, Henry Shelton. "Report on the Annual Meeting of the African International Association, in Brussels, in June, 1877," *Journal of the American Geographical Society of New York* 9 (1877): 103–108.

"Sanitary Reform Society: A Conference with the Board of Health," *New York Times*, 11 January 1880.

"Sanitary Reform Society," *New York Times*, 19 November 1880.

Schneider, William H. *An Empire for the Masses: The French Popular Image of Africa, 1870–1900*. Westport, CT: Greenwood Press, 1982.

Schulten, Susan. *The Geographical Imagination in America, 1880–1950*. Chicago: University of Chicago Press, 2001.

"Seeing the Eothen Sail," *New York Sun*, 20 June 1878.

"Shall We Have a North Pole Expedition? An Appeal to Congress," and "The Polar Mystery: An Appropriation for Its Exploration to be Made by Congress," *New York Herald*, 1 March 1875.

Shapin, Steven. *The Scientific Revolution*. Chicago: University of Chicago Press, 1996.

Shapin, Steven. "Placing the View from Nowhere: Historical and Sociological Problems in the Location of Science," *Transactions of the Institute of British Geographers* 23 (1998): 5–12.

Sidaway, James. "Postcolonial Geographies: An Exploratory Essay," *Progress in Human Geography* 24 (2000): 591–612.

Smith, Matthew Hale. "Chief Justice Daly," *Successful People and How They Win*. New York, 1877.

Smith, Neil. *American Empire: Roosevelt's Geographer and the Prelude to Globalization*. Berkeley: University of California Press, 2003.

Smith-Rosenberg, Carol. *Disorderly Conduct: Visions of Gender in Victorian America*. New York: Oxford University Press, 1985.

"Sons of Liberty: America's Successful Revolutionists and Ireland's Struggling Patriots," *New York Herald*, 23 May 1887.

Southworth, Alvan S. "The Soudan and the Valley of the White Nile," *Journal of the American Geographical Society of New York* 5 (1874): 95–111.

Spann, Edward K. "Union Green: The Irish Community and the Civil War." In *The New York Irish*, edited by Ronald H. Bayor and Timothy J. Meagher, 193–212. Baltimore: Johns Hopkins University Press, 1996.

Stanley, Henry M. "Explorations of Central Africa," *Journal of the American Geographical Society of New York* 7 (1875): 174–282.

"Stanley Banquet of the Geographical Society at Delmonico's," *New York Herald*, 28 November 1872.

"Stanley's Discoveries," *New York Herald*, 14 December 1875.

"Stanley Reception: Meeting of the American Geographical Society at the Cooper Institute Last Night – A Large and Fashionable Attendance," *New York Herald*, 27 November 1872.

Steedman, Carolyn. "The Space of Memory: In an Archive," *History of the Human Sciences* 11 (1998): 65–83.

Steinberg, Philip. *The Social Construction of the Ocean*. Cambridge: Cambridge University Press, 2001.

Sternstein, Jerome. "King Leopold II, Senator Nelson W. Aldrich, and the Strange Beginnings of American Economic Penetration of the Congo," *African Historical Studies* 2 (2, 1969): 189–204.

Stevens, John D. *Sensationalism and the New York Press*. New York: Columbia University Press, 1991.

Stockton, Charles H. "The Commercial Geography of the American Inter-Oceanic Canal," *Journal of the American Geographical Society of New York* 20 (1888): 75–93.

"Street Cleaning Question," *New York Times*, 12 April 1881.

"Streets of New York Must Be Cleaned," *The Sun*, 15 April 1881.

"Struggle is Ended: Nicaragua Reorganization Can Now Go On Unimpeded," *New York Tribune*, 3 March 1894.

"Sunset Sunshine for Daly: The Nicaragua Bill Stirs Up the House of Representatives," *The World*, 15 December 1888.

Tammiksaar, E., N.G. Sukhova, and I.R. Stone. "Hypothesis versus Fact: August Petermann and Polar Research," *Arctic* 52 (3, 1999): 237–244.

Taylor, H.C. "The Nicaragua Canal," *Journal of the American Geographical Society of New York* 18 (1886): 95–97.

"Tenement Reform," *New York Herald*, 11 January 1880.

Thompson, Rev. Joseph P. "The Value of Geography to the Scholar, Merchant, and Philanthropist," *Journal of the American Geographical Society of New York* 1 (4, 1859): 98–107.

Thompson, Rev. Joseph P. "The Physique of Different Nationalities," *Proceedings of the American Geographical and Statistical Society* 1862–1863: 84–93.

Tichi, Cecelia. *Civic Passions: Seven Who Launched Progressive America (and what they teach us)*. Chapel Hill: University of North Carolina Press, 2009.
"To Avert a Panic" [Nicaragua Canal], *The Star*, 15 December 1888.
"To Civilize the Indians," *New York Times*, 3 April 1886.
"To Have a New Home," *New York Tribune*, 26 September 1897.
"To Strike at Pauperism," *New York Times*, 8 December 1883.
Tosh, John. *Manliness and Masculinities in Nineteenth-Century Britain: Essays on Family, Gender and Empire*. Harlow, England: Pearson Longman, 2005.
Tuason, Julie. "The Ideology of Empire in National Geographic Magazine's Coverage of the Philippines, 1898–1908," *The Geographical Review* 89 (1999): 34–53.
Turner, Hy B. *When Giants Ruled: The Story of Park Row, New York's Great Newspaper Street*. New York: Fordham University Press, 1999.
"Uncle Sam, How About France? Our National Legislators Unanimously Opposed to Allowing Foreign Ownership of the Panama Canal" and "Dig that Ditch: the Interests of the Country Demand that Congress Charter the Nicaragua Canal Company, Let France Stand Aside," *New York Herald*, 12 December 1888.
"Up in Arms!" *New York Herald*, 19 March 1881.
"Urging Sanitary Reform," *New York Daily Tribune*, 19 November 1880.
"Valley of the Congo, Practical Steps Toward the Opening to Trade of a Rich Territory, Action of the Chamber of Commerce, Judge Daly's Address – the King of Belgium and His Neutrality Project," *New York Herald*, 11 January 1884.
Vaughan, Richard. *The Arctic: A History*. Dover: Alan Sutton Publishing Inc., 1994.
Veiller, Lawrence. *Tenement House Reform in New York, 1834–1900. Prepared for the Tenement House Commission of 1900*. New York: The *Evening Post* Job Printing House, 1900.
"Views from the Rostrum, Discussing the Evils of Tenement-House Life," *New York Times*, 19 November 1880.
Villarejo, Oscar. *Dr. Kane's Voyage to the Polar Lands*. Philadelphia: University of Philadelphia Press, 1965.
Ward, Stephen V. *Planning and Urban Change*, 2nd ed. London: Sage, 2004.
Watson, F. Dekker. *The Charity Organization Movement in the United States: A Study in American Philanthropy*. New York: Macmillan, 1922.
White, Richard. *"It's Your Misfortune and None of My Own": A History of the American West*. Norman: University of Oklahoma Press, 1991.
Wiebe, Robert. *The Search for Order, 1877–1920*. New York: Hill and Wang, 1967.
Wilder, Rev. H.A. "A Description of Natal," *Bulletin of the American Geographical and Statistical Society* Vol. 1, Part III (1854): 45–61.
Williams, Glyndwr. *Voyages of Delusion: The Northwest Passage in the Age of Reason*. London: Harper Collins, 2002.

Withers, Charles. "Towards a History of Geography in the Public Sphere," *Hist. Sci.* xxxvi (1998): 1–39.

Withers, Charles. *Geography, Science and National Identity: Scotland Since 1520.* Cambridge: Cambridge University Press, 2001.

Withers, Charles. "A Partial Biography: The Formalization and Institutionalization of Geography in Britain since 1887." In *Geography: Discipline, Profession and Subject Since 1870*, edited by Gary Dunbar, 79–119. Dordrecht, Netherlands: Kluwer Academic, 2001.

Withers, Charles W. "Constructing 'The Geographical Archive'," *Area* 34 (2002): 303–311.

Withers, Charles W. "History and Philosophy of Geography 2003–2004: Geography's Modern Histories? – International Dimensions, National Stories, Personal Accounts," *Progress in Human Geography* 30 (2006): 79–86.

Withers, Charles W.J. and Robert J. Mayhew. "Rethinking 'Disciplinary' History: Geography in British Universities, *c.* 1580–1887," *Transactions of the Institute of British Geographers* 27 (2002): 11–29.

Wright, John K. *Geography in the Making: The American Geographical Society 1851–1951.* New York: American Geographical Society, 1952.

Wright, John K. "British Geography and the American Geographical Society, 1851–1951," *Geographical Journal* 118 (2, 1952): 153–167.

Wylie, John. "Earthly Poles: The Antarctic Voyages of Scott and Amundsen." In *Postcolonial Geographies*, edited by Alison Blunt and Cheryl McEwan, 169–183. New York: Continuum, 2002.

Wynne, James. "Benevolent Societies," *Journal of the American Geographical and Statistical Society* 1 (10, 1859): 298–303.

"Year's Explorations" [Africa], *New York Herald* and *New York Times*, 28 February 1878.

Zinn, Howard. *A People's History of the United States 1492–Present*, 20th ed. New York: HarperCollins, 1999.

Index